The final third of the book brings the analysis to the present day, examining the new technological and competitive environment within which U.S. firms now operate. The authors examine the implications of the organization of R&D in Japan, one of the key competitive factors in this new environment. Although a number of features of the Japanese R&D system have been cited as meriting emulation by U.S. firms and public policy, this system appears to be changing in response to the new technological and competitive environment in which Japanese firms now find themselves. The authors suggest some reasons for caution in imitating organizational arrangements that are believed to be key components of the Japanese success story of recent decades. Also discussed are the implications of "internationalization" of the global R&D system for the organization of innovation in the United States and for trade and technology policies.

This book will be an important addition to the general debate over the role of technological innovation in economic growth.

DAVID C. MOWERY is Associate Professor of Business Administration at the School of Business Administration, University of California, Berkeley.

NATHAN ROSENBERG is Fairleigh Dickinson Professor of Economics at Stanford University. He is the author of *Inside the Black Box: Technology and Economics* (1983).

Technology and the pursuit
of economic growth

Technology and the pursuit of economic growth

DAVID C. MOWERY
University of California, Berkeley

NATHAN ROSENBERG
Stanford University

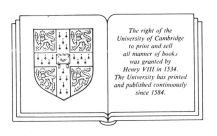

Cambridge University Press

Cambridge

New York   Port Chester   Melbourne   Sydney

Published by the Press Syndicate of the University of Cambridge
The Pitt Building, Trumpington Street, Cambridge CB2 1RP
40 West 20th Street, New York, NY 10011, USA
10 Stamford Road, Oakleigh, Melbourne 3166, Australia

First published 1989

Printed in the United States of America

Library of Congress Cataloging-in-Publication Data
Mowery, David C.
Technology and the pursuit of economic growth / David C. Mowery,
Nathan Rosenberg.
p.   cm.
Includes bibliographical references.
ISBN 0-521-38033-2
1. Technological innovations – Economic aspects – United States –
History.   2. Technological innovations – Economic aspects – Great
Britain – History.   3. Science and industry – United States – History.
4. Science and industry – Great Britain – History.   I. Rosenberg,
Nathan, 1927–   . II. Title.
HC110.T4M68   1989
338′.064′0973 – dc20   89–17294
                                                              CIP

British Library Cataloguing in Publication Data
Mowery, David C.
Technology and the pursuit of economic growth.
1. Economic development.   Role of Technology
I. Title   II. Rosenberg, Nathan, *1927–*
330.9

ISBN 0-521-38033-2

Contents

Preface

Technological innovation has been one of the most important contributors to the growth in employment and incomes in the U.S. economy. Yet the institutional and organizational factors that lead to differences among nations and firms with respect to innovative performance are not well understood. In particular, it has seemed apparent to the authors that the intellectual framework long employed by economists for the analysis of these issues is distinctly inadequate. Above all, it is incomplete. Instead of focusing exclusively, as is the present practice of economic theory, on the conditions under which the economic returns to research may be appropriated, we believe that much more attention needs to be devoted to the conditions influencing the utilization of the results of the scientific and technological research that lead to innovation.

For the past decade, we have been engaged, individually and jointly, in research on the organization of the process of innovation that underpins economic growth in the modern era. Our work has been empirical, historical, and comparative in its approach and concerns; it has drawn on a number of disciplines, including the history of science, policy analysis, and economic history. This volume presents the results of that work. We hope that it will be received as a constructive attempt to expand the range of relevant variables in the economic analysis of the innovation process.

It is a pleasure to acknowledge the support, both intellectual and financial, that we have received in the course of this work. Our intellectual debts are particularly great to Moses Abramovitz, Masahiko Aoki, Alfred Chandler, Wesley Cohen, Paul David, Christopher Freeman, Stephen Kline, Ralph Landau, Richard Nelson, Keith Pavitt, Richard Rosenbloom, Edward Steinmueller, and David Teece. Significant financial support for this work was provided by the Technology and Economic Growth Program of the Stanford University Center for Economic Policy Research; the Policy Research and Analysis Division of the National Science Foundation; the American Enterprise Institute; the Council on Foreign Relations; the Panel on Technology and Employment of the National Academy of Sciences, National Academy of Engineering, and Institute of Medicine; the Department of Social and Decision Sciences, Carnegie-

Mellon University; and the Center for Research on Management of the Walter A. Haas School of Business Administration, University of California, Berkeley.

Support of a very different variety was provided by our families in the course of drafting, and, in some cases, endlessly redrafting the pages in this volume. Our wives, Janet and Rina, shared in many ways in the creation and the writing of this book. We are grateful for their assistance and encouragement.

PART I

Introduction

1

A new framework for research and development: Analysis and policy implications

Technology's contribution to economic growth and competitiveness has been the subject of a large and growing literature in recent years. This debate has been spurred in part by a recognition of the importance of innovation in an economy that is increasingly open to the products of foreign firms that have proven to be the technological and economic equals of U.S. firms in a number of industries. Many contributors to this literature and a growing number of policymakers are concerned with the design of public policies that can improve the innovative performance of U.S. firms and with the training of U.S. managers to better manage technological change.

Economists have contributed a great deal to the identification of the importance and (imprecisely) the measurement of the contribution of technological change to economic growth. It is therefore surprising that economists have not played a more prominent role in recent debates of science and technology policies. In our view, the potential contributions of economics to the development of improved public and private policies for innovation have been hampered by the limitations of the theoretical framework employed by most economists for the analysis of innovation. This book is intended to aid the development of an alternative framework for the analysis of innovation and the design of policies for its support and management.

The chapters in this book do not develop a comprehensive alternative theory of innovation; indeed, the analytic insights offered here complement those of the neoclassical economic framework. Nevertheless, our analysis is based on several premises that depart in varying degrees from those of the neoclassical framework and its descendants. Rather than focusing exclusively on the conditions affecting the supply of research and development, we are concerned with the utilization of research findings and their translation into commercial innovation. It is only through this conversion of research into innovation that the economic payoffs from scientific research are realized, and recent history suggests that strength in research alone may be insufficient to guarantee that the economic benefits of research investment will be realized by the nation making the investment. Our concern with utilization also motivates an extensive dis-

3

cussion of the processes linking scientific research and commercial innovation.

Because the structure and organization of the institutions of research heavily influence the utilization of research results and their translation into commercial innovations, our analysis examines the development of the U.S. R&D "system" in some detail and compares this system with those of other industrial nations. The neoclassical economic framework for the analysis of R&D and innovation says very little if anything about the institutional structure of the research systems of advanced industrial economies, yet this structure heavily influences the ability of nations to realize the economic payoffs from research. Not only does the structure of institutions matter, but their historical development affects innovative performance.

The performance of a given institutional structure for R&D clearly depends on the technological and economic environment of that research system. As the environment changes, the research system must adapt, if its performance is to remain strong. The U.S. research system has undergone at least one upheaval thus far this century (the rise of federal funding of research during and after World War II) in response to a significant change in its environment. This system may be in the midst of a second transformation, as new structures for the performance of research, including domestic and international cooperative research, now are emerging in response to change in the environment. It is impossible to understand and evaluate the causes and implications of these structural shifts without an understanding of their historical origins.

The first section of this chapter discusses the neoclassical economic framework for the analysis of R&D, focusing on its limitations for policy and for the analysis of the organization and management of research. The next section presents an alternative framework for the analysis of innovation, one that emphasizes the interactions among basic research, applied research, and commercial development. The final section discusses the role of basic research within this schema, arguing that current analytic distinctions (distinctions that are reflected in current data collected by the National Science Foundation) between basic and other forms of research lack a substantive basis.

Appropriability and policy

The vast economics literature on technological innovation, market structure, and government policy is reviewed in Scherer (1980), Cohen and Levin (1988), and Kamien and Schwartz (1982). This section sketches the conceptual framework for the organization of R&D and for public policies toward innovation that has developed out of this literature.

The economist's theory of the firm is actually a theory of markets; theoretical understanding of the basis for the existence of the firm, to say nothing of the factors that determine its boundaries, is not well advanced, despite important work by Williamson (1975, 1985), Chandler (1962, 1975, 1988), and Teece (1982, 1986). This deficiency is particularly significant in the analysis of the organization of research and development. Neoclassical theory's emphasis on the appropriability of the results of research must be complemented with an analysis of the conditions supporting the utilization of these results. In the absence of an analysis of the utilization of the fruits of R&D, economic theory is hard pressed to provide answers to a broad array of increasingly urgent policy questions.

The key elements of the neoclassical economic theory of R&D are contained in articles by Nelson (1959) and Arrow (1962) that considered the economics of knowledge production through investment in industrial research (Mowery, 1983b, contains a more detailed discussion of this work). Research was portrayed in these papers as an activity resulting from an investment decision made by the profit-maximizing firm. The critical element in the research investment decision of the firm was the returns to this investment. Consistent with the tenets of microeconomic theory, the firm was treated as a "black box" whose internal workings and structure could be ignored. The critical element in the firm's decision on R&D investment was the returns to the investment. Nelson and Arrow argued that the social returns to research investment exceeded the private returns faced by the individual firm, a condition leading to underinvestment by the firm (from the societal point of view) in research.

The reasons adduced for this market failure illustrate the deficiencies of the appropriability framework. Arrow in particular argued that although firms incurred costs in producing scientific or technical knowledge, the costs of transferring this knowledge once discovered were effectively zero. That the consumption by another firm of the knowledge produced by a firm did not diminish or degrade it made the information a public good. From the social point of view, the widest possible diffusion of this knowledge is optimal. The price necessary to achieve this goal, however, one equal to the costs of transfer, was so low as to bankrupt the discoverer. The supply of socially beneficial research in civilian technologies, and basic research in particular, therefore was insufficient because of the disjunction between the privately and socially optimal prices for the results:

> Thus basic research, the output of which is only used as an informational input into other inventive activities, is especially unlikely to be rewarded. In fact, it is likely to be of commercial value to the firm undertaking it only if other firms are prevented

from using the information. But such restriction reduces the efficiency of inventive activity in general, and will therefore reduce its quantity also. (Arrow, 1962, p. 618)

Although this theoretical analysis identified an important source of market failure in the generation of new knowledge through private investment, it is deficient. The fruits of research do not consist solely of information that can be utilized by others at minimal cost for innovation. As Pavitt (1987) and others (Rosenberg, 1982; Mowery, 1983b; Cohen and Levinthal, 1989) have noted, transferring and exploiting the technical and scientific information that is necessary for innovation constitute a costly process that itself is knowledge intensive. The neoclassical analysis of innovation focuses largely on the conditions of appropriability of the returns to innovation in concluding that market failure results in too little R&D investment. The critical factor for commercially successful innovation, however, may well be the utilization of the results of R&D. The market-failure analysis must be supplemented by an analysis of the conditions affecting the utilization of the results of R&D. Utilization of the results of research is heavily influenced by the structure and organization of the research system within an economy, a topic on which the neoclassical theory is either silent or incorrect.[1]

For example, the appropriability analysis of R&D investment provides no basis for explaining a topic discussed at some length below, namely, why is most U.S. industrial research conducted in laboratories that are a part of manufacturing firms? Why did industrial research develop in this fashion rather than being provided through contract by independent firms? The growth of industrial research within U.S. manufacturing was part of a broader process through which manufacturing firms absorbed functions previously carried out and organized through the market and developed entirely new activities within the firm (Chandler, 1977). In-house research allowed for the development and exploitation of firm-specific knowledge, reflecting the superiority of the quality and quantity of intra-firm communications to those between contractual partners, as well as the fact that production and the acquisition of detailed technical knowledge frequently are joint activities. Among other things, these factors meant that the activities of independent, contract research organizations and the relationship of contract research to in-house research differed substantially from the predictions of such distinguished proponents of neoclassical theory as George Stigler (see Chapter 4).

Moreover, for policy purposes, the distribution and utilization of the

[1] An important and interesting exception to this characterization of the economics literature is the recent paper by Clark, Chew, and Fujimoto (1987), which compares the performance of European, Japanese, and U.S. auto firms in developing new designs and emphasizes the roles of internal communication and organization in explaining differences in performance.

results of R&D, rather than solely the sufficiency or insufficiency of its supply, are critical. Although it pinpoints a critical source of underinvestment in R&D, the appropriability analysis does not yield useful policy guidance of a more specific sort. Its failure to address issues of utilization means that the appropriability framework ultimately can provide very little analysis or prediction about the distribution of the benefits of cooperative R&D among industries and firms – but such distributional issues are crucial in this context. Moreover, this analytic framework ignores many of the key characteristics of the process of technological change.

Rather than a page from a book of blueprints, a new technology is a complex mix of codified data and poorly defined "know-how."[2] A richer analysis of the economics and organization of R&D must stress the costs to the individual firm of finding and adopting new techniques. This perspective also allows for different levels of technical performance among firms in the same industry and differences in the technical performance of the same industry in different nations. It places greater weight on internal firm structure and issues of utilization in a more explicit analysis of the implementation and distribution of R&D results than does the appropriability paradigm.

We agree with the argument of the neoclassical analysis that research services and technical knowledge have unique characteristics that distinguish them from such commodities as wheat. Our critique of market mechanisms is in some ways a more fundamental one than the market-failure analysis of the appropriability paradigm. Even if the specific market failure identified by the appropriability analysis could be remedied, the distributional consequences would still be unacceptable (i.e., certain firms and industries would not be served). Further, the distributional consequences of such markets for R&D may not be remediable through public subsidization of the supply of contract research.

The processes of innovation

The focus on appropriability also leads to a distorted view of the process of innovation. The neoclassical analysis focuses largely on the incentives

---

[2] Research on government demonstration projects carried out by a team at the Rand Corporation emphasized the costs and difficulties of knowledge transfer; see Baer, Johnson, and Merrow (1977) for a summary. Surprisingly, the Rand analysis says rather little about the role of client firms' in-house expertise as an influence on the success or failure of such demonstrations. The authors of the study cite as important for demonstration projects' success "the existence of a strong industrial system for commercialization" and the "inclusion of all elements for commercialization" (p. 955), both of which criteria presumably include in-house technical expertise among client firms. However, these categories as they are employed by the authors are nearly vacuous. In the wake of a failed demonstration project, it may be obvious that "all elements needed for commercialization" were not present. However, the policy problem is one of prediction; for this task, more precise criteria are needed.

of firms to invest in R&D and views internal structure and process as unimportant. As a result, it devotes little if any attention to the process through which research is converted into commercial innovation. According to this view, new technologies represent the application of previously acquired scientific knowledge – usually meaning "recently acquired" scientific knowledge. Thus, technological innovation is regarded as essentially the application of "upstream" scientific knowledge to the "downstream" activities of new product design and the development of new manufacturing processes.

In reality, however, many of the primary sources of innovation are located "downstream," without any initial dependence on or stimulus from frontier scientific research. These sources involve the perception of new possibilities or options for efficiency improvements that originate with working participants of all sorts at, or adjacent to, the factory level. The participants include professional staff such as engineers and those who have responsibilities for new product design or product improvement, and may include customers as well, as von Hippel (1978) has noted.

The acquisition of knowledge for innovation is not a once-and-for-all matter. Rather than a unidirectional, one-time occurrence of transfer of basic scientific knowledge to application, the processes of innovation and knowledge transfer are complex and interactive ones, in which a sustained two-way flow of information is critical. The ability to adopt a new technology, to evaluate a new technique, or even to pose a feasible research problem to an external research group may require substantial technical expertise within the firm.[3]

The process of technical innovation has to be conceived of as an ongoing search activity that is shaped and structured not only by economic forces that reflect cost considerations and resource endowments but also by the present state of technological knowledge, and by consumer demand for different categories of products and services. Successful technological innovation is a process of simultaneous coupling at the technological and economic levels – of drawing on the present state of technological knowledge and projecting it in a direction that brings about a coupling with some substantial category of consumer needs and desires.

[3] Arrow's famous 1969 set of "Classificatory Notes on the Production and Transmission of Technical Knowledge" noted, "When the British in World War II supplied us with the plans for the jet engine, it took ten months to redraw them to conform to American usage" (1969, p. 34). Concerning Japanese technology imports from the industrialized West, Caves and Uekusa (1976) stated: "The level and pattern of research and development within Japan are closely related to the import of technology from abroad. Firms must maintain some research capacity in order to know what technology is available for purchase or copy and they must generally modify and adopt foreign technology in putting it to use. A 1963 survey of Japanese manufacturers showed that on average one-third of the respondents' expenditures on R&D went for this purpose. The moderate level, wide diffusion, and applied character of Japan's research effort are consistent with a facility for securing new knowledge from abroad" (p. 126).

The choice among technological alternatives and the decision as to how much performance improvement is worth acquiring involve commercial and economic judgments, not only technological criteria. There are typically many ways of strengthening a bridge or reducing the weight of a commercial aircraft or improving the conductivity of an electrical transmission system. The exchange of information among specialists in establishing the optimal trade-off is therefore a central part of the firm's decision-making process.

Work by Nelson and Winter (1982) contains an excellent statement of these characteristics. A central component of their view of innovation is the portrayal of the discovery of alternatives, as in research, and the choice among alternatives, as in the decision to pursue development of a discovery, as a single process, rather than separate activities.[4] Research and development is portrayed as a particular type of search activity, consisting of repeated "draws" from a distribution of possibilities that may be more or less "distant" from a firm's existing endowment of skills and technological capabilities. This view of innovation, and of knowledge more generally, has two central elements. A great deal of the knowledge that is important to the operation and improvement of a given process or product technology is "tacit," that is, not easily embodied in a blueprint or operating manual. A closely related characteristic of technical knowledge is that much of it is highly firm specific and results from the interaction of R&D and other functions within the firm.

The process of R&D has often been equated with innovation. If innovation consisted solely of R&D, understanding innovation would be far simpler and the real problems would be far less interesting. Successful innovation requires the coupling of the technical and the economic, rather than being solely a matter of "technology push" or "market pull" (see Mowery and Rosenberg, 1979), in ways that can be accommodated by the organization while also meeting market needs, and this implies close cooperation among many activities in the marketing, R&D, and production functions. The research that goes on within this internal cooperation and communication process is not usually considered as science, but it is essential to successful innovation. The importance of these types of research has been underestimated in the recent past, probably in part because of the use of an oversimplified linear model of innovation that entirely omits them as categories of research.

---

[4] "Orthodox theory treats 'knowing how to do' and 'knowing how to choose' as very different things; we treat them as very similar. Orthodoxy assumes that somehow 'knowledge of how to do' forms a clear set of possibilities, bounded by sharp constraints, and that 'knowledge of how to choose' somehow is sufficient so that choosing is done optimally; our position is that the range of things a firm can do at any time is always somewhat uncertain prior to the effort to exercise that capability, and that capabilities to make good choices in a particular situation may also be of uncertain effectiveness" (Nelson and Winter, 1982, p. 52).

The role of basic research

Basic research occupies a central place within both the appropriability framework for the analysis of R&D and the science and technology policy structure that has developed under the influence of this intellectual schema. The appropriability analysis of R&D investment essentially equates research activity with basic research: The payoff is uncertain and distant, and the knowledge quickly moves into the public domain. Historically, federal support of nonmilitary research and technology development has focused on the support of basic research, since this activity was assumed to display the greatest divergence between a modest private and high social payoff.

Our analysis of innovation questions many of these assumptions and policy prescriptions and undercuts the basis for the definition of basic research. In this section, we examine the role of basic research within the innovation process. If the returns from this activity are largely nonappropriable by the performer, why do private firms invest in this activity? Our discussion stresses the hazy distinction between basic research and other innovation activities that underpins a portrayal of the innovation process as a linear sequence of phases stretching from scientific discovery to application. In fact, basic research has a complex relationship with most of the other phases of the innovation process.

In 1985, industry performed nearly 20 percent of all basic research within the United States (universities and colleges performed the largest share of basic research, 48 percent). Industry performed nearly 38 percent of all "nonacademic basic research" (a category including basic research by nonprofit institutions, federally funded research and development centers (FFRDCs), and the federal government). A slightly smaller share, roughly one-third (32.9 percent) of nonacademic basic research (total nonacademic basic research was $5.7 billion in 1985), was financed by industry.[5] Incomplete data compiled by the National Science Foundation (NSF) for 1984 indicate that 61 percent of the industry-financed basic research was concentrated in four sectors – chemicals, electrical equipment, aircraft and missiles, and nonelectrical machinery (an industry classification that includes computers) (NSF, 1986).

In understanding why some private firms do basic research, it is necessary to recognize that businesses do not live in a neat, orderly world where causal relationships are clearly defined and where causality works in one direction. The business environment is much more interactive, full of "feedbacks" where some "downstream" development reacts back on, and alters, behavior "upstream." Perhaps most important, it is full of

---

[5] All data are from National Science Foundation (1987).

unplanned or accidental developments that then turn out to have important consequences of their own.

It is essential to emphasize the unexpected and unplanned, even if – or especially if – it renders serious quantification impossible. In fact, the difficulties in precisely identifying and measuring the benefits of basic research are hard to exaggerate. The point has been expressed succinctly: "Project selection methodologies of a formal, quantitative nature reduce the tendency to perform basic research" (Nason, 1981, p. 24). Difficulties in applying quantitative techniques to basic research planning stem in part from the distinction between risk, where probabilities can be assigned to each of a number of possible outcomes, and uncertainty, where the very nature of outcomes is unknown. As one moves from applied research and development toward basic research, risk declines and uncertainty increases. Most quantitative techniques for investment analysis and planning that are relevant to basic research resource allocation decisions are designed to manage and minimize risk, and cannot deal effectively with uncertainty. Indeed, corporations that support basic research programs rarely subject these activities to the same type of quantitative analyses that are employed for their product development or manufacturing investments.[6]

A second source of difficulty with the quantitative evaluation of basic research investment stems from the fact that the output of basic research is rarely if ever a final product to which the marketplace can attach a price tag. Rather, the output is some form of new knowledge that has no clear dimensionality. The output is a peculiar kind of intermediate good that may be used, not to *produce* a final good, but to play some further role in the *invention* of a new final good. These connections are extraordinarily difficult to trace with any confidence, even ex post. But even if these difficulties could be overcome, the problems of evaluating the knowledge and of providing an appropriate incentive system to reward the knowledge producers appear to be insuperable.

The application of quantitative techniques to the analysis of basic research is further complicated by problems in defining basic research. The distinction between basic research and applied research is highly artificial and arbitrary. The distinction usually turns on the motives, or goals, of the person performing the research. But this is not a very useful distinc-

---

[6] See the study by the Office of Technology Assessment, *Research as an Investment: Can We Measure the Returns?* (1986), and the testimony in the 1986 hearings of the Science Policy Task Force of the Science, Space, and Technology Committee of the U.S. House of Representatives (1986). One of the most ambitious efforts to trace the payoffs to defense research, Project Hindsight, was unable to compute any measure of the returns on the investment in defense research, ultimately rejecting "the possibility that any simple or linear relationship exists between cost of research and value received." (Office of the Director of Defense Research and Engineering, 1969, p. xxii).

tion. Pasteur in 1870 was trying to solve some practical problems connected with fermentation and putrefaction in the French wine industry.
He solved those practical problems – but along the way he invented the
modern science of bacteriology. Sadi Carnot, fifty years earlier, was trying
to improve the efficiency of steam engines.[7] As a by-product of that particular interest, he created the modern science of thermodynamics.

Other examples of the workaday nature of the motives for and influences on the basic research agenda can be drawn from the history of Bell
Telephone Laboratories, a major industrial performer of basic research.[8]
Jansky's pioneering research on the sources of static in the new transatlantic radiotelephone service was motivated by the need to reduce or
eliminate the background noise. Based on work with a rotatable antenna,
Jansky concluded in 1932 that there were three sources of noise: local
thunderstorms, more distant thunderstorms, and a third source, which he
identified as "a steady hiss static, the origin of which is not known." It
was the discovery of this "star noise," as he labeled it, which marked the
birth of radio astronomy.

Jansky's experience underlines one of the reasons why it is so difficult
to distinguish between basic research and applied research. Researchers
often make fundamental breakthroughs when dealing with applied or
practical concerns.[9] Attempting to draw the line between basic and applied research on the basis of the motives of the person performing the
research – whether there is a concern with acquiring useful knowledge
(applied) as opposed to a purely disinterested search for new knowledge
(basic) – is hopeless. Whatever the ex ante intention in undertaking re-

[7] Carnot made this utilitarian concern perfectly clear in the title of his short but immensely
influential book, published in 1824: *Réflexions sur la Puissance Motrice du Feu et sur les
Machines Propres a Développer cette Puissance*.

[8] Hoddeson (1981), pp. 512–44, argues that the decision to strengthen the in-house research
capabilities of the Bell System in the early 1900s stemmed from the perception of senior
management that the solutions to operating problems could be found only through fundamental research: "Out of Vail's nonscientific goal to create a universal system grew his
decision to build a transcontinental line, from which came the technological problem of
developing a nonmechanical repeater, and this problem in turn contributed crucially to
the start of Bell's formal commitment to in-house basic research. 'Basic' industrial research
was now [1910–11] recognized as intrinsically dual in nature, being fundamental from the
point of view of the researchers while at the same time supported by the company for its
possible applications" (pp. 534–5). Interestingly, the decision to expand fundamental research within the predecessor of Bell Labs followed the discharge in 1907 of two of the
firm's senior scientists (both of whom held Ph.D.s), Hammond V. Hayes and William
Jacques (Hoddeson, p. 529).

[9] Birr (1966) argues that one of the distinguishing characteristics of industrial research was
the use of scientific research methodologies to address technological problems and concerns. As the in-text argument suggests, the merger of the technological and scientific
research agenda within the industrial research laboratory makes it possible to exploit an
interactive relationship between basic research and technological concerns: Not only can
the methods of research be applied to technological problems, but technological issues can
also structure and inform the scientific research agenda.

search, the kind of knowledge actually acquired is highly unpredictable. Fundamental scientific breakthroughs have come from people like Jansky or Pasteur or Carnot, who thought they were doing very applied research, and who would undoubtedly have said so if they had been asked.

But the distinction breaks down in another way as well. We have to distinguish between the motives of the individual scientists and the motives of the firm that employs them. Many scientists in private industry could honestly say that they are attempting to advance the frontiers of basic scientific knowledge, without any applied interest. At the same time, the managers who finance research in basic science may be strongly motivated by expectations of useful findings. Thus, Bell Labs decided to support basic research in astrophysics because of its relationship to the field of microwave transmission and to the use of communication satellites for such purposes. It turned out that at very high frequencies, rain and other atmospheric conditions interfered significantly with transmission. This source of signal loss was a continuing concern in the development of satellite communications. It was out of such practical concerns that Bell Labs scientists Arno Penzias and Robert Wilson conducted fundamental research in radio astronomy. Penzias and Wilson first observed the cosmic background radiation, which is now taken as confirmation of the "Big Bang" theory of the formation of the universe, while they were attempting to identify and measure the various sources of noise in their antenna and in the atmosphere. Penzias and Wilson justifiably shared a Nobel Prize for this finding. Their finding was about as basic as basic science can get, and it is in no way diminished by observing that the firm that employed them did so because it hoped to improve the quality of satellite transmission.

The fact that basic research may be financed for profit-seeking motives has other implications. When basic research is isolated from the rest of the firm, whether organizationally or geographically, it is likely to become sterile and unproductive. The history of basic research in industry suggests that it is most effective when it is highly interactive with the work of applied scientists and engineers. This is because the high-technology industries are always throwing up problems, difficulties, and anomalous observations that may occur only within these sectors. In order for scientists to exploit the potential of the industrial environment it is necessary to create opportunities and incentives for interaction with other components of the industrial world.

Basic research should be thought of as a ticket of admission to an information network. This network includes a variety of information flows that fit equally well into the basic or applied categories. There is a high degree of interactivity, embracing work that goes on within the realm of development as well as research.

The attempt to classify research into basic and applied categories is hard to take seriously in some areas and disciplines, for example, in the realms of health, medicine, and agriculture. A strict application of the most common criterion for basic research – research that is undertaken without a concern for practical applications – could easily lead to the conclusion that the National Institutes of Health are not deeply involved in basic research, which is absurd.[10]

There are a number of activities that are essential to the success of business firms that depend heavily on a basic research capability, even if that capability does not play a direct role in solving industrial problems. For one thing, firms need to do basic research to understand better how and where to conduct research of a more applied nature. For another thing, a basic research capability is essential for evaluating the outcome of much applied research and for perceiving its possible implications. In providing a deeper level of understanding of natural phenomena, basic research can provide valuable guidance to the directions in which there is a high probability of payoffs to applied research.

A basic research capability also is indispensable in order to monitor and to evaluate research being conducted elsewhere. As we noted earlier, most basic research in the United States is conducted within the university community (see Chapter 6), but in order to exploit the knowledge that is generated there, a firm must have an in-house capability. It may be difficult for a firm to benefit from university research unless it performs similar research. This observation has some important implications for the fate of cooperative research organizations. Since a larger in-house investment may be necessary to utilize basic research performed outside the firm's boundaries (Cohen and Levinthal, 1989), participants in cooperative research programs often shift the collaborative research agenda away from basic research. These pressures appear to have contributed to recent decisions by such well-known cooperative research institutions as the Electric Power Research Institute (EPRI) and the Microelectronics and Computer Technology Corporation (MCC) to reduce their basic research commitments.[11]

---

[10] In conducting its resource surveys, the NSF defines basic research as research that has as its objective "a fuller knowledge or understanding of the subject under study, rather than a practical application thereof." By contrast, applied research is directed toward gaining "knowledge or understanding necessary for determining the means by which a recognized and specific need may be met" (National Science Foundation, 1985, p. 221). These definitions appear to mean that if NIH directed a major research thrust into cellular biology to provide the knowledge necessary for the development of a vaccine against AIDS (or a cure for specific forms of cancer), none of the resulting research could be classified as basic. It is hard to see why the determination to deal with a particular disease cannot give rise to research that provides "a fuller knowledge or understanding of the subject under study," even when there is a "practical application" in mind. Here again the introduction of motives or goals is less than useful.

[11] The EPRI primarily serves electric utilities, which support modest in-house research staff and facilities. Historically, EPRI member firms have not been direct competitors, serving different geographic areas – a factor that contributed to the formation of EPRI in 1973.

These arguments about the role of basic research underline the limitations of the economists' view that knowledge is "on the shelf" and costlessly available to all comers once it has been produced. This model is seriously flawed because it takes a research capability to understand, interpret, and appraise knowledge that is placed on the shelf – whether basic or applied. The cost of maintaining this capability is high because it requires a cadre of in-house scientists who can do these things. And in order to maintain such a cadre, the firm must be willing to let them perform basic research. The only way to remain plugged in to the scientific network is to be a participant in the research process.

The mere existence of spillovers and nonappropriabilities that allow competitors a free ride is not a decisive argument against the performance of basic research by private firms. If the production of new knowledge generates commercial opportunities to the performer, the relevant calculation involves not the size of the spillovers but whether the performing firm can capture enough of the benefits generated to yield a high rate of return on the investment. Even in the extreme case of basic research where there is no prospect of establishing proprietary control over the research findings, commercial benefits may nevertheless be very great.

Conclusion

A century ago organized innovation was rare, and with the exception of Thomas Edison and early efforts in the German chemicals industry (Beer, 1958, 1959), individual, independent inventors were the major sources of innovation (see Chapter 4). Organizing and managing the innovation was an issue of far less importance in such a world. With the development of organizations dedicated to research and the steady rise of public and private investment in R&D, however, issues of structure and management have become far more salient. Moreover, the structure of current U.S. research is now undergoing far-reaching change as public policymakers

EPRI originally was charged with focusing on "a small number of large, long-range projects. This was in part due to the industry's concern that EPRI not duplicate or compete with the product development work of the commercial vendors, for fear of undermining their incentives to pursue R&D. The intention was to complement the work of others" (Barker, 1983, p. 6). Since its foundation, however, EPRI's research agenda appears to have adopted a shorter time horizon. In 1976, "short-," "medium-," and "long-term" research accounted for 45, 45, and 10 percent of total expenditures, respectively. By 1981, "short-term" R&D had risen to 50 percent of the total, and "mid-term" research had been cut to 40 percent. In 1982, "short-term" research accounted for 69 percent of the total EPRI research budget, "long-term" research absorbed 3 percent, and "medium-term" research accounted for 28 percent of the total.

MCC is experiencing a similar shift. A recent article on its new chairman, Grant Dove, noted his concern with developing applications more rapidly for members: "To carry out Dove's directive, MCC is restructuring its largest program – Advanced Computer Architecture – to enable its members to focus resources on areas that promise immediate paybacks" (Lineback, June 25, 1987, p. 32).

and private managers reevaluate the ends and means of their research agenda. As the number of technologically adept international competitors has expanded and the rate at which technological and scientific knowledge is transferred across international boundaries has increased, innovation has become essential to stay even in the marketplace. Increased demands on research institutions for rapid innovation have been a key factor behind recent corporate and public research initiatives.

We have several goals in writing this book. By examining key episodes and institutions in the development of the U.S. research system and in the development of the research systems of other industrial economies, we wish to provide additional material for the analysis and evaluation of the organization of R&D. We also hope that the conclusions of this work will spur economists to expand their theoretical analysis of R&D. Expansion and enrichment of this framework are needed because of the weak guidance provided by the appropriability analysis for public policymakers and managers alike. This framework's lack of attention to the utilization of the results of research and to the ways in which the organization of research affects utilization means that it can contribute little to such debates as the effects on the performance of Bell Telephone Laboratories of the divestiture by AT&T in 1984 of its regional operating companies, or to the design of cooperative organizations for the performance of research. The considerable potential contributions of economics to the empirical and analytic challenges mentioned here have been constrained by the narrow theoretical framework employed within neoclassical economics. A richer framework may support a more fruitful dialogue among economists, policymakers, and managers on the organization of public and private institutions for innovation.

Plan of the book

Our discussion of the organization of innovation relies heavily on historical and institutional analysis. We begin with a discussion of the relationship between science and industrial technology in the nineteenth century, focusing on the initially modest contribution of scientific research to industrial technology (Chapter 2), and follow with an analysis of the development of industrial research in the United States before 1940 (Chapters 3 and 4). The contrasting evolution of the U.S. and British industrial research systems is considered in Chapter 5. Both Chapters 4 and 5 build on and advance our critique in Chapter 1 of the neoclassical treatment of R&D investment and organization.

Chapters 6 and 7 consider the transformation of the U.S. R&D system that resulted from World War II. Chapter 6 describes the growth of the federal role within industrial and academic research within the United

States and discusses the complex role of military research as a source of technological "spillover" to commercial applications. Chapter 7 presents a detailed case study of a single industry, commercial aircraft, that illustrates many of the analytic and historical arguments concerning the organization of innovative activity and the rise of the U.S. system for research and innovation. This chapter also examines the transformation of the R&D system within the U.S. commercial aircraft industry that has occurred in the past fifteen years as a result of the rise of international collaborative ventures, since it may prefigure similar structural changes now occurring in other U.S. industries.

Chapters 8–11 bring the analysis to the present day, examining the ways in which the changing environment is leading to institutional innovation in the U.S. research system. Chapter 8 discusses the new technological and competitive environment within which U.S. firms now operate, focusing on the implications of this environment for the organization of innovative activity and considering the implications of the organization of R&D in Japan, one of the key competitive factors in this new environment. Although a number of features of the Japanese R&D system have been cited as worthy of emulation by U.S. firms and public policy, this system also appears to be changing in response to the changing technological and competitive environment in which Japanese firms now find themselves. Chapter 9 extends the discussion of collaborative activity that was begun in Chapter 7, describing the growth of international and domestic collaborative ventures in a widening range of U.S. manufacturing industries and considering the implications of collaborative activities for innovation and competitiveness. A central theme of both Chapters 8 and 9 is the increased technological and economic interdependence that are both cause and effect of the phenomena described in these chapters. Expanding on this theme, Chapter 10 discusses the increasingly close relationship between domestic science and technology policies, on the one hand, and the international trade policies of the United States and other industrial nations, on the other. This relationship is being managed awkwardly at best within the federal government at present. Chapter 11 presents some concluding thoughts.

PART II

The development of the institutional structure, 1860–1940

2

The growing role of science in the innovation process

A revolution in science, 1859–74

Simon Kuznets has stated that "the epochal innovation that distinguishes the modern economic epoch is the extended application of science to problems of economic production" (1966, p. 9). Although there is general agreement with the view that the dependence of technological progress on science has increased substantially in the course of industrialization, there is considerable disagreement, or at least considerable difference in emphasis, concerning the extent of that dependence. On the one hand, A. E. Musson and E. Robinson (1969) have argued forcefully that technological progress was already heavily dependent on science in the early stages of the British industrial revolution.[1] Their research has provided a wealth of evidence showing, in the British case, the intimate and multitudinous networks that linked the business community to scientists. Robert Schofield has advanced the claim, based on a careful study of the Lunar Society in Birmingham, that the society was really an eighteenth-century "industrial research group" (Schofield, 1963, p. 437).

On the other hand, a long and influential tradition in the history of technology stresses the crude, trial-and-error, hit-or-miss nature of technological progress (Gilfillan, 1935, 1970). During the preindustrial period, this interpretation argues, scientific and technological research and advancement were social processes that were almost hermetically sealed off from one another. As A. R. Hall has stated, with respect to preindustrial technology:

> We have not much reason to believe that, in the early stages, at any rate, learning or literacy had anything to do with it; on the contrary, it seems likely that virtually all the techniques of civilization up to a couple of hundred years ago were the work of men as uneducated as they were anonymous.[2]

[1] See also Musson's extended introduction to his *Science, Technology and Economic Growth in the 18th Century* (1972).
[2] Hall, *The Historical Relations of Science to Technology*, inaugural lecture.

21

Clearly a central issue in the formulation of such divergent views is how one goes about defining science. If by science one means rigorously systematized knowledge within a consistently formulated theoretical framework, the role of such knowledge is likely to have been small before the late nineteenth and twentieth centuries. But if one defines science more loosely in terms of procedures and attitudes, including the reliance on experimental methods and an abiding respect for observed facts, it is likely to appear universal in industrializing societies.

Discussion of the role of science in the innovative process inevitably raises a more fundamental question: Where does this science come from? Can the economist or historian be content with treating science as some exogenous force, some *scientia ex machina*, which is of interest only for its industrial applications? However attractive, such an approach fails to capture a large part of what scientific progress is all about. Science, after all, when considered as a social process in a social context, is an activity that is powerfully shaped by day-to-day human concerns. One does not need to be an economic determinist to believe that these concerns are, to a considerable extent, shaped and even often defined by the needs of the economic sphere and by the technologies that prevail in any given social context. Indeed, the growth of scientific knowledge has itself been decisively shaped by technological concerns.

Repeatedly, scientific knowledge of great generality has developed from the examination of a particular problem in a narrow context. Such a recitation, however, conveys a very limited sense of the exact nature and extent of the interplay between science and technology. That sense is totally suppressed in the prevailing tendency to view the causal relationships as if they ran exclusively from science to technology – and in which it is common to think of technology as if it were reducible to the application of prior scientific knowledge. Yet this view is no more valid today than in the second half of the nineteenth century, a period of extraordinary scientific creativity that was scarcely if at all coupled to the equally productive processes of technological innovation occurring simultaneously.

The period beginning in 1859 was one of remarkable scientific progress. If one had to choose any fifteen-year period in history on the basis of the density of scientific breakthroughs that took place, it would be difficult to find one that exceeded 1859–74. Of course, 1859 was the landmark year in modern biology, the year of publication of Darwin's monumental *Origin of Species*. Mendel was already at work by 1859 in his monastery garden, performing experiments with peas that were to lead, in a few years' time, to a mathematical formulation of the laws of genetics. Mendel's findings, which were long neglected, were announced in an article published in 1866, "Experiments with Plant Hybrids." During the

1860s, Pasteur was formulating the germ theory of disease, which was quickly followed up by Koch's remarkable work in identifying the microbial basis of some of the most dreadful diseases that afflict the human race.

During the 1860s, Kekule discovered and described the structure of the benzene molecule, a theoretical breakthrough that was to provide guidance for wide-ranging experimental research in organic chemistry. In 1871, Mendeleyev imposed a wonderful unity on the entire field of chemistry with his presentation of the periodic table of the elements. So great was Mendeleyev's confidence in his assertion of the periodic recurrence of certain chemical properties that he left holes in his table and predicted, correctly, that elements possessing specific characteristics would be discovered that fit into those locations. In 1873, Maxwell published his *Electricity and Magnetism,* the culmination of a line of research going back to Faraday's empirical discovery of the relationship between electricity and magnetism, an announcement he had described in a paper to the Royal Society in 1831. Maxwell's mathematical formulations and predictions in turn pointed the way to further research (such as Hertz's discovery of radio waves) that provided the intellectual foundation for all the electricity-based industries. Also in 1873, Josiah Willard Gibbs published the first two of a series of papers in which the laws of thermodynamics were applied to chemistry. Truly 1859–74 represented a remarkable fifteen years! (See Bode, 1965; and Sharlin, 1966, Chapter 8.)

The relation between scientific and technological advance

The post-1859 period, however, was not only one of numerous and remarkable developments in fundamental science. It was also a period of widespread innovation and productivity growth, sufficient to warrant the expression "second Industrial Revolution." What was the connection between these two sets of events?

The short and inevitable answer is, of course, that these connections were complex. No single characterization can encompass the relations between science and technological change during that period. This is not only because the relationships themselves changed over time, and at any moment in time varied considerably from sector to sector (although these statements are both true and important). It is also because – and this is why the question cannot be pursued solely through the study of the history of science – the relationships depended at least as much on developments in the realm of technology as in the realm of science. Although major scientific breakthroughs and an extensive application of science to industry did emerge during this period, the two classes of events were much more loosely coupled than is commonly thought.

The construction of a bridge between recent scientific discoveries and technological innovation is typically a very protracted affair, although that is not always the case. In the realm of medical science, specific advances were sometimes exploited rapidly. Roentgen's announcement of the discovery of X-ray phenomena in 1895 led to immediate applications because the technology that was required for exploitation of the new scientific knowledge already existed and its usefulness was immediately apparent. In other fields of medical science, such as the research of Pasteur and Lister, the necessary technologies were either easily achievable or unnecessary. Knowledge of the ways in which infectious diseases were transmitted would often yield benefits by inciting simple changes in medical procedures, alterations in certain hospital practices, or new public-sanitation measures. Spectacular reductions in the incidence of puerperal fever could be achieved simply by persuading attending doctors or medical students to wash their hands before visiting each of their patients in hospital maternity wards. Nevertheless, the sad experience of Ignaz Semmelweis, who was hounded out of the Viennese medical profession for suggesting this practice, is powerful testimony to the difficulty of gaining acceptance for new knowledge that runs counter to long-standing practice.[3] Semmelweis's assertion of the connection between unwashed hands and the frequency of puerperal fever is also extremely interesting for present purposes because he never actually explained the vector of transmission. Rather, he simply inferred some connection from extensive observation. One does not necessarily need a good scientific theory to adopt some appropriate modification of behavior. Lister, after all, was the founder of antiseptic surgery, even though he believed that there was only one kind of germ producing many diseases.[4]

[3] Semmelweis was forced to resign his professorship and moved to Budapest, where he published his book, *The Cause and Prevention of Puerperal Fever*, in 1861. Oliver Wendell Holmes had been teaching essentially similar ideas in Boston. He too encountered skepticism and hostility, but it was less intense than that which drove Semmelweis to an early and tragic death.

[4] Speaking of intestinal-tract diseases, Burnet and White (1972) point out: "The method of preventing such diseases is obvious to everyone. Indeed, the one indubitable blessing of modern civilized life is the development of the technical methods and mental attitude required to eliminate them. . . . Decent sewage disposal, pure water supply, pure food laws, control of milk supply and pasteurization, plus the cult of personal cleanliness have rendered most of these diseases rare in any civilized community. An outbreak of typhoid fever or a high infantile mortality from diarrhoeal disease is rightly regarded as a civic disgrace.

"It is interesting to look back on the development of such a civic conscience and to realize that its all-important beginnings were based on a completely wrong idea of how infections like typhoid fever arose. In the early nineteenth century it was recognized that typhoid fever and filthy drains went together, but the stress was laid more on the smell than on possible infective principles (bacteria were, of course, unknown) in the objectionable drainage. By some transference of ideas, bad-smelling drains were also blamed for

Nevertheless, although some scientific breakthroughs experienced rapid application, in other cases the applications came slowly. Sometimes the reasons were simple. Mendel's writings, for example, were ignored for three decades, until his findings were independently rediscovered. An understanding of the laws of heredity was eventually to have profound effects in the twentieth century, especially in agriculture, with the development of new and superior hybrid varieties.[5] But unfortunately, unread scientific papers exercise no technological consequences.[6]

In the case of Faraday and electromagnetic induction, there were no major technological innovations for several decades after his announcement of the discovery of the phenomenon in 1831, with the exception of the telegraph. There were numerous reasons for this, both scientific and technological. Faraday's discovery did not profoundly advance scientific understanding of a complex phenomenon, nor did it unambiguously point to specific directions for exploitation. More than forty years later, Maxwell's formulation brought electrical phenomena to a level of understanding that was systematic and mathematical and that pointed in specific useful directions. Thus, Maxwell's prediction of the existence of radio waves was experimentally confirmed by Hertz in 1887, and this confirmation led directly to the use of radio waves for the transmission of sound.

In addition to the need for more sophisticated scientific understanding, the technological exploitation of electricity required the development of a complex system of innovations – including the dynamo for the generation of electricity, techniques for the transmission of electricity over long distances, a small and efficient electric motor for converting the electricity into useful work in factory and home, and a range of alloys possessing specialized performance characteristics that were substantially different from anything required by other industries.

As the preceding example suggests, technological exploitation of new scientific understanding often requires considerable time because of the

---

the incidence of diphtheria, and the incentive to remove these two diseases was largely responsible for the development of modern sanitary engineering. The process was under way by the time the infectious nature of typhoid fever was clearly recognized, and it was a good deal later that the typhoid bacillus was found. Both these discoveries, of course, accentuated the necessity for keeping drinking water and sewage, to put it bluntly, out of each other's way" (p. 106).

[5] Here, too, it is worth recalling that selective breeding was a very old practice, carried on with considerable success long before a scientific analysis of the laws of heredity was available.

[6] Gibbs's astonishingly complete formulation of the theory of "chemical thermodynamics" in the 1870s attracted no scientific interest whatever for some time. This may have been due partly to its obscure place of publication, the *Transactions of the Connecticut Academy of Arts and Sciences*. It was only when Ostwald translated the work into German in 1892 that it began to command the attention it so richly deserved.

need for additional applied research before the economically useful knowledge can be extracted from a new but abstract formulation. According to Cyril Stanley Smith:

> Perhaps the greatest achievement of nineteenth century science was the thermodynamics of Gibbs. This was exploited by metallurgists in the form of the phase rule – but not, it must be noted, until after they had catalogued and puzzled over innumerable structures and change of structure observed empirically under the microscope in alloys of various compositions and treatment. The simple phase rule not only enabled metallurgists quickly to understand their binary and ternary systems and to limit the range of the possible, but it also provided the background against which various transformations could be studied. (1961, p. 363)

In other important cases, the exploitation of advances in scientific understanding required the development not only of new technology but even an entirely new discipline, such as chemical engineering. Perkin's accidental synthesis in 1856 of mauveine, the first of the synthetic aniline dyes, gave rise to a new synthetic dyestuffs industry and exercised a powerful impact on research in organic chemistry. At the same time, the exciting developments in the science of chemistry often had no effect on the capacity to produce something on a commercial basis. Discovering or synthesizing a new material under laboratory conditions was usually the first of many steps toward the possession of a marketable final product. The discipline of chemical engineering arose during the period as a systematic way of designing and manufacturing industrial process techniques, without which many chemical discoveries would have remained no more than laboratory curiosities.

Even when important technological breakthroughs were based on recent scientific developments, subsequent improvements in that field were not necessarily science based. Although chemical science was vitally important to industrial developments during the period, much of the actual timing of innovation (i.e., the translation of scientific discoveries into commercial products) depended on advances in chemical engineering. Speaking of the problems of the chemical industries during the First World War, L. H. Baekeland, who had patented the first synthetic resin, Bakelite, stated:

> When the present crisis came, we had no trouble finding chemists and chemical engineers in the field of acids and heavy chemicals. Our lack of experience was mostly evident in the newer problems of coal-tar dyes and other organic industries. Here, like in other fields of chemical industry, it is not enough to know a

chemical reaction on a laboratory scale. It makes an enormous difference whether you are manufacturing by the ounce or by the ton. In a laboratory, operations can be performed in little glass vessels, or in porcelain or expensive platinum. On a manufacturing scale, all this becomes totally different and the difficulty is no longer the chemical reaction itself, but the vessels and the methods of carrying it out. Acids and other substances which attack iron and other metals have to be handled in machinery which can withstand their action and insure not only the highest yields but great purity, and exclude the possibility of accidents. An entirely new industry had to be created for this purpose – the industry of chemical machinery and chemical equipment. (1917, p. 394)

Finally, it needs to be emphasized that the coupling between science and technological innovation remained very loose during this period because, in many industrial activities, innovations did not require scientific knowledge. This was true of the broad range of metal-using industries in the second half of the nineteenth century, in which the United States took a position of distinct technological leadership. Indeed, following the American display at the Crystal Palace Exhibition in 1851, the British came to speak routinely of "the American system of manufactures." The distinctive aspect of the American system was the production of large quantities of metal components to a high degree of precision by the use of a sequence of specialized machines. This high degree of precision made it possible to avoid the costly process of fitting, which consumed much time and effort in craft-dominated industries. Components produced under the American system were sufficiently precise and standardized that they could be easily assembled rather than laboriously fitted.[7] In the second half of the nineteenth century, America provided the leadership in developing a new production technology for manufacturing such products as reapers, threshers, cultivators, repeating rifles, hardware, watches, sewing machines, typewriters, and bicycles. These developments also necessitated a great deal of innovation at the level of machine tools – turret lathes, universal milling machines, precision grinders, and so on. In some cases, such as the well-known Lincoln miller, the machines themselves were produced by the same mass-production techniques to which their own development had given rise.[8]

The development of this new machine technology rested on mechanical skills of a high order, as well as considerable ingenuity in conception and

---

[7] See introduction to Rosenberg (1969).
[8] Referring to the Lincoln miller, Fitch (1880) states that between 1855 and 1880, "nearly 100,000 of these machines or practical copies of them have been built for gun, sewing-machine and similar work" (p. 26).

design. It did not typically require much recourse to the scientific knowledge of the time. The notion of "Yankee ingenuity" has been overworked by generations of authors who have approached the writing of American history in a celebratory mood. The negative aspect of the notion, however, is worth recalling in this context: Whatever the extent or the source of that ingenuity, it did not draw substantially on a scientific education.

The application of technological knowledge in industry

The preceding section has suggested reasons that account for the fact that, although great progress was being made at the scientific frontier after 1860, the research at that frontier was still only rather loosely coupled to industrial innovation. This is not to say that science was only loosely tied to innovation but rather that *recent* scientific research was loosely tied to innovation. To appreciate the importance of this distinction, we can consider the interaction of science and technology from the side of industry and the needs of the innovative process in major sectors of the economy. Viewed from this perspective, it appears that within many economic sectors, the knowledge required for moving out the *technological* frontier was rather elementary scientific knowledge of a kind that had been available for a long time. This is true in the key sectors of the First Industrial Revolution: metallurgy and the metal-using and metal-shaping sectors. In these sectors, the needs of the innovation process created a high payoff to elementary science and its applications. These needs led to the first entry by science into the industrial establishment in an organized way. The more sophisticated industrial scientific research of the twentieth century evolved out of those simple and prosaic beginnings (see Chapters 3 and 4 for additional discussion).

The transformation of the iron and steel industry – and in fact its transformation from an iron industry to a steel industry – began with Bessemer's striking announcement to the 1856 meeting of the British Association for the Advancement of Science of a new technique for refining iron. Bessemer's process offered opportunities for great cost reductions, in part by taking advantage of the impurities in pig iron and using them as a fuel. Indeed, Bessemer's paper bore the rather compelling title "Manufacture of Malleable Iron and Steel without Fuel."[9]

Bessemer had developed his process without the benefit of any training

---

[9] Writing on the use of the Bessemer process in the American rail industry, Temin (1964) has pointed out: "It took 7 tons of coal to make 1 ton of cast (crucible) steel from pig iron by the old method: 2½ tons of coal to make blister steel and 2½ tons of *coke* to make cast steel. The same process with a Bessemer converter required ⁹⁄₁₀ of a ton of coal to heat the converter plus about ⁹⁄₁₀ of a ton to melt the iron. One part fuel in the Bessemer process equaled 6 ot 7 parts in the old method of steelmaking, and a comparison of labor and machinery requirements would yield similar results." (p. 131, emphasis in the original).

in the chemistry of his day. Neither he nor his contemporaries had a very precise idea of the chemical transformations that occurred inside the converter. In fact, the Bessemer process failed to produce a satisfactory product when it was first adopted in Britain – to the considerable indignation of ironmakers who had paid handsome royalties for access to Bessemer's innovation. The blowing of air through the molten iron removed some of the impurities – the carbon and silicon. Unfortunately, as was eventually established by chemical analysis, it did not remove the phosphorus. As a result, the Bessemer process was confined for some years to the use of nonphosphoric ores. The fact that Bessemer's process could refine only materials that fell within certain narrow bounds of chemical composition had important economic consequences, imparting a strong comparative advantage to regions possessing nonphosphoric ores. Britain's use of the (acid) Bessemer process grew rapidly with the exploitation of her large deposits of nonphosphoric hematite ores located in the Cumberland-Furness region, supplemented by imports of nonphosphoric ores from the Bilbao region of Spain. Germany and France had only very limited deposits appropriate for the Bessemer process, and Belgium had none. The Bessemer technique was useless for the exploitation of the massive deposits of high-phosphorus ore in Lorraine and Sweden.

As was eventually established, Bessemer had conducted his original experiments using a highly purified form of pig iron, Swedish charcoal iron. The determination to establish the cause of the failure of the technique with certain British ores eventually led to a systematic analysis of the chemical processes involved in iron and steel production.

Other related events following Bessemer's innovation also dramatized the importance of chemical analysis. Users of Bessemer steel eventually encountered additional problems of reliability; Bessemer steel tended to become brittle as it aged. This deterioration in quality had much to do with the declining popularity of Bessemer steel as other methods of steel production became available and as new products were introduced that required steel of high quality and reliability. Although nineteenth-century metallurgists never succeeded in establishing the cause, it turned out that the blowing of air through the molten iron not only removed impurities but also added one: The brittleness was caused by the presence of minute quantities of nitrogen from the air, which dissolved into the iron during the blowing.

The peculiarities of the post-1860 steel industry placed a premium on basic chemical knowledge. This knowledge was of great economic value, not only in assuring quality control in manufacturing, but in the selection of the raw materials – the coal and the iron ore – to be employed in the productive process. In considering the use of scientific research in industry, one must distinguish between what is "interesting" to the historian of science and what has a high economic payoff. Manufacturers who used this elementary chemical knowledge could gain significant economic advantages over their competitors through a more informed selection of raw material sources. Andrew Carnegie could scarcely conceal his delight at the benefits that accrued from the chemical assays performed by his first trained chemist:

> We found . . . a learned German, Dr. Fricke, and great secrets did the doctor open up to us. [Ore] from mines that had a high reputation was now found to contain ten, fifteen, and even twenty per cent less iron than it had been credited with. Mines that hitherto had a poor reputation we found to be now yielding superior ore. The good was bad and the bad was good, and everything was topsy-turvy. Nine-tenths of all the uncertainties of pig iron making were dispelled under the burning sun of chemical knowledge.
> What fools we had been! But then there was this consolation: we were not as great fools as our competitors. . . . Years after we had taken chemistry to guide us [they] said they could not afford to employ a chemist. Had they known the truth then, they would have known they could not afford to be without one.[10]

Carnegie, with his customary business acumen, had quickly perceived the vast possibilities of chemical analysis in evaluating ores and in attaining better control over metallurgical processes.

The increasing introduction of steel into new uses, such as structural engineering, created a compelling need for precise information concerning the performance of structural steel members under a variety of specific circumstances. The existing theory of the behavior of steel did not provide sufficiently detailed guidance for design and construction purposes. The need for such guidance in numerous specific industrial contexts provided a powerful impetus for the establishment of new testing facilities.[11] These issues are discussed further in Chapter 3.

Although the seminal microscopic researches of Henry Clifton Sorby

---

[10] Quoted in Livesay (1975), p. 114.
[11] As Timoshenko (1953) has pointed out: "The introduction of steel into structural engineering produced problems of elastic stability which became of vital importance . . . The simplest problems of this kind, dealing with compressed columns, had already been investigated theoretically in sufficient detail. But the limitations under which the theoretical results could be used with confidence were not yet completely clear. In experimental work with columns, inadequate attention had been paid to the end conditions, to the accuracy with which the load was applied, and to the elastic properties of material. Hence, the results of tests did not agree with the theory, and engineers preferred to use various empirical formulas in their designs. With the development of mechanical-testing laboratories and with the improvement of measuring instruments, fresh attacks were made on experimental investigations of columns" (pp. 293–4).

had begun before 1860 and would eventually provide a scientific basis for much of twentieth-century metallurgy, the great metallurgical innovations of the period drew primarily on elementary science when they drew on science at all.[12] None of the three great technological innovations in ferrous metallurgy in the second half of the nineteenth century – Bessemer's converter, Siemens's open-hearth method, or the Gilchrist–Thomas basic lining, which made it possible to make steel with high-phosphorus ores – drew on anything but elementary chemical knowledge that had already been available for a long time. Indeed, only Siemens had had the benefit of a university education.[13] Sidney Gilchrist Thomas, for example, was a clerk in a London police court, with no more than a smattering of knowledge of chemistry that he had gained by attending evening classes. To be sure, Thomas eventually called in his cousin, Percy Gilchrist, who was employed as a chemist in South Wales. Gilchrist came to assist Thomas in some experimental trials in 1877, but Thomas had concluded, at least as early as 1875, that "a lining conducive to the formation of a basic slag which would combine with and hold phosphoric acid was the chemical basis for the use of phosphoric ores in steelmaking; and he . . . had concluded that the best material for the purpose was lime or a substance with similar chemical affinities" (Carr and Taplin, 1962, p. 99). Thus, the exceedingly simple chemical insight that the addition of lime would result in the removal of phosphorus from molten iron resulted in a complete redrawing of the industrial map of Europe by the end of the nineteenth century, making feasible the exploitation of the Continent's huge high-phosphorus ore deposits.

Although the introduction of basic steelmaking involved the beginning of the use of scientific knowledge in metallurgical innovation, the development of the science of metallurgy in the second half of the nineteenth century owed much to *prior* technological innovations in metallurgy. This scientific research developed because of the great commercial importance of understanding the behavior of metals that were being produced by the

---

[12] By 1863, Sorby had developed a technique for examining metals under a microscope by the use of reflected light. This technique opened the door to an understanding of the microstructure of steel. The vast significance of this technique has been described by Cyril Stanley Smith (1965): "From steel, the technique spread to show the behavior of microcrystals of the nonferrous metals during casting, working and annealing. By 1900 it has been proved that most of the age-old facts of metal behavior (which had first been simply attributed to the nature of the metals and had later been partially explained in terms of composition) could best be related to the shape, size, relative distribution and inter-relationships of distinguishable microconstituents" (p. 915).

[13] As Bernal (1953) has pointed out, "None of the scientific ideas used by Bessemer, Siemens and Thomas were more recent than 1790" (p. 110). What was true in an old industry like iron and steel was not necessarily true elsewhere. The Hall–Heroult method of aluminum production, developed simultaneously in America and France in the 1880s, made use of an electrolytic technique that in turn had been made possible by more recent developments in science. The same was true of the Mond nickel process.

Bessemer and post-Bessemer technologies. Particularly fruitful scientific research analyzed the specific properties of steel produced by certain technologies or utilizing specific resource inputs. Such phenomena as the deterioration of certain metals with age or the brittleness of metals made with a particular fuel were both intriguing to scientifically trained people and objects of great concern to manufacturers and users of the metals.

At the same time, the development of a science of metallurgy – or "materials science," as it has recently come to be called – was a slow process and was by no means completed by the outbreak of the First World War. New alloys continued to be developed by essentially trial-and-error methods, or by sheer accident, well into the twentieth century. A new and superior aluminum alloy like Duralumin was more or less accidentally developed and used for years before anyone really understood the phenomenon of "age hardening." That understanding came later and depended on the introduction of improved instrumentation, including X-ray diffraction techniques and the electron microscope.

In 1906, Wilm discovered the phenomenon of age hardening (a finding of major significance in metallurgy) as a result of inconsistencies of hardness measurements in some aluminum alloy specimens. At the time, it was impossible to connect age hardening with structural changes that could be observed under a microscope, and no satisfactory explanation of the phenomenon was forthcoming.[14] Nevertheless, Duralumin underwent considerable exploitation in the aircraft industry (including the construction of Zeppelins) during the First World War. Age-hardened and precipitation-hardened alloys[15] were used in a widening circle of commercial application during the interwar years, and the obvious commercial value of new and superior alloys gave a powerful impulse to fundamental research that would link performance characteristics of the alloys to their underlying crystallographic and atomic structures. Nevertheless, it was the practical metallurgists who made available to the scientists and engineers an array of new materials of much greater strength, superior strength–weight ratios, strength–conductivity combinations, and magnetic properties many years before performance could be explained at a deeper level. Indeed, the determination to account for the performance characteristics discovered by the metallurgist and already incorporated into numerous industrial practices was a major stimulus to fundamental research: "From these studies have arisen a better insight into deforma-

---

[14] "Although he must be considered a successful applied researcher and careful experimentalist even by modern standards, Wilm did not express any deep curiosity concerning the reasons for the hardening and preferred to leave to others even the speculation concerning its nature" (Hunsicker and Stumpf, 1965, p. 279).

[15] An alloy that ages at room temperature is considered an age-hardening alloy, whereas one that requires precipitation at a higher temperature is classed as a precipitation-hardening alloy. Alexander and Street (1968), p. 176.

tion and strengthening mechanisms, additional support for dislocation and magnetic theories and verification of the existence and importance of lattice vacancies" (Smith, ed., 1965, p. 309; see also O'Neill, 1965).

Well into the twentieth century, metallurgy was a sector in which the technologist typically "got there first," developing powerful new technologies in advance of systematic guidance by science. The technologist demanded a scientific explanation from the scientist of certain properties or performance characteristics. Such technological breakthroughs as Taylor and White's development of high-speed steel (1898), and the subsequent development, in the 1920s, of sintered tungsten carbide, are classic instances of technological improvements that preceded and gave rise to scientific research. Indeed, Frederick Taylor had been concerned with questions of shop management and organization, and was unfamiliar with even the rudimentary metallurgical knowledge available to the technologists of his own time.[16] Nevertheless, the discovery of the heat treatment that was necessary to impart "red hardness" to cutting tools resulted in remarkable improvements in productivity throughout the machine-tool industry.[17]

The sequence of technological knowledge preceding scientific knowledge has by no means been eliminated in the twentieth century. Much of the work of the scientist today involves systematizing and restructuring in an internally consistent way the knowledge and practical solutions and methods previously developed by the technologist. Technology has shaped science in important ways because it acquired some bodies of knowledge first and, as a result, provided data that in turn became the "explicanda" of scientists, who attempted to account for or to codify these observations at a deeper level.

A deepening of the understanding of how science has influenced and

[16] Frederick Taylor is, of course, better known as the father of scientific management, and his discovery of high-speed steel was the outcome of some protracted time-and-motion studies. His extraordinary report on his twenty-six years of experimentation in his presidential address to the American Society of Mechanical Engineers in 1906 is entitled, significantly, "On the Art of Cutting Metals." On the opening page, Taylor states: "There are three questions which must be answered each day in every machine shop by every machinist who is running a metal-cutting machine, such as a lathe, planer, drill press, milling machines, etc., namely: 'a. What tool shall I use? b. What cutting speed shall I use? c. What feed shall I use?'

"Our investigations, which were started 26 years ago with the definite purpose of finding the true answer to these questions under all the varying conditions of machine shop practice have been carried on up to the present time with this as the main object still in view" (Taylor, 1907, p. 3).

[17] The operation of high-speed steel was demonstrated at the Paris Exhibition of 1900. "At that exhibition they exhibited tools made of this steel, in use in a heavy and powerful lathe, taking heavy cuts at unheard of speeds – 80, 90, or 100 feet per minute, instead of the 18 to 22 feet per minute that previously had been the maximum for heavy cuts in hard material" ("Metal-working Machinery," in *Special Reports of the Census Office*, 1905, Part IV, p. 232).

shaped technological innovation requires that attention be given to the interactive relationship between those two sets of forces, as well as a recognition that the technological needs of a rapidly expanding industrial society were often satisfied by very simple science, rather than by knowledge at the forefront of scientific research. The direction of scientific research and the uses of scientific knowledge in the late nineteenth century were increasingly dictated by the needs of a growing industrial establishment. The nature and results of this influence are discussed in Chapters 3 and 4.

3

The beginnings of the commercial exploitation of science by U.S. industry

The extensive changes of the last century in (1) the nature of production technologies and inputs generally, and (2) the composition of industrial output have raised the payoff to investment in scientific knowledge. The growing proximity of science and industry was intimately bound up with these changes. This chapter attempts to account for the growing application of science to industry by identifying the forces at work in the industrial sector that generated an increasing demand for scientific knowledge.

The relevant forces were not confined to small sectors of the economy nor were they restricted to a few distinctive technologies, although individual technologies (e.g., electrification) were sometimes extremely important. These forces of change were pervasive and expressed themselves in the most basic and elemental of economic activities. They were based, first, on a metallurgical revolution beginning after the Civil War, a revolution flowing from remarkable reductions in the cost of steel that were made possible by the application of the "old" science, as the preceding chapter argued.

This cheapening of steel made possible an immense increase in its use as a substitute for wood and iron, for example, in machinery and rails. Cheaper iron and steel were fundamental to the emergence of national markets for branded, packaged products because such markets required a low-cost transportation system that became available with a dense network of railroads in the closing decades of the nineteenth century. The emergence of that market, in turn, was a critical component in the growth in the size and range of functions performed by individual firms (see Chandler, 1977).

At the same time, the cheapening of steel and the availability of other new materials for construction purposes (e.g., reinforced concrete) made possible entirely new techniques of construction that transformed the urban environment. This involved building on a vastly larger scale and departing from earlier limitations on design and construction that were imposed by the nature of available materials. Out of these new possibilities emerged the high-rise living environment of cities, skyscrapers, and suspension bridges across wide rivers and bays.

Finally, the growing productivity of agriculture and the large-scale urbanization of the American population led to a complete restructuring of the production and preparation of food. Agriculture became a much more specialized activity, involving a declining proportion of the labor force and an increasing degree of geographic specialization. The reorganization of the food supply and its distribution to a geographically dispersed but increasingly urbanized population of consumers required fundamental changes in the technology of food production, processing, preservation, and transportation.

Although these three sectors – metallurgy (and metal-using industries), construction, and food processing, packing, and canning – are not fully representative of the rest of the economy, they constitute a sufficiently large part of the national economy for significant trends within them to be, at the very least, important for the economy as a whole.

A set of common forces operated within all of the sectors examined here. Improvements in transportation in the post–Civil War years ended the earlier isolation of small local markets that were served by small-scale, locally oriented firms and created a large, internal market of continental scale. This market was also growing rapidly in terms of population, per capita income, and extent of urbanization. For a number of cultural, social, and economic reasons, the U.S. market was apparently prepared to absorb products of a higher degree of standardization and uniformity than was the case in Europe. U.S. firms in these industries grew larger and on the whole attained large size earlier than elsewhere. (In the construction industry, the growth of firm size was particularly conspicuous among the suppliers of construction materials.) Bigness in this respect was critical to the issues at hand because bigness created a vast range of problems, but also opportunities, that required much closer control of inputs and their qualities.[1]

Larger scale also required careful attention to numerous aspects of the new production processes in which more precise regulation and control were essential to successful performance. This was notoriously the case with the new, large-scale production technologies in metallurgy. Moreover, throughout these sectors, significant changes in the nature of the final product transformed or established a need for greater precision in its performance characteristics. These changes in turn made necessary much more careful monitoring of the materials employed to manufacture the product. Thus, the baker producing on a larger scale could not make purchases from the miller, the Pennsylvania Railroad could not buy steel products from the rolling mill, nor could the urban construction firm make purchases from the cement manufacturer, without the assurance of pre-

---

[1] This discussion does not require growth in size of firm to the extent of involving a significant degree of market concentration, although this kind of growth did indeed frequently occur.

cise performance or quality specifications for these purchased inputs. Failure to meet precise specifications could be commercially disastrous and was increasingly likely to pose a threat to life and limb.

As we pointed out in the preceding chapter, the pattern of industrial development that began to emerge in the late nineteenth century has to be understood not only – and perhaps not even primarily – as the emergence of new bodies of scientific knowledge that were subsequently applied to industry. Rather, a rapidly growing and industrializing economy encountered all sorts of situations in newly emerging technologies where further improvement and progress required drawing on the existing fund of scientific knowledge.

Although a number of laboratories had been established by 1900, even well after that date industrial research laboratories were not yet performing activities that should be regarded as research. Rather, they were engaged in a variety of routine and elementary tasks such as the grading and testing of materials, assaying, quality control, and writing of specifications. These were the primary initial applications of science in the industrial context. Science, when it entered the industrial establishment, came to perform tasks that were elementary *from the point of view of their scientific content.*

Very little of the work of scientists in industry before the First World War was of interest to anyone concerned *exclusively* with science and its progress. From the point of view of industrial growth, however, the work of these scientists was absolutely vital. It is difficult to envision how the emerging industrial technology could have functioned successfully without the vital information that could only be readily supplied by scientifically trained personnel. Competitive success increasingly went to those industrialists who were the quickest to perceive and exploit these opportunities.

The industrial growth of the United States coincided with a geographic expansion over a vast continent. One of the most distinctive aspects of American industrialization was the extraordinary richness of the natural resource environment within which it took place. Such mundane scientific techniques as chemical analysis, evaluation, and assaying played a crucial role in identifying and providing guidance to the speedy and efficient exploitation of hitherto unexplored and untapped mineral resource deposits.[2]

The ability to grade and sort with a high degree of precision played, and continues to play, a major role in the structure and operation of markets for specific products. Historically, futures markets have been estab-

---

[2] A useful introduction to this history may be found in Williamson, ed. (1951), Chapters 23 and 24.

lished only for those commodities that could be easily sorted and graded. For example, small differences in coal composition are very important for metallurgical purposes. The Chicago Board of Trade still does not deal in long-term coal contracts because of the difficulty of acceptable, standardized grading of metallurgical coal.

Metallurgy

The spectacular developments in the iron and steel industry that emerged in the mid-nineteenth century are a forceful demonstration that the new directions – including the very transformation of the industry from an iron industry into a steel industry – did not originate in advances in new scientific knowledge.

The dramatic growth in steel production that was made possible by the Bessemer process was not due to recent scientific discoveries because there had been no such recent addition to scientific knowledge. Once installed, however, the major technological innovations in steelmaking raised immensely the *payoff* to the use of existing science in this industry and to the development of new scientific knowledge. This became immediately apparent with the introduction and rapid diffusion of the Bessemer process.

The very success of the Bessemer process in lowering the price of steel and in introducing steel to a rapidly expanding array of new uses made it necessary to subject the inputs of the process to quantitative chemical analysis. This was because, as was quickly discovered, the quality of the output was highly sensitive to even minute variations in the composition of the inputs.

The first Bessemer steel produced in the United States was made in Wyandotte, Michigan, in 1864. In anticipation of the problems associated with chemical variations in inputs, a chemical laboratory was established at Wyandotte in 1863. This was the first chemical laboratory established in the metallurgical sector of the United States, as well as one of the first laboratories attached to any industrial firm (see Clark, 1929, pp. 70, 78).[3]

Similarly, large *users* of Bessemer steel were likely to set up testing laboratories to ensure that the steel met appropriate specifications. Such was the case of the railroads, where the larger companies established their own central testing laboratories – as did the Burlington in 1876 when it

---

[3] Clark (1929), vol. 2, pp. 70, 78. Wide (1985) argues that the need to analyze and ensure uniform quality in materials and outputs led a number of individual plants within General Electric to establish laboratories for materials testing in the early 1870s. A similar set of concerns led to the foundation of Eastman Kodak's Experimental and Testing Laboratory in 1890 (see Sturchio, 1985).

adopted the steel rail,[4] and the Pennsylvania Railroad, which established a chemical laboratory at Altoona, Pennsylvania, in 1874.[5]

The new uses to which cheaper steel was introduced defy a summary description. It was employed in a wide range of machines in which cast iron or wood had been used before. As a result, the machines could be made larger, stronger, and capable of higher operating speeds, all of which improved their performance. Steel played a major role in agriculture, as a bewildering number of machines were introduced that raised the acreage that could be cultivated by a single farmer. Low-cost steel was increasingly employed in mining machinery as well.

Steel was also a vital part of the transportation revolution, as it became a basic material input in the structure of oceangoing vessels and in the rapidly expanding network of railroads. At the outbreak of the Civil War, rails were made of iron that wore out in a couple of years and that could support rolling stock of only about eight tons. By 1905, steel rails might last as long as ten years and could support rolling stock of seventy tons. The railroad network was now able to exploit steel bridges of far greater span and capacity than previous materials had permitted.[6]

With the introduction of the automobile in the opening years of the century, there was a huge increase in the demand for steel as well as for a large number of specialty steels with many different kinds of high-performance characteristics. Development of alloy steels began before the turn of the century, but their use was mostly limited to armor and ordnance until after the First World War. In the 1920s the growth of the automobile, the airplane, and petroleum-refining industries brought rapid increases in demand.[7] In cities, the availability of steel as a structural material made possible the construction of skyscrapers (i.e., high-rise buildings with no dependence on masonry) beginning in Chicago and New

---

[4] Olson (1971), p. 45. "Railroad men used and developed chemical analysis, microscopic study, physical tests, and statistical methods in their attempt to obtain longer lasting rail. They devised laboratory and manufacturing tests that would identify defective rails before they were put in track" (ibid., p. 46).

[5] See *The Life and Life-Work of Charles B. Dudley, 1842–1909* (Philadelphia: American Society for Testing Materials, n.d.). Dudley was a leading figure in the field of materials testing and was subsequently first president of the American Society for Testing Materials, as well as president of the American Chemical Society. By the end of the First World War, the Altoona laboratory had a staff of more than 600 men, "half of whom are engaged in inspection work." See also Greene (1919), p. 588.

[6] American builders had shown remarkable daring and ingenuity in constructing even quite large railroad bridges out of timber. Nevertheless, the increase in the weight and speed of locomotives had earlier made the transition to iron, with its far greater tensile strength and rigidity, inevitable. Thus, many steel bridges were constructed as replacements for iron ones. Condit (1968), Chapter 8.

[7] Bartlett (1941) points out that the output of alloy steels grew from 570,000 tons in 1910 to about 4 million tons in 1930 (p. 161).

York in the early 1890s.[8] A series of other major innovations exploited the properties of steel in important ways – sewing machines, bicycles, typewriters, and barbed wire, to name a few.

The ability to deliver steel according to the precise specifications required by different classes of final users was substantially improved by two developments. First was the rapidly expanding use of the open-hearth process. Although the Bessemer process first made cheap steel possible, the Bessemer process did not permit precise control over quality, partly because of the sheer speed of the process. The open-hearth process, by contrast, did permit such control and could exploit a wider range of ores than the Bessemer process.[9] Second, the development of new steel alloys, especially those utilizing nickel, chromium, and tungsten, immensely improved the ability of metallurgists to manufacture steel according to precisely designed quality characteristics, such as toughness and hardness (see Clark, 1929, pp. 80–1; Barlett, 1941).

In effect, therefore, the manufacturer of steel may be said to have had both an internal and an external motivation to assert a precise, more scientific control over his manufacturing process. Internally, the manufacture of steel involved elaborate chemical transformations in which such control enabled the manufacturer to minimize the cost of producing any given output mix and to ensure quality control. Externally, a critical aspect of the competitive process was to develop new products that optimally achieved the specific combination of performance requirements of a growing number of specific users of steel. These production requirements brought trained chemists and metallurgists into the industry in increasing numbers. Thus, the increasing dependence on science in metallurgy was a consequence of two sets of prior and ongoing changes: in production technology, largely thanks to "old" science; and in the peculiarities and special performance requirements of new products.

As the new production technologies made steel cheaper, its widening diffusion and application to new uses strengthened the economic importance of understanding its characteristics and performance properties. In this respect, developments in the late nineteenth and early twentieth centuries intensified a concern about metallurgical phenomena that had

---

[8] "Skyscraper construction . . . began in 1891, when the Columbia Iron and Steel Company, of Uniontown, Pennsylvania, was awarded the contract for supplying the structural steel for the new Masonic Temple in Chicago. This building, twenty stories high and at the time the loftiest business structure in the world, required between 3,500 and 4,000 tons of steel for its skeleton frame. As in the case of bridges, each piece was exactly fitted, holes drilled, connections dove-tailed, and all connections adjusted for ultimate use before leaving the factory" (Clark, 1929, vol. 2, p. 345).

[9] Bessemer steel output reached its all-time peak in the United States in the first decade of the twentieth century, after which the period of dominance of the open-hearth method began.

become central to machinery designers and engineers during the "first" Industrial Revolution. The capacity to sustain higher temperatures and pressures, for example, had been a continuing preoccupation since the invention of the steam engine in the eighteenth century.

It became an increasing concern with the introduction of locomotives, steamboats, and steamships, which attached much greater importance to fuel efficiency (as evidenced by the introduction of the compound engine) as well as safety. With the introduction of electricity and steam turbine generators, the diesel engine, the automobile, the modern oil refinery, and eventually the airplane, the capacity to sustain very high temperatures and pressures, and therefore to understand the metallurgical conditions that would make them possible, increased incessantly (Clark, 1929, vol. 3, pp. 150–3).

Wherever steel was used as a structural material, as well as in the emerging mass-production metal-fabricating industries generally, similar tensions arose. It was not enough to be able to produce steel cheaply. In both the construction and the manufacture of increasingly complex products, the metal inputs needed to be produced to a high degree of uniformity and predictable reliability. Such conditions were essential to the possibility of designing and manufacturing high-performance products. Failure to achieve such reliability could, under certain circumstances, be disastrous, as was obviously the case with respect to large gun forgings, steam turbines aboard oceangoing vessels, or the structural members of large-span bridges.

As steel became cheaper, it not only served as a substitute for iron in many established structural uses; it also provided the possibility of far more audacious construction designs. But, here again, as a material was pushed to new and previously unexplored limits by skyscrapers and large-span bridges, the ability to predict its performance limits with a high degree of accuracy became indispensable.[10] Furthermore, even the mere substitution of steel for iron in a product of more conventional design called for a thorough exploration of its performance possibilities. For, without that information, excessive amounts of steel were likely to be committed to any given purpose, with consequent waste and inefficiency.

The economic importance of these relationships between cheaper metal and its more intensive utilization would eventually play a significant role in expanding the frontiers of metallurgical science. Their shorter-run and

[10] "Without the development of a science of structure and materials, construction in iron and steel could never have been accomplished on the scale necessary to modern urban life. As the engineer was faced with constantly increasing demands for higher buildings and heavier, longer bridges, he was increasingly compelled to turn to science in order to solve the structural problems thrust upon him. Building could no longer be treated as an art or a craft; it had to become a branch of theoretical and applied science" (Condit, 1968, pp. 76–7).

more pervasive effect was to increase the industrial payoff to a wider application of the existing body of scientific knowledge.

The innovative activity that led to the production of cheap steel, and the resulting substitution of steel for iron, calls attention to a phenomenon of pervasive economic importance in the twentieth century. It was to occur over and over with a widening range of materials exploited by industrializing societies. That is, the growth of knowledge with respect to the behavior of materials was to lead, in myriad ways, to a prolongation of the useful lives of the products made of these materials. This has been one of the most decisive impacts of the expanding body of useful knowledge – and it is also an impact that is, by its very nature, undramatic and not readily observable.

A large part of the history of alloys is the development of new materials with a number of more useful properties or combinations of properties – one of which was commonly greater strength and durability and a longer life expectancy than the simpler metal that it replaced. Similarly, an increase in the potential useful life of all products of the construction industry, to which we now turn, flowed from this kind of deepening understanding of the whole range of material inputs.

Construction

Construction has already received frequent mention in the discussion of metallurgy because steel had become a major construction material in the late nineteenth century. Construction nevertheless warrants further consideration because, at a time when its materials were far from standardized, it became an important focal point for the introduction of trained scientists into industry quite independently of the increasing reliance on structural members made of metal.

Concrete has an unusually long history going back to the ancient Romans, who had even discovered how to prepare a cement that would harden under water. But its use as a construction material has some striking parallels to that of steel. Like steel, it was not extensively used as a building material until late in the nineteenth century. Like steel, its large-scale use came after the introduction of a new European technology – in this case the rotary kiln, which had been invented in England in 1873.[11] Like the earliest British experience with the Bessemer process, its introduction was beset by difficulties that were ultimately traceable to the failure to exercise sufficient chemical control over the composition of the raw material inputs. As in the case of steel, its eventual performance was

---

[11] Although the rotary kiln is of European origin, it is interesting to note that the smaller-scale vertical kiln is still used by European manufacturers, whereas "cement plants in the United States have used the rotary kiln almost exclusively since its invention in 1873" (Huettner 1974, p. 101; see also Clark, 1929, vol. 3, pp. 253–6).

extremely sensitive to variations in the processing as well as to variations in the quality and composition of the inputs, since the transformation of a wet plastic into a rigid material involves some complex chemical reactions.

In addition to its low cost as a building material, concrete has great compressive strength and durability and can be made to assume an unlimited number of possible structural shapes. When supplemented by its reinforced and prestressed forms, concrete came to far exceed (by weight) the use of steel for structural purposes in the course of the twentieth century.[12]

These achievements were made possible by the systematic application of chemical analysis to the raw materials employed in the manufacture of concrete – lime, silica, alumina, iron oxide, and associated impurities.[13] The first major step was identification of the aluminum and silicon oxides as the active ingredients in the production of hydraulic lime, even though "the full understanding of the chemical reactions that occur in the setting of concrete was not to come until well into the twentieth century."[14]

That cement would be required to function for long periods of time in very different kinds of environments meant that exhaustive chemical studies were necessary to develop a cement that behaved appropriately in each of those environments. Whether a process worked or not, and whether the cement eventually behaved as expected, might depend on very small variations in the chemical components or in timing, the percentage of specific impurities and the specific forms of chemical compounding in the raw materials, the degree of fineness to which the raw materials were ground, and so forth. Separate studies were necessary to examine the causes of failure and of insufficient stability over time. From this chemical analysis had emerged a body of knowledge that was eventually capable of "designing" different kinds of cement to suit each of a wide range of eventual end uses.[15]

---

[12] There is a further interesting link between concrete and metallurgy. For prestressed concrete to perform properly, "the cable wire must be made of high quality steel so that it will maintain its tension throughout the life of the structure. The success of pre-stressing thus depended as much on progress in the metallurgy of steel as on the technology of concrete construction" (Condit, 1968, p. 248).

[13] "The major structural innovations of the twentieth century have been the products of concrete technology, and many of these have led to radical changes in the form and action of structural systems. No building material was treated to a more scientific investigation than concrete, with the consequence that by midcentury its chemistry, its internal structure, and its behavior under every condition are as well understood as the properties of familiar metals. Indeed, the engineers regard it as the most scientific material, one that allows the closest approach to the organic ideal, in which structural form exactly corresponds to the pattern of internal stresses" (Condit, 1968, p. 240).

[14] Ibid., p. 158.

[15] "Out of this research work has come the ability of the cement chemist to produce products with special properties, such as high-early strength for concrete that must be put into service quickly; low-heat cement that hardens slowly but develops less heat during hy-

In its reinforced and, more recently, prestressed form, concrete has become the predominant twentieth-century building material. Its performance characteristics were gradually established through patient and sustained empirical analysis, usually without the benefit of a larger theoretical framework to provide specific guidance to the research process.[16] As in metallurgy, the actual practices – structural achievements as well as problems and failures of the users of the material – provided the intellectual challenge for the deeper scientific understanding that eventually followed practice rather than preceded it. Although the work of trained chemists in all this would provide only occasional footnotes in a history of science, the economic importance of their achievements may be encapsulated in the observation that a larger quantity of concrete by weight is currently embodied in American construction than all other building materials combined.

Concrete was not the only example of scientists being drawn into work for the construction industry by the growing use of a material. Scientific knowledge (primarily chemical) also was applied to the industrial uses of wood. This took place at several levels. The Department of Agriculture had long included a Division of Forestry that had emphasized the use of scientific principles (or what they thought were scientific principles) in growing timber as a crop ("silviculture"). The problems confronted by industrial users of wood went far beyond the application of such principles, however. This was recognized by the establishment of a federally financed Forest Products Laboratory at the University of Wisconsin in Madison. This laboratory, which opened in 1910, conducted research on all questions pertaining to the use of woods for industrial purposes.[17]

The prominent role played by the railroads is again noteworthy. Even though the railroads gave up the use of wood as a fuel in the post–Civil War years, it is estimated that they accounted for between 20 and 25 percent of the country's annual timber consumption between 1870 and 1900.[18] The largest single use was for crossties.

dration in large masses of concrete; sulphate-resistant cement, which is free from the distintegrating action of sulphate soils or waters; and special oil well cements able to withstand very high temperatures and pressures before the mixture of cement and water can be placed around the casing in the bottom of oil wells from ten to fifteen thousand feet in depth" (Glover and Cornell, 1951, p. 629; see also Clark, 1929, vol. 3, pp. 253–6).

[16] "Because concrete by itself can work only in compression, it will quickly fail if it is used for members subject to high bending forces, such as beams and floor slabs. If it is reinforced with iron or steel bars, however, the elastic metal will take the tensile and shearing stresses, and the rigid concrete will sustain the compressive forces. Exactly why this nice division of labor occurs is not entirely understood, but it can be made exact if the metal is concentrated in the region of maximum tension" (Condit, 1968, p. 168).

[17] For a detailed institutional history, see Nelson, "A History of the Forest Products Laboratory" (1964). It is worth mentioning that in the year 1910, the lumber industry was, by a wide margin, the largest single industrial employer in the United States with 700,000 workers (Bureau of the Census, 1913, vol. 8, p. 40).

[18] Olson (1971), pp. 11–14.

The economic benefits flowing from the systematic chemical testing, grading, and classifying of the woods of the immense and heterogeneous forestlands of the United States were considerable. A more exact determination of the composition of woods, and the linking of composition to performance characteristics, made it possible to utilize resources far more efficiently. One immediate result of chemical testing was to establish that some tree species were much more useful than previously believed. Although white oak was strongly preferred for the making of crossties before 1890, subsequent research revealed that chestnut oak and post oak were "perfectly interchangeable" with white oak.[19]

Similarly, "studies of southern pines demonstrated that bleeding trees for turpentine in no way damaged the strength of the timber. Trees that had been bled for many years were therefore no longer excluded from the bridge timber market."[20]

More significantly, the research that led to important improvements in techniques of wood preservation by chemical treatment eventually made it possible to make routine use of wood that was abundant in many regions and that was unsuitable for use on crossties in an untreated condition.[21] By far the most important chemical treatment was impregnation with creosote, a coal-tar derivative. Treatment with creosote rendered "inferior" woods usable and substantially prolonged the useful life of the better woods. The proportion of crossties treated with chemical preservatives rose to over 20 percent in 1910, over 75 percent in 1930, and over 95 percent by 1950. The number of wood-preserving plants in the United States increased from 14 in 1900 to more than 70 in 1907, to 102 in 1914.[22]

Finally, chemical and physical testing identified the precise performance requirements of each end use so that a finer matching of specific end use with specific wood input became possible. With such information, the high-quality woods were used only where they were needed, and cheaper, lower-quality woods were introduced wherever higher-quality wood could be dispensed with:

> About 1908–1910 the Santa Fe, Pennsylvania, Northern Pacific, and Burlington, among others, established definite systems of geographical distribution in track for ties of several species and

---

[19] Ibid., p. 17.
[20] Ibid., p. 50.
[21] "Wood preservation enlarged the supply of timbers suitable for crossties. The 'inferior species,' that is, the cheaper kinds of wood that if untreated decayed rapidly, were treated and substituted for the relatively durable white oak. The red oaks were abundant in the same regions as the white oaks, and their use increased. Treated hemlock and tamarack entered production in large volumes in the states bordering on the Great Lakes, nearly five million ties in 1905. The use of cedar began to decline, displaced by treated timbers. Durable foreign woods from Japan, Hawaii, and Australia were tested and found more expensive than the treated 'inferior species' " (Olson, 1971, p. 100; see also p. 186).
[22] Ibid., pp. 104, 111.

treatments. Hardwood ties were reserved for curves and grades, softwood ties for tangent track. The untreated white oak was reserved for steep grades, sharp curves, and heavy traffic zones where it would wear out before decay destroyed it. The treated species, if given such punishment, would have worn out before their added life could be realized because many of the new timbers were softer. The cellular structures that made them absorb preservatives readily also gave them less desirable mechanical properties. Ties treated with zinc chloride were placed in arid districts, while those treated with creosote or zinc chloride and creosote were reserved for the wet areas. The same principle of careful allocation was also applied to large timber structure. The soft shortleaf and loblolly pines were utilized for temporary structures (falsework), and the denser, harder, and stronger pieces and longleaf pine were treated and reserved for permanent structures.[23]

Thus, a detailed knowledge of physical properties made possible a more efficient matching of specific grades of wood to the wide range of possible end uses.

Materials testing

There is an important common denominator running through much of the discussion of metallurgy and construction so far: Commercial as well as technological success increasingly depended on the ability to predict accurately the performance of both inputs and outputs. The growth of mass-production, metal-using industries and the remarkable new feats of construction all relied on the ability to push materials to new limits and to predict the performance of these materials with a high degree of confidence. This involved bringing together in a systematized way the knowledge of the behavior of materials that had been gleaned from the work of

[23] Ibid., pp. 110–12; see also p. 119. In the pulp and paper industry, research conducted at the Forest Products Laboratory laid the technical basis for the southern pulp and paper industries that emerged during the 1930s by making possible new uses for previously "inferior" woods. "Previously Southern pines had been used to make 'kraft' paper, a strong, brown paper, useful for wrapping exclusively. During the 1920s the FPL experts discovered a modified sulfate process which, in combination with a new two-stage bleaching process, permitted the manufacture of strong, white paper from Southern pines good for book and magazine paper. The so-called 'semichemical' process, which ranks among the most outstanding of the many FPL accomplishments, was also developed at FPL during the 1920s. This process featured a combination of the chemical and mechanical pulping methods of reducing wood substance to fiber form. The process revolutionized the pulp and paper industry by providing a method for the successful pulping of hitherto useless hardwoods" (Nelson, 1964, p. 223).

scientists and engineers working on these materials in innumerable industrial contexts. These activities were crystallized in the formation, in May 1902, of the American Society for Testing Materials (ASTM).[24]

The charter of the ASTM states that "the corporation is formed for the Promotion of Knowledge of the Materials of Engineering, and the Standardization of Specifications and the Methods of Testing." The kinds of concerns that led to the new organization are well summarized by the topics that were proposed for the Paris meeting of the International Association for Testing Materials in 1900. "Of the nineteen problems to be considered by the nineteen international committees, six are on iron and steel, one on stone and slate, eight on mortars, one on tile pipe, one on paints, one on lubricants, and one on the dry rot of wood."[25]

By 1908 the members of the ASTM were being presented in their annual proceedings with a wide range of reports dealing with the behavior of metals and building materials. Steel rails were still a major topic – including "Some Results of the Tests of Steel Rails in Progress at Watertown Arsenal," "A Microscopic Investigation of Broken Steel Rails: Manganese Sulphide as a Source of Danger," and "Rail Failures, Mashed and Split Heads." Tests and standards for road-building materials, fireproofing, waterproofing, and boilers were also prominent. But so also were papers discussing equipment and methods for testing.[26]

This was an inevitable outgrowth of the attempt to set objective standards. For, assuming one could demonstrate the relevance of given standards in quantitative terms, such standards were of limited usefulness unless tests and instruments could be developed that predicted reasonably well the actual performance in service,[27] and unless these tests and instruments yielded at least roughly uniform results in different places and in different hands. This codification of knowledge concerning the performance of materials formed the basis for writing specifications that covered a large part of the economy. It provided a scientific basis, in terms of uniformity and reliability of materials, for the design and manufacture of complex capital goods and the high-performance, consumer-durable goods that have played a great role in the economic history of the twentieth century.

---

[24] The society was an outgrowth of the American section of the International Association for Testing Materials that had been organized in June 1898.

[25] International Association for Testing Materials (1899), p. 22.

[26] American Society for Testing Materials (1908), vol. 8 (see table of contents).

[27] In his presidential address to the society in 1911, Henry Howe stated: "The shakiness of our foundations is only too evident. In order to determine whether a given steel is fitted for a given use, for instance for rails, we prescribe certain reception tests, the conditions of which are very far removed from the conditions under which that steel is to do its work. The results of these tests are not quantitatively convertible into terms of service usefulness" (American Society for Testing Materials, 1911, p. 24).

Food processing, packing, and canning

Although it is possible to label a particular aggregation of industries as "food processing," it is obvious that such a classification includes a very diverse collection of industries. Nevertheless, these industries have shared a common shift in the locus of the preparation of food products after they have left the farm. That shift has been from preparation (including preservation) in individual households or by small-scale entrepreneurs catering to local markets to factory processing on a much larger scale, involving a high degree of regional specialization in production and preparing products for eventual distribution over a vast geographic region, perhaps even the entire nation.

This transformation was set in motion by specific economic, social, and technical forces quite independent of science. None of these major transformations was *initiated* by a scientific breakthrough. Nevertheless, at critical junctures in the transition to large-scale factory production, scientific knowledge and analytic procedures had to be invoked because the new, large-scale production technologies, or the nationwide distribution of perishable products, encountered problems or constraints that could be dealt with more effectively by scientifically trained personnel.

Although the biological nature of the raw materials and therefore their high degree of variability presented certain unique difficulties that distinguished them from steel or concrete, the demands on science of food processing were similar to those of metallurgy and construction. They included, above all, a detailed understanding of the composition of inputs because that composition was highly relevant to the success of certain subsequent large-scale production technologies, and also because the highly specific needs of purchasers of intermediate inputs required both precise predictability and uniformity of composition.[28] Thus, along with the new technologies, markets were becoming increasingly sensitive to even small variations in taste, texture, and size, and the development of national markets, national distribution networks, advertising and brand names, and trademarks intensified these trends (see Chandler, 1977).

---

[28] Consider the Babcock test, an extremely simple way of measuring the butterfat content of milk. All that is required is a small amount of sulfuric acid, a properly graduated container, and a sample of milk. The test was introduced by Professor S. M. Babcock of the University of Wisconsin in 1890. Its use made it possible for dairy processors (creamery men, cheese makers, etc.) to make more informed purchasing decisions and to control their own production processes more effectively; it provided farmers with a means of measuring the productivity of their dairy cows in a more economically significant fashion than was possible before. More than incidentally, it also discouraged the adulteration of milk.

Canning

The preservation of food by canning began in the first decade of the nineteenth century. In fact, the term "canning" is a misnomer with respect to the original process. Nicholas Appert, a Parisian confectioner, managed to preserve certain foods by placing them in glass bottles that had been immersed in boiling water. He published his findings in a treatise in 1810 bearing the title *L'Art de conserver, pendant plusiers années, toutes les substances animales et végétales*.[29] No one could explain exactly how this heat-sterilization process, and subsequent airtight sealing, prevented food deterioration. Indeed, the process was not completely reliable. Spoilage was to remain the great nemesis of the canning industry for a century or more. Nevertheless, the industry grew. Tin-coated steel cans were introduced in the 1830s, and the autoclave, offering higher and more precise temperature control, was adapted to canning in 1852. Pasteur discovered the role played by microorganisms in food spoilage in 1873, effectively establishing the new science of bacteriology. Nevertheless, spoilage persisted as a major problem for several decades more, as chemists and bacteriologists wrestled with the particularities of individual food products and the specific roles, not only of microorganisms but also of oxidation, dehydration, and enzyme action. "The form of spoilage to which a food is susceptible depends on its composition, structure, specific microorganisms, and storage conditions. Micro-organisms themselves are affected by temperature, moisture, oxygen concentration, available nutrients, degree of contamination with spoilage organisms, and the presence or absence of growth inhibitors."[30]

Chemists, biochemists, and bacteriologists thus spent much time identifying the role played by each of a large number of variables in food spoilage and how they interacted in the case of each canned product. Chemists gradually established the connections between temperature, length of cooking time, and desirable food characteristics such as flavor, aroma, and texture. Careful bacteria counts established how it was possible to attain acceptable bacterial levels and more attractive food properties by shorter periods of cooking at higher temperatures. Out of this came the precise, food-specific information on which the control over the preservation technologies was dependent, as well as a gradual expansion of the varieties of fruits and vegetables that could be successfully canned. This increasingly effective knowledge led also to greater discrimination in

---

[29] Appert's method secured for him a prize of 10,000 francs that had been offered in 1797 by Napoleon's Society for the Encouragement of Industry for the development of a technique of food preservation that could be used by the military.

[30] *Encyclopaedia Britannica*, 15th ed., "Food Preservation."

the selection of crops for canning and to greater geographic specialization as knowledge of optimal soil and climatic conditions was also established.

Eventually, the need of the canners, as well as of other food processors, were to exercise a great deal of influence on the work of geneticists and plant breeders. Twentieth-century science was able to move from the passive selection activities of earlier scientists to the active shaping of plant varieties that conformed better to the needs of the food processors: fruit and vegetable varieties that yielded more uniform size, ripened simultaneously, and resisted the bruising effect of mechanical picking.

Milling

The technological changes that occurred in milling beginning in the 1870s highlight the subtle relationship between technology and national resources on the one hand and the changing economic role of science on the other. Although milling technology became very complex, involving the use of a large number of specialized machines, two basic innovations (plus, of course, the availability of new power sources) dominated the transition from the local, small-scale grist mill to the large-scale, mass-production catering to huge and distant, urban markets. The first was the replacement of millstones by a system of rollers. These rollers had a capacity many times greater than technologies based on mill stones.[31] The second major innovation was the introduction of a technique exploiting air currents to separate the flour from the bran. The older method had relied exclusively on sifting. Both of these techniques were of European origin, the rollers having been developed mainly in the Danubian basin and the air-separation technique (purifier) in France. By the time these two innovations had been thoroughly assimilated in the United States in the early twentieth century, the milling capacity of the United States was concentrated in ten or twelve cities in close proximity to the major wheat-growing areas of the Midwest.[32]

The impact of this new technology cannot be expressed simply in terms of conventional measures of productivity improvement. Such measures are too static to encompass the effects of the new milling methods. Before their introduction, there was a strong preference for flour made from winter wheat, a preference reflected in a higher price. Spring wheat had a variety of inferior milling qualities:

---

[31] "The size of American mills was increasing in all sections of the country, but nowhere more rapidly than in Minneapolis, where the average daily capacity per mill, which had been 25 barrels in 1860, rose to 1,837 barrels in 1890 and reached 3,623 barrels thirty years later" (Storck and Teague 1952, p. 210).
[32] For a detailed rendering of changes in milling technology, see Storck and Teague (1952).

Its kernel was rich in gluten, but very hard. To grind it satisfactorily it was necessary to run the millstones with a great pressure
and at high speed. The heat thus generated tended to discolor
the flour, and also injured its keeping qualities. Moreover, the
husk of the spring-wheat kernel was thin and brittle; hence, it
tended to crumble into fine particles which it was difficult to sift
from the flour. Winter wheat, on the contrary, had a thick, tough
bran which in milling, was more likely to separate from the kernel in large flakes which could be easily sifted out. Winter wheat
was softer and so ground more easily. There was not the same
pressure and speed of stones with resulting heating and discol-
oration. Winter wheat flour was therefore whiter, stronger, and
less likely to spoil; hence it was everywhere preferred and this
preference was extended to the winter wheat. (Kuhlmann, 1929,
p. 114)[33]

As a result, only small quantities of spring wheat were produced before
the advent of the new milling techniques, and wheat growing was therefore largely confined to those regions that were well suited to the cultivation of winter wheat. The new technology, however, could produce a
quality of flour from spring wheat as good as the flour from winter wheat.
Consequently, wheat with good milling quality (the new techniques had
redefined "good milling quality") could now be grown for the first time
across a vast land area where *only* spring wheat could be grown – Minnesota, the Dakotas, and Montana. It was these developments that made
Minneapolis the leading flour-milling city of the world by the 1880s. But,
more important, they expanded immensely the land area over which a
basic cereal crop could be grown.

The conditions of the new milling technology created a number of difficulties not encountered under the older technological regime. There is
considerable variation among different types of wheat, variations that require somewhat different methods of processing.[34] As mills became larger
and used wheats from an increasing number of locations, the flour could
exhibit wide variations in strength and quality. The new markets for flour,

[33] See also Temporary National Economic Committee (1940), pp. 135–8.
[34] "Different varieties of wheat are quite unlike in their characteristics, the same wheats
will vary considerably from season to season and from district to district, and bulk grain
comes to the mill mixed with all manner of alien substances – tiny sticks and stones, wire
and mud and dust, other seeds and spores, excess moisture, parasitic infestations, and a
thousand unsuspected surprises. As little as 0.2 percent of fine outside dirt can discolor a
straight flour. If badly stored, wheats go through a change known as sweating. In a modern mill, the storage of wheats, their cleaning and preparation for grinding, and their
reduction demand constant vigilance and an instant resourcefulness" (Storck and Teague,
1952, p. 199).

however, demanded an increasing degree of uniformity for each of various types of flour that were utilized for specific purposes within bakeries or households. A high degree of predictability in the properties of the flour was essential in making breads, pastries, crackers, biscuits, and baking powders that were produced and marketed on a large scale. Large bakeries operate with formulas that require gluten measurements. Any deviation is unacceptable. "A big baker would have just as little use for a batch of flour of slightly higher gluten content as for one that was slightly deficient – both would disturb his formulas."[35] Furthermore, the internal requirements of the new milling process demanded more precise measurement and control to attain the important goal of uniform grinding characteristics.[36]

All of this required chemical analysis and control, and the new technology therefore brought with it the establishment of laboratories for testing the wheat and the flour to establish their precise chemical composition – protein content, gluten content, moisture, ash, and so forth.[37] Chemistry soon discovered that earlier criteria were misleading. "The great difficulty is that the system of wheat-grading now in use emphasizes certain external factors, such as hardness, plumpness of kernel, color, and weight, which do not always correlate closely with milling quality. This the cereal chemists have shown is largely dependent on the chemical composition of the wheat; its protein content and the quantity and quality of the gluten it contains."[38]

Finally, the use of rollers, together with other improvements, gave millers a much greater degree of control over the grinding process than was previously possible. It thereby offered them an enhanced capacity for making more exacting choices. Millers could, by incurring an additional cost, increase the proportion of high-grade to low-grade flour. But to determine the optimum composition of output it was essential to be able to measure a number of relevant magnitudes with greater accuracy than was previously attainable, and to exercise a more informed control over each stage of the milling process.[39]

[35] Ibid., p. 312.
[36] Ibid., p. 232.
[37] "The need for quality control along scientific rather than merely empirical lines was felt at least as early as 1886, when A. W. Howard founded a commercial testing laboratory at Minneapolis to which millers sent their flours for baking tests and for analyses of their contents. Stimulated by Jago's work on the chemistry of flour, the Washburn Crosby Co. set up a testing room in 1893 – the first such step to be taken by an American miller. Today every large miller determines precise quality standards for his products, of whatever kind, and bends every effort to see that they are maintained" (Storck and Teague, 1952, p. 315; see also Kuhlmann, 1929, p. 231).
[38] Kuhlmann (1929), p. 231.
[39] Ibid.

Meat packing

The meat-packing industry was the product of two innovations – the railroad and the expansion of the railroad network throughout the Midwest, and the introduction of mechanical refrigeration. Before the 1870s, meat packing was primarily a local business confined to pork products, and the dominant preservative techniques were salting and smoking. Cattle were necessarily slaughtered near the place of final consumption. Within a couple of decades meat packing had become a national, year-round industry, no longer merely seasonal, highly concentrated in Chicago and a few other Midwestern livestock centers, and providing beef as well as pork to a rapidly growing and rapidly urbanizing population.[40]

Some winter shipments of dressed beef to eastern cities were made in the late 1860s, but artificial refrigeration was not successfully introduced until the mid-1870s. In short order the major packers – Swift, Hammond, Armour, and others – entered the refrigerated beef trade, and by 1890 a national distribution system was firmly in place. In that year also a federal meat-inspection system was introduced.

The employment of scientists (mainly chemists and bacteriologists) in meat packing involved certain functions basically analogous to those in canning.[41] Refrigeration as a technique of food preservation involved a distinctive set of problems of its own. Full-time chemists began to be employed in the industry in the second half of the 1880s (see MacDowell, 1921; Clemen, 1923, Chapter 16). Chemical control of meat packing production involved the setting of numerous chemical standards and extensive sampling procedures in fulfilling criteria that were relevant to health, taste, and appearance. Specific agents entering into the various meat-curing processes were analyzed for uniformity and quality, and then the curing process itself was monitored. Chemical analysis was eventually extended to provide rigorous guidance from the initial purchase of livestock to the eventual flow of finished products.

What was most distinctive about the role of science in meat packing,

---

[40] "In 1890, according to the census, meat packing establishments located in five cities – Chicago, Kansas City, Omaha, St. Joseph and St. Louis – accounted for 69 percent of the total domestic cattle slaughtered, 49 percent of the hogs and 52 percent of the sheep. Chicago alone contributed 30 percent of the cattle slaughter, 23 percent of the hogs and 30 percent of the sheep" (*Encyclopedia of the Social Sciences*, 1933, "Meat Packing and Slaughtering").

[41] Some meat was, of course, preserved by canning. Here, too, change initiated by trained scientists played a very significant role, in spite of the extreme simplicity of their suggested innovations. "A change in the process of canning, which consisted in precooking the meat before it went into the container and in making the latter wedge-shaped so the contents could be removed in a loaf, eliminated the disagreeable taste and appearance of meats cooked in the can and packed floating in their juices, and thus gave a great impetus to this form of food preparation" (Clark, 1929, vol. 2, p. 507).

however, was not its control over the preservation processes or the assurance of uniformity of quality in the final product. Rather, it was the part played in the development of by-products. Indeed, if the term "by-product" is defined to include everything other than edible meat, then it constituted almost one-half of the weight of the live animal. In the early days of the industry before refrigeration, when slaughterhouses and packing plants were separate establishments, most of the nonedible portions of the animal were dumped into a convenient waterway, or even buried.[42] The rendering of lard was only a partial exception because lard was made primarily from portions of the hog that would not be thrown away. Whether the pork was packed or rendered into lard depended on the relative prices of pork and lard. When lard prices were high, a larger fraction of the hog was converted into lard.[43]

The development of the by-products industries in the 1880s and after is a remarkable story of the creative use of techniques of chemical analysis to transform an enormous quantity of meat-packing waste materials into a very long list of valuable products. Although the nearby glue factory indeed antedated the chemical laboratory in the packing industry, the by-products industry was basically an outgrowth of the huge increase in scale of plant that accompanied the introduction of the railroad and refrigeration. These two innovations made much larger markets accessible to the packer (who also absorbed the activities of the slaughterhouse) and led directly to a high degree of geographic concentration and a large scale of operation of individual plants. The large scale of operation in turn made possible the diverse range of highly specialized activities exploiting what had formerly been mainly waste materials.

Although the earliest work of chemists focused on food products such as oleomargarine and beef extract,[44] before the turn of the century the chemists' attention also turned to more distant fields that would expand dramatically in the early decades of the twentieth century: pharmaceuticals,[45] commercial fertilizers, soap, explosives, lubrication oils, cosmetics,

[42] "As long as the slaughtering was done at an establishment which was conducted independently of the packing plants, the offal, head, internal organs, blood, hair, and other trimmings of the slaughtered animals were considered a part of the waste material which the slaughterer must dispose of. The packer did not want to be bothered with it, and for that matter, neither did the slaughterer. In fact, at Cincinnati all this material was dumped into the Ohio River, and since the current was swift enough to carry it away that proved to be an easy method of getting rid of it" (Clemen, 1923, p. 127; see also Armour, 1895, p. 388).
[43] Clemen (1923), p. 129.
[44] Ibid., pp. 360–2.
[45] Writing in the early 1920s, Clemen stated: "At present, for the medical profession only, 48 pharmaceutical preparations are made, glands and membranes being utilized, while fresh, in the plant laboratories. Among the most important medical agents produced in the packinghouse laboratories are pepsin, pancreatin, thyroids, rennet, benzoinated lard, suprarenals, and pituitary liquids" (ibid., p. 370).

and so forth. The development of these by-products involved systematic chemical analysis to determine the exact chemical composition of former waste materials. But, in addition, the new markets that were being targeted often required a high degree of uniformity in the final product. In pharmaceuticals it turned out that

> the products being manufactured in the pharmaceutical department were by no means standard and that uniform results were not being obtained by physicians in prescribing and using those compounds, due to the variation of the content of the active principle. The laboratory was asked to develop standards for all of the medicinal products and to undertake to check each day's product against these standards, so that an absolutely uniform medicine would be produced. (MacDowell, 1921, p. 218)

Even for an older and more traditional product such as beef extract, however, better chemical analysis played an essential role in achieving a marketable product:

> For many years beef extract had been one of the standard by-products of the packing industry. It was known that various batches apparently handled in the same manner differed widely as to color, odor and taste. Nothing was known, however, of the nutritive value; nothing was known as to the actual reasons for the above mentioned variations. This problem was put up to the laboratory and it was discovered that certain minor changes in the methods of making beef extract and certain separations of raw materials would enable the factory to produce a uniform product of standard nutritive value. (Ibid.)[46]

By-products in industries other than meat packing

Although the issue has not been explicitly formulated in such terms, our discussion has several times disclosed how sensitive the concept of an economic resource is to the progress of technological knowledge. In fact, the waste materials of one generation have become the valued by-products of the next. This transformation of waste materials into valuable resources has been one of the most pervasive of all the effects of the application of science to industry. It is widely observable throughout the sectors that we have been considering, but it has been by no means confined to them. We have seen, over and over, how elementary scientific

---

[46] Products such as fertilizers were usually sold with guarantees to the buyer concerning composition, strength, and so forth. In this respect, the guarantees were similar to those available for flour and steel products.

knowledge, often involving little more than the most basic tools of analytic chemistry, has provided essential information that has raised the efficiency of resource utilization (often including the initial selection process), product design, and materials processing.

Although the exploitation of by-products involved scientific techniques very similar to those we have been considering, they involved some other basic economic considerations as well. One of these is, of course, relative prices. Whether it pays to utilize a previously discarded by-product depends on its price and the price of the products for which it may be a close substitute. Indeed, what is a product and what is a by-product (or potential by-product) depends on the cost of bringing it to market, the prices of other products for which it is a potential substitute, and the level of technological and scientific knowledge. Although the hide of a cow and the tallow were regarded as valuable by-products of the meat-packing industry in Chicago, on the Argentine pampas earlier in the nineteenth century cattle were slaughtered merely for their hide or tallow – as Marx indignantly observed in *Capital*.[47] More recently, natural gas, a high-quality fuel, was flared for many years because of the absence of satisfactory techniques of pipe manufacture. In the early history of petroleum, everything aside from kerosene (which was highly desired as an illuminant) was considered a by-product. Petroleum was not regarded as an energy source. Subsequent technological change – in the form of internal combustion and diesel engines – changed all that.

The ability and the financial incentive to exploit waste materials depended, in addition to the availability of scientific knowledge, on a central trend in the process of industrial development: the growth in scale of production operations. Marx saw this clearly in the last years of his life (he died in 1883).[48] Indeed, in the history of individual industries we find

[47] "While simple cooperation leaves the mode of working by the individual for the most part unchanged, manufacture thoroughly revolutionises it, and seizes labour-power by its very roots. It converts the labourer into a crippled monstrosity, by forcing his detail dexterity at the expense of a world of productive capabilities and instincts; just as in the States of La Plata they butcher a whole beast for the sake of his hide or his tallow" (Marx, 1936, p. 396).

[48] Production on a large scale, Marx pointed out, offers certain decisive advantages. Among them: "We refer to the reconversion of the excretions of production, the so-called waste, into new elements of production, either of the same, or of some other line of industry; to the processes by which this so-called excretion is thrown back into the cycle of production and, consequently, consumption, whether productive or individual. This line of savings . . . is . . . the result of large-scale social labour. It is the attendant abundance of this waste which renders it available again for commerce and thereby turns it into new elements of production. It is only as waste of combined production, therefore of large-scale production, that it becomes important to the production process and remains a bearer of exchange-value. . . . In the chemical industry, for instance, excretions of production are such by-products as are wasted in production on a smaller scale; iron filings accumulating in the manufacture of machinery and returning into the production of iron as raw materials, etc." (Marx, *Capital*, 1959, p. 100).

case after case in which the increasing scale of production operations eventually gave rise to an awareness that certain materials of great potential usefulness were being discarded in large quantities. Since techniques for utilizing these materials did not yet exist, this awareness often led to the necessary research activities, sometimes to the original establishment of a research laboratory. Thus, growth in scale commonly raised the private financial returns to investment in research, leading to the acquisition of new techniques for the utilization of by-products.

Such developments were particularly common in the growth of chemical-processing industries such as petroleum refining. The origin of the central research laboratory for the Royal Dutch Shell Oil Company's American subsidiary has been characterized as "an attempt to make profitable uses of the tremendous amounts of oilfield and refinery gases which had up to then been flared into the air or, at best, burned for boiler fuel." The importance of developing a research thrust to use these by-products was closely linked to the growth in scale of plant: "The quantities of these gases were at first insignificant, but with rapid expansion of cracking facilities in the second half of the Twenties, the volume of cracking gases became enormous."[49]

Nevertheless, although the search for by-products led to systematic laboratory research in the twentieth century, the earlier search for petroleum by-products in the nineteenth century was the work of practical people or those with only a smattering of chemical training.[50] Before the turn of the twentieth century the value of these "by-products" (gasoline, naphtha, paraffin, petroleum jelly, and lubricants) was equal to the value of the main product – illuminating oil.[51]

Conclusion

Most R&D even today is not directed to the creation of knowledge, if by knowledge one means *scientific* knowledge. Some two-thirds of R&D in recent years has been development, and only about one-twelfth has been basic research. Similarly, the work of most scientifically trained people has historically been, in this sense, devoted to the application rather than the creation of knowledge. To a much greater extent than is generally

---

[49] Beaton (1957), pp. 502–3, as quoted in Mowery (1981), p. 123.

[50] This was true only of the early search for by-products. "Most improvements in the refining process were the work of practical refiners rather than trained chemists. The most serious chemical problem facing refiners before the end of the century, the sulfur content of crude from the Lima, Ohio, fields, was solved by Herman Frasch, a German-born technician with only minimal formal training in chemistry" (Birr, 1966, p. 61). Birr points out that Standard Oil Co. had begun hiring trained chemists in 1882 "primarily for analytical and control purposes."

[51] Clark (1929), vol. 2, p. 519.

recognized, economically valuable knowledge has been old, rather than new, scientific knowledge.

These facts and their implications have been neglected because of the preoccupation with the generation of new knowledge, a preoccupation that has been especially strong in the academic world. Obviously, if in the long run no new knowledge is created, the application of knowledge will fall to low levels as the returns to the application of this knowledge decline. Nonetheless, in order to understand science as a social phenomenon, it is essential to examine the entire system of activities that contribute to its advance, rather than focusing on a few such activities in isolation.

The economics of science requires a study of both the relationships and incentives that lead to the production of knowledge and the relationships and incentives for the application of that knowledge. As this chapter has suggested, the industrial application of scientific knowledge in the U.S. economy was shaped by the peculiar needs and special problems confronting the production technologies of a rapidly expanding economy. Over the past century changes in production technologies and the inputs employed in them have been associated with major changes in the nature and composition of industrial output. These changes raised the payoff to scientific knowledge. As a result, science has provided its economic benefits through a number of channels, but most commonly by assisting in the exploitation of innovations that did not have their origins in recent science.

To a much greater extent than we have acknowledged, science has become the servant of industrial technology in industrializing societies. Industrial applications of scientific knowledge in turn have been driven in large part by technological developments that have shaped the industrial demand for scientific knowledge. If we are to understand the functioning of the "scientific epoch" and the growth in productivity associated with this epoch, we must study the ways in which industrial technologies have shaped the demand for scientific knowledge.

4

The U.S. research system before 1945

As we noted in the preceding chapters, the expansion of the American economy during the late nineteenth and early twentieth centuries combined with innovations in transportation, communications, and production technologies to yield manufacturing operations of unprecedented scale. The materials-analysis and quality-control laboratories that were established within many of these factories were among the first industrial employers of scientists and research personnel. Over time, these plant-level laboratories expanded and were supplemented by the foundation of central laboratories devoted to longer-term research.[1] Although the development of much of the original testing and materials-analysis research was a response to changes in the structure of production, the expansion and elaboration of these activities reflect changes in the organizational structure of the firm. The development of these research facilities was associated with changes in the structure of the parent firm that expanded and diversified its activities and products and substituted intrafirm control of these activities for market control.

These developments transformed the processes of invention and innovation within American manufacturing during the early twentieth century. Formerly carried out largely by inspired individuals, the process of innovation increasingly took place in research facilities under the control of manufacturing firms. Schumpeter argued that "innovation is being reduced to routine. Technological progress is increasingly becoming the business of teams of trained specialists who turn out what is required and make it work in predictable ways. The romance of earlier commercial

---

[1] Lewis (1967) argues that "testing and analysis have continued to be of major importance in the industrial application of science down to the present time. . . . The significance of such work in providing employment for scientists, however, gradually declined in a relative sense. Although the development of testing procedures and the determination of physical constants often required considerable ingenuity and imagination, routine testing itself tended to be monotonous and unattractive to highly trained personnel; in time it was increasingly assigned to nonprofessional employees and even handled by mechanical or electronic devices. Meanwhile, the efforts of industrial researchers came to be applied to an ever greater degree to eliminating production bottlenecks, exploring different processes, finding substitute raw materials from which goods could be turned out at lower cost, finding profitable uses for by-products, and improving the quality of various manufactured commodities" (p. 622).

adventure is rapidly wearing away" (1954, p. 132).[2] Although a number of major manufacturing firms had emerged during the late nineteenth century from the innovations of such individual inventor-entrepreneurs as Eastman, Edison, Bell, and Westinghouse, in the twentieth century innovation became too important to be left to the whims of the market and the wiles of the individual inventor.[3]

In this chapter we describe the development of the pre-1945 research system within the United States. We analyze the pattern of growth in the number of research laboratories and in research employment within U.S. industry and examine the distribution of employment across sectors. The growth of industrial research also affected the performance of firms, and we discuss the contribution of research to performance.

The growth of research within U.S. industry was primarily an increase in research within the firm.[4] Independent research organizations not affiliated with manufacturing firms declined in importance during the first decades of this century. As we noted in Chapter 1, neoclassical economic theory predicts the development of a very different structure of industrial research. Accordingly, this chapter analyzes the relationship between intrafirm and contractual research during the prewar period in order to illuminate some of the reasons for this clash between theory and evidence.

Research within both academic and public-sector laboratories also expanded (albeit at lower rates) during this period. What relationships if any developed between academic and industrial, or between academic, public, and industrial research facilities? What influences common to academia, government, and industry might explain this parallel pattern of

---

[2] Beer's description of the activities of one of the first industrial research laboratories in the German chemicals industry also is apposite: "Of the research work done in the Bayer laboratories, only a fraction was devoted to the search for dyes of radically new chemical composition. By far the largest amount of time was devoted to experiments of an unspectacular or routine nature in which the theoretical principle was well understood. Only on rare occasions in the course of this work did a reaction refuse to go as predicted and thus point up a new theoretical problem. The number of routine experiments that had to be conducted to find a single promising color was large. . . . This tedious, meticulous experimentation, in which a thousand little facts were wrenched from nature through coordinated massed assault, admirably illustrates the method and spirit introduced into scientific inquiry by the rising industrial laboratory of the late nineteenth century" (1958, p. 130).

[3] Schmookler's analysis of patent data (which measure only inventive, rather than innovative, activity) concluded that "During the [1900–50] period invention changed from an activity overwhelmingly dominated by independent individuals to one less overwhelmingly dominated by business enterprise" (1957, p. 333).

[4] See later discussion in this chapter; Wise (1985) notes that this structure contrasts with the organization of much of the industrial research of the late nineteenth century, which he describes as the "putting-out" method: "Companies supplied independent inventors with the money needed to do a specific R&D job, and took possession of the results. Those companies did not employ the inventors permanently" (p. 4).

growth? Despite the fact that nonindustrial research employment and funding grew during this period, the nonindustrial component of the national research system experienced its greatest expansion only after World War II.

Trends in the growth of industrial research, 1899–1946

Tables 4.1 through 4.6 present data on laboratory foundations and employment during 1899–1946 in manufacturing, drawn from the National Research Council survey data reported in Mowery (1981). Table 4.1 displays foundation rates by two-digit manufacturing industry for the 1899–1946 period in terms of numbers of new laboratories established during each of five periods rather than in terms of cumulative growth in total laboratories within each industry. Nearly all of the industries represented in Table 4.1 exhibit patterns of laboratory formation that peak in 1919–28, the next most active period being 1929–36. The influence of wartime (the 1909–18 and 1937–46 periods) on laboratory formation varies across these industries. The decade including World War I is substantially more important than the 1937–46 period for petroleum, rubber, glass, primary metals, and nonelectrical machinery. The laboratory foundations in the rubber, petroleum, and glass industries during this early period may well have reflected the rapid expansion of automobile-related production of tires, auto glass, and gasoline and lubricants during the early growth of the U.S. automobile industry.

By contrast, instruments, transportation equipment, and electrical machinery all display dramatic increases in laboratory formations during 1937–46. This upsurge almost certainly reflects the expansion of the federal government's role as a source of research funding during and after World War II, a topic we discuss in greater detail in Chapter 6. These three industries were among the largest recipients of federal research support in wartime and benefited as well from major procurement programs.

The chemicals industry, which in Germany played a central role in the development of industrial research (Beer, 1958), contributed more than one-quarter of all laboratory foundations during 1899–1946. The group of industries including chemicals, glass, rubber, and petroleum products, identified by Chandler (1969, p. 261) as "more chemical than mechanical," account for nearly 40 percent of the total foundations of laboratories during the period.

Tables 4.2 through 4.6 provide data on research laboratory employment for 1921, 1927, 1933, 1940, and 1946 within each of nineteen two-digit manufacturing industries and in manufacturing overall. From a level of less than 3,000 in 1921, employment of scientists and engineers in industrial research within manufacturing grew to nearly 46,000 by 1946.

Table 4.1. *Laboratory foundations within manufacturing, 1899–1946*

		Prior to 1899	1899–1908	1909–18	1919–28	1929–36	1937–46	Total (% of total mfg.)
Food & beverages	number	11	20	32	50	48	40	201
	% of row	5.5	10.0	15.9	24.9	23.9	19.9	(8.7)
Tobacco products	number	0	0	1	2	3	1	7
	% of row	0.0	0.0	14.3	28.6	42.9	14.3	(0.3)
Textile products	number	3	4	11	16	28	17	79
	% of row	3.8	5.1	13.9	20.3	35.4	21.5	(3.4)
Apparel	number	0	0	1	1	0	2	4
	% of row	0.0	0.0	25.0	25.0	0.0	50.0	(0.2)
Lumber products	number	0	1	1	2	5	5	14
	% of row	0.0	7.1	7.1	14.3	35.7	35.7	(0.6)
Furniture	number	0	0	0	2	1	1	4
	% of row	0.0	0.0	0.0	50.0	25.0	25.0	(0.2)
Paper	number	4	6	15	38	26	13	102
	% of row	3.9	5.9	14.7	37.3	25.5	12.7	(4.4)
Publishing	number	0	0	0	2	3	1	6
	% of row	0.0	0.0	0.0	33.3	50.0	16.7	(0.2)
Chemicals	number	40	56	88	178	146	107	615
	% of row	6.5	9.1	14.3	28.9	23.7	17.4	(26.7)
Petroleum	number	5	3	15	25	31	10	89
	% of row	5.6	3.4	16.9	28.1	34.8	11.2	(3.9)
Rubber products	number	2	2	16	19	13	5	57
	% of row	3.5	3.5	28.1	33.3	22.8	8.8	(2.5)

Leather products	number	3	0	4	9	3	1	20
	% of row	15.0	0.0	20.0	45.0	15.0	5.0	(0.9)
Stone, clay, glass	number	5	12	24	54	39	12	146
	% of row	3.4	8.2	16.4	37.0	26.7	8.2	(6.3)
Primary metals	number	9	19	30	42	29	14	143
	% of row	6.3	13.3	21.0	29.4	20.3	9.8	(6.2)
Fabricated metals	number	0	17	24	53	37	28	159
	% of row	0.0	10.7	15.1	33.3	23.3	17.6	(6.9)
Nonelectrical machinery	number	6	14	49	65	63	30	227
	% of row	2.6	6.2	21.6	28.6	27.8	13.2	(9.9)
Electrical machinery	number	12	18	28	53	64	44	219
	% of row	5.5	8.2	12.8	24.2	29.2	20.1	(9.5)
Transportation equipment	number	4	4	12	16	10	20	66
	% of row	6.1	6.1	18.2	24.2	15.2	30.3	(2.9)
Instruments	number	6	4	17	23	32	36	118
	% of row	5.1	3.4	14.4	19.5	27.1	30.5	(5.1)
All manufacturing	number	112	182	371	660	590	388	2,303
	% of row	4.9	7.9	16.1	28.7	25.6	16.8	(100.0)

Table 4.2. *1921 Survey, total employment, scientific personnel, research intensity, and employment concentration*

	Staff (% of total)	Scientific personnel (% of total)	Research intensity[a]	Scientific personnel in bottom 10% of laboratories (in %)	Scientific personnel in top 10% laboratories (in %)
Food/ beverages	204 (3.0)	116 (3.2)	.19	2.5	24.2
Tobacco	—	—	—	—	—
Textiles	16 (.23)	15 (.41)	.015	—	—
Apparel	—	—	—	—	—
Lumber products	70 (1.0)	30 (.83)	.043	—	—
Furniture	—	—	—	—	—
Paper	115 (1.7)	89 (2.5)	.49	1.2	38.1
Publishing	—	—	—	—	—
Chemicals	1,627 (24.3)	1,102 (30.4)	5.2	1.4	44.8
Petroleum	246 (3.7)	159 (4.4)	1.83	1.8	49.1
Rubber products	522 (7.8)	207 (5.7)	2.04	0.5	49.8
Leather	29 (0.4)	25 (0.7)	0.09	4.0	40.0
Stone, clay, glass	146 (2.2)	96 (2.6)	.38	2.1	50.0
Primary metals	592 (8.8)	297 (8.2)	.78	1.0	40.7
Fabricated metals	185 (2.8)	103 (2.8)	.27	2.9	41.7
Nonelectrical machinery	148 (2.2)	127 (3.5)	.25	2.4	36.2
Electrical machinery	2,049 (30.6)	199 (7.2)	1.11	1.6	53
Transportation equipment	464 (6.9)	83 (2.3)	.204	2.4	51.8
Instruments	238 (3.5)	127 (2.5)	.396	1.6	52.0
Total[b]	6,693	2,775	.56	1.1	47.4

[a] Scientific personnel/1000 wage earners.
[b] Excluding miscellaneous manufacturing.

Table 4.3. *1927 Survey, total employment, scientific personnel, research intensity, and employment concentration*

	Staff (% of total)	Scientific personnel (% of total)	Research intensity[a]	Scientific personnel in bottom 10% of laboratories (in %)	Scientific personnel in top 10% laboratories (in %)
Food/ beverages	425 (3.5)	354 (5.6)	.53	2.1	31.1
Tobacco	7 (0.06)	4 (0.06)	.031	—	—
Textiles	121 (1.01)	79 (1.25)	0.07	2.5	32.9
Apparel	—	—	—	—	—
Lumber products	96 (.80)	50 (.79)	.16	3.1	58.5
Furniture	—	—	—	—	—
Paper	306 (2.54)	189 (2.99)	.87	1.6	37.0
Publishing	—	—	—	—	—
Chemicals	3,150 (26.19)	1,812 (28.67)	6.52	1.3	47.5
Petroleum	788 (6.55)	465 (7.36)	4.65	1.1	36.5
Rubber products	907 (7.54)	361 (5.71)	2.56	0.8	54.4
Leather	40 (0.33)	35 (0.55)	.11	2.9	28.6
Stone, clay, glass	683 (5.68)	410 (6.49)	1.18	1.6	37.8
Primary metals	909 (7.56)	538 (8.51)	0.93	1.2	51.9
Fabricated metals	555 (4.61)	334 (5.28)	0.63	1.9	25.9
Nonelectrical machinery	1,232 (10.24)	421 (6.66)	0.65	1.8	28.6
Electrical machinery	1,652 (13.73)	732 (11.58)	2.86	1.1	42.8
Transportation equipment	778 (6.47)	256 (4.05)	0.52	1.6	42.0
Instruments	425 (3.53)	234 (3.7)	0.63	1.8	52.0
Total[b]	12,028	6,320	0.83	1.3	43.5

[a] Scientific personnel/1000 wage earners.
[b] Excluding miscellaneous manufacturing.

Table 4.4. *1933 Survey, total employment, scientific personnel, research intensity, and employment concentration*

	Staff (% of total)	Scientific personnel (% of total)	Research intensity[a]	Scientific personnel in bottom 10% of laboratories (in %)	Scientific personnel in top 10% laboratories (in %)
Food/ beverages	839 (4.29)	651 (5.96)	.973	2.2	31.5
Tobacco	21 (0.11)	17 (0.16)	0.19	—	—
Textiles	185 (0.95)	149 (1.36)	0.15	2.7	29.5
Apparel	—	—	—	—	—
Lumber products	93 (0.48)	65 (0.59)	0.22	3.2	22.6
Furniture	9 (0.05)	5 (0.05)	0.041	—	—
Paper	461 (2.36)	302 (2.76)	1.54	1.8	32.7
Publishing	4 (0.02)	4 (0.04)	0.015	—	—
Chemicals	5,239 (26.8)	3,255 (29.79)	12.81	1.1	48.2
Petroleum	2,809 (14.37)	994 (9.1)	11.04	0.7	51.7
Rubber products	1,434 (7.34)	564 (5.16)	5.65	1.5	48.0
Leather	80 (0.41)	67 (0.61)	0.24	1.6	25.4
Stone, clay, glass	889 (4.55)	569 (5.21)	3.25	1.8	37.5
Primary metals	1,356 (6.94)	850 (7.78)	2.00	1.1	41.6
Fabricated metals	777 (3.97)	500 (4.58)	1.53	2.0	27.0
Nonelectrical machinery	1,484 (7.59)	629 (5.76)	1.68	2.2	29.5
Electrical machinery	2,340 (11.97)	1,322 (12.1)	8.06	1.5	44.7

Table 4.4. *Cont.*

	Staff (% of total)	Scientific personnel (% of total)	Research intensity[a]	Scientific personnel in bottom 10% of laboratories (in %)	Scientific personnel in top 10% laboratories (in %)
Transportation equipment	858 (4.39)	394 (3.61)	1.28	1.3	47.5
Instruments	657 (3.36)	581 (5.32)	2.69	1.1	60.1
Total[b]	19,548	10,927	1.93	1.3	47.7

[a] Scientific personnel/1000 wage earners.
[b] Excluding miscellaneous manufacturing.

The ordering of industries by research intensity is remarkably stable throughout this period: Chemicals, rubber, petroleum, and electrical machinery were among the most research-intensive industries, leaving leather and textiles among the least research-intensive during 1921–46. The major exception to this portrait of stability in relative research intensity is transportation equipment. From a research intensity well below the manufacturing average in 1921, transportation equipment expanded its research intensity throughout the period, and by 1946 was ranked within the five most research-intensive manufacturing industries.

The upward movement in this industry's relative research intensity reflects the effects of federal support of research and federal procurement in this industry (which includes aircraft) during 1940–6, in addition to those of rapid growth in the automobile industry throughout the 1921–46 period. Research employment during the wartime period of 1940–6 grew most rapidly in transportation equipment, instruments, and electrical machinery, all of which were major recipients of procurement contracts and research funds.

Research activity, measured in terms of either total employment or research intensity, grew most rapidly within the chemicals industry during 1921–46. As Chandler has noted, however, these data also hint at a shift in the major employers of research personnel from chemicals-based industries to physics-based industries (1985, p. 56). In 1921, the chemicals, petroleum, and rubber industries accounted for slightly more than 40 percent of total research scientists and engineers in manufacturing. Electrical machinery and instruments, both of which drew more heavily on physics for their scientific and technological knowledge bases, accounted for less than 10 percent of total research employment. By 1946, however, these two industries employed more than 20 percent of all re-

Table 4.5. *1940 Survey, total employment, scientific personnel, research intensity, and employment concentration*

	Staff (% of total)	Scientific personnel (% of total)	Research intensity[a]	Scientific personnel in bottom 10% of laboratories (in %)	Scientific personnel in top 10% laboratories (in %)
Food/ beverages	3,141 (5.38)	1,712 (6.16)	2.13	1.2	49.2
Tobacco	87 (0.15)	54 (0.19)	0.61	3.5	57.9
Textiles	523 (0.9)	254 (0.91)	0.23	1.6	32.8
Apparel	11 (0.02)	4 (0.01)	0.005	—	—
Lumber products	235 (0.40)	128 (0.46)	0.30	1.3	40.5
Furniture	41 (0.07)	19 (0.07)	0.10	15.8	26.3
Paper	1388 (2.38)	752 (2.71)	2.79	1.5	36.4
Publishing	12 (0.02)	9 (0.03)	0.03	—	—
Chemicals	14,156 (24.26)	7,675 (27.63)	27.81	0.9	54.6
Petroleum	7,632 (13.08)	2,849 (10.26)	26.38	0.5	58.5
Rubber products	2,163 (3.71)	1,000 (3.6)	8.35	0.5	48.6
Leather	118 (.20)	68 (.24)	.21	3.6	30.4
Stone, clay, glass	2,509 (4.3)	1,334 (4.8)	5.0	1.0	50.8
Primary metals	3,989 (6.84)	2,113 (7.61)	3.13	0.8	38.6
Fabricated metals	2,187 (3.75)	1,332 (4.8)	2.95	1.6	41.3
Nonelectrical machinery	5,915 (10.14)	2,122 (7.64)	3.96	1.3	46.5
Electrical machinery	7,013 (12.02)	3,269 (11.77)	13.18	0.9	58.3

Table 4.5. *Cont.*

	Staff (% of total)	Scientific personnel (% of total)	Research intensity[a]	Scientific personnel in bottom 10% of laboratories (in %)	Scientific personnel in top 10% laboratories (in %)
Transportation equipment	5,032 (8.62)	1,765 (6.35)	3.24	0.2	53.5
Instruments	2,196 (3.75)	1,318 (4.74)	4.043	0.8	52.6
Total[b]	58,348	27,777	3.67	0.8	56.8

[a] Scientific personnel/1000 wage earners.
[b] Excluding miscellaneous manufacturing.

search scientists and engineers in U.S. manufacturing, and the chemicals-based industries had increased their share to slightly more than 43 percent of total research employment.

Growth in industrial research employment exhibits little sensitivity to the dramatic economic fluctuations of the 1921–46 period. Although employment growth for wage earners within manufacturing was negative during 1927–33, employment of research scientists and engineers continued to expand: Employment of research scientists and engineers grew by 72.9 percent during 1927–33, while wage earner employment in manufacturing fell by 26.2 percent.[5] Moreover, the growth of research employment during the 1933–40 recovery period (154 percent) considerably exceeded that for wage earners in manufacturing (35 percent). Employment growth for research scientists and engineers was less rapid than that for wage earners, however, during World War II. According to the Steelman Report, industry R&D expenditures increased throughout the 1930s and accelerated their growth near the end of the decade. Measured in 1930 dollars, R&D expenditures were more than twice as large in 1940 (more than $295 million) as they had been in 1930 ($116 million).[6]

The expansion of industrial research within the American firm was closely linked as both cause and effect with the reorganization of the American corporation during the late nineteenth and early twentieth centuries.

[5] Other studies, however, suggest that research employment was interrupted during 1931–3. See Cooper (1941).
[6] *Science and Public Policy* (1947), vol. 1, p. 10. Implicit GNP deflators were employed in the calculation.

Table 4.6. *1946 Survey, total employment, scientific personnel, research intensity, and employment concentration*

	Staff (% of total)	Scientific personnel (% of total)	Research intensity[a]	Scientific personnel in bottom 10% of laboratories (in %)	Scientific personnel in top 10% laboratories (in %)
Food/ beverages	5,308 (4.5)	2,510 (5.46)	2.26	1.6	41.4
Tobacco	108 (0.09)	67 (0.15)	0.65	2.2	57.8
Textiles	1,229 (1.04)	434 (0.94)	0.38	2.6	22.4
Apparel	55 (0.05)	25 (0.05)	0.026	—	—
Lumber products	359 (0.31)	187 (0.41)	0.31	1.9	41.5
Furniture	53 (0.05)	19 (0.04)	0.068	—	—
Paper	1,764 (1.5)	770 (1.68)	1.96	1.7	38.3
Publishing	48 (0.04)	28 (0.06)	0.064	—	—
Chemicals	32,560 (27.67)	14,066 (30.62)	30.31	1.1	51.9
Petroleum	12,412 (10.55)	4,750 (10.34)	28.79	0.6	52.4
Rubber products	2,418 (2.06)	1,069 (2.33)	5.20	0.7	40.5
Leather	174 (0.15)	86 (0.19)	0.25	2.1	18.7
Stone, clay, glass	3,692 (3.14)	1,508 (3.28)	3.72	1.3	47.9
Primary metals	5,539 (4.71)	2,460 (5.35)	2.39	1.2	42.3
Fabricated metals	3,355 (2.85)	1,489 (3.24)	1.81	1.1	37.3
Nonelectrical machinery	8,261 (7.02)	2,743 (5.97)	2.20	1.5	38.9
Electrical machinery	18,421 (15.66)	6,993 (15.22)	11.01	1.1	53.0

Table 4.6. *Cont.*

	Staff (% of total)	Scientific personnel (% of total)	Research intensity[a]	Scientific personnel in bottom 10% of laboratories (in %)	Scientific personnel in top 10% laboratories (in %)
Transportation equipment	14,897 (12.66)	4,491 (9.78)	4.58	0.9	42.3
Instruments	7,007 (5.96)	2,246 (4.89)	3.81	1.0	55.9
Total[b]	117,660	45,941	3.98	1.0	61.1

[a] Scientific personnel/1000 wage earners.
[b] Excluding miscellaneous manufacturing.

Technically trained managers, a strong central office staff able to focus on strategic, rather than operating, decisions, and the integration within the firm of functions such as marketing – all were associated with the growth of R&D within the firm. In-house research was better able to combine the heterogeneous inputs necessary for commercially successful innovation, to use and increase the stock of firm-specific knowledge gleaned from marketing and production personnel, and to exploit the close link between manufacturing and the acquisition of certain forms of technical knowledge.

Because of this relationship between the changing organizational structure of the firm and the growth of industrial research, the mergers and corporate reorganizations of the late nineteenth and early twentieth centuries hastened the growth of industrial research. The firms emerging from the numerous horizontal mergers of the period were among the largest in the American economy. Many of these giant enterprises reorganized and rationalized their internal structure following their creation and developed a strong central office staff to coordinate the activities of their many component parts. Such internal rationalization was of critical importance to the subsequent incorporation within the firm of major nonmarketing activities such as marketing and industrial research. In firms such as American Telephone and Telegraph, General Electric, U.S. Steel, or Du Pont, the development of a strong central office was closely associated with the establishment or significant expansion of a central research facility. As we note in Chapter 5, the lack of comparable changes during this period in the ownership and structure of many British firms was associated with lower levels of R&D employment and investment within industry.

The growing body of work on the historical development of industrial research within individual firms emphasizes the ways in which industrial research strengthened and broadened the technological portfolios of these firms and thereby contributed to their commercial survival. A factor that contributed significantly to the growth of industrial research was the development of stronger protection for intellectual property, which both increased the appropriability of the returns from innovation and facilitated the development of a market for the acquisition and sale of patents. Beer (1958) argues that the growth of German industrial research was spurred by the passage in 1876 of a national patent law.[7] Jenkins (1975) also emphasizes the increased enforcement of patent rights within the United States in the late nineteenth century as a factor motivating Eastman Kodak's business strategy and industrial research investment.

The impending expiration of patents that protected core technologies of established firms also led to the foundation or expansion of research laboratories with the responsibility of renewing or improving patent protection for these technologies. Reich and Brock argue that Bell Telephone Laboratories protected the dominant position in telecommunications of the American Telephone and Telegraph Company, which was threatened in the early twentieth century by the expiration of its basic patents in telephony and by the development of radio. Bell Labs research contributed to AT&T's efforts to contest Pupin's patent on the loading coil, a critical innovation for long-distance transmission, and also influenced AT&T's eventual purchase of this patent. The impending expiration of patents covering light bulb products and processes also led General Electric to expand its research significantly (see Reich, Summer 1977, 1980; Brock, 1981).[8]

In addition to motivating the internal development of new technologies, industrial research (in conjunction with strong patent protection) also supported the acquisition by firms of new technologies from external sources. A number of scholars have described the important role played by Du Pont's research laboratory in guiding the firm's post–World War I

---

[7] "Almost overnight the copying practices, used heretofore with telling success by the German firms, came to an end. Factories would now have to find their own new colors or be threatened with extinction" (p. 127).

[8] Frank Jewett, the first president of Bell Labs, argued that the firm's research was "a currency which is more potent than gold in insuring complete freedom of action and in some cases even the right to live . . . which can be used in a bartering operation of cross-licensing and as an aid to charting out progress in the future, enabling better and more economical planning" ("The Laboratory – A Potent Source of Progress in Industry," speech before the Association of Life Insurance Presidents annual convention, December 2, 1938, cited in Hoddeson, 1981, p. 541).

diversification efforts.[9] Mueller (1955) argues that many of Du Pont's major product and process innovations were purchased by the firm from outside inventors at an early point in their development, often on the advice of the central research laboratory (see also Mueller, 1962).

Appropriability concerns, reflected in the drive to strengthen patent positions through internal development or acquisition of innovations, played an important role in the early development of industrial research. With the growth of in-house research, however, patents appear to have declined somewhat in importance within the research strategies of some of the corporate pioneers of industrial research. Research made a growing contribution to a stock of firm-specific knowledge that often was not patentable but that served nonetheless to strengthen the firm against competitors. Both Eastman Kodak and AT&T, for example, which had placed great emphasis on patent strategies in the early years of development of their industrial research strategies, increasingly focused on developing a strong knowledge base through in-house research and gave less weight to patents.[10] The role of patents within Bell Labs declined in importance as

[9] Chandler and Salsbury (1971); Chandler (1962). Hounshell and Smith (1985), along with these other scholars, attribute much of the firm's diversification drive to federal antitrust scrutiny before and after World War I. One federal antitrust suit against Du Pont had led to the loss of the firm's monopoly over the dynamite and gunpowder businesses, and threats to the firm's dominance of the smokeless powder market remained: "Threatened again after 1907 with the loss of their market for smokeless powder [if the federal government established its own plant], executives determined to diversify the company to make it less dependent upon government business. The extraordinary expansion of smokeless powder capacity during the Great War made diversification all the more imperative.

"Diversification and R&D were closely coupled as early as 1908. Du Pont's research organization provided executives with the technical resources to evaluate diversification opportunities" (Hounshell and Smith, 1985, p. 4).

[10] Maclaurin (1949) quotes an interview with Frank Jewett, director of Bell Labs during the 1920s: "Mr. Vail [Theodore N. Vail, chief executive officer of AT&T during 1907–19] was not satisfied with the kind of service the parent company was getting from its laboratories in the Western Electric Company, and asked me to find out where the trouble lay. I soon discovered that the method that was being followed in rewarding engineers for their technical accomplishments was not satisfactory. The situation was an outgrowth of the conditions in the telephone industry in the 1880's and 1890's. This had been the 'era of the inventor' when it was vital to the future of the company to control the basic patents in the telephone art. In order to stimulate invention, the Western Electric Company had offered a reward of $100 for every patent issued. And this practice had continued into a period when the Bell Telephone System had become firmly established ahead of all rivals and the need for patents was no longer acute. The engineers would get together from time to time to discuss some new development, in which they were all interested. Each man would then go off by himself and try to develop the idea in secrecy to the point where a patent application could be made. Moreover, wherever it was possible to make a number of divisional patent claims, instead of one broad claim, this was done, even though a patent on one broad claim would usually be more valuable to the company. This method of remuneration was therefore abandoned and any special rewards that were given thereafter were in the form of a bonus for exceptional inventive accomplishment" (pp. 156–7).

Jenkins (1975) notes in his discussion of Eastman Kodak's research activities that "the

new techniques were developed by Bell personnel for both research and the management of technological development. Examples of such firm-specific knowledge include the algorithms developed by Harold Black in his studies of the behavior of electronic waves, and the management and analytic techniques of systems engineering. Much of the early theory of solid-state physics also was developed within Bell Labs. The growth of a strong firm-specific knowledge base that was not patentable served as a barrier to the entry of competitors.

Industrial research, firm size, and performance

Schumpeter, along with other scholars and analysts, emphasized the relationship between industrial research (organized, or in Schumpeterian terms nonentrepreneurial, innovation) and the growth of large firms in oligopolistic markets. Indeed, this link was central to the argument in Schumpeter's late work.[11] The association between industrial research and market power has been examined intensively in the recent work of the historians discussed earlier on the development of industrial research within manufacturing corporations before World War II. The strength and significance of this linkage within a broader sample of the largest firms in the economy or within manufacturing as a whole, however, have not been examined rigorously. How important were the largest U.S. manufacturing firms as employers of industrial research personnel before World War II? How if at all did research affect the development of these firms and their acquisition or maintenance of market power?

One of the only empirical analyses of industrial research activity in the pre–World War II American economy was carried out by the Works Progress Administration's (WPA) National Research Project (Perazich and Field, 1940). The study analyzed data on industrial research activity during 1921–37, concluding that research employment was concentrated in large laboratories (the majority of which were in turn controlled by large firms).[12] Drawing on the WPA study, the Temporary National Economic

mid-1890s represented a period of significant policy shift from dependence upon patents and litigation as the principal method of protection of an established market position to substantial dependence upon the institutionalization of continuous technological innovation" (p. 185).

[11] "Perfect competition is not only impossible but inferior, and has no title to being set up as a model of ideal efficiency. It is hence a mistake to base the theory of government regulation of industry on the principle that big business should be made to work as the respective industry would work in perfect competition" (Schumpeter, 1954, p. 106).

[12] "[Thirteen] companies with the largest research staffs, representing less than 1 percent of all companies reporting in the National Research Council survey, employed in 1938 one-third of all research workers" (pp. 9–10), and "of the 45 largest research laboratories employing half the total laboratory personnel, all but 9 are owned or controlled by companies which are among the 200 largest leading non-financial corporations" (ibid., p. 11).

Committee (TNEC) concluded in 1941 that "since industrial research is much more characteristic of large than of small concerns, and since it gives a competitive advantage to firms able to pursue it, technology in this second way imparts impetus to the concentration of economic power" (TNEC, 1941, p. 212).

The high level of concentration of research activity suggested in these two studies does not, of course, control for the size distribution of manufacturing firms during this period, nor does it allow for the possibility that many large firms may have lacked research laboratories. Neither study discusses the development over time of the relationship between corporate size and research activity. Despite their conclusions, these studies say nothing about whether large firms were investing proportionately more in research, relative to their size, than were small firms. The nature of the competitive advantage realized by firms investing in research also is neither defined nor measured in this analysis.

Data from the National Research Council surveys of industrial research employment in 1921, 1933, and 1946 were used, along with data on firm size (measured as the book value of assets) from *Moody's Industrials*, to analyze the relationship between research employment and firm size during 1921–46.[13] Analysis of the relationship between employment and firm size within the two hundred largest manufacturing firms in these three years yields several conclusions:[14] (1) the minimum or threshold firm size associated with an industrial research facility declined steadily throughout the 1921–46 period, indicating that smaller firms within the two hundred largest were increasingly significant performers of research; (2) the elasticity of research employment with respect to firm size was less than 1 for nonchemicals manufacturing firms throughout the period; (3) industries differed significantly in both the threshold firm size associated with the existence of a research facility and the elasticity of research employment with respect to firm size; and (4) chemicals firms displayed a significantly lower threshold firm size in the 1921 and 1933 data samples and were characterized by a research employment–firm size elasticity larger than 1 in 1921 and 1933, suggesting that the largest firms in this industry indeed were disproportionately intensive employers of research personnel during 1921–33.

Throughout the 1921–46 period, the chemicals industry was the most research-intensive in U.S. manufacturing. The threshold size associated with the existence of a research laboratory within chemicals firms is both smaller than that for other manufacturing firms and relatively stable

---

[13] This discussion draws on Mowery (1983c).

[14] The listing of the two hundred largest manufacturing firms was compiled by Takashi Hikino under the direction of Professor Alfred D. Chandler, whose assistance in making these data available is greatly appreciated.

during 1921–33, suggesting that chemicals firms were among the very first to adopt the in-house form of industrial research. Industrial research employment had already grown significantly within the cohort of smaller chemicals firms among the two hundred largest manufacturing firms by 1921.

With the exception of the chemicals industry in 1921 and 1933, large firms within the two hundred largest manufacturing firms do not appear to be disproportionately research-intensive during this period. Indeed, large firms outside the chemicals industry employed fewer research professionals, relative to their size, than did smaller firms throughout 1921–46. The exceptionally high research intensity of large chemicals firms is consistent with the conclusions of empirical analyses of postwar data on firm size and research (see Mansfield, 1964). The contrast between the chemicals and other industries has been ascribed to the high fixed costs of research within this industry (introducing economies of scale into the research process), the greater ability of diversified chemicals firms to exploit the results of research, or the higher technological opportunity in this industry, raising the returns to investment in research. Nevertheless, the relative research intensity of the largest firms within chemicals declined during 1921–46, and the differences between chemicals and other industries in the relative research intensity of large firms also declined during this period.

The changes during 1921–33 and 1933–46 in the elasticity of research employment with respect to firm size suggest that changes occurred during these periods in the relative research intensity of smaller and larger firms within the two hundred largest manufacturing firms. Throughout the 1921–46 period, the research intensity of smaller firms increased relative to that of larger firms within the chemicals industry. The behavior of this elasticity for firms outside the chemicals industry, however, suggests that smaller firms' research intensity did not grow relative to that of larger firms during 1921–33. During 1933–46, the research intensity of smaller firms increased relative to that of the largest manufacturing firms within the two hundred largest.

This analysis suggests that large firms within chemicals were among the earliest adopters of large-scale industrial research within the largest U.S. manufacturing firms. Research intensity then increased among the largest firms in other industries and among smaller firms within chemicals. By the 1930s, smaller firms in other manufacturing industries within the top two hundred had begun to establish research laboratories and the research intensity of smaller chemicals firms was also growing. These trends, as well as the concentration of research employment within the chemicals and chemicals-related industries (discussed earlier in this chapter), may have reflected the diffusion of production techniques originally identified with the chemicals industry, such as high-pressure, high-temperature reactions, and continuous-flow processes, to other industries, including petroleum, foodstuffs, and paper. Chemicals in the prewar U.S. economy, like machine tools in the nineteenth-century U.S. economy, operated as a source of innovations and production techniques that were adopted by a wide range of other industries (see Rosenberg, 1963). The adoption of chemicals industry technologies and innovations by other industries was associated with the adoption of large-scale industrial research. In addition, of course, research employment grew in industries relying on physics, especially during the 1930s and 1940s, further reducing the "outlier" status of the chemicals industry.

Changes in the relationship between research employment and firm size during 1921–33 and 1933–46 for nonchemicals firms reflect changes in this relationship for firms remaining within the two hundred largest manufacturing firms and the influence of new entrants to this group. New entrants to the 1933 top two hundred, which were smaller than the survivors from the 1921 top two hundred, do not display any statistically significant relationship between research employment and firm size. The research employment–firm size elasticity increased significantly, however, for those firms remaining among the top two hundred during 1921–33. Firms entering the top two hundred during 1933–46 exhibit a far more significant relationship between research employment and firm size, however, suggesting that industrial research was a more important factor in such upward mobility during this period than during 1921–33.

During the 1921–46 period, the largest firms in American manufacturing do not appear to have been disproportionately intensive research employers, suggesting that the conclusions of the WPA and TNEC studies should be qualified. If anything, the opposite was true. The one exception to this conclusion is in the chemicals industry for 1921 and 1933; even within this industry, however, the trend during 1921–46 was one of growing relative research intensity among smaller firms. Overall, the evidence on firm size and research employment for firms in the chemicals and other manufacturing industries suggests a gradual spread of industrial research laboratories from large chemicals firms to other firms within chemicals and other industries. Comparison of the research employment–firm size relationship in 1921, 1933, and 1946 indicates some change during this period in the relative importance of large and small firms within the top two hundred as research employers. This change may reflect the differential impact of the Depression on the growth of industrial research employment among various firm-size classes and industries. During the 1933–46 period, the opposite occurred: The research employment–firm size elasticity was affected by the entry into the ranks of the largest firms of smaller, relatively research-intensive enterprises.

Did industrial research support increased economic concentration and rigidity in market structure, for example, by giving large firms the capability to offset the disruptive impact of technological change? Data on the two hundred largest firms and research employment were used in Mowery (1983c) to analyze the influence of research activity on the probability that firms would remain among the ranks of the two hundred largest during 1921–46. The results support the hypothesis that industrial research significantly aided firms' survival in the ranks of the two hundred largest firms during 1921–33, 1933–46, and during 1921–46, controlling for the effects of initial firm size and for interindustry differences in survival rates not elsewhere measured. The growth of industrial research during 1921–46 among the two hundred largest firms is associated with a drop in turnover within this group. Combined with the findings of other scholars that the post–World War I period witnessed a significant decline in change and instability in market structure (see Collins and Preston, 1961; Kaplan, 1964; Edwards, 1975), this analysis suggests that industrial research may have played a role in the stabilization of market structure in the unstable economic environment of the 1921–46 period.

Another measure of the distribution of the benefits of industrial research concerns the effects of research investment on the growth of large and small firms. Were large firms better able to reap the benefits of research, measured as growth in the value of their assets? Analysis of this issue for the 1933–46 period in Mowery (1983c) yielded a mixed verdict. Controlling for initial firm size, research employment appears to have exerted a positive impact on firm growth that was similar in magnitude for large and small firms during this period: Firm size had a small and negative effect on the growth in the value of firms' assets during 1933–46. There nevertheless is some evidence of a growth-enhancing interaction between research investment and initial firm size, although this effect is exhausted at modest levels of firm size. Industrial research is associated with higher rates of growth in the value of firms during 1933–46. This effect is similar for both large and small firms, however, contradicting the implications of the WPA and TNEC analyses.

Research activity also influenced the growth of industrial productivity. Within U.S. manufacturing, interindustry differences in total factor productivity growth between 1921 and 1946 were significantly and positively related to interindustry differences in research intensity.[15] These results are of interest in view of the fact that labor productivity growth in American manufacturing substantially exceeded productivity growth in British manufacturing for much of the 1900–50 period. The gap in labor produc-

---

[15] See Terleckyj (1961), as well as the results presented in Mowery (1986a).

tivity increased during the 1920s, a period of rapid growth in the number and size of American industrial research laboratories.[16]

The role of intrafirm and contract research

Industrial research in American manufacturing during the 1900–40 period developed a dualistic structure. Employment of professional scientists and engineers grew rapidly within manufacturing concerns and in independent research firms not affiliated with a manufacturing enterprise. Between 1900 and 1940, according to data from the National Research Council (NRC), nearly 350 independent laboratories were established.[17] Employment of scientists and engineers within these independent organizations grew rapidly during the period for which data are available. Total employment of scientists and engineers in independent research laboratories was 3,300 in 1940 and more than 5,000 by 1946.

Contemporary observers and practitioners of industrial research hailed the growth of independent research laboratories as a development that would allow small firms without in-house laboratories to reap the benefits of industrial research. The comments in 1916 of John J. Carty, the first director of the reorganized Bell Telephone Laboratories, are representative:

> Conditions today are such that without cooperation among themselves the small concerns can not have the full benefits of industrial research, for no one among them is sufficiently strong to maintain the necessary staff and laboratories. Once the vital importance of this subject is appreciated by the small manufacturers many solutions of the problem will promptly appear. One of these is for the manufacturer to take his problem to one of the industrial research laboratories already established for the purpose of serving those who cannot afford a laboratory of their own. Other manufacturers doing the same, the financial encouragement re-

[16] See Rostas (1948). Kendrick (1961, p. 136) concludes that total-factor productivity in U.S. manufacturing grew at an average annual rate of 5.3 percent from 1919 to 1929 and 1.9 percent from 1929 to 1937. Matthews et al. (1982, p. 229) estimate that total-factor productivity in British manufacturing grew at an average annual rate of 1.9 percent from 1924 to 1937. Although some tendency for British productivity growth to catch up with that of American manufacturing thus is indicated for the 1930s (possibly because of the severe impact of the Great Depression on output growth in the United States), these estimates are broadly consistent with those of Rostas in pointing to a large gap in the 1920s. For additional comparative discussion of U.S. and British R&D investment and innovative performance, see Chapter 5.

[17] The source and nature of these data are discussed later in this chapter. For additional analysis, see Mowery (1981, Chapter 2).

ceived would enable the laboratories to extend and improve their facilities so that each of the small manufacturers who patronized them would in the course of time have the benefit of an institution similar to those maintained by our largest industrial concerns. (Carty, 1916, p. 512)

Carty's faith in the ability of market mechanisms to handle research is echoed in a statement forty years later by George Stigler, who argued that

> with the growth of research, new firms will emerge to provide specialized facilities for small firms. It is only to be expected that, when a new kind of research develops, at first it will be conducted chiefly as an ancillary activity by existing firms. . . . We may expect the rapid expansion of the specialized research laboratory, selling its services generally. The specialized laboratories need not be in the least inferior to "captive" laboratories. (Stigler, 1956, p. 281)[18]

As we suggested in Chapter 1, however, the peculiar characteristics of R&D and commercial innovation may hamper the sale of research services by means of contracts. In order to analyze and to understand more fully the factors that influenced the development of the U.S. R&D system, we examined the relationship between the activities of independent research organizations and those of the in-house research laboratories of manufacturing firms during 1900–40. Archival data from three major independent research organizations and the National Research Council data on industrial research employment were used in Mowery (1983a) to analyze employment growth in independent and in-house laboratories, the extent to which independent research laboratories were utilized by firms lacking in-house research facilities, and the nature of the research performed within independent and within in-house research facilities. Before presenting the data and results of this analysis, however, a more detailed discussion of the factors influencing the relationship between in-house and contractual research is necessary.

The role of independent research laboratories is influenced by factors affecting the supply of such services and by factors affecting the demand for these services, that is, the ability of firms to exploit the available contract research services. The supply of contract research is affected by two factors. The first is the degree to which specialization in the performance of research reduces costs per unit of research output, that is, economies of scale in specific types of research that cannot be fully exploited by in-

---

[18] A more skeptical view of the role of the independent research organization may be found in Baldwin (1962).

house research laboratories. Independent research organizations should specialize in research services characterized by declining unit costs. The second factor concerns the degree of interdependence between specific research activities and other manufacturing and nonmanufacturing functions within the firm. Strong interdependence between research and other functions within the firm favors in-house research.[19] Scale economies are most significant for routinized, relatively simple research tasks, such as materials testing, since these often utilize specialized equipment and facilities. Interdependence between research and other activities within the firm will be more important in research projects requiring knowledge of a highly specialized, idiosyncratic variety specific to a given firm, or in research requiring that a wide range of research and other nonresearch activities be coordinated in the innovation process.[20]

As firms grow in size and structural complexity, the more complex, riskier research project with severe requirements for interaction and information exchange among various corporate functions should form the core of their in-house research activities.[21] As Chapter 3 and a number of statements we cite in this chapter point out, much of the early activity of in-house research facilities focused on routinized, low-risk materials analysis and testing. Over time, however, the complexity and range of projects undertaken by in-house laboratories expanded. Much of the necessary knowledge for such research and development projects may be highly

[19] Armour and Teece (1981) discuss "contractual difficulties in the market for technological know-how" (p. 470), arguing, among other points, that "the transactions costs associated with buying and selling engineering and scientific manpower are reduced when personnel can move from R&D to one or several stages of production within an enterprise. Furthermore, a common coding system, or language, can develop within the vertically integrated enterprise which facilitates the transfer of technical information. The existence of a common coding system and the attendant dialogue between departments or divisions facilitates both technology transfer and the formulation of appropriate research objectives. As a result, the research activity is likely to be better directed and hence more productive" (p. 471). Although these authors are discussing the effects on R&D of a vertically integrated firm structure, it is clear that many of the advantages to which they refer result as well from the location of an industrial research facility within the manufacturing firm.

[20] An idea of the different corporate functions that must be brought together in the innovation process is conveyed by the estimates by the U.S. Department of Commerce Panel on Invention and Innovation (1967) of the typical distribution of costs in successful product innovations. "Research, Advanced Development, and Basic Invention" accounted for 7.5 percent; "Engineering and Designing and Product" accounted for 15 percent; "Tooling and Manufacturing Engineering" accounted for 50 percent; "Manufacturing Start-up Expenses" accounted for 10 percent; and "Marketing Start-up Expenses" comprised 17.5 percent of total costs (p. 9).

[21] Variables measuring the ex ante complexity of a specific research project are difficult to devise, even in the absence of data constraints. One broad measure is the extent of technological advance embodied in a research project; this measure has been employed by Mansfield et al. (1971), Summers (1967), and Marshall and Meckling (1962) in studies of R&D project cost overruns. A second measure, drawing on Summers, consists of an estimate of the duration of a research project. Both the degree of technological advance and the duration of a project are expected to be positively correlated with complexity and risk.

specific to a given firm or production process and cannot be produced by an organization not engaged in both production and research. The specificity of such technical knowledge stems ultimately from the fact that production and acquisition of detailed technical knowledge, or the use and acquisition of such knowledge, are frequently joint activities.

Independent research organizations are most likely to supply research services characterized broadly by two features. Research supplied by means of contract will be generic in character, applicable to a relatively wide range of industries and firms, and exploiting little or no firm-specific knowledge. Second, contract research services will deal primarily with isolated or independent components of the firm's operations. Projects focused on the improvement of production processes employed by many firms or analyses of materials, rather than projects developing new products, are likely to be supplied by independent research organizations.

The independent research organization thus may be unable to supply certain research services. On the demand side, the ability of manufacturing firms to exploit contract research may be undercut by two factors. The client firm requires substantial in-house expertise to pose a feasible research problem to an independent laboratory, or to evaluate and utilize the results of externally performed research.[22]

Contracting problems also limit the role of independent research organizations. The effectiveness of contracts in the provision of research is undermined by the highly uncertain nature of the research enterprise, the imperfect character of knowledge about a given project, and the thin market for specialized research services. These contractual difficulties are likely to be greater the more technically complex and uncertain the proposed research. Assessment of the value of the results produced by an independent contractor also is difficult without complete revelation of these results; but revelation removes any incentive for the client to pay for the research.[23] The small number of suppliers of specialized research services

---

[22] The argument that an in-house research facility enhances the ability of firms to exploit external research receives support from analyses of industrial research in other nations. Discussing the development of cooperative industrial research laboratories in Great Britain, Varcoe (1974) noted that "the relations [of the cooperative research facilities] with the industries and the extent to which the latter availed themselves in practice of the results were not the straightforward matters they were at first imagined to be. Smaller firms frequently had no one capable either of articulating research needs and putting them into scientifically meaningful terms or of understanding the concepts and terminology of technical literature and of relating these ideas to their own problems" (p. 30; see Chapter 5 for a more detailed discussion). Similarly, Caves and Uekusa (1976) note that Japanese firms invested heavily in research during the postwar period as a means of absorbing and modifying technologies from external sources: "Firms must maintain some research capacity in order to know what technology is available for purchase or copy and they must generally modify and adapt foreign technology in putting it to use – a 1963 survey of Japanese manufacturers showed that on average one-third of the respondents' expenditures on R&D went for this purpose" (p. 126).

[23] This argument was first made by Arrow (1962).

Table 4.7. *Employment of scientific*
professionals in independent research
organizations as a percentage of employment
of scientific professionals in all in-house and
independent research laboratories, 1921–46

1921	15.2
1927	12.9
1933	10.9
1940	8.7
1946	6.9

Source: Mowery (1981, Chapter 2).

means that opportunistic behavior by one or the other party to such a contractual agreement is likely.[24] Finally, the difficulty of specifying all contingencies and the uncertainty associated with complex research projects will reduce firms' reliance on external providers for such research.

How did these factors affect the relationship between independent and in-house research organizations? Consistent with the arguments made earlier in this and other chapters, the growth of industrial research in the United States reduced the importance of independent research organizations. Table 4.7, which is drawn from the National Research Council surveys of industrial research, displays the proportion of total employment of research professionals in both in-house and independent research organizations accounted for by independent research organizations (excluding the research laboratories of trade associations). Over time, contract research laboratories account for a declining share of total scientific and engineering research employment in manufacturing and independent research laboratories. Whereas employment in both forms of industrial research organization was growing rapidly during this period, employment growth for in-house research substantially outstripped that for the independent research organizations.

The National Research Council surveys of industrial research discussed earlier and archival data from three major independent research organizations were employed to analyze the relationship between in-house and independent research during 1900–1940. The NRC surveys provided a comprehensive tabulation of research facilities within more than 7,300 manufacturing firms. Since the 1940 and 1946 surveys contained foundation dates for in-house laboratories within these firms, the presence or

[24] Williamson (1981) argues: "That economic agents are simultaneously subject to bounded rationality and (at least some) are given to opportunism does not by itself, however, vitiate autonomous trading. On the contrary, when effective ex ante and ex post competition can both be presumed, autonomous contracting will be efficacious" (p. 554).

absence of an in-house research laboratory could be confirmed. Archival data from three major independent research organizations provided a comprehensive list of client firms for each organization and information for an assessment of the types of research performed for client firms.[25] The three firms are the Mellon Institute in Pittsburgh, Pennsylvania, the Battelle Memorial Institute in Columbus, Ohio, and Arthur D. Little, Inc., of Cambridge, Massachusetts.

The choice of these three firms was based on several criteria. All three were active during all or a substantial part of the 1900–40 period. Arthur D. Little was founded in 1896, the Mellon Institute opened in Pittsburgh in 1911, and the Battelle Institute began operations in 1929. The firms were also among the largest independent research organizations in the United States during this period. In 1933, according to data from the National Research Council survey, Arthur D. Little and the Mellon Institute were the two largest independent contract research organizations in the United States, and the three organizations together represented 12.3 percent of total professional scientific employment in independent research organizations (of 223 such organizations). In 1940 these three organizations were among the five largest such laboratories, accounting for 13.6 percent of total scientific employment, and by 1946 they included 16 percent of independent research organizations' scientific and engineering staff. These three firms were among the largest independent research organizations and accounted for a growing share of employment within such organizations. They are therefore likely to have offered the broadest possible range of research facilities and service.

The relationship between in-house and contract research can be inferred from the existence or absence of an in-house laboratory in client firms. The existence of a research facility within a client firm was taken as a case in which contract research functioned as a complement, rather than a substitute, for in-house research. Where no laboratory was found within the client firm, one may infer that contract research substituted for the research that otherwise would be performed within the firm.

The descriptions of the research projects performed by these independent research organizations provide another insight into the relationship between contract and in-house research. Only the Mellon Institute data contained detailed project descriptions that allowed a categorization of research projects. For the Battelle Institute and Arthur D. Little, a division of the project population into "analysis" and "nonanalysis" projects was based largely on the project title. "Analysis" projects were defined to consist of analysis of chemical or other substances, including coal. Both

---

[25] In obtaining these data, invaluable aid was provided by Ms. Rena Zeffer at the Mellon Institute, Ms. Kathy Kelland and Dr. Michael Michaelis at Arthur D. Little, and Dr. George McClure at the Battelle Institute.

Table 4.8. *Structural complementarity between
in-house and contract research at the Mellon Institute
of Industrial Research*

Years	Firms sponsoring research at Mellon Institute[a]	Sponsoring firms with in-house labs at time of sponsorship[b]
1910–40	187	71 (38%)
1910–19	73	15 (20.5%)
1920–29	60	28 (46.7%)
1930–40	54	28 (51.8%)

[a]A number of firms sponsored more than one fellowship, at several different dates. In such cases, the first occurrence is the only one counted, biasing downward the number of firms in later periods.
[b]"Time of sponsorship" is taken to be the date at which the fellowship began.

the Battelle and Little organizations were heavily involved in performing such routinized analysis projects. In the discussion below, analysis projects are assumed to be less technically complex. This assumption is based on the likelihood that the degree of uncertainty about costs, technical feasibility, and outcomes for such tasks is much lower for materials and chemical analysis projects.

Tables 4.8 through 4.10 present data on the proportion of clients of each independent research organization that had in-house research laboratories. The independent research organizations are complements to, rather than substitutes for, in-house research in a substantial proportion of the client firms. Such complementarity is most pronounced in the Mellon Institute and Battelle Institute data (where, respectively, 38 percent and 47 percent of the manufacturing client firms during this period have in-house laboratories). The results from the Little data, however, especially those for the special reports series, where by 1930–40 over 69 percent of the client firms have in-house labs, also suggest that contract research was not used extensively as a substitute for an in-house research facility.

For both Arthur D. Little and the Battelle Institute, the share of client firms with in-house laboratories is higher for the more complex (i.e., nonanalysis) projects than for analysis projects. A much higher proportion of the firms sponsoring special reports at Little, projects that are more complex and riskier, have in-house laboratories than is true of the firms spon-

Table 4.9. *Structural complementarity between in-house and contract research at the Battelle Memorial Institute*

Proportion of client firms at the Battelle Institute with in-house research laboratories (as recorded in the NRC survey), 1929–40:
All client firms: 43.6% ($n = 241$)
Manufacturing firms only: 47.9% ($n = 217$)
Mining firms: 4.2% ($n = 24$)
Analysis contracts ($n = 60$)
Percentage sponsored by firms with in-house laboratories: 33.3%
Nonanalysis contracts ($n = 181$)
Percentage sponsored by firms with in-house laboratories: 47.0%

Table 4.10. *Structural complementarity between in-house and contract research at Arthur D. Little, Inc.*

1896–1940
Technical reports
All client firms: 5.5% ($n = 5,027$)
Clients for whom analyses were carried out: 3.8% ($n = 2,709$)
Clients for whom other research projects were done: 7.4% ($n = 2,318$)
Special reports: 28.4% ($n = 134$)

1896–1909
Technical reports
All client firms: 3.8% ($n = 390$)
Clients for whom analyses were carried out: 4.1% ($n = 49$)
Clients for whom other research projects were done: 3.8% ($n = 341$)
Special reports: 0.0% ($n = 9$)

1910–19
Technical reports
All client firms: 3.6% ($n = 1,309$)
Clients for whom analyses were carried out: 3.4% ($n = 585$)
Clients for whom other research projects were done: 3.7% ($n = 724$)
Special reports: 17.4% ($n = 23$)

1920–29
Technical reports
All client firms: 22.8% ($n = 260$)
Clients for whom analyses were carried out: 9.5% ($n = 21$)
Clients for whom other research projects were done: 24.0% ($n = 239$)
Special reports: 69.6% ($n = 23$)

soring simple chemical analyses. The difference in the proportions of structural complementarity for the analysis and special report clients at Little is significant at the 0.01 level for the entire 1896–1940 period, as well as for the 1910–19, 1920–9, and 1930–40 subperiods. At the Battelle Institute, the share of client firms with in-house laboratories varies between analysis and nonanalysis projects; one-third of the firms contracting for chemical or metallurgical analysis have in-house laboratories, whereas among the nonanalysis population of contracts, this proportion rises to 47 percent. The difference is significant at the 0.10 level, but not at the 0.05 level.

Rather than declining over time, as one would predict if the research function were being "spun off" à la Stigler, the proportion of client firms with in-house laboratories increased for both Little and the Mellon Institute, the only two of the three for which longitudinal data are available. The increase in this proportion between the 1910–19 and 1920–9 periods is significant at the 0.01 level for the Mellon Institute. Looking at these proportions for the special reports prepared by Arthur D. Little, one observes an increase from 17.4 percent in 1910–19 to 22.8 percent in 1920–9, and 69.6 percent in 1930–40; the increase in this proportion from the 1920–9 to the 1930–40 period is statistically significant at the 0.01 level. Consistent with the data in Table 4.7, there is no evidence of growing reliance by manufacturing firms on independent research organizations for research services during this period.

To assess the statistical significance of the results of the structural complementarity analysis, three control populations of manufacturing firms were constructed for comparison with the client firm populations at each of the three independent research organizations during the 1930s. The client firm populations were restricted to clients listed in *Moody's Industrials* during the year in which they first appeared as a client.[26]

The proportion of firms in the control populations was compared with the level of structural complementarity observed at each independent research facility. This comparison tested the null hypothesis that the proportion of client firms with in-house laboratories at each independent research organization matched the proportion of firms within the larger population of manufacturing firms with in-house laboratories.[27] Tests for

---

[26] Firms in the control samples were also drawn from *Moody's*, by taking firms from pages matching the last four digits of each of a series of random numbers. This generated a large list of candidate firms for the control population, out of which a subset was selected. The control samples were chosen so as to replicate the distribution of the client firm population among years, firm size classes, and across two-digit standard industrial classifications (SICs). Where a surplus of candidate firms for a specific year, size class, or SIC was encountered, the firms were ranked by size. Firms whose rank order matched the last two digits of a random number were included in the control sample population.

[27] The test of the null hypothesis assumed that the difference in the proportions of the firms with research laboratories in the two populations was normally distributed. The use of

Table 4.11. *Types of research sponsored by the Mellon Institute*

New use for materials	Process improvement	Product improvement	By-product utilization
18 (19.3%)	75 (38.9%)	11 (5.7%)	11 (5.7%)

differences between the proportion of firms in the control and client firm samples with in-house laboratories for each of the three independent research laboratories allowed rejection in each case at the 0.001 level of confidence of the null hypothesis that the proportion of firms with in-house laboratories in the control and client firm populations was identical. The proportion of manufacturing firms utilizing contract research services during the 1930s that had in-house research facilities was significantly greater than the proportion of firms with such research laboratories in a sample of all manufacturing firms.

A more detailed examination of the characteristics of projects performed by these independent research organizations can illuminate the supply side of contract research. We discuss the available data on the types of projects carried out at each of these three independent research organizations next (Tables 4.11 through 4.13).

Mellon Institute: Table 4.11 contains data on the projects performed for clients of the Mellon Institute. Only those projects whose titles are sufficiently clear were classified; the percentages thus do not sum to 100. The overall tabulation of projects by type reveals that process improvement (e.g., "problems in cement manufacturing processes") is the most important single category of project. With the possible exception of some of the projects dealing with new uses for materials (e.g., "utilization of milk and butter by-products," covering an early phase of product development), new product development activities at the Mellon Institute were minimal. Projects dealt primarily with improvement of existing processes or the utilization of by-products.

Battelle Institute: The Battelle data have descriptions that are less informative than those for the Mellon Institute. Both Arthur D. Little and Battelle, unlike Mellon, did a good deal of work in the provision of analyses of metals and/or chemicals for clients. Battelle was heavily involved in providing such services to the coal industry as well, which involved testing samples of coal for smoke and clinkering characteristics. Nearly 25 percent of all projects undertaken by the institute during 1929–40 were

the normal approximation drew its justification in part from the size of the combined populations (36, 150, and 180 firms), as well as the fact that the control and experimental populations had been constructed to contain equal numbers of firms in various size classes.

Table 4.12. *Types of research sponsored at the*
Battelle Institute: Manufacturing firms only
(in %)

"Analysis"	24.9
Other	75.1

analyses or tests of metals (see Table 4.12), minerals, or coal, and as such were lower-risk undertakings. Among mining firms (excluded from Table 4.12), few of which had in-house labs, two-thirds of the projects were analyses. Clarence Lorig, who joined the institute in 1930, noted that during the first decade of Battelle's existence, "problems were clearly defined and had objective solutions" (quoted in Boehm and Groner, 1972, p. 20); these data tend to support his views.

Arthur D. Little: Chemicals analysis was a mainstay of this firm's activities through the 1900–40 period. The project descriptions allowed only for classification of the technical reports into analysis or nonanalysis categories. The "special reports" were more fundamental and long-term projects. The data in Table 4.13 indicate the importance of analysis work for the Little firm, especially during the 1910–19 and 1920–9 periods, which are the most complete in their coverage. Once again, the activities carried out by an independent research organization are concentrated at the low-risk end of the continuum of research projects.

The extent to which independent research organizations may be said to have substituted for in-house research during 1900–40 appears to be limited. The independent research organizations examined here did not offer a full menu of research services for purchase, and were especially limited in product research and development. These limitations reflect difficulties of contracting, idiosyncratic knowledge, and the need for the involvement of many components of the firm in such activities as new product development.

As in-house research facilities grew in size and number during 1900–40, contract research institutions increasingly functioned as complements rather than substitutes (in the "structural" sense defined here). Increasingly, firms without in-house research facilities were not the primary clients for independent research organizations. Moreover, firms without in-house laboratories apparently used contract research only for the simplest types of research projects. This complementary relationship between in-house and contract research reflects the fact that knowledge and technology transfer are themselves knowledge-intensive processes. Much of the important expertise for innovation also is highly specific to a given firm.

Table 4.13. *Types of research sponsored at*
Arthur D. Little (percentage of total clients)

1896–1943	
Analyses	52.4
Nonanalytic technical reports	44.9
Special reports	2.6
1896–1909	
Analyses	12.3
Nonanalytic technical reports	85.5
Special reports	2.3
1910–19	
Analyses	43.9
Nonanalytic technical reports	54.3
Special reports	1.7
1920–29	
Analyses	65.6
Nonanalytic technical reports	31.9
Special reports	2.5
1930–40	
Analyses	7.6
Nonanalytic technical reports	84.0
Special reports	8.4

Thus, in-house and contract research are complements on the demand side.

If the only factor affecting the relationship between in-house and contract research were the need for in-house expertise to evaluate and exploit the services of an independent contractor, one would observe a wide range of research services offered on a contract basis. In this case, increasing in-house research employment would reflect the growth of a staff within the firm to monitor and evaluate the activities of independent research organizations. The conclusions of this empirical analysis, however, suggest that the firm undertaking complex or risky projects during this period had little choice but to do so in-house. In addition, the ability of firms to exploit even the limited services that were available through contracts was affected critically by the presence of an in-house laboratory. Firms lacking such in-house expertise utilized contract research primarily for simple analysis projects. The establishment of an in-house laboratory thus was a response to forces affecting both the supply of research services and the characteristics of the demand for contract research.

During the twentieth century, industrial research developed within both the nonmarket and the market sectors of the American economy. Although research employment grew most rapidly in laboratories located within manufacturing firms, a substantial network of independent research organizations also emerged. These independent research organizations were viewed by many important practitioners of industrial research during the 1900–40 period as possible substitutes for the in-house research facilities believed to be lacking among smaller firms. Such faith in the frictionless performance of market mechanisms in distributing the fruits of industrial research to large and small firms alike, faith that was echoed in the predictions of economic theory, appears to have been misplaced.

Rather than functioning as substitutes, the independent and in-house research laboratories were complements during this period and performed different research tasks. The foundation of an in-house laboratory resulted not in a "spinning in" of the research activities previously performed on a contract basis but in a substantial expansion in the range of research possibilities and projects open to the firm.[28] The growth of industrial research within U.S. manufacturing reflected the shortcomings of market institutions as mechanisms for the conduct and distribution of research and development. The effects of R&D on firm performance that we discussed elsewhere in this chapter thus were largely inaccessible to firms lacking in-house research laboratories.

For all but the most prosaic and standardized activities, the evidence discussed in this section suggests that industrial research is most efficient and effective when conducted in-house. Commercially successful innovation requires the combination of skills and information from a wide range of functions within the firm and often exploits firm-specific knowledge emerging from complex production processes. To obtain information about such processes at arm's length is exceedingly difficult, fraught as it is with uncertainties and moral hazard, and frequently does not permit the effec-

---

[28] Balbien and Wilde (1982) suggest that a manufacturing firm is more likely to contract for research with an independent laboratory the greater the manufacturing firm's state of technical knowledge (represented in their model as a lower level of initial unit costs). Such a hypothesis suggests a complementary relationship between in-house and contract research; *ceteris paribus*, the presence of an in-house research facility is likely to endow a firm with greater technical expertise relative to its peers. The authors also suggest that the independent research laboratory will exhibit the greatest veracity in reporting the results of very short term projects. Such a proposition is consistent with the data presented here concerning the importance of short-term routinized analysis projects in the activities of the independent research laboratories. In reaching these results, the authors rely on a very strong and somewhat questionable assumption, viz., that the marginal returns to reductions in unit costs reaped by the firm increase as the initial level of unit costs declines. This assumption raises the possibility that, as production costs decline, the firm's research expenditures may increase without limit. Such an assumption is difficult to support with empirical evidence.

tive exploitation of firm-specific knowledge. The efficient organization of industrial research has historically been associated with the growth of a strong central staff in charge of functions such as marketing or production engineering. To be effective, industrial research requires complementary changes in the structure and organization of firms and markets. Where these changes have not occurred (see Chapter 5 for a discussion of industrial research in an economy where these changes occurred much later, Great Britain), industrial research has been more modest in scope and less effective.

Publicly funded research and the universities

In spite of the permissive implications of the "general welfare" clause of the U.S. Constitution, federal support for science prior to World War II was limited by a strict interpretation of the role of the federal government. Support for research in agriculture, one of the oldest commitments of the federal government, was also opposed by states' rights advocates and strict constructionists who until the Civil War continued to view the American national government as the loosest possible form of federation, with minimal powers at the national center. The Morrill Act, establishing the land-grant colleges, had passed both houses of Congress in 1859 in spite of bitter opposition by the South, but was vetoed by President Buchanan. It became law only in 1862, with a new president holding different views on the nature of the federal union and with a Congress that had recently lost the sectional representation that supported the states' rights view most strongly. The Department of Agriculture (USDA) was established the same year.

During World War I, the military largely operated the research and development facilities and other advanced production assets of importance to the war effort; the private-sector expertise to support an alternative institutional design did not exist outside the munitions sector. Such advanced facilities as the Muscle Shoals nitrate production complex were government-constructed and -owned. When one of the armed services identified a particular urgent scientific need, a person with the appropriate qualifications was drafted into that branch.

Until the Second World War, agriculture continued to occupy a privileged position in the American political scheme. No other sector of the economy was the recipient of the sort of research support granted by the federal government, through the Department of Agriculture, to the agricultural experiment stations. Even as late as the 1930s, when a presidential science advisory board recommended that the federal government award grants to private institutions as a way of alleviating unemployment among scientists, the proposal was rejected as involving an excessive exercise of federal power.

For 1940, the last year that was not dominated by the vast expenditures associated with a military buildup, total federal expenditures for research, development, and R&D plant amounted to $74.1 million. Of that, Department of Agriculture expenditures amounted to $29.1 million, or 39 percent. As some measure of how drastically the prewar world differed from the postwar, it should be noted that, in 1940, the Department of Agriculture's research budget exceeded that of the agencies now included in the Department of Defense, whose total research budget amounted to $26.4 million. Between them, these two categories accounted for 75 percent of all federal R&D expenditures. The claimants on the remaining 25 percent, in descending order of importance, were the Department of the Interior ($7.9 million), the Department of Commerce ($3.3 million), the Public Health Service ($2.8 million), and the National Advisory Committee on Aeronautics ($2.2 million).

Federal expenditures for R&D throughout the 1930s constituted between 12 and 20 percent of estimated total R&D expenditures. By far the largest contributor was private industry, which accounted for about two-thirds of the total. The remainder came from universities, state governments, private foundations, and research institutes. There are insufficient data to assess the relative importance of state and federal government research funds. At least one estimate, however, suggests that state funds accounted for at least 14 percent of university research funding during 1935–6. Moreover, the contribution of state governments to nonagricultural university research appears from these data to have exceeded the federal contribution.

The most reliable prewar estimate (for 1935–6) of total university research funding employs what was described as the "broadest definition" of research in all disciplines and obtains an estimate of $50 million. Again, the dominance of the agricultural experiment stations is apparent, accounting for $16 million, or almost one-third of the total budget, and a much larger fraction of the research funds that were earmarked for specific purposes.[29]

There is a point of larger significance, however, concerning the role of universities in American economic life and research before the Second World War. It does not emerge from data on research expenditures alone. The American higher education system has been highly decentralized and remarkably diverse. Within this diversity it has found ways to provide constructive responses to a wide variety of changing economic needs. In-

---

[29] National Resources Planning Board (1942), vol. 1, p. 178. The $50 million estimate was broken down into the following sources: "Appropriation by States, Department of Agriculture, experiment stations, $7,283,000; Estimate of other State appropriations spent for research, 7,000,000; Federal grants to universities for agricultural experiment stations, 4,995,000; Sales and other income for research, 2,000,000; General endowment income, 17,000,000; Grants from foundations for research, 8,000,000; Special gifts from outside the foundations, 4,000,000; Total (approximate) $50,000,000."

deed, the term "vocational" has long been an epithet employed by foreigners and members of elite American universities in criticizing what they have regarded as an excessive willingness to modify the teaching curriculum in response to changes in the needs of the marketplace.

But the responsiveness to the needs of business and industry has been only part of the story. Another part has been the remarkably high degree of *accessibility* of higher education to such a large fraction of the population who would not have had such access elsewhere. The innovative manner in which the American higher education system accommodated itself to the needs of the farm population is well known. A further essential part of the story needs to be told in terms of teachers' colleges, junior colleges, and municipal institutions such as Wayne State University, the University of Akron (which catered to the needs of the city's large rubber industry), the University of Cincinnati (where, at the close of the First World War, the Tanners' Council established a laboratory for cooperative research on problems pertaining to the preparation of leather), and the City College of New York, which in the late 1930s had scholarly admission standards that were among the most rigorous in the nation (Levine, 1986, Chapter 4).

The very diversity of the higher education system, its relative ease of access, and the absence of a system of centralized funding at the federal level all contributed to a form of academic entrepreneurship in which both curriculum and research were more closely geared to commercial opportunities than was true in many European systems of higher education. This was most evident with respect to agriculture and the research conducted on the needs of local agriculture at the state agricultural experiment stations. But the state universities were also closely linked to the changing needs of industry.

Although the Morrill Act provided for the establishment of "colleges of agriculture and the mechanic arts," the mechanic arts did not, in fact, receive much attention. Very little research of any kind was undertaken by the new land-grant colleges for the first twenty-five years after the passage of the Morrill Act. When the Hatch Act was passed into law in 1887, it provided federal funds for agricultural experiment stations, but not, significantly, for engineering experiment stations.

Nevertheless, especially within emerging subfields of engineering and, to a lesser extent, within mining and metallurgy, state university systems often introduced new programs as soon as the requirements of the local economy became clear. Although they were never to receive federal financial support, the first engineering experiment stations were established early in the twentieth century. The first one was founded at the University of Illinois in State College in 1904. Other land-grant colleges followed suit. By 1910, there were five engineering experiment stations, and by 1925 there were twenty-six. In 1938 there were thirty-eight.

The University of Minnesota had a Mines Experiment Station with its own blast furnace and foundry for work with iron ore refining and treatment (see Davis, 1964, pp. 135, 137). Purdue University, which maintained a locomotive-testing station, was nicknamed "The Boilermakers" for obvious reasons. The engineering college at the University of Illinois

> . . . in the early 1920s offered undergraduate degrees in architecture, architectural engineering, ceramic engineering, civil engineering, electrical engineering, mechanical engineering, mining engineering, municipal and sanitary engineering, general engineering, physics, railway civil engineering, railway electrical engineering, and railway mechanical engineering. Nearly every industry and government agency in Illinois had its own department at the state university in Urbana-Champaign. (Levine, 1986, p. 52)

Although a detailed discussion cannot be undertaken here, it is worth noting that the close connection with the needs of the local economy sometimes led to a research initiative that yielded significant technological or intellectual consequences. The Massachusetts Institute of Technology, for example, originally a public institution, played a major role in the development and diffusion of the new discipline of chemical engineering (see Servos, 1980). The increasingly complex needs of agricultural experiment stations for statistical analysis led to the establishment of statistics departments at such institutions as Iowa State University and later at the University of North Carolina. These institutions became important centers of statistical research well before this subject received department recognition and status in Western European universities (Ben-David, 1971, pp. 147–52).

This is the background against which the American university system and its dramatic transformation due to the infusion of federal funds during and after World War II must be seen. Before 1940 federal research support for any but agricultural research was very limited and was exceeded by state government support. Although university research budgets before 1940 were minuscule by later standards, the system was one in which the requirements of industry, agriculture, and mining were recognized and accommodated. The system may have been excessively vocational in orientation as a result, but judged by narrowly utilitarian criteria, higher education achieved significant accomplishments during this period. These accomplishments went beyond responses to industrial needs; as research within industrial establishments grew in importance, university research during this period often involved various forms of collaboration with private industry.

Conclusion

Much of the structure of the private-sector components of the U.S. national research system took shape during the 1900–40 period. Closely linked with the rise of the giant multiproduct corporation that began at the turn of the century, industrial research contributed to the stability and survival of these firms. During the pre-1940 period, however, the largest firms do not appear to have "dominated" the practice of industrial research in a statistically meaningful sense. Industrial research in the United States had a particular feature that distinguished it, at least in some degree, from Western European patterns. A large fraction of privately supported research was conducted *within* the firm, rather than by an industrywide association or other arrangement. To a greater extent than appears to have been the case, say, in Britain, the growth of research in the United States was directly linked to considerations of business strategy at the level of the individual firm (see Chapter 5 for additional discussion). Over time, industrial research was governed increasingly by nonmarket institutions and allocation mechanisms, as this activity was integrated into the boundaries of the firm. The neoclassical theory of R&D investment and organization does not satisfactorily explain this characteristic of the U.S. industrial research system.

The diversity of institutional mechanisms that were involved in the development of industrial research during this period is striking, and the underlying rationale for the particular pattern that emerged requires more scholarly attention. Not only did it include a huge growth of in-house industrial research and university-based research; by the outbreak of the First World War there were also a number of diverse, specialized organizations such as the National Bureau of Standards, the National Advisory Committee on Aeronautics, the Forest Products Laboratory, and the American Society for Testing Materials – the last an interesting example of interfirm cooperation sponsored by a professional engineering society. Nevertheless, the importance of public sources of research support remained marginal throughout this period. Outside of agriculture, state funding of research, channeled largely through public institutions of higher education, may have exceeded federal funding.

The growing utilization of scientific knowledge and methodology in industry was vastly accelerated by an expanding pool of technically trained personnel – especially engineers. Associated with this expansion was the growth in the number of engineering schools, engineering programs, and engineering subspecialties in the second half of the nineteenth century. U.S. engineers were trained in the scientific knowledge and scientific methodology of the time. That training was, to be sure, often elementary in character and did not prepare engineers for work at the scientific frontier. But it was the larger body of scientific knowledge, and not merely frontier science, that was relevant to the needs of an expanding industrial establishment.[30]

Thus, engineers and other technically trained personnel served as valuable carriers of scientific knowledge. As a result, the number of people bringing the knowledge and methods of science to bear on industrial problems was vastly greater than the limited number of individuals that society chose to label "scientists" at any particular time. Moreover, the scale of the U.S. higher educational system considerably exceeded those of other industrial nations during this period. As we note in Chapter 5 and in the subsequent discussion of the Japanese research system, this broad-based system of training scientists and engineers served effectively as a device for diffusion and utilization of advanced scientific and engineering knowledge. Even where it did not advance the knowledge frontier, the higher education system appears to have been an important instrument for scientific and engineering "catch-up" in the United States during the early twentieth century and in the postwar Japanese economy. the postwar Japanese economy.

[30] Moreover, to a much greater extent in the United States than elsewhere, engineers moved into positions of industrial leadership. See Chandler (1962), p. 317, and the discussion in Chapter 5.

5

The organization of industrial research in Great Britain, 1900– 1950

A central factor in Britain's uneven economic fortunes since 1900 has been the poor innovative record of its industry. Partly because innovation lagged, British manufacturing productivity and exports grew more slowly than those of its industrial competitors.[1] The innovative performance of British firms was affected by low levels of industrial research, in which British firms invested fewer resources than did American enterprises during 1900– 50. The organization of British industrial research, which contrasted with that of the United States during this period, may also have undermined its effectiveness. The persistence of extramural research within Great Britain, in addition to the lower levels of overall industrial investment in research, appears to have impaired the innovative performance of British firms. The different histories of corporate development in these two econ- omies produced different R&D systems, with direct consequences for in- novative and competitive performance. Comparing the development and organization of industrial research in these two economies can therefore illuminate some of the issues that are discussed elsewhere in this volume.

During the 1900–50 period, the share of British exports in total world trade declined substantially more than did the British share of world man- ufacturing output; even more dramatic was the absolute decline in British exports during the 1920s. Declining exports reflected the continued de- pendence of British foreign trade on such staple commodities as coal, iron, and textiles (see Matthews, Feinstein, and Odling-Smee, 1982).[2] The development of alternative export industries was impeded by low levels of R&D. Productivity growth in the British economy during this period also lagged behind that of other European countries and the United States (see Rostas, 1948; Brown, 1973). Clearly, R&D investment and innovative performance were not the only causes of these disturbing trends.

---

[1] A recent exploration of this argument may be found in Pavitt (1980).
[2] See esp. pp. 436–7. Lewis (1949) noted that "the largest category of British exports was in those commodities expanding least in world trade. The leader par excellence in world trade was the United States; only 17.1 per cent of her manufactures exports were in the lowest category (in terms of growth in world trade during 1913–29) compared with Brit- ain's 42.1 per cent, and 28.6 per cent were in the highest category, compared with Britain's 4.3 per cent. Germany also was well ahead" (p. 79).

Nonetheless, the empirical evidence on the links between export performance and R&D investment[3] suggests that a more vigorous R&D effort might have offset this spiral of economic decline. The persistence of low levels of R&D investment in British industry is especially striking in view of the many official and unofficial acknowledgments of the technological failings of British industry during this period.

The effects of low levels of R&D investment were exacerbated by the organization of the British industrial research system, which reduced the returns on this investment. Reliance on government-funded cooperative research organizations, the scarcity of engineers (as opposed to scientists) in British industrial research, the weak links between academic and industrial research, and individual firms' failure to organize industrial research effectively and coordinate it with other internal functions all undermined the effectiveness of the modest British investment in R&D.

Three related factors contributed to the low level and inefficient organization of British industrial research during this period. The first is the structure of the British manufacturing firm. In the United States, as we noted in Chapter 4, the development of industrial research was closely associated with the reorganization of the American corporation described by Chandler (1977). In Britain, the transformation and reorganization of major firms occurred later than in the United States and was less complete in important respects. British firms thus depended to a greater extent on market institutions for the organization and conduct of industrial research. The effectiveness of R&D within British firms was often limited by the incomplete rationalization of internal firm structure. In short, the structural development of American industrial enterprises allowed for a more effective exploitation of the complementarities between research activity and production activity.

Government policy was another important influence affecting both the development of the British firm and the organization of British industrial research. A weak British antitrust policy influenced the development of R&D in two ways. Anticompetitive price and market-sharing agreements among British firms, particularly after the end of free trade, undercut the incentives for the pursuit of competitive advantage through innovation. Moreover, the British government's rationalization policies of the late 1920s

---

[3] Several studies have shown that innovative activity – measured in terms of inputs (e.g., expenditures or employment in R&D) or outputs (e.g., patents) – can improve productivity growth and export performance at the firm and industry levels of analysis. Mansfield (1968) and Terleckyj (1974) present empirical evidence on the links between industry and firm productivity growth and R&D investment. Keesing (1967) and Gruber, Mehta, and Vernon (1967) found a significant statistical linkage between export performance and R&D investment within industrialized nations during the postwar period. Although their findings cover only the post–1950 period, research activity almost certainly made a similar contribution to export performance during the earlier period as well.

and 1930s worsened the situation by supporting cartel agreements among small and inefficient firms.[4] British antitrust policy also may have reduced the incentives of British firms to pursue large mergers, which in the United States were closely associated with the development of modern corporate management structures. Government support for cooperative research within industry just after World War I appears to have had little if any positive impact on innovative performance.

A third major influence on the development of British R&D was the structure of technical and managerial education at the secondary and university levels – and here again government policy played a central role. A tradition of minimal public financial support for such education in Britain did nothing to improve the number or the professional training of British engineers, who are still much scarcer than in Germany or the United States (see Peck, 1968). In addition, Britain did not develop the informal links between higher and technical education and industry that were important in the industrial research systems of the United States and Germany. Both as a provider of technical expertise and a producer of technical manpower, the British educational network did not support and promote industrial research as effectively as the American system, which received much more public financial support.

These three explanatory factors interacted in a complex fashion. The structure of British firms and industries enforced dependence on the market (rather than the firm) to coordinate transactions. This industrial structure reduced British industrial demand for technical and managerial personnel. Government policy avoided (especially before World War I) any interference with the operations of the market. A different set of government policies might have increased the level and effectiveness of British industrial research. Even the more interventionist policies of British governments since 1945, however, have not raised industrial research activity and technological performance to American levels. Indeed, a striking aspect of this comparative analysis is the stability over a long period of both the gap in R&D investment and the factors contributing to it. Throughout the 1900–50 period, the nature and degree of the differences between British and American firm structure, educational systems, and government policies were largely unchanged.

A comparison of R&D investment in Great Britain and the United States

Neither the U.S. nor the British data on research activity permit a quantitative comparison covering the entire 1900–50 period. The data consis-

---

[4] Allen (1979) argued that "the measures taken to deal with this condition of excessive capacity must be classed among the noteworthy failures of economic policy of the interwar period" (p. 74).

tently suggest, however, that during and after this period, British manufacturing firms lagged substantially behind their American counterparts in average research intensity (measured as either the share of research employees in employment or as the share of R&D expenditures in sales). Freeman's analysis of data on expenditures from the 1950s and Sanderson's analysis of employment data from the 1930s both conclude that research intensity in British firms averaged about one-third that of American manufacturing firms. Lower levels of research activity in British manufacturing are not well explained by transatlantic differences in the mix of industries in the manufacturing sectors of these two nations.[5] Other data on American and British industrial research from the 1930s and 1940s also suggest that R&D investment in British manufacturing was well below that of American manufacturing.

Estimates of research employment in U.S. manufacturing during the 1930s and 1940s from the surveys of the National Research Council, for example, suggest that research intensity in American manufacturing was roughly four to five times that of British manufacturing during the 1930s and 1940s.[6] Although the British data may understate research employment during the 1930s, as Sanderson (1972) has argued, his analysis suggests that U.S. firms were on average at least three times as research intensive as British enterprises during and after this period.

These differences in manufacturing research intensity reflect different levels of public funding of research in the two countries and differences in the structure of publicly funded research. In Britain, government research installations such as the National Physical Laboratory and the quasi-public research associations accounted for a higher percentage of R&D

[5] Freeman (1962) stated that U.S. industry's R&D expenditures per employee were three times as great as British industry's. Industrial research employed 0.13 percent of the U.S. work force, compared with 0.05 percent in Britain in 1961. See also Sanderson (1972). Both Freeman and Sanderson found electrical machinery, chemicals, and petroleum products to be among the most research-intensive industries in the United States and Great Britain during the 1930s and 1950s. Freeman concluded in addition that the most research-intensive industries in his analysis (including aircraft, chemicals, electrical and nonelectrical machinery, and instruments) accounted for a larger percentage of net manufacturing output in Great Britain (32 percent in 1935 and 45 percent in 1958) than in the United States (28 percent in 1935 and 40 percent in 1958).

[6] Employment of research professionals in the laboratories of American manufacturing firms stood at 10,900 in 1933 (0.18 percent of total manufacturing employment), rising to nearly 28,000 in 1940 (0.35 percent), and 45,900 in 1946 (0.39 percent). On the basis of surveys conducted by the Federation of British Industries, research employment in manufacturing can be estimated at 1,724 in 1933 (0.030 percent of the total manufacturing work force), 2,575 in 1935 (0.042 percent), 4,505 in 1938 (0.066 percent), and 5,200 in 1945–46 (0.080 percent). For additional details, see the data in National Research Council, Bulletins 91, 104, and 113 (1933, 1940, and 1946), reported and analyzed in Mowery (1981). The American data for 1946 reflect the impact of high levels of wartime federal support of industrial research. Nevertheless, the prewar data suggest that the gap between British and American manufacturing in-house research activity may have been greater than in the postwar period.

expenditures than they did in the United States. Bernal estimated in 1939 that R&D expenditures by British industry amounted to £2.2 million and that total research expenditures by the British government (including financial support of the research associations) totaled £2.95 million. In contrast, Perazich and Field estimated total expenditure on research within U.S. industry at $175 million in 1937; total federal research expenditures in that year were $72 million, of which $38 million was spent within industry.[7] It is possible that publicly funded research in Britain partially compensated for the lower levels of in-house research employment in British manufacturing. Very little British government-supported R&D, however, was conducted within industrial firms during this period. Indeed, the government's focus on research associations (discussed later in this chapter) and national laboratories may have weakened the impact of public R&D funding on industrial innovation.

Although the available data suggest that British manufacturing was considerably less research intensive than that of the United States, this comparison does not control for transnational differences in the size distribution of firms. If anything, however, the largest British firms appear to have been even further behind their American counterparts in research intensity than were the smaller British manufacturers. In 1933, 116 of the firms in a sample of 160 U.S. firms listed among the two hundred largest manufacturing firms had R&D laboratories; in 1936, only twenty of the two hundred largest British firms had such research facilities. The contrast for the postwar period is similarly dramatic: 164 of the two hundred largest U.S. manufacturing firms in 1948 had research laboratories, and forty of the top two hundred British firms had in-house R&D facilities as of 1946.[8]

The structure of the British firm: The delayed managerial revolution and its consequences

The structure of British firms had much to do with the lower level of industrial research in British manufacturing, as well as with its frequently dysfunctional organization. The wave of structural change that transformed the structure of many U.S. corporations and provided an impetus to industrial research occurred later and was less significant within British industry.

---

[7] See Bernal (1939); Perazich and Field (1940); and Senate Military Affairs Committee, Subcommittee on War Mobilization (1945), p. 8.

[8] The data on U.S. firms are taken from the National Research Council surveys of industrial research and the tabulations of the two hundred largest firms compiled by Chandler that are discussed in Chapter 4. The British R&D and firm data are drawn from Chandler's unpublished tabulations and Andrade (1946).

In Britain, the merger wave of the late nineteenth and early twentieth centuries was smaller than the U.S. merger movement of the same period. Fewer firms and assets were absorbed than in the United States (see Hannah, 1974, esp. p. 10). The British merger wave also involved a narrower range of industries, primarily brewing (reflecting the development of tied houses in response to licensing restrictions) and textiles. Both British and American manufacturing experienced another wave of mergers after World War I. In the United States this merger wave had a less dramatic impact on firm and market structure than its predecessor (see Salter and Weinhold, 1980, esp. p. 4). The British merger wave of the 1920s, in contrast, resulted in the formation of such major modern firms as Imperial Chemical Industries (ICI) and Unilever. The giant centralized firm thus did not develop in Great Britain until well after the first American merger wave. Since the development of the large multifunction firm is linked to the rise of industrial research, the slower pace of change in British firm structure contributed to the differences between American and British industrial research activity during this period.

As the previous chapter noted, the initial U.S. merger wave was followed by substantial growth in the industrial research activities of many firms. Moreover, the post–World War I reduction in turnover among the ranks of the largest U.S. corporations may have been associated in part with investments in industrial research. In British industry, there was no comparable transition from instability to stability in market structure after World War I. The survival rate of large British firms appears to have been substantially lower than that of the largest American firms in the early years of this century; an increase in British firms' survival rates comparable to that of the early twentieth century in the United States appears in Great Britain only in the 1940s (Hannah, 1976, pp. 117, 167). Lower levels of industrial research in British manufacturing thus are associated with lower levels of firm survival and a more unstable market structure during much of the 1900–50 period.

Even where large mergers among British firms took place, they often produced an awkward collection of poorly coordinated, fiercely independent subsidiaries, rather than a streamlined or efficient structure (Payne, 1967; Hannah, 1974; Chandler, 1980). The opposition of directors to the extinction of their firms or the closing of their factories often meant that inefficient and excess capacity survived the merger. One of the most famous examples of incomplete rationalization of internal firm structure is the Calico Printers' Association, a "lumbering leviathan" formed in 1902 with a board of directors numbering no fewer than eighty-four (Macrosty, 1907, p. 147). Interestingly, a committee appointed by the firm in 1907 to recommend ways of improving its poor performance strongly advocated the establishment of a central research department

. . . equipped with necessary appliances for research and experimental work, conducted by the ablest and best-trained chemists, specially qualified to pursue investigations, in which chemical processes and mechanical and electrical appliances are involved. This department would form a "Clearing House" for difficulties experienced in any branch works in carrying out complicated processes, and in the introduction of new colours and methods of production. It would inquire into, and test if necessary, all new inventions, and obtain information from other countries of new developments in calico printing. It would be the brains of the business. (Macrosty, 1907, p. 152)

Despite this eloquent recommendation, no central research facility was established.

Incomplete internal rationalization was not confined to firms in the older staple industries. William Lever was known for supporting competition among the subsidiaries of his firm – a leader in the rapidly growing consumer goods market of twentieth-century Britain.[9] The development of United Steel, one of the more progressive firms in the British steel industry, suggests that the formation of that firm was not motivated by a desire for greater efficiency or rationalization of industry structure.[10] Nor was the firm destined to acquire a strong central office. Only in the early 1930s, some seven years after the United Steel merger, did the firm establish a central office and a central research department and adopt a more systematic policy of internal rationalization. Despite these reforms, the entire central sales and administrative staff of the company numbered only 150 persons in 1950, when the work force totaled more than 28,000.

Major new firms in two of the "new industries" – chemicals and electrical machinery – experienced severe difficulties in the central coordination of their newly merged subsidiaries and frequently failed in the strategic management and coordination of research activities. In a technically progressive industry, ICI – a firm that consciously emulated many of the management techniques of Du Pont – achieved a unified organizational structure only in the 1950s. As a result, according to ICI's historian, even after "ICI had been in existence for a dozen years . . . the central research organization was still far from fully developed. Indeed, its funda-

---

[9] "Within his own business he [Lever] salved his Victorian economic conscience by the application of competitive principles; all associated companies should 'compete strongly with Lever Brothers in every line' " (Wilson, 1954, vol. 1, p. 273).

[10] "United Steel was not intended to be a very centralized business. . . . There is no record of the founders of the business having as their object the achievement of increased productive efficiency horizontally as between the businesses which were to become branches of the combine through what was later to be called 'rationalization,' and an enforced specialization upon different parts of their joint product" (Andrews and Brunner, 1951, p. 121).

mental principles had hardly been laid down, apart from the somewhat negative one of leaving the Groups alone as much as possible"(Reader, 1975, vol. 2, p. 93).[11]

Associated Electrical Industries (AEI) – the product of a 1928 merger of British Thomson Houston and Metropolitan Vickers – also was racked by fierce internal rivalries between its formerly independent constituent units. Indeed, the firm's historians attribute British industry's slow development of a commercial jet engine in part to the lack of cooperation between its two components, each of which had made significant progress in jet engine development in the late 1930s (Jones and Marriott, 1975, p. 155). The Marconi firm, which was absorbed in 1946 by English Electric after being controlled for many years by Cable and Wireless, operated with a similarly chaotic internal structure through the late 1940s (see Baker, 1970, p. 332).[12]

Even within large British firms in technically progressive industries, then, powerful centrifugal forces prevented the development of the strong central staff associated with industrial research in American manufacturing firms. Where such firms were, by American standards, research intensive (in the late 1930s, ICI was spending 2.8 percent of its total sales on R&D, compared with 2.4 percent at Du Pont), weak central managerial control often led to internal duplication and rivalry in the research effort (see Reader, 1975, vol. 2, p. 414). Possibly more significant were the persistently weak links between research and the other staff functions and between the research laboratory and the production units. As previous chapters noted, these links are critical to innovative performance.

The presence of these structural problems within firms in both technically progressive and stagnant industries suggests that their causes were related to the structure and institutional environment of the British economy. An important feature of the economic environment was the absence of a strong antitrust policy, which slowed the emergence of large firms through mergers in Great Britain. British firms interested in reaping the benefits of industrywide coordination of price or output could choose from alternatives ranging from trade associations to a complete merger. In Great Britain throughout this period, legal sanctions against such interfirm cooperation were minimal.[13] Trade associations were a primary vehicle for

[11] Reader argues further (p. 461) that ICI, in contrast to Du Pont, failed to master the integration of product diversification with its internal structure until the late 1950s, because of an inability to reorganize existing divisions within the firm to take advantage of new product opportunities and strategies.

[12] Yet another large firm formed in the 1920s, Metal Box, also was characterized by a lack of internal cohesion (see Reader, 1976, pp. 40–1).

[13] Hannah (1980) states that "in important respects – particularly in coordinating sales policies and securing monopolistic control over prices – cartels were an alternative to merger that was open to European entrepreneurs but closed to their counterparts in the United

such arrangements, which spread throughout the manufacturing sector. In many cases these agreements were encouraged by the government in industrial rationalization programs.

Louis Galambos and other scholars have noted that such trade associations were also important in the United States in the late nineteenth century (Galambos, 1966, p. 35). After the passage and increasingly stringent judicial interpretation of the Sherman Antitrust Act, however, the number and effectiveness of such interfirm agreements declined. Some scholars have suggested that the merger wave of the 1892–1904 period, particularly the surge in mergers after 1897, was in part a response to this new juridical environment. Finding that the legality of informal or formal price-fixing and market-sharing agreements was under attack, firms resorted to mergers, creating (with the aid of the rapidly expanding New York financial community) firms that substituted intrafirm for interfirm methods to control prices and markets.[14]

Although it may be claiming too much to argue that the mild antitrust climate failed to encourage mergers or the rationalization of such mergers in British industry as did occur, this cartelized environment reduced firms' incentives to pursue technological change as an instrument of competition, especially after the demise of free trade. Informal or formal interfirm cooperation allowed the survival of firms that were smaller and less efficient. Schumpeterian competition (i.e., the aggressive introduction of new products or improved versions of old ones – a process heavily dependent on research) was discouraged by such agreements among firms.[15]

States. Firms that preferred to maintain a single-unit structure in Britain were therefore free to do so while, at the same time, reducing competition by joining a cartel; in the 1930s and during World War II, in fact, these arrangements were actively encouraged by the government. United States industrialists like Gerald [sic] Swope, the dynamic president of the American General Electric Company, accustomed to the antitrust tradition, were advised by bankers in Britain that they need not create large, centralized corporations through mergers for their European operations; market competition could be regulated through agreement with other firms, and there was thus no need to acquire them" (p. 67). Macrosty (1907) and Lucas (1937), among others, provide detailed accounts of price and output agreements among firms in a wide range of industries.

[14] This argument is stressed in Stigler (1968). The Supreme Court ruled in the *Trans Missouri Association* case in 1898 and the *Addyston Pipe* case in 1899 that the Sherman Act made illegal all agreements among firms on prices or market sharing. According to Thorelli a total of 84 mergers occurred from 1890 to 1897, followed by 24 in 1898, 105 in 1899, and a total of 83 from 1900 to 1902. See also Chandler (1977), pp. 331–6.

[15] Reader (1979) notes that "it was settled policy in ICI (Imperial Chemical Industries) to avoid competition with customers or suppliers which meant, in effect, avoiding competition with virtually every manufacturing company of any importance in the United Kingdom. For many years, accordingly, ICI kept clear of the range of chemical products associated with industrial alcohol, which were supplied by the Distillers' Company Ltd. and which were of considerable importance in the fields of organic activity opening up in the late 1920s and early 1930s. Similarly, in order to avoid giving offence to Courtaulds, important customers for caustic soda, ICI, unlike Du Pont, kept well clear of rayon and cellophane" (p. 174).

Another factor contributing to the relatively slow pace of the British managerial revolution before 1950 was the limited involvement of financial institutions in corporate management and mergers. In the United States, by contrast, financiers and banks played a significant role in the finance and organization of such forerunners of the modern corporation as the railroads. Financial institutions also were important, especially after 1900, in the development of U.S. industrial corporations. Outside financiers facilitated many large mergers and often imposed new organizational and management structures on the firms that they created. The size of the firms resulting from these mergers, the mergers' financial requirements, and their organization by major financial houses also hastened the replacement of owners by managers. In Great Britain through much of the early twentieth century, on the other hand, industrial firms seeking long-term financing had little alternative to floating new issues on the stock market or relying on nonbank sources for borrowing. The supervision of corporate growth and organization by financial institutions, which was even more pronounced in Germany than in the United States, was largely absent from Britain, and family owners retained managerial control of major firms far longer.[16]

British firms of all sizes thus remained far more dependent on the market for the organization and control of their activities than was true of the largest American firms. In industries such as textiles, the production process was carried on through a highly developed interfirm division of labor. The nonelectrical machinery and steel industries also were populated by relatively small firms that were not involved in product marketing or distribution (see Lazonick, 1981, 1983).[17]

This British reliance on market mechanisms was also reflected in the importance of the consulting engineer, whose negative influence on innovation and export performance has been cited by a number of observers and official committees. Although the importance of the American independent research organization declined during this period, the independent consulting engineer continued to play a significant part in such British industries as heavy electrical and nonelectrical machinery. The importance of the consulting engineer, who designed and supervised the production of complex capital goods for a particular customer, impeded the development of more efficient corporate organization and in-house research in at least two ways. First, custom design and production of

[16] The Committee on Finance and Industry's *Report* (1931) remarked on the absence of such close links (p. 165).
[17] The share of industry capacity accounted for by "combined" firms (firms that carried out both weaving and spinning operations) declined substantially between 1884 and 1914, according to data in Tyson (1968). See the Committee on Commercial and Industrial Policy after the War (1918), Saul (1968), and Tolliday (1979).

machinery prevented sufficient standardization of product lines to support the development of larger firms capable of exploiting scale economies in design and production. In addition, the consulting engineer assumed an important mediating role in the research and development process, reducing the incentive for engineering firms to invest in research within their boundaries and making it more difficult for them to exploit information received directly from customers or suppliers in the innovation process. S. B. Saul's comment illustrates these difficulties:

> The consulting engineer all too often was deprived of the opportunity of combining his theoretical knowledge with a deep practical understanding. The industrialist, for his part, called in the consulting engineer whenever calculations had to be made – fixing the proper thickness of wall for a hydraulic cylinder, or determining the strains in a simple lattice girder or workshop crane. Things had so fossilized that if the poor consultant tried to give the manufacturer a free hand, there was a chorus of protest. . . . There is little point in arguing that German locomotive makers were more advanced in ideas of design than were the British, for by and large the use of consulting engineers meant that the British maker was concerned with organizing his works to the best of his ability, not with design. The consultant's aim tended to be to design a product of high technical quality which would do him credit in his profession. Executing the work in the most economical manner was not the prime object by any means. Not being in close contact with any one firm, he failed to design in a manner which fitted in with any particular manufacturing facilities. Standardization was extremely difficult to achieve and the method inhibited continued development work on plant when it was in operation. (Saul, 1968, pp. 117–8) [18]

This analysis suggests the dangers of extensive reliance on contractual arrangements in the innovation and design processes. The consulting engineer hampered the emergence of large corporations that incorporated research and other functions within their boundaries by reducing incentives for firms to invest in in-house research and by preserving an industry structure characterized by small firms and low levels of product standardization. Furthermore, the efficiency and effectiveness of the innovation process were reduced.

[18] Byatt (1979), pp. 177–8, argues that the reliance on consulting engineers in the British electrical machinery industry reduced the flow of incremental innovations and adaptations resulting from the actual operation of the machinery. On the northeast coast, where consulting engineers were not widely used, this feedback channel was not obstructed, and important innovations resulted.

In the United States, the interaction between evolving firm structure and in-house research was of great importance to the development of the modern industrial firm. In Britain, this interaction was largely absent. The modest importance of intrafirm industrial research reflected the lack of dramatic change in the structure of the British firm. As a result, the independent consulting engineer continued to play a major role in such industries as electrical and nonelectrical machinery. Firms in other industries also were unlikely to establish large-scale, centralized research facilities covering the full range of current and future activities because of the weakness of the central office structure and because of the lack of technical expertise of managers.

Neither British nor American firms developed in a vacuum, of course. The structure of the British firm, and its modest commitment to industrial research, were both responses to and influences on the broader institutional environment. Important elements of this environment were the higher educational system and the government, both of which are considered in the following section.

Scientific and managerial education in Great Britain and the United States

A key factor in the growth of industrial research in U.S. manufacturing was the parallel growth of a large higher education establishment. As we have noted, the development of research within academia in the late nineteenth century was closely followed by the emergence of industrial research. A complex web of connections linked the two kinds of research, including personnel, ideas, and financial, as well as political, support.[19]

In Britain, on the other hand, fewer strong links developed between academia and industry. In comparison with the United States, Britain suffered a shortage of professional engineers for industrial research and a shortage of professionally trained managers. Moreover, there was little of the informal involvement of academic personnel in industrial research that developed during the 1920s and 1930s in the United States. The educational system clearly was not the sole factor behind these developments; the lack of professional training for managers reflected the continued managerial control by owners of many British firms. Indeed, the educational system may be viewed more generally as the supply response to the demand for research investment by firms. The weak British industrial demand for technical personnel reduced pressure for changes in the

---

[19] For a discussion, see Thackray (1982). Graham (1983) provides a description of the relationship between academic and industrial research during and after the interwar period in the United States.

structure of the institutions supplying research and managerial personnel.[20]

Perhaps the most important difference between the British and American systems was their size. In the early 1920s, roughly 24,000 students were enrolled in British universities; the figure rose to 50,000–60,000 by the late 1930s. By contrast, American institutions of higher learning awarded over 48,000 degrees in 1913 and more than 216,000 in 1940. With a total population 35 percent that of the United States, Britain had only about 6 percent as many students in higher education in the late 1930s (see U.S. Bureau of the Census, 1975, vol. 1, p. 386; Briggs, 1981).[21]

The small size of the higher education sector in Great Britain reflected the modest level of government support for higher education during the first half of the twentieth century. In the United States, in contrast, state government provided substantial support for higher education. Using data from the University Grants Committee, Bernal estimated total government support of British university education at £2.7 million (slightly more than $9 million) in 1934–5. Total government appropriations for American higher education, most of which came from state governments, are estimated by the Carnegie Foundation to have been $340 million in 1929–30 (Bernal, 1939; Carnegie Foundation for the Advancement of Teaching, 1976, p. 35). One result was the development of a much larger higher education system in the United States that was in many cases better suited to provide technical education for the needs of industry. The American system of higher education placed much more emphasis on the training of engineers, a group of great importance for the industrial research and innovation process.

Britain lagged far behind other industrialized nations in its output of engineers. One scholar noted in 1968 that "no other country trains as engineers such a low proportion of its total professional manpower" (Peck, 1968, p. 450). The chronic shortage of university-trained engineers is well illustrated by the experience of Nobel Industries, a key component of ICI. As late as World War II, there were no engineers in the firm's chief research laboratory or (of equal or greater importance) in its management. According to its historian:

---

[20] Sanderson (1972), p. 117, argues that the demand on the part of industry for technically trained personnel was weak, especially before 1914.

[21] The size of the higher educational system was an important "supply-side" influence on the growth of industrial research; Beer (1959) cites the high rate of production of chemistry Ph.D.s by German higher education in the late nineteenth century as an important influence on the growth of industrial research in the German chemicals industry. As the supply of professional chemists exceeded available academic employment opportunities, emigration and industrial research were the only alternatives open to the German graduate chemist.

This was to some extent the result of the decision made long before and hardened into a tradition at the end of the century, that the factory should be in the hands of chemists; but even if the attempt to employ qualified engineers had been made it must have failed, for engineers trained in the same way and to the same degree as chemists could not have been found in any number. Despite the fact that British industries were in the main engineering industries or conducted by engineers, the engineering profession had been very little concerned with full-time academic training, and indeed had a prejudice against any form of training other than that of the workshop and the evening school. (Miles, 1955, p. 58)

It was only after World War II that Nobel established a laboratory devoted to engineering research on manufacturing processes.

To compound the problem, the training of engineers in Britain tended to reinforce, rather than bridge, the barriers between science and industrial practice. The dominant form of British engineering education well into the twentieth century was a combination of night school and apprenticeship, both of which were conducted outside the major research universities. This system facilitated vertical mobility between the skilled trades and professional engineering, but it perpetuated the gap between the universities and the engineering profession (see Wickenden, 1929, esp. pp. 140–2).[22] In the United States, by contrast, engineers functioned as critical links between advanced scientific research and industrial practice.[23] Both the content and the modest scale of British engineering education made such links less effective.

The American engineer also performed the important function of fusing managerial and technical skills. Engineer-managers such as Frederick W. Taylor, Charles Kettering and Alfred Sloan of General Motors, and Pierre Du Pont played a major role in the integration of industrial research with the business practices of the American firm. Engineers trained in the United States received far more managerial instruction than did their British

---

[22] Floud (1978) focuses largely on the ability of this system of engineering education to respond to increasing industrial demand during the late nineteenth century, rather than considering the content and the implications for innovation of this form of engineering education, in arguing that British technical education during this period was adequate.

[23] The importance of this linkage is underlined in Reich (1983). He observes that at General Electric's central research facility in the early years, "many industrial researchers were both scientists and engineers by training. Five of the best people at Bell in the early years had taken undergraduate degrees in engineering, then proceeded to Ph.D.'s in science. Irving Langmuir received a B.S. in metallurgical engineering before acquiring his Ph.D. in physical chemistry, and William Coolidge, his well-known contemporary at GE, began with a B.S. in electrical engineering, then went on to a physics Ph.D." (p. 200).

or European counterparts (see Wickenden, 1929, p. 258; Chandler, 1962, p. 317).

A major factor in the close links between American higher education and industrial research was the state university, founded with federal support (through the 1862 Morrill Act) and supported by local legislatures. These universities sought, for obvious political reasons, to be helpful to local industry. Many state universities established organizations – analogous to their agricultural extension and research services – to provide industry with applied engineering skills and expertise on a consulting basis. Examples of such organizations include the Bureau of Industrial Research at the University of Washington, founded in 1916, and the Industrial Research Department at the University of Oklahoma, founded in 1917.[24] State universities supplied consulting services to industry, trained engineers, and, increasingly, trained Ph.D.s in chemistry or physics for industrial research positions. Public funds for the support of higher education in the United States were supplemented by the grants of the large private foundations that grew rapidly in the early twentieth century. Much of the funding from such institutions as the Rockefeller Foundation was intended to bolster the research links between university and industry. In Britain, cooperation between academia and industry was more informal, less widespread, and received much less public or private financial support.

The higher education complex in the United States also played a much more important role in training managers than the British system did. As Charlotte Erickson (1959) and Alfred Chandler (1977) have noted, American managers were more likely to have received a university degree than their British counterparts. Moreover, American managers often had greater technical training and expertise; those British managers who received any postsecondary education tended to be arts majors. Indeed, it has been argued that the technical background of top-level British managers actually declined in the 1900–50 period – a period in which the proportion of this group trained in either the public schools or the ancient universities increased sharply (Coleman, 1973). In neither of these training grounds were future British managers given a strong background in either man-

[24] For additional discussion, see Thackray (1982). Servos (1980), pp. 531–49, discusses the rise and decline of a similar organization, the Research Laboratory for Applied Chemistry, at the Massachusetts Institute of Technology during the period 1910–35, arguing that advocates of pure academic research eventually eclipsed such industrially oriented research activity at MIT. Although such conflicts undoubtedly occurred elsewhere, several points should be noted. Even after the influence of the applied chemistry laboratory waned, links between MIT and industry remained strong, and certainly were far stronger than those between British industry and elite institutions of higher education. The laboratory's decline was also a reflection of the fact that such applied research facilities were much more widespread in American industry in the 1930s than before World War I, as was noted in our discussion in Chapter 4.

agement techniques or the technological basis of modern manufacturing industry. The lack of professional and technical training among British managers reflects the persistence of management control by founding families of many British manufacturing firms well into the 1940s, as well as the absence within British manufacturing of an extensive middle-management hierarchy. As Chandler (1977) has observed, it was the growth of middle management, in response to the increasing size and range of functions performed by the American manufacturing firm, that increased the demand for professional management education and aided the shift in control of the large firm from owners to managers. The lack of industry demand for professional engineers was a significant factor in Britain's failure to achieve more far-reaching reforms and greater state support for higher education. The continued weakness of Britain's technical and professional management training capacity, then, cannot be separated from the delayed and incomplete reorganization of British corporate structure.

The role of government

As the many studies of British industry, education, and industrial research cited earlier in this chapter make clear, it was generally recognized during the early twentieth century that British industry was lagging behind German and American practice in the exploitation of new technologies and scientific knowledge and in the development of new institutional mechanisms to encourage such exploitation. Popular and official discussion of foreign (especially German) competition was particularly intense immediately before the outbreak of World War I. The extent of British dependence on foreign sources of supply for various critical chemical and optical products became excruciatingly clear in wartime:

> The outbreak of war found us unable to produce at home many essential materials and articles. We were making less than a dozen kinds of optical glass out of over a hundred made by our enemies. We could hardly make a tithe of the various dyestuffs needed for our textile industries with an annual output of over 250,000,000 pounds. We were dependent on Germany for magnetos, countless drugs and pharmaceutical products, even for the tungsten used in our great steel works and for the zinc smelted from the ores which our own empire produced. (Advisory Council to the Committee for Scientific and Industrial Research, 1916)

The British government's response to the supply crisis in technologically sophisticated matériel took several forms. A state-owned corporation, British Dyestuffs, was established to expand the production of synthetic dyestuffs and intermediates. This new corporation proved to be a mixed success. Events (notably the 1915 shell crisis) forced British Dyestuffs to devote much of its effort to the production of explosives rather than dystuffs. It remained for two private firms, British Alizarine and Levinsteins Ltd., to produce most of the synthetic dyes for the war effort. Although British Dyestuffs did establish a research department, the firm's in-house technical staff devoted most of its efforts to process engineering and improvement (concerned primarily with the manufacture of explosives). The firm attempted to use research contracts with senior chemistry faculty at Oxford, Cambridge, Leeds, and Liverpool universities for more fundamental research, but "as late as October 1917 nothing much had come of it and apparently nothing ever did" (Reader, 1970, vol. 1, p. 275). Rather than encouraging research within the firm, government policy promoted reliance by British Dyestuffs on external research organizations. British Dyestuffs did not prosper after the war, despite the imposition of a prohibitive tariff on imports of dyestuffs, and the firm was merged with Brunner Mond, Nobel, and United Alkali to form Imperial Chemical Industries in 1926.

The second major wartime policy initiative in industrial research was the establishment in 1916 of the Department of Scientific and Industrial Research (DSIR), which assumed responsibility for the control of such civilian governmental research establishments as the National Physical Laboratory. An important new policy associated with the DSIR was financial support for industrial research associations (RAs) – cooperative research organizations that firms within an industry were free to join. According to P. S. Johnson, a central concern in the discussions leading to the RA scheme was the belief that cooperative research could substitute for the in-house research facilities absent in British industry at the time:

> One of the principal impediments to the efficient organisation of industrial research was the small scale on which much of British industry operated. The investigation, for instance, of the fundamental properties of cotton fibres was outside the reach of all except the very large firms, and even in the latter management might only be prepared to spend a very small amount on it. . . . The implications were that, even apart from the traditional attitudes of British management to research, a certain minimum turnover was required before a firm could support a research department or even, at the lowest level of indivisibility, a research worker. (Johnson, 1973, p. 19)

First established in 1918, the RAs were to be funded jointly by government and industry for a five-year period, after which industry support was expected to be sufficient to allow the RAs to continue with private funding alone.

The research association scheme initially appeared to be a success. Over the first five years of the program (1918–23), twenty-four RAs were established in industries ranging from woolen textiles to laundering. No groundswell of industry financial support materialized, however, and by 1923, when state aid was expected to cease, only one RA, devoted to research on portland cement, was able to continue on the basis of industry support alone. Public support of the remaining associations was renewed for an additional five years, but the level of funding was intended to shrink over the period.

The 1920s were a difficult period for the RAs. A number of the associations failed as their income declined and industrial contributions dwindled. By the end of the second five-year trial in 1928, it was clear that the RAs would collapse without increased public support. Financial aid was increased for a period ending in the early 1930s, when budgetary crises forced major reductions. In 1933, D. W. Hill observed, "The average expenditure of the associations was only 14,500 pounds a year and this average included a few very large associations so that the average for thirteen associations was less than 7,000 pounds a year" (Hill, 1947, p. 54). The DSIR significantly increased its expenditures in support of the RAs through the rearmament years of the late 1930s. During and after World War II, state support of the cooperative research scheme expanded dramatically, and the future of the RAs was assured.

Despite their long history, the RAs have had a modest impact on the innovative performance of British manufacturing. As early as 1929, the Balfour Committee remarked on "the admittedly inadequate extent to which the results [of the RAs' research work] have been utilised up to the present by British industries." The committee argued that "at present, it is too often the case that the information, compiled with great skill and labour, simply runs to waste for want of a properly equipped 'receiving mechanism' within the works" (Committee on Industry and Trade, 1929, pp. 215, 217). With this statement, the committee accurately diagnosed one of the central difficulties of the RA scheme. Cooperative or extramural research institutions could not entirely substitute for in-house research facilities because client firms needed in-house technical expertise in order to use the results of such extramural research effectively. Without such a "receiving mechanism," as we noted in Chapter 4, the firm was far less likely to benefit from the activities of the research associations.[25]

---

[25] Albu's (1980) description of the research association in marine engineering is illustrative: "By the time of the last war Parsons [marine engine and turbine] designs had become conservative. . . . The anxiety of the Admiralty led to the setting up of the Parsons and Marine Turbine Research and Development Association (PAMATRADA) in 1944, but although it had a well-staffed research department the marine engine builders, most of whom were adjacent to the shipyards, were too small to be able to support it, and lacked

Thus the RAs could do little to solve the central problem to which they were addressed – the lack of in-house research activity within British industry. Writing long after the foundation of the first RAs, Johnson argued:

> The government was mistaken in its view that the RAs' work would be primarily concerned with research for the small firm which was unable to do any for itself. . . . What has happened is that the RAs now derive their main support from the larger firms. Thus, one of the original aims of the scheme – to overcome the difficulties associated with the small firm – has gone largely unmet. (Johnson, 1973, pp. 51–2)

The RA scheme was intended to deal with the supply of research and development, rather than the use of the results of research. Inasmuch as the utilization, more than the supply, of R&D was critical to improving the technical performance of British industry during this period, the program was not a great success.

The research associations, the British government's primary policy response to the perceived technical shortcomings of manufacturing, became a more formal version of the interfirm cooperation that characterized the behavior of British industrial firms in other areas, in sharp contrast to the developing American research system. During a period of growth in intrafirm industrial research within American manufacturing, government policy encouraged the opposite trend in Britain. The research associations were an extension of the organizational structure typified by the consulting engineer, rather than a significant change in the technological organization or foundations of British industry.

British government policies, both those directly concerned with industrial research and those focusing on factors indirectly affecting research, did little to advance, and may have retarded, the development of modern industrial research within British manufacturing. Policies influencing the structure of British industry, which was admittedly antiquated, had little impact. Both the weak antitrust policies of the British government and its industrial rationalization efforts of the 1920s and 1930s removed incentives for mergers and the internal governance of transactions that played a major role in the development of large American manufacturing firms with in-house research facilities. The competitive environment resulting from the mild antitrust posture of the British government also reduced the incentives of British firms to pursue product and process innovation. The small size of the higher-education complex in England and low levels

the level of technical management to be interested in the results of research. The Association declined into a licensing organization for Parsons design" (p. 175).

of state financial support for this system impeded the development of links between academia and industry and produced a system that trained too few professional engineers for the needs of British industry.

The DSIR and its associated research associations also do not appear to have had a major impact on either the research activity or the innovative performance of British industry. It is difficult to know what would have occurred had the RAs not been established, or had they received greater funding. There is widespread agreement, however, that the RAs were not effective as substitutes for in-house research facilities.

Rather than addressing the underlying causes of lagging technical performance and underinvestment in R&D by British industry, the British government used public funds to support industrial research directly, in the research associations. The RAs were an industrial policy that would disturb none of the institutions that hampered industrial research and innovation within British industry.[26] In view of the great obstacles to the development of a more progressive industrial and educational system, a more inventive set of government policies would have been necessary to improve industrial research and innovative performance in British industry. Such policy initiatives did not emerge.

The contrast with the role of government in the United States is striking. The federal policies that proved to be crucial for the development of a vigorous American industrial research infrastructure evolved in an atmosphere in which the federal government paid relatively little attention to the technical strengths or shortcomings of industry. Although they were not consistently enforced with great energy, the federal antitrust statutes were enacted in the late nineteenth century with little explicit consideration of their implications for dynamic efficiency. The complex system of public higher education in the United States, with its vast size and numerous local sources of financial support, was originally established to meet the technical needs of industry and agriculture. At the state level especially, the support of state universities and other institutions of higher education was increasingly seen as a means of providing technical services and support to local industry. At the federal level, government policies explicitly directed at the support of industrial research were conspicuously absent before 1941, with the possible exception of the National Ad-

---

[26] British public policy toward R&D since World War II bears some striking similarities to that of the interwar period. A high level of government spending on R&D has been overwhelmingly concentrated (or overcommitted – see Peck, 1968) in two sectors that have important military applications but are isolated from the rest of the British economy: nuclear energy and aircraft. This policy has reduced the resources (both financial and human) available for R&D elsewhere in the economy. As our discussion of postwar federal research support in Chapter 6 points out, military R&D programs in the U.S. economy have been similarly concentrated among industries and may have weakened the innovative performance of the economy.

visory Committee on Aeronautics (see Chapters 6 and 7 for additional discussion). The fortunes of British and American industrial research suggest that American government policy, which affected the proximate influences on industrial research investment, ultimately proved more effective than that of the British government, which attempted to deal directly with a perceived shortfall of industrial research activity without disturbing the foundations of the existing industrial and educational systems.

Conclusion

During the first half of the twentieth century, the British manufacturing sector invested significantly less in industrial research than did the American manufacturing sector. The low level of industrial research, and the fact that much of it was performed outside manufacturing firms, reflected British firms' continued reliance on markets as a primary means for organizing economic activity. In the United States, on the other hand, more and more products and functions were absorbed within the boundaries of the developing firm. The establishment of in-house research was a central component of this reorganization of the American firm. The fact that far fewer British firms underwent a similar transformation before 1950 is critical in explaining the substantially higher levels of research activity in American manufacturing. Several factors contributed to the delay of the managerial revolution in British industry: a weak antitrust policy, government rationalization policies, a lack of involvement of financial institutions and their operatives in the internal management and reorganization of British firms, and persistent family control of British firms. Between 1940 and 1960, as the structure of the British firm and manufacturing sector changed, the level of industrial research activity rose, but remained well below the American level.

Firm structure was not the sole factor influencing the low level of industrial research in Britain. The educational system, particularly higher education, remained small, in part because of low levels of government financial support. The training of engineers in particular was deficient. The lack of engineers in research and management reduced the effectiveness of industrial research and may have constrained its growth. The small supply of engineers and the nonacademic character of their training perpetuated the separation of British laboratory science and British technological practice. The former was of extremely high quality, but the latter often was severely deficient.

The organization of British industrial research on a contractual, interfirm basis meant that the modest research investments that British firms did make may have yielded lower returns than they might have, had the research been organized differently. The advantages resulting from the combination of research and other activities within a single firm could not be realized by either the consulting engineer or the research associations. The structural development of the British firm, the lack of educational support for industrial research, and the growth of the research associations all were influenced by government policy, which was conservative in design and modest in impact. Despite the many perceptive critical analyses of British industry's technical performance, successive governments avoided major policy shifts aimed at improving this performance. In the United States, the fundamental factors influencing the structure of industry and the supply of technical personnel were considered to be either beyond the direct control of the federal government or already so well established that no activist policy was needed. Nevertheless, state government support of education proved to be very important in the development of U.S. industrial research.

Britain's failure to match the level of industrial research achieved in U.S. manufacturing reflected the institutional legacy of an earlier era of industrial activity and organization – as well as the failure of government policy to change this institutional environment. In the United States the private firm had essentially preempted any government role in direct control or funding of industrial research before World War II. British firms did not assume this role to the same extent. Both during and after the period we have examined, the British government's efforts to fund and direct industrial research and innovation have been largely unsuccessful.

PART III

The development of the postwar system, 1940–1987

6

Postwar federal investment in research and development

The Second World War transformed the U.S. R&D system. Wartime led to a dramatic increase in government involvement as a supporter of industrial and academic research – in some contrast to other nations, however, responsibility for the performance of much of this R&D remained with these nongovernmental institutions. World War II also transformed the global technological and competitive environment within which U.S. firms operated. The U.S. emerged from wartime as an unchallenged leader in a much broader range of technologies than was true at any point before 1940. Moreover, the demands of reconstruction were to prolong the period of U.S. technological, as well as economic, supremacy. Because the central point of contrast between the prewar and postwar research systems is this upsurge in federal government involvement in the national R&D system, in this chapter we devote considerable attention to the contours of federal R&D support in basic, commercial, and military research.

During the past forty-five years, the federal government has assumed major responsibilities for decision making, for finance, and even for the use of the "output" of scientific research. Since the Second World War the U.S. research system has been transformed from one in which the federal government was a minor participant to one in which it has become a major purchaser of R&D, albeit without at the same time becoming a primary performer of R&D. Rather than being performed mainly in government laboratories, federally funded R&D is largely carried out by private industry; the university community is the main performer of the basic research component. Furthermore, federal support of R&D has been provided within an institutional framework dominated by contractual relationships between the federal government and private performers.

World War II and its aftermath

With war preparations and the U.S. entry into World War II in December 1941, the distinctly bucolic picture of federal R&D expenditures we discussed in Chapter 4 was transformed permanently. Funding for the primary categories of prewar R&D, which were not war related, grew only slightly during the war in dollar terms and declined substantially in real terms (see the appendix to this chapter). Total federal R&D expenditures (in 1930 dollars) rose from $83.2 million in 1940 to a peak of $1,313.6 million in 1945. Over the same period, the research expenditures of the Department of Defense rose from $29.6 million to $423.6 million (in 1930 dollars).

Two novel organizational features characterized wartime R&D expenditures and presaged important postwar changes. First was the massive Manhattan Project, whose research budget in the peak years 1944 and 1945 substantially exceeded that of the Department of Defense. The successful completion of the Manhattan Project and the role of the atomic bomb in bringing the war against Japan to a swift and awesome conclusion ushered in the age of truly "big science." The Manhattan Project also shaped postwar perceptions of the constructive possibilities of large-scale science applied to the pursuit of human goals.

Far smaller in financial terms, but highly significant as an institutional innovation, was the Office of Scientific Research and Development (OSRD), a civilian agency directed by Vannevar Bush. The OSRD was not under military control. Although it employed federal funds on wartime scientific research projects, OSRD entered into contracts with the private sector for the performance of that research and allowed full reimbursement of research costs. The contrast with the situation during the First World War is instructive and reflects the far more advanced state of development of private-sector research capabilities. The contractual arrangements developed by OSRD during the Second World War allowed the office to tap the far wider range of private-sector scientific capabilities that had developed during the interwar period. Members of the scientific community were called on to recommend and to guide as well as to participate in scientific research with military payoffs. Not only did they not work through or become subordinated to the military, they had direct access to the president and to the pertinent congressional appropriations committees.

The success of these contractual arrangements with the private sector would exert a great influence over the organization of American science in the postwar period. It also serves to highlight a distinctive feature of postwar American R&D, as compared with both the prewar period and other countries.[1] In 1940 almost all federal R&D went to support research performed within the federal establishment itself – by government civil servants, as in the National Bureau of Standards, the Department of Agriculture, and the Public Health Service, or by state institutions financed

---

[1] For a careful, although now somewhat dated, treatment of these contractual issues, see Danhof (1968).

by federal grants, as in the agricultural experiment stations. In the postwar period, by contrast, although the proportion has varied substantially over time, the vast majority of federal R&D funds, about 75 percent in 1984, has been allocated to support research performed by organizations in the private sector. This structure preserves federal control of broad research priorities while expanding the capabilities of private institutions and professionals. The postwar arrangement placed overall allocation decisions in the hands of the government while allowing the scientific community considerable autonomy in problem formulation and approach.

Postwar R&D expenditures

The two most distinctive features of postwar R&D spending are the magnitude of the overall investment and the size of the federal R&D budget. Throughout this period, federal R&D spending has been a large fraction of the very large total budget that is characteristic of the American economy since World War II. The total volume of resources devoted to R&D activities since the end of the Second World War has been very large, not only by comparison with our earlier history, but also by comparison with other Organization for Economic Cooperation and Development (OECD) member countries. Indeed, for many years, not only in the war recovery period but well beyond it, total U.S. R&D expenditures were greater than the total for all other OECD countries combined. As late as 1969, when the combined R&D expenditures of the largest foreign industrial economies (West Germany, France, and the United Kingdom, and Japan) were $11.3 billion, those for the United States were $25.6 billion. Not until the late 1970s did the combined total for those four countries exceed that of the United States. By 1979, the four countries were spending $58.3 billion, compared with $55 billion for the United States.[2]

The national R&D budget includes two separate components – private and federal spending. The share of federal spending has been the more volatile component, reaching a peak of about two-thirds of total R&D in the mid-1960s and declining substantially after this point. Over the same period, private R&D has tracked GNP growth more closely and therefore has grown more steadily (see Table 6.1). Total R&D spending was slightly more than 1 percent of GNP in the immediate postwar years. The percentage grew very rapidly in the second half of the 1950s and peaked at almost 3 percent in the mid-1960s, after which it declined until the second half of the 1970s (see Table 6.2).

In absolute terms, there was a sharp decline in the immediate postwar years from the wartime highs of 1944 and 1945, a decline attributable

---

[2] National Science Board (1983), p. 192.

Table 6.1. *Federal, private, and total R&D, 1953–84, constant 1972 dollars (millions)*

Year	Total	Federal	Private	% Federal
1953	8,702	4,675	4,027	53.7
1954	9,456	5,247	4,209	55.7
1955	10,121	5,473	4,648	54.1
1956	13,296	7,714	5,582	58.0
1957	15,034	9,397	5,637	62.5
1958	16,214	10,262	5,952	63.3
1959	18,303	11,917	6,386	65.1
1960	19,693	12,725	6,968	64.6
1961	20,664	13,351	7,313	64.6
1962	21,820	14,048	7,772	64.4
1963	23,829	15,651	8,178	65.7
1964	25,930	17,241	8,689	66.5
1965	26,896	17,443	9,453	64.8
1966	28,442	18,180	10,262	63.9
1967	29,241	18,176	11,065	62.2
1968	29,833	18,108	11,725	60.7
1969	29,586	17,209	12,377	58.2
1970	28,613	16,316	12,297	57.0
1971	27,814	15,615	12,199	56.1
1972	28,477	15,808	12,669	55.5
1973	29,147	15,594	13,553	53.5
1974	28,736	14,826	13,910	51.6
1975	28,153	14,537	13,616	51.6
1976	29,510	15,072	14,438	51.1
1977	30,506	15,382	15,124	50.4
1978	32,002	15,878	16,124	49.6
1979	33,612	16,407	17,205	48.8
1980	35,133	16,541	18,592	47.1
1981	36,859	17,124	19,735	46.5
1982	38,742	17,841	20,901	46.1
1983 (est.)	40,568	18,622	21,946	45.9
1984 (est.)	42,951	19,577	23,374	45.6

Source: The figures for 1953–64 are from *National Patterns of Science and Technology Resources, 1953–1977*, and the later figures are from *National Patterns of Science and Technology Resources, 1984* (Washington, D.C., National Science Foundation).

Table 6.2. *National expenditures for performance of R&D as a percent of gross national product by source, 1953–84*

Year	Total	Federal	Nonfederal
1953	1.40	.75	.65
1954	1.54	.85	.69
1955	1.54	.88	.66
1956	1.98	1.15	.83
1957	2.20	1.38	.82
1958	2.38	1.51	.87
1959	2.53	1.65	.88
1960	2.67	1.73	.94
1961	2.73	1.76	.97
1962	2.72	1.75	.97
1963	2.86	1.88	.98
1964	2.96	1.97	.99
1965	2.90	1.88	1.02
1966	2.89	1.85	1.04
1967	2.89	1.80	1.09
1968	2.82	1.71	1.11
1969	2.72	1.58	1.14
1970	2.63	1.50	1.13
1971	2.48	1.39	1.09
1972	2.40	1.33	1.07
1973	2.32	1.24	1.08
1974	2.29	1.17	1.12
1975	2.27	1.17	1.10
1976	2.27	1.16	1.11
1977	2.23	1.13	1.10
1978	2.22	1.10	1.12
1979	2.27	1.11	1.16
1980	2.38	1.12	1.26
1981	2.43	1.13	1.30
1982	2.61	1.21	1.40
1983 (est.)	2.65	1.22	1.43
1984 (est.)	2.66	1.22	1.44

Source: National Science Foundation and Department of Commerce.

mainly to a reduction in expenditures on the Manhattan Project and, to a lesser degree, to the phasing out of OSRD and a cutback in Department of Defense expenditures (see the appendix). Nevertheless, in the early postwar years, federal R&D expenditures resumed growth from a point that was already several times higher, in real terms, than prewar levels.

Shifts in the size and composition of the federal budget have been driven by external events and changing domestic concerns and social priorities, among which the most significant have been national security issues. Among the most influential international events were the prolonged cold war posture of higher defense spending and military readiness; the Soviet nuclear explosion in 1948 and thermonuclear explosion in 1951; the outbreak of the Korean War in June 1950; the development of strategic nuclear missiles in the mid-1950s; Sputnik and the subsequent commitment to a space program; the Vietnam War; the changing social priorities associated with Great Society programs; the growth of environmental, safety, and health concerns in the 1970s; the "War on Cancer"; massive growth in energy research by the Energy Research and Development Administration and, later, the Department of Energy; and more recently, a widening concern over the apparent decline in U.S. international competitiveness, especially in high-technology industries.

The single peacetime event with the greatest effect on the federal R&D budget during the postwar years was undoubtedly the Soviet launch of Sputnik in 1957, which resulted in considerable growth of many items in the federal R&D budget. Most striking, of course, was the transformation of the modest National Advisory Committee on Aeronautics (NACA) into the giant National Aeronautics and Space Administration (NASA), which administered an enormous R&D program over a ten-year period – a program that assumed somewhat more modest proportions after the first lunar landing in 1969 (see Table 6.3). The rise of OPEC's power over energy supplies and prices caused energy R&D to expand from slightly over 3 percent of federal R&D spending in 1971 to a peak of 12 percent of the federal R&D budget in 1980, declining subsequently to less than 5 percent.[3]

Within the postwar R&D system, federal expenditures have financed somewhere between one-half and two-thirds of total R&D, the great bulk of which is performed by private industry. This pattern partly reflects the dominance of military R&D in the federal R&D budget. Military R&D is development intensive and therefore finds a natural home in private industry. In 1985, 73 percent of all R&D was performed in private industry, and only 12 percent in federal intramural laboratories (although 47 percent of all R&D was financed by the federal government). The remaining

[3] Ibid., p. 52.

Table 6.3. *Trends in federal and nonfederal R&D outlays, 1953 and 1960–84 (in %)*

| Year | Total | Federal | | | Non-federal |
		Defense related	Space related	Civilian related	
1953	54	48	1	5	46
1960	65	52	3	9	35
1961	65	50	6	9	35
1962	64	48	7	9	36
1963	66	41	14	11	34
1964	66	37	19	9	34
1965	65	33	21	11	35
1966	64	33	19	12	36
1967	62	35	14	13	38
1968	61	35	13	13	39
1969	58	34	11	13	42
1970	57	33	10	14	43
1971	56	32	9	15	44
1972	56	32	9	15	44
1973	53	30	8	15	47
1974	51	27	8	16	49
1975	51	26	8	17	49
1976	51	26	8	17	49
1977	50	25	8	17	50
1978	50	24	7	19	50
1979	49	23	7	19	51
1980	47	22	7	18	53
1981	46	23	7	16	54
1982	46	25	7	14	54
1983 (est.)	46	27	6	13	54
1984 (est.)	46	29	6	11	54

Note: Detail may not add to 100 because of rounding.
Source: National Patterns of Science and Technology Resources, 1984 (Washington, D.C., National Science Foundation).

15 percent is a very critical component of federal R&D spending. Within this component, approximately 3 percent supports federally funded research and development centers (FFRDCs) administered by universities and colleges; 3 percent is allocated to other nonprofit institutions; and 9

percent supports university research (National Science Foundation, 1985, p. 3).[4]

Although federal funds have been important in all areas of research, they have been most important by far in basic research. The federal government's dominance of the financing of basic research may be seen in Table 6.4. Although that share has been declining for the past several years and in 1984 was at its lowest level for the past twenty years, federal funds still represent two-thirds of total basic research spending. As in other areas of the U.S. research system, however, the federal government's dominant role in financing basic research does not imply a dominant role in the performance of basic research. Only 15 percent of basic research currently is performed within the federal establishment, although the relative importance of industry and government as basic research performers has shifted over time. Until the 1970s, basic research performed by private industry exceeded that of the federal government substantially. During the 1970s, the levels were quite similar. In the 1980s, however, industry performance again is exceeding that of the federal government. Universities have increased in importance as basic research performers during this period. In 1953, less than one-third of all basic research was performed in universities and FFRDCs at universities and colleges. In recent years, however, these institutions have performed more than one-half of all basic research.

Support for basic research is concentrated in a few agencies within the federal budget. By far the largest federal obligations are in the Department of Health and Human Services, where the basic research budget consists overwhelmingly of the expenditures of the National Institutes of Health. The next largest obligations, in descending order, are in NSF, DOD, DOE, and NASA (see Table 6.5).

Military R&D funding

Although the share of the defense budget within total federal spending has fluctuated over time, it has dominated the federal R&D budget for the last quarter century, falling below 50 percent of federal R&D obligations only in the single year 1966 (see Table 6.6). In 1960 defense research constituted no less than 80 percent of federal R&D funds. It declined sharply from that level (a decline offset by the growth of the space program) and hovered around the 50 percent level until the early 1980s, when it rose swiftly again. If expenditures on space-related activities and atomic energy are added to the defense budget (since these activities often are motivated largely by defense concerns), defense-related categories

---

[4] For a listing of FFRDCs by location and sponsoring agency, along with federal obligations for 1981, see National Science Board (1983), p. 310.

Table 6.4. *Sources of funds for basic research by sector, 1953, 1960,*
and 1965–84 (dollars in millions)

Year	Total	Federal government	Industry	Universities and colleges	Other nonprofit institutions
Current dollars					
1953	441	251	153	10	27
1960[a]	1,197	715	342	72	68
1965[b]	2,555	1,809	461	164	121
1966	2,814	1,978	510	197	129
1967	3,056	2,201	492	223	140
1968	3,296	2,336	535	276	149
1969	3,441	2,441	540	298	162
1970	3,549	2,489	528	350	182
1971	3,672	2,529	547	400	196
1972	3,829	2,633	563	415	218
1973	3,946	2,709	605	408	224
1974	4,239	2,912	651	432	244
1975	4,608	3,139	705	478	286
1976	4,977	3,436	769	475	297
1977	5,537	3,823	850	527	337
1978	6,392	4,445	964	605	378
1979	7,257	4,044	1,091	711	411
1980	8,039	5,559	1,265	805	460
1981	9,217	6,236	1,585	909	487
1982	9,886	6,588	1,805	983	510
1983 (est.)	10,610	6,970	2,025	1,075	540
1984 (est.)	11,850	7,775	2,270	1,220	585
Constant 1972 dollars[c]					
1953	742	421	259	17	45
1960[a]	1,729	1,030	497	103	99
1965[b]	3,416	2,415	620	219	162
1966	3,660	2,571	665	256	168
1967	3,853	2,774	622	281	176
1968	4,001	2,837	649	335	180
1969	3,985	2,829	623	346	187
1970	3,895	2,733	578	384	200
1971	3,836	2,644	570	418	204
1972	3,829	2,633	563	415	218
1973	3,768	2,589	573	391	213

Table 6.4. *Cont.*

		Constant 1972 dollars[c]			
Year	Total	Federal government	Industry	Universities and colleges	Other nonprofit institutions
1974	3,757	2,589	567	386	215
1975	3,720	2,540	582	388	230
1976	3,770	2,604	581	360	225
1977	3,939	2,718	607	374	240
1978	4,250	2,956	641	402	251
1979	4,438	3,085	667	435	251
1980	4,548	3,128	709	453	258
1981	4,727	3,199	813	466	249
1982	4,749	3,160	872	471	246
1983 (est.)	4,886	3,205	938	494	249
1984 (est.)	5,229	3,427	1,006	537	259

[a] Data for 1954–9 can be found in *National Patterns of R&D Resources, 1953–77* (NSF 77-310).
[b] Data for 1961–4 can be found in *National Patterns of Science and Technology Resources, 1981* (NSF 81-311).
[c] Based on GNP implicit price deflator.
Source: National Science Foundation.

have dominated the federal R&D budget for the past thirty years. In 1982, DOD, DOE, and NASA accounted for 97 percent of all federal R&D funds to industrial firms.

The National Science Foundation was established in 1950. During the 1950s, the National Institutes of Health began to support basic as well as more applied research. Their expenditures were minuscule, however, by comparison with defense and defense-related expenditures. Beginning in the mid-1960s, the decline in the space budget was offset by growth in R&D expenditures for medicine, energy, and agriculture. Nevertheless, defense and space have accounted for at least 60 percent or a great deal more of the federal R&D budget for the past twenty-five years. In the 1980s, the sharp increase in military R&D has reversed the rise in the share of civilian-related R&D that occurred during the 1970s (see Table 6.7).

The dominant role of the defense budget within the total federal R&D budget has another important implication. As we noted earlier, the defense R&D budget is far more development intensive than the rest of the

Table 6.5. *Federal obligations for basic research, by selected agency, fiscal years 1975–85 (dollars in millions)*

Agency and subdivision	1975	1976	1977	1978	1979	1980	1981	1982	1983	Estimates 1984	Estimates 1985
Total, all agencies	2,588.4	2,767.5	3,258.6	3,698.6	4,192.7	4,674.2	5,041.3	5,481.6	6,260.1	6,931.0	7,637.6
Dept. of Agriculture, total	154.2	171.4	204.5	242.7	256.4	275.7	314.1	330.8	362.0	386.4	419.7
Agricultural Res. Serv.[a]	91.2	101.7	125.6	142.4	148.2	157.8	186.4	192.9	215.3	232.5	240.1
Cooperative State Res. Serv.[b]	38.4	43.1	48.4	65.6	70.5	75.2	83.9	91.3	98.8	100.8	123.6
Econ. Stat. & Coop. Serv.[c]	NA	NA	3.8	3.9	6.4	NA	NA	NA	NA	NA	NA
Economic Res. Serv.	3.2	3.6	NA	NA	NA	NA	3.6	3.9	3.9	4.4	4.7
Economics & Statistics Serv.[d]	NA	NA	NA	NA	NA	6.6	NA	NA	NA	NA	NA
Forest Service	21.1	22.6	26.7	30.8	31.4	33.7	38.1	38.7	38.8	41.3	40.2
Off. of Int. Coop. & Devt.	NA	NA	NA	NA	—	2.3	1.7	1.1	2.3	4.2	2.8
Off. of Trans.	NA	NA	NA	NA	—	—	.5	.5	.5	.5	.5
Stat. Reporting Serv.	.3	.4	NA	NA	NA	NA	—	2.3	2.5	2.7	2.8
Dept. of Commerce, total	8.1	11.0	12.3	11.8	11.9	15.9	16.2	16.9	19.2	20.5	18.4
National Bureau of Standards	5.4	5.8	6.9	5.9	8.8	12.8	15.6	16.5	18.4	19.2	17.8
Other Commerce	2.8	5.2	5.4	5.9	3.1	3.1	.6	.3	.9	1.3	.6
Dept. of Defense, total	300.1	326.9	373.3	410.4	471.5	540.3	604.3	686.7	785.6	816.6	913.2
Army	71.7	81.4	99.0	104.1	115.0	132.2	148.1	187.7	208.3	209.2	233.5
Navy	118.7	129.7	153.8	172.1	192.1	214.9	233.0	280.3	305.4	308.5	359.9
Air Force	78.9	83.9	84.8	95.1	105.0	108.2	125.8	145.8	164.2	187.9	206.2
Defense agencies	30.7	31.9	35.6	39.1	59.3	85.1	92.4	72.9	107.7	111.0	108.6
Dept. of Education, total	NA	NA	NA	NA	20.6	17.6	20.6	14.2	14.2	12.4	14.3
Dept. of Energy, total	NA	NA	389.5	440.5	463.0	523.1	586.3	642.2	767.7	841.7	944.5

Table 6.5. *Cont.*

Agency and subdivision	1975	1976	1977	1978	1979	1980	1981	1982	Estimates 1983	1984	1985
Dept. of Health, Ed., & Welfare, total	903.7	986.2	1,119.5	1,292.3	NA	NA	NA	NA	NA	NA	NA
Alcohol, Drug Abuse, & Mental Hlth. Admin.	66.2	52.6	62.7	79.9	NA	NA	NA	NA	NA	NA	NA
Nat. Institute of Education	1.9	5.1	11.9	18.3	NA	NA	NA	NA	NA	NA	NA
NIH	823.5	920.3	1,032.8	1,181.1	NA	NA	NA	NA	NA	NA	NA
Other HEW	7.1	8.2	12.2	13.1	NA	NA	NA	NA	NA	NA	NA
Dept. of Hlth. & Human Serv., total	NA	NA	NA	NA	1,576.0	1,762.7	1,900.4	2,144.7	2,475.4	2,793.1	2,925.9
Alcohol & Drug Abuse, & Mental Hlth. Admin.	NA	NA	NA	NA	94.6	104.7	116.3	117.3	145.0	165.4	169.3
NIH	NA	NA	NA	NA	1,463.7	1,642.3	1,766.8	2,020.7	2,313.0	2,607.7	2,738.1
Other HHS	NA	NA	NA	NA	17.7	15.6	17.3	6.7	17.4	20.0	18.5
Dept. of the Interior, total	54.9	54.3	63.6	65.9	72.5	71.6	80.7	76.5	103.0	124.7	102.8
Bureau of Mines	1.9	.8	4.0	8.6	13.7	11.5	13.6	15.9	23.5	45.5	32.3
Geological Survey	33.6	39.5	40.3	46.3	49.0	47.3	53.5	52.6	64.7	69.9	63.9
Other Interior	14.4	14.0	19.3	11.0	9.8	12.8	13.6	7.9	14.8	9.3	6.5
Dept. of Justice, total	9.5	4.5	5.1	14.7	7.9	9.5	4.6	3.1	3.6	4.0	2.6
Off. of Justice Asst., Res., & Stat.	9.5	4.5	5.1	14.7	7.9	9.5	4.6	3.1	3.6	4.0	2.6
Dept. of Labor, total	.9	1.0	.7	3.7	2.3	3.9	3.7	6.5	5.3	4.5	4.5
Dept. of State, total	1.5	—	—	—	*	—	—	—	—	—	—

Agency for Inter. Dev.	1.5	—	—	—	NA	NA	NA	NA	NA	NA	NA
Other State	—	—	—	—	*	—	—	—	—	—	—
Dept. of Trans., total	.1	—	—	—	—	—	1.2	1.0	.9	.6	.4
Other Trans.	.1	—	—	—	—	—	1.2	1.0	.9	.6	.4
Dept. of the Treasury, total	—	—	—	—	.2	1.7	2.3	2.2	3.5	4.0	7.6
Other agencies											
Agency for Inter. Dev.	NA	NA	NA	NA	NA	NA	—	—	4.1	2.7	3.9
Energy Res. & Dev. Admin.	312.8	345.8	NA	NA	NA	NA	NA	NA	NA	NA	NA
EPA	17.4	13.7	8.3	6.0	10.1	13.6	10.5	32.7	22.2	22.7	25.5
NASA	309.3	293.2	413.8	479.7	512.8	559.1	531.1	535.7	617.0	689.1	826.7
NSF	486.0	523.6	624.9	678.0	733.3	815.2	896.6	916.1	999.1	1,172.5	1,335.8
VA	3.9	8.9	9.1	8.9	9.5	14.3	15.0	12.9	14.1	15.2	15.0
All other agencies	26.1	27.0	34.2	43.9	44.6	49.8	53.6	59.6	63.1	70.5	76.8

Note: NA (not applicable) indicates that the agency or agency subdivision did not exist as such in that year.

[a] Includes the former Agriculture Research Service of the Science and Education Administration for fiscal years 1978–80.

[b] Includes the former Cooperative State Research of the Science & Education Administration for fiscal years 1978–80.

[c] Includes programs of the Economic Research Service, the Statistical Reporting Service, and the Farmer Cooperative Service for Fiscal Years 1977–79.

[d] Includes programs of the Economic Research Service and the Statistical Reporting Service for fiscal year 1980.

An asterisk indicates amount less than $50,000.

Source: National Science Foundation.

Table 6.6. *Federal funds for R&D by major budget function, 1960–84*

Fiscal year	Dollars in billions			As percent of total obligations	
	Total	Defense	All other	Defense	All other
1960	8	6	2	80	20
1961	9	7	2	77	23
1962	10	7	3	70	30
1963	13	8	5	62	38
1964	14	8	6	55	45
1965	15	7	7	50	50
1966	15	8	8	49	51
1967	17	9	8	52	48
1968	16	8	8	52	48
1969	16	8	7	54	46
1970	15	8	7	52	48
1971	16	8	7	52	48
1972	17	9	8	54	46
1973	17	9	8	54	46
1974	17	9	8	52	48
1975	19	10	9	51	49
1976	21	10	10	50	50
1977	24	12	12	50	50
1978	26	13	13	50	50
1979	28	14	14	50	50
1980	30	15	15	50	50
1981	33	18	15	55	45
1982	36	22	14	61	39
1983 (est.)	38	25	14	66	34
1984 (est.)	46	32	14	70	30

Note: Detail may not add to totals due to rounding. Estimates given for 1984 may change significantly as the result of congressional action on agency budget requests. Data for 1960–77 are shown in obligations; data for 1978–83 are shown in budget authority.
Source: Executive Office of the President, Office of Management and Budget, "Special Analysis K," *Budget of the U.S. Government, 1984* (1983).

federal R&D budget. This characteristic of the dominant component of federal R&D spending imparts a strong bias in the overall federal R&D budget in favor of development. If the 1982 federal budget is broken down into defense and nondefense components, the share of basic, applied, and development expenditures within each total is as shown in Table 6.8.

The largest items in the DOD R&D budget involve the development of advanced weapons systems, construction and testing of prototypes, and so on.[5] Conversely, the share of DOD's R&D budget that goes to basic and applied research is less than that of any major federal R&D funding agency.[6]

As a result of the development emphasis in defense R&D and the large size of the defense R&D budget, the distribution of the federal R&D budget across industry sectors is highly concentrated. Nearly 75 percent of all federal R&D in 1981 went to two industry sectors – aircraft and missiles (almost 50 percent) and electrical machinery (almost 25 percent).[7] Nonelectrical machines was a distant third, and motor vehicles and other transportation equipment fourth (see Table 6.9).

Aircraft and missiles also make up the only major industry sector that derives substantially more than half of its R&D funding from federal sources (73 percent in 1981, down from 79 percent in 1971). In the electrical equipment sector, by contrast, although the federal contribution is large, it represents a much smaller fraction of total R&D spending in the industry. In 1981, private funding accounted for 62 percent of industry R&D, a sizable increase over the 1971 ratio of 49 percent. In communications equipment and electronic components, which account for most of electrical equipment R&D, 66 percent of 1981 R&D funding was financed privately, up from the 1971 share of 46 percent.

Technological "spillovers" from military R&D

Have military expenditures strengthened the R&D capabilities of private firms? At issue in any assessment of the commercial benefits of military

---

[5] In addition to the expenditures of the Department of Defense, defense research includes expenditures for military programs in the Department of Energy.

[6] Although no more than 3.2 percent of federal defense R&D in 1982 went to basic research, the absolute size of this budget is still very large, and basic research supported by military agencies has been a significant component of federally supported basic research. The Office of Naval Research has been a supporter of basic research for forty years, and the Defense Advanced Research Projects Agency (DARPA) has played a crucial role in the early stages of several research programs that have yielded significant civilian applications, most notably in computer technology (Flamm, 1988b).

[7] Ergas (1987) argues that this concentration is a common feature of "mission-oriented" R&D programs: "The goals of mission-oriented R&D are centrally decided and clearly set out, generally in terms of complex systems meeting the needs of a particular government agency. . . .

"Concentration also extends to the range of technologies covered. Virtually by its nature, mission-oriented research focuses on a small number of technologies of particular strategic importance – primarily in aerospace, electronics, and nuclear energy. As a result, government R&D funding in these countries is heavily biased toward a few industries that are generally considered to be in the early stages of the technology life cycle" (p. 194).

Table 6.7. *Federal funds for R&D by budget function, fiscal years 1971–86* (dollars in millions)

Function[a]	1971	1972	1973	1974	1975	1976	197‹
	Current dollars						
Total	15,542.5	16,495.9	16,800.2	17,410.1	19,038.8	20,779.7	23,45‹
National defense	8,109.9	8,901.6	9,001.9	9,015.8	9,679.3	10,429.7	11,86
Health	1,287.8	1,546.7	1,585.0	2,068.6	2,170.2	23,502.6	2,62
Space research & technology	3,048.0	2,931.8	2,823.9	2,701.8	2,764.0	3,129.9	2,83‹
Energy	555.8	574.0	629.7	759.2	1,363.4	1,648.5	2,56‹
General science	512.5	625.3	657.6	749.4	813.3	857.7	97‹
Transportation	727.9	558.2	571.5	693.4	634.9	630.5	70‹
Natural resources & environment	415.5	478.5	553.8	516.0	624.3	683.0	75
Agriculture	259.0	294.4	308.1	313.1	341.8	382.5	45‹
Education, training, employment & social services	215.4	235.3	290.4	236.4	238.6	254.8	23‹
International affairs	31.9	28.6	28.3	23.8	29.0	42.4	6‹
Veterans benefits & services	62.9	69.1	74.3	84.8	94.8	97.7	10‹
Commerce & housing credit	89.5	49.7	50.2	50.8	64.9	68.7	7‹
Income security	144.9	106.3	106.3	70.9	71.9	48.3	5‹
Administration of justice	10.4	23.4	33.2	34.7	44.3	48.3	2‹
Community & regional development	64.6	65.8	78.4	82.1	92.5	108.5	10‹
General government	6.6	7.6	7.4	9.3	11.7	11.9	1‹
	Constant 1972 dollars[b]						
Total	16,254.4	16,495.9	16,084.4	15,536.4	15,446.0	15,758.5	16,65‹
National defense	8,481.4	8,901.6	8,618.4	8,045.5	7,852.8	7,908.5	8,42‹
Health	1,346.8	1,546.7	1,517.5	1,846.0	1,760.7	17,821.2	1,86
Space research & technology	3,187.6	2,931.8	2,703.6	2,411.0	2,242.4	2,373.3	2,01‹
Energy	581.3	574.0	602.9	677.5	1,106.1	1,250.0	1,82‹
General science	536.0	625.3	629.6	668.7	659.8	650.4	69
Transportation	761.2	558.2	547.2	618.8	515.1	478.1	50‹
Natural resources & environment	434.5	478.5	530.2	460.5	506.5	517.9	53‹
Agriculture	270.9	294.4	295.0	279.4	277.3	290.0	32‹
Education, training, employment & social services	225.3	235.3	278.0	211.0	193.6	193.2	16‹
International affairs	33.4	28.6	27.1	21.2	23.5	32.2	4‹
Veterans benefits & services	65.8	69.1	71.1	75.7	76.9	74.1	7‹
Commerce & housing credit	93.6	49.7	48.1	45.3	52.7	52.1	5‹
Income security	151.5	106.3	101.8	63.3	58.3	36.6	3‹
Administration of justice	10.9	23.4	31.8	31.0	35.9	36.6	2‹
Community & regional development	67.6	65.8	75.1	73.3	75.0	82.3	7‹
General government	6.9	7.6	7.1	8.3	9.5	9.0	‹

Note: Detail may not add to totals because of rounding.
[a] Listed in descending order of 1986 budget authority. Data for the period 1971–7 are shown in obli‹ tions; data for 1978–84 are shown in budget authority.

78	1979	1980	1981	1982	1983	1984	1985	1986
			Current dollars					
76.0	28,208.0	29,773.0	33,735.0	36,115.0	38,768.0	44,214.0	50,479.0	58,257.0
99.4	13,791.0	14,946.4	18,413.0	22,070.0	24,936.0	29,287.0	34,332.0	42,360.0
67.7	3,401.3	3,694.3	3,870.8	3,869.0	4,298.0	4,779.0	5,408.0	5,108.0
39.0	3,136.0	2,738.0	3,111.0	2,584.2	2,134.0	2,300.0	1,693.0	3,144.0
34.4	3,461.4	3,603.2	3,501.4	3,012.0	2,578.0	2,581.0	2,401.0	2,183.0
50.2	1,119.1	1,232.6	1,340.0	1,359.0	1,502.0	1,676.0	1,873.0	1,990.0
67.5	798.2	887.5	869.5	791.0	876.0	1,040.0	1,051.0	952.0
03.9	1,009.6	999.3	1,060.5	965.0	952.0	963.0	1,033.0	905.0
01.3	551.6	585.3	658.5	692.7	745.0	762.0	819.0	778.0
45.1	353.5	468.0	298.4	228.0	189.0	200.0	215.0	210.0
57.2	116.8	127.3	160.0	165.0	177.0	192.0	217.0	225.0
11.1	122.8	125.8	142.9	139.2	157.0	218.0	193.0	187.0
76.7	92.7	102.1	105.5	103.9	106.9	110.0	116.0	106.0
67.3	56.8	77.2	42.6	31.6	32.0	26.0	25.0	24.0
43.7	46.5	45.1	33.8	30.9	37.0	24.0	45.0	40.0
91.9	127.3	119.4	104.3	62.5	44.0	46.0	43.0	28.0
20.3	23.2	22.0	22.1	10.0	5.9	8.0	17.0	18.0
			Constant 1972 dollars[b]					
79.3	17,256.8	16,762.2	17,269.9	17,252.7	17,814.5	19,571.5	21,546.4	23,901.3
80.7	8,436.9	8,414.8	9,426.1	10,543.2	11,458.5	12,964.0	14,654.0	17,379.2
74.1	2,080.8	2,079.9	1,981.6	1,848.3	1,975.0	2,115.4	2,308.3	2,095.7
55.0	1,918.5	1,541.5	1,592.6	1,234.5	980.6	1,018.1	722.6	1,289.9
85.0	2,117.6	2,028.6	1,792.5	1,438.9	1,184.6	1,142.5	1,024.8	895.6
98.6	684.6	694.0	686.0	649.2	690.2	741.9	799.5	816.4
10.5	488.3	499.7	445.1	377.9	402.5	460.4	448.6	390.6
01.3	617.6	562.6	542.9	461.0	437.5	426.3	440.9	371.3
33.5	337.5	329.5	337.1	330.9	342.3	337.3	349.6	319.2
29.6	216.3	263.5	152.8	108.9	86.8	88.5	91.8	86.2
38.0	71.5	71.7	81.9	78.8	81.3	85.0	92.6	92.3
73.9	75.1	70.8	73.2	66.5	72.1	96.5	82.4	76.7
51.0	56.7	57.5	54.0	49.6	49.1	48.7	49.5	43.5
44.8	34.7	43.5	21.8	15.1	14.7	11.5	10.7	9.8
29.1	28.4	25.4	17.3	14.8	17.0	10.6	19.2	16.4
61.1	77.9	67.2	53.4	29.9	20.2	20.4	18.4	11.5
13.5	14.3	12.4	11.3	4.8	2.7	3.5	7.3	7.4

P implicit price deflators used to convert current dollars to constant 1972 dollars.

ce: National Science Foundation, *Federal R&D Funding by Budget Function, Fiscal Years* –86 (1985 and earlier years).

Table 6.8. *1983 federal R&D expenditures*
(% share)

	Defense	Nondefense
Basic	3.2	33.7
Applied	11.0	35.3
Development	88.5	31.0
Total	100.0	100.0

Source: Congressional Budget Office (1984), p. 53.

R&D are questions that go beyond the direct transfer to commercial applications of specific pieces of hardware – as in jet engines, semiconductors, and new materials. What are the second-order spillover effects of military R&D on other industries? Much of the "output" of military R&D is incorporated in improved products and processes that have been diffused widely throughout the economy. Military and space programs, for example, have developed new materials with improved performance characteristics (such as light weight, high strength, durability, and electrical conductivity). Similarly, military programs have aided the development of electronic components (especially semiconductors) that are used in a broad array of sectors. Measuring the full civilian benefits of military R&D requires that one trace thousands of small improvements in a great many economic sectors.

Other issues that demand attention in any systematic assessment of the commercial effects of military R&D include: What commercial benefits flow from military spending on "upstream" basic research or applied research of a more generic nature, and to what extent do U.S. firms capture these benefits? Do military R&D expenditures in specific industries or technologies allow for the exploitation of scale economies as research facilities reach some minimum efficient size? For contractors performing military R&D who also design and sell civilian products, does "learning" on military contracts benefit their civilian-oriented activities?[8]

Even more difficult than tracing out the interindustry flow of military-funded technological improvements is establishing the content of the "learning process" in the sectors that receive the majority of military R&D. Product designers and technical specialists working on defense projects in fact may "learn" an indifference to cost in the pursuit of performance

---

[8] Later in this chapter we discuss the possibility that in some industries technological benefits may flow from the commercial to the military sphere.

Table 6.9. *Company and federal funding of industrial R&D for selected industries, 1971 and 1981*

Industry	Total 1971	Total 1981	Federal 1971	Federal 1981	Company[a] 1971	Company[a] 1981
			Millions of current dollars			
Total	18,320	51,830	7,666	16,468	10,654	35,362
Chemicals and allied products	1,832	5,325	184	383	1,648	4,942
Industrial chemicals	1,009	2,553	159	367	850	2,186
Drugs and medicines and other chemicals	823	2,770[b]	25	20[b]	798	2,756
Petroleum refining and extraction	505	1,920[b]	17	140[b]	488	1,777
Rubber products	289	800[b]	69	190[b]	221	616
Primary metals	272	889	6	182	266	707
Ferrous metals and products	144	560[b]	2	140[b]	142	414
Nonferrous metals and products	128	330[b]	4	40[b]	124	293
Fabricated metal products	242	638	11	80	230	558
Nonelectrical machinery	1,860	6,800	315	739	1,545	6,061
Electrical machinery	4,389	10,466	2,258	3,962	2,131	6,502
Communication equipment and electronic components	2,731	6,396	1,479	2,167	1,252	4,228
Motor vehicles and other transportation equipment	1,768	5,089[b]	309	704[b]	1,461	4,381
Aircraft and missiles	4,881	11,702	3,864	8,501	1,017	3,201
Professional and scientific instruments	746	3,685	164	638	583	3,047
Scientific and mechanical measuring instruments	133	1,680[b]	14	400[b]	120	1,285
Optical, surgical, photographic, and other instruments	612	2,000[b]	150	240[b]	463	1,762
All other manufacturing industries	2,889	8,325[b]	395	963[b]	2,494	7,368
Nonmanufacturing industries	704	2,080[b]	452	880[b]	252	1,199
			Millions of constant 1972 dollars[c]			
Total	19,081	26,511	7,984	8,423	11,097	18,087
Chemicals and allied products	1,908	2,724	192	196	1,716	2,528
Industrial chemicals	1,051	1,306	166	188	885	1,118
Drugs and medicines and other chemicals	857	1,410[b]	26	10[b]	831	1,410

Table 6.9. *Cont.*

Industry	Total 1971	Total 1981	Federal 1971	Federal 1981	Company[a] 1971	Company[a] 1981
	Millions of current dollars					
Petroleum refining and extraction	526	980[b]	18	70[b]	508	909
Rubber products	301	410[b]	72	97[b]	230	315
Primary metals	283	455	6	93	277	362
Ferrous metals and products	150	290[b]	2	70[b]	148	212
Nonferrous metals and products	133	170[b]	4	20[b]	129	150
Fabricated metal products	252	326	11	41	240	285
Nonelectrical machinery	1,937	3,478	328	378	1,609	3,100
Electrical equipment	4,571	5,353	2,352	2,026	2,220	3,326
Communication equipment and electronic components	2,844	3,272	1,540	1,108	1,304	2,163
Motor vehicles and other transportation equipment	1,841	2,602[b]	322	360[b]	1,522	2,241
Aircraft and missiles	5,084	5,985	4,025	4,348	1,059	1,637
Professional and scientific instruments	777	1,885	171	326	607	1,558
Scientific and mechanical measuring instruments	139	860[b]	15	210[b]	125	657
Optical, surgical, photographic, and other instruments	637	1,020[b]	156	120[b]	482	901
All other manufacturing industries	3,009	4,260[b]	411	490[b]	2,598	3,769
Nonmanufacturing industries	733	1,060[b]	471	450[b]	262	613

[a] Includes all sources other than the federal government.
[b] Estimated.
[c] GNP implicit price deflators used to convert current dollars to constant 1972 dollars.
Source: National Science Foundation, *Research and Development in Industry, 1980* (NSF 82-317), pp. 11, 14, and 17, and National Science Foundation, preliminary data.

improvements. Military (and space) programs have notoriously subordinated cost considerations to the improvement of performance – often incurring very high costs for very small improvements, few of which are relevant to civilian markets. Military R&D programs may also encourage "learning" of expensive and ultimately inefficient habits, for example, a predisposition to substitute large-scale experimentation and computation for rigorous thought. Such learning "spillovers" may reduce the effectiveness of R&D personnel in competitive commercial markets where close attention to cost considerations can be a matter of commercial success or failure.

It is important to distinguish between cost discipline in the *performance* of R&D and similar discipline in the *design* of the finished product – or "gold plating," as it is sometimes called. The purely economic impact of the gold plating of military hardware may be very large. In addition, however, defense procurement policies may provide insufficient incentives for R&D in manufacturing *process* technology. Military suppliers have learned over the years that contracts are won on the basis of actual or promised product performance, not on the basis of cost-reducing innovations in process technology. Thus, the military procurement system may create a strong bias in favor of product innovation and against process innovation.[9]

Assessing the impact of military R&D spending is further complicataed by the fact that the influence of military R&D spending can easily be confounded with that of federal procurement. Most military R&D is obviously directed at the development of products that are designed for eventual purchase by the military itself. Indeed, the allocation of military R&D expenditures may be taken as an excellent guide to military procurement intentions.

This point is critical to any evaluation of the effects of American military R&D in the past forty years. The benefits that are sometimes perceived to flow from military R&D are in fact the product of military R&D plus frequently massive military procurement. The willingness of private in-

---

[9] See the 1986 report by the National Research Council, *The Role of the Department of Defense in Supporting Manufacturing Technology Development*, especially Chapter 2. According to this report: "Seldom can contractors attribute lack of success in a competition . . . to lack of manufacturing excellence. In such an environment, suppliers focus on designing new products with new performance features, not on improving production efficiencies.

"Once contracts are awarded, moreover, the conventional commercial pressures to improve efficiency do not prevail. On the contrary, there are significant disincentives for making process improvements. Reducing the cost of manufacturing lowers the base on which profits are calculated. Short-term procurement contracts permit the government to capture the full savings from process improvements during the negotiation for each new increment of acquisition" (p. 11).

dustry to commit substantial resources to innovation in a particular sector has been dominated by an awareness of the potentially large markets for military products of superior design and performance capability. Without the pull of defense procurement in such sectors as jet aircraft, integrated circuitry, and computers – especially in the critical early years of development of these technologies – the impact of military R&D spending alone would have been far smaller.

The example of semiconductors illustrates an instance in which the role of military procurement may well have outweighed the direct influence of military R&D expenditures. Following the wartime demonstration of the importance of electronics for communications and many other military applications, the military services were intensely aware in the 1940s of the potential military applications of semiconductors and followed developments in this technology closely. "Followed," however, is the operative word. The major scientific and technological breakthroughs in semiconductors were achieved in the private sector with private funds, and not, in the most important instances, with military R&D support. Yet much of this privately funded work on semiconductors was motivated by an awareness that military electronic equipment was plagued by equipment failures that stemmed in part from the systems' complex circuitry and reliance on vacuum tubes. The continual lure and the eventual reality of vast procurement contracts drove much of the R&D effort in this sector.

The invention of the transistor at Bell Labs was achieved without government financial support but with an awareness of the large potential market within the telephone industry for a solid-state substitute for vacuum tubes. Although Bell was well aware of the great military interest in its discoveries of 1947–48, its more immediate concern was to prevent that interest from imposing restrictions on civilian diffusion of the new technology. According to one authority, "There was substantial concern in early 1948 that disclosure of the transistor to the military prior to public announcement might lead to restriction of its use or to its classification for national defense purposes. Thus, Bell did not disclose the invention to the military until one week prior to public announcement" (Levin, 1982, p. 58).

During the 1950s the military supported a number of R&D projects in microelectronics as part of broader research programs in radar, missile guidance systems, and fire control systems. Some but by no means all of these programs focused on semiconductors; most attempted to improve the ruggedness, miniaturization, and reliability of radio tube technologies. As it happened, these projects, such as Tinkertoy and Micromodule, were not successful, and none of the major technological breakthroughs of that period were directly supported by the military. This failure reflected the dominant role within the military research programs of established producers of electronics, such as General Electric or RCA, who were weak in semiconductor technologies. Nevertheless, some of the most important breakthroughs, such as the silicon transistor and the integrated circuit, were undertaken with the needs of the military foremost in the minds of the successful inventors.[10]

The large procurement needs of the military and NASA and the increasing concern with the importance of miniaturization were vital in the early years of new product development in electronics. The Signal Corps was the largest military purchaser of semiconductors in the early and mid-1950s. A major expansion in demand occurred in 1958 with the Air Force's decision to employ semiconductors in the guidance system of the Minuteman missile. In 1962 NASA made public its intention to introduce integrated circuits into the guidance computer of the Apollo spacecraft. Soon after, the Air Force announced that the guidance system of the improved Minuteman intercontinental ballistic missile would make extensive use of integrated circuits.

From the mid-1950s to the late 1960s, the federal government (overwhelmingly the military and NASA) accounted for a large, although declining, share of the output of semiconductor devices (see Table 6.10). In the first year of integrated circuit production, the federal government purchased the entire $4 million of output (Table 6.11). It remained the largest buyer for the first five years, although the government share declined rapidly. By the end of the 1960s the rapidly growing computer industry displaced the military as the largest end-user market for integrated circuits.

Several conclusions can be drawn from a review of the military role in the development of the semiconductor industry in America during the 1950s and 1960s: (1) The major early innovations were achieved largely without military R&D support;[11] (2) military R&D projects that pursued

[10] "By his own account, Gordon Teal . . . turned his attention to the growth of single-crystal silicon in 1951 because silicon offered the potential for fabrication of transistors capable of meeting high-temperature performance specifications for military equipment. A conscious aim of the management of Texas Instruments when it hired Teal in late 1952 was to be the first to make a silicon transistor available to the military. . . . The breakthrough in silicon secured for TI its position as the largest merchant supplier of semiconductor devices" (Levin, 1982, p. 61). Similarly for the integrated circuit: "Kilby's . . . own account of his invention makes clear that TI had the military clearly, indeed exclusively, in mind during the course of early R&D work on the integrated circuit" (ibid., p. 62).

[11] The record of defense R&D support in microelectronics contrasts with the role of military R&D in computers, where the financial support of the Advanced Research Projects Agency (ARPA), the Office of Naval Research (ONR), and other military agencies proved indispensable to advances in both civilian and military technological applications. A further interesting contrast between these two technologies is the far more significant role of academic research (much of which was funded by ARPA, ONR, and other military agencies) in the development of advanced computing technologies (Flamm, 1988b).

Table 6.10. *Government purchases of semiconductor devices, 1955–77*

Year	Total semiconductor shipments (millions of dollars)	Shipments to federal government (millions of dollars)[a]	Government share of total shipments (%)
1955	40	15	38
1956	90	32	36
1957	151	54	36
1958	210	81	39
1959	396	180	45
1960	542	258	48
1961	565	222	39
1962	575	223	39
1963	610	211	35
1964	676	192	28
1965	884	247	28
1966	1,123	298	27
1967	1,107	303	27
1968	1,159	294	25
1969	1,457	247	17
1970	1,337	275	21
1971	1,519	193	13
1972	1,912	228	12
1973	3,458	201	6
1974	3,916	344	9
1975	3,001	239	8
1976	4,968	480	10
1977	4,583	536	12

[a] Includes devices produced for Department of Defense, Atomic Energy Commission, Central Intelligence Agency, Federal Aviation Agency, and National Aeronautics and Space Administration equipment.
Source: Richard C. Levin, "The Semiconductor Industry," in Richard R. Nelson, ed. (1982), p. 60.

alternatives to miniaturization through semiconductors were largely unsuccessful; and (3) the procurement needs of the military resulted in considerable firm-financed R&D spending. Profits and overhead from military procurement contracts supported company-funded R&D and thereby may have generated more civilian spillover than R&D that was directly funded by the military. In addition, direct financial support from the Pentagon was available for the construction of production facilities by winners of contracts under the provisions of the Defense Production Act.

Table 6.11. *Government purchases of integrated circuits, 1962–68*

Year	Total integrated circuit shipments (millions of dollars)	Shipments to federal government (millions of dollars)[a]	Government share of total shipments (%)
1962	4[b]	4[b]	100[b]
1963	16	15[b]	94[b]
1964	41	35[b]	85[b]
1965	79	57	72
1966	148	78	53
1967	228	98	43
1968	312	115	37

[a] Includes circuits produced for Department of Defense, Atomic Energy Commission, Central Intelligence Agency, Federal Aviation Agency, and National Aeronautics and Space Administration.
[b] Estimated by Tilton (1971).
Source: Richard C. Levin (1982), p. 63.

Defense procurement may have lowered marketing-based barriers to entry. Lower entry barriers allowed small firms, such as General Radio, Texas Instruments, and Transitron, to direct their development efforts to meeting the performance and design requirements of a single large customer in the 1950s. The relatively modest barriers to entry were associated with the entry and rapid growth of numerous young, relatively small firms in the industry. This pattern contrasts sharply with the development of the biotechnology industry, where young firms have relied heavily on linkages with larger firms in order to obtain capital and marketing expertise (see Pisano et al., 1988).

Are spillovers increasing or decreasing?

Granted that spillovers have, at certain times and in certain industries, been a significant economic phenomenon, are they as large today as they were twenty or thirty years ago, and are spillovers from the military to the civilian sector likely to be rising or falling in the years ahead? The answers to these questions vary across different technologies. The commercial spillovers from defense research and procurement also appear to fluctuate over time within a specific technology. A number of factors influence the magnitude of such spillovers, but among the most important is the generic similarity of civilian and military requirements for a technology. Frequently, commercial and military requirements for performance, cost, ruggedness, and so forth more closely resemble one another early in the development of a new technology. This broad similarity in requirements appears to have been associated with significant spillovers in microelectronics in the early 1960s, when the demands of the commercial and military markets for miniaturization, low heat in operation, and ruggedness did not diverge too dramatically. During the 1950s and 1960s, the jet engine was applied in military strategic bombers, transports, and tankers, all of which had fuselage design and engine performance requirements that resembled some of those for commercial air transports. The jet engine was a prime instance of a military spillover to the civilian economy.

Over time, however, the size and even the direction of spillovers in these technologies appear to have changed. As military fighter and strategic bomber aircraft moved into the world of supersonic speeds, they began to assume performance and associated cost characteristics that were inappropriate for the cost-conscious world of commercial travel. The absence of substantial procurement programs for large subsonic military transports has exacerbated this trend. Indeed, the most conspicuous airframe technology spillover in recent years has flowed from the civilian sector to the military. The largest purchase of military tankers is currently for the KC-10, a direct derivative of McDonnell Douglas's wide-bodied commercial jet, the DC-10.[12]

In communications satellites, where spillovers from the military and NASA were once very significant, military priorities now differ considerably from civilian needs. Civilian applications of communications satellites utilize geosynchronous orbits and deal with a diverse range of demands for voice, visual, and data transmission. Commercial satellites must have sufficient power to redirect strong signals back to earth. Military communications and intelligence applications, on the other hand, attach great importance to covert operation of satellites and therefore have very different requirements. These satellites often operate in random orbits rather than in a stationary geosynchronous orbit. Military satellite signal transmission and reception facilities and equipment are largely ground based, rather than incorporated into the satellite, in order to protect these assets. Military satellites are designed to transmit and receive weak signals of a kind that cannot readily be detected by actual or potential adversaries – as when communicating with a far-flung submarine fleet. Military and civilian performance requirements in remote sensing also have di-

---

[12] A recent study (1985) of the commercial aircraft industry by the National Research Council noted that "commercial engines gain service experience 10 to 15 times faster than military engines, even military transport engines . . . some of the improvements in the CF6 turbofan engine (derived from the TF39 used in DOD's large C5A cargo airplane), developed during commercial service, are being incorporated in later versions of the TF39" (National Research Council, 1985, p. 101).

verged. Military requirements have demanded improvements in resolution beyond what has been commercially justifiable for most civilian applications. In addition, some of these remote sensing technologies have been classified because of national security considerations.

In microelectronics, the declining share of the market accounted for by the military and the increasing length of time needed to insert new devices into weapons systems have made U.S. military microelectronics dependent on progress in commercial technologies. This trend has affected military R&D priorities and funding in microelectronics. Funding for the Pentagon Very High Speed Integrated Circuit (VHSIC) R&D program that was begun in 1979 was partially justified on the grounds that it would generate large commercial spillovers and thereby strengthen the American position in an increasingly competitive industry. In fact, the operation of the program provides additional evidence that the two sectors confront increasingly divergent needs. The program also demonstrates the tendency of defense R&D programs to stress applied and development objectives, rather than basic research.[13] Combined with divergent requirements, this focus on development means that the commercial spillovers of VHSIC are likely to remain modest. U.S. government export restrictions in "dual use" technologies may further restrict the possibilities for exploitation of civilian derivatives of military VHSIC technologies.[14]

The unique performance requirements of the military, whose products must perform reliably in hostile environments, has led to many costly design tradeoffs that are of little use or relevance to manufacturers of civilian products. As one observer has noted in discussing integrated circuits:

> Consumers have no expectation that their product will continue to work in temperatures over two hundred degrees Fahrenheit while being bathed in ionizing radiation. Military systems must continue operating in such environments. This has always caused

[13] Fong's recent discussion (1988) of the VHSIC program's impacts concludes that "one of VHSIC's objectives – that of immediate system applications . . . has come to dominate all others. The program has become 'system driven' with emphases on technology insertion and on the analysis, demonstration, and construction of radar, sonar, communications, fire control, and guidance systems" (p. 94). This shift in emphasis, Fong notes, has reduced the possibilities for commercial spillovers from VHSIC that might have resulted from greater involvement by the major commercial merchant producers: "The demise of device technologies has undermined the program's third major objective, that of encouraging the participation of merchant semiconductor producers in defense work. The Pentagon wanted to reverse the growing division between commercial and military work in integrated circuitry, and reestablish the close Pentagon-merchant industry relations of the 1950s. A VHSIC program that promoted semiconductor advances was to be the device to bring the merchants back into the fold. Initially progress was made along these lines. But as device technologies moved down the list of VHSIC priorities, the Pentagon concentrated its attention on the military system houses, rather than the semiconductor merchants" (p. 95).

[14] These issues are discussed in Brueckner and Borrus (1984), pp. 56–68.

military specifications to be higher and the resulting cost of production of military specifications components to exceed those of civilian components. (Steinmueller, 1988, p. 344)

The changing relationship between military and commercial technologies in microelectronics contributed to a recent federal initiative in this sector, the Defense Department's contribution of as much as $600 million over six years to the Sematech (Semiconductor Manufacturing Technology) research consortium. Interestingly, the Sematech consortium is dedicated to the development of advanced manufacturing processes for commercial memory chips, not military components. The Pentagon decision appears to be based on the perception that the health (both technological and economic) of the defense electronics industrial base depends on the health of the commercial sector of the industry and that technological advances in process technologies for commercial components will spill over to affect the state of the art in military components, a complete reversal of the situation in the 1950s. Similar concerns led to the announcement in early January 1989 by the Defense Advanced Research Projects Agency that $30 million would be allocated to support research in high-definition television (HDTV) technologies by U.S. firms (Davis, 1989). Many (although not all) of the applications of HDTV will be in civilian markets.

University research and federal funding

Another dramatic shift in the structure of the postwar U.S. research system from its prewar outlines is the expansion of research in U.S. institutions of higher learning. Much of this growth in research of course reflects the expansion in federal support for university research during and after World War II; indeed, industrial funding conceivably could account for a smaller share of university research than was true during the 1930s (the industry share of university research funding in the 1970s was well below that of the early 1950s). By any measure, however, the expansion of academic research was immense. From an estimated level of nearly $420 million (1982 dollars) in 1935–6, university research (excluding FFRDCs) grew to more than $2 billion (1982 dollars) in 1960 and $8.5 billion in 1985, nearly doubling as a share of GNP during 1960–85 (from .13 to .25). The federal share of postwar university research funding, however, was virtually constant at 63 percent throughout the 1960–85 period.

Expanded federal support of university science can be traced back to the wartime experiments of OSRD (and to the views articulated by Vannevar Bush, its director, in his influential report, *Science, the Endless Frontier* [1945]), to the formation of new military research agencies such as the Office of Naval Research in 1946 and the National Science Foundation in 1950, and to budget support from established agencies such as the Department of Agriculture. The increase in federal support of university research is a dramatic change in the institutional structure of the U.S. research system. It has transformed the major universities into centers for the performance of scientific research. As we noted in Chapter 4, the assumption by universities of a major responsibility for basic research is at most a century old. The rise of universities to a position of primacy within basic research since 1945 in the United States was aided considerably by expanded federal funding.

The huge increase in federal expenditures on university research has taken the form of contracts and grants for specific research projects. Most of the "demand" for scientific research has emanated from a centralized federal authority, although a number of federal departments and agencies with distinctly separate missions and goals have contributed to this demand. On the supply side has been a highly dispersed and heterogeneous range of institutions, public and private, committed to both research and education, dependent on the federal government for financial support but otherwise determined to maintain their independence and autonomy.

The expanded role of the government as a supporter of university research coincided roughly with the arrival of Big Science. The essential feature of Big Science was that reearch at certain frontiers of science absolutely required access to equipment and instrumentation of unprecedented costliness. Cosmological questions dealing with the formation of the universe can be explored, and relevant hypotheses tested, only through access to immensely expensive astronomical equipment. At the microcosmic level, the fundamental nature of matter can be examined only by access to particle accelerators that cost hundreds of millions of dollars. The establishment of CERN, the European Organization for Nuclear Research, confirmed that the most sophisticated equipment in particle physics was too costly for even a single large and affluent Western European country. The proposals of the next generation of particle research technology, the superconducting supercollider (SSC), involve a capital outlay of several billion dollars.

There is an additional element that is essential to this picture. The federal government did not confine itself to generating a demand for university research. On the contrary, federal actions on the supply side enlarged vastly the pool of scientific competence as well as the physical equipment and facilities essential to the performance of high-quality research. The effects of these actions, many of which peaked in the late 1960s and have declined drastically since, are essential to an evaluation of the impact of federal R&D programs.[15]

---

[15] There was, of course, one wholly exogenous supply-side phenomenon of major significance to the growth in the pool of scientific talent: the intellectual diaspora triggered by Hitler and the Nazi onslaught. For some aspects of the benefits that flowed to U.S. science from that diaspora, see Fleming and Bailyn, eds. (1969). In particular, see Chapter

After the Second World War, the federal government undertook programs that increased the number of students who were able to pursue a higher education. The best known of these was the GI Bill, which provided substantial financial support to all veterans who enrolled in college-level educational programs. The bill made educational opportunities available on a greatly expanded scale. At the same time, other postwar programs expanded educational opportunities at the graduate and professional levels. Shortly after the war, the Atomic Energy Commission introduced fellowship programs for doctoral students in the sciences. The National Science Foundation introduced fellowship programs in 1952 and devoted a substantial fraction of its budget to science education programs. The National Institutes of Health introduced traineeships as each new health institute was established (and had sponsored a training program as far back as 1930). The National Defense Education Act, passed in 1958 shortly after the launch of Sputnik, increased federal support for education in science and engineering.

As Figure 6.1 shows, the composition and size of federal graduate student support have changed dramatically since the 1960s. Funding for graduate fellowships has declined considerably, and graduate student support increasingly has depended on research funding and loans. As several recent studies have pointed out (Office of Technology Assessment, 1985; Office of Scientific and Engineering Personnel, 1988), the decline in graduate fellowship support has been associated with a sharp drop in the share of the science and engineering baccalaureate degree-holder population that pursues graduate studies in science and engineering, and an increase in the proportion of foreign nationals in the entry-level ranks of the engineering faculties of U.S. research universities (Figures 6.2 and 6.3, respectively). In light of other evidence suggesting that baccalaureate degree holders are very responsive to the expected costs and benefits of different career paths and funding packages for graduate study, it appears likely that declining federal support for graduate fellowships led to this decline in U.S. degree holders' enrollment in graduate studies in science and engineering programs.

Federal funds also supported the development of a major university research infrastructure. This support made it possible for universities to purchase increasingly expensive scientific equipment and advanced instrumentation, central to the expansion of both research and teaching functions of the university scientific community. Access to such equip-

4 by Charles Weiner, "A New Site for the Seminar: The Refugees and American Physics in the Thirties." Weiner stresses the heightened sophistication of U.S. physics in the period immediately before the arrival of the refugee physicists and argues that this was an essential precondition to the spectacular intellectual progress that followed. On the role of refugees in the United States as recipients of Nobel Prizes, see Zuckerman (1977).

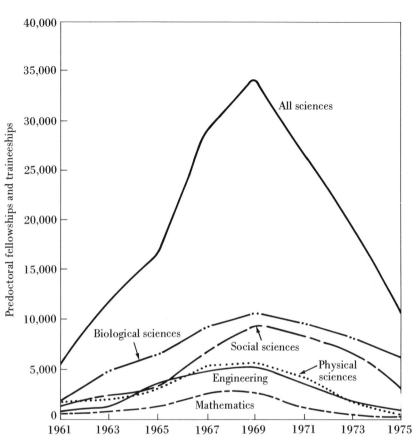

Figure 6.1. Federal predoctoral fellowships and traineeships by field, fiscal years 1961–75. *Source:* Office of Technology Assessment (1985), p. 47.

ment has become a sine qua non for research at the frontiers of science, as we discuss in Chapter 9, and eroding federal financial support for research facilities has been an important motivating factor in recent university–industry cooperative research initiatives.

Federal expenditures on university research and graduate student support had an additional significant benefit. By simultaneously providing funds for university education and for the support of research within the university community, the federal government strengthened the university commitment to research (a commitment that, before World War II, ran a very poor second to teaching) and reinforced the link between research and teaching. That link, which is strengthened by conducting

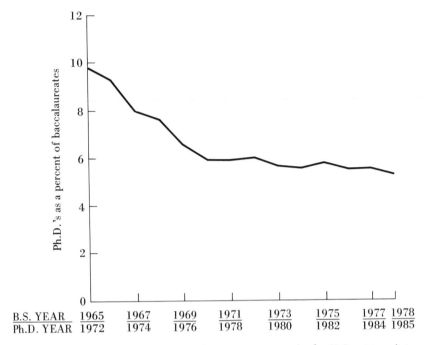

Figure 6.2. Share of baccalaureate degree recipients (male U.S. citizens) in natural science and engineering receiving a doctorate in these fields, 1972–85. *Source:* Government-University-Industry Research Roundtable (1987), p. 21.

graduate and professional training and basic research in the same organizational context (departments and laboratories), with advanced students participating in research, exploits a great potential complementarity between research and teaching. Under the appropriate set of circumstances, each may be performed better when they are done together.

The combination of research and teaching has been carried much further in the United States than elsewhere. In Europe and Japan, for example, a larger fraction of research is carried out in specialized research institutes not connected directly with higher education, and in government-operated laboratories.[16] The U.S. practice of combining research and teaching did not originate in the postwar period. Rather, it goes back to the late nineteenth century, to the agricultural experiment stations that were, from the start, attached to the agricultural schools of

[16] See National Research Council (1982); Okimoto and Saxonhouse (1987).

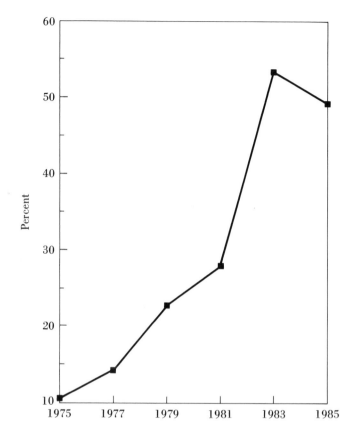

Figure 6.3. Foreign nationals as a share of U.S. assistant professors of engineering (thirty-five years of age and younger), 1975–85. *Source:* Office of Scientific and Engineering Personnel, National Research Council (1988), p. 62.

the land-grant colleges. In Europe, by contrast, government-sponsored research stations, such as the distinguished British agricultural station at Rothamsted, were less likely to be tied to the educational process. Nevertheless, although the joining of research and teaching did not originate in the postwar period, it came to fruition in large measure as a result of federal financial-support policies.

The practice of providing large amounts of research funding from a centralized source, but making it available on a competitive basis to a highly dispersed, decentralized system of institutional performers, seems to have owed much of its success to another distinctive feature of the U.S. R&D experience, namely, the great diversity of American higher education institutions combined with their relative accessibility to a larger fraction of the population than has been typical of other industrial countries. The U.S. system of higher education and research also is unusual in combining strong public and private institutions. Financial support for the state universities depends to some extent on their provision of useful services to state constituencies, a system that has had its most tangible benefits (although far from the only ones) in the agricultural sector, where state funds have been supplemented by considerable federal funding. Private universities, on the other hand, have not been tied to local constituencies and have been less constrained in pursuing research of no obvious or immediate utilitarian value. They also may have had greater flexibility in responding to changes in the research or funding environment. It is interesting to note that, during the Second World War, the great majority of the universities holding the largest OSRD contracts for research were private universities. Indeed, of the top ten universities with the largest OSRD research contracts during the war, all – with the sole exception of the University of California at Berkeley – were private institutions.[17]

Research in industry

As the preceding discussion makes clear, private industry retained its dominance as a performer of research amid dramatic shifts in the sources of the funding for this research. In 1985, although it performed 73 percent of total U.S. research and development, industry accounted for slightly more than 50 percent of total funding. Its continued primacy as a performer of R&D, however, meant continued growth in employment within industrial research – from fewer than 50,000 in 1946 to roughly 300,000 scientists and engineers in 1962 (Birr, 1965), 376,000 in 1970, and almost 600,000 in 1985 (*Statistical Abstract of the U.S.*, 1987, p. 570). Moreover, the industries that accounted for the vast majority of research employment in 1940 remained by far the most significant performers of R&D in the postwar period. Although there were shifts in ranking within the group, the chemicals, electrical machinery, instruments, and transportation equipment industries accounted for more than 70 percent of total research in 1982, compared with 50 percent in 1940.

---

[17] The universities, ranked by size of OSRD contracts, were the Massachusetts Institute of Technology, the California Institute of Technology, Harvard University, Columbia University, the University of California at Berkeley, Johns Hopkins University, the University of Chicago, George Washington University, Princeton University, and the University of Pennsylvania. See Baxter (1946), pp. 456–7. MIT and Harvard did fundamental work on the improvement of radar. Columbia, Chicago, and Berkeley made major contributions to nuclear physics research that culminated in the atomic bomb.

Changes did occur, however, within the industrial research facilities of many of the pioneers of research, such as General Electric, Du Pont, RCA, and Kodak. The wartime demonstration of the significant possibilities of scientific research for fundamental advances in applications, combined with vast increases in the government funds available for research in defense-related technologies, led a number of these firms to expand their central research facilities and to decentralize applied research to the product divisions.

Especially during the early postwar period, buoyant domestic and international markets supported robust profits and rapid expansion of R&D in both the central laboratories and the divisional laboratories. Central R&D facilities focused increasingly on fundamental research in many of these large firms, leaving the development and application of new technologies, as well as the improvement of established products and processes, to the divisional laboratories. Federal research contracts often were awarded to the central research facility or to a dedicated divisional laboratory – for reasons of both policy (accounting regulations governing federal contracts) and security, government research contracts often had to be carried out in separate facilities. In some cases, as in that of Du Pont, the use of the central laboratory and development department as "scanning devices," searching out promising technologies or firms for acquisition, was ruled out by senior management as a result of increasing antitrust restrictions on expansion through acquisition. As a result, internal discovery and development of new products became paramount (Hounshell and Smith, 1985). Although the data are insufficient to support a rigorous longitudinal analysis, the share of total U.S. basic research performed within corporate research laboratories may well have been at its peak during the 1950s and early 1960s (see the discussion of university–industry research collaboration in Chapter 9).

However, as the fundamental research activities of the central research laboratories expanded (expansion that in many cases depended on federal funds), and as these and other large manufacturing firms diversified into new product lines through acquisition and internal development, the ties between the central research laboratory and the increasingly diverse and in some cases geographically distant product divisions of these and other firms were weakened (see Hounshell and Smith, 1985; Rosenbloom, 1985; Sturchio, 1985; Wise, 1985; Graham, 1986). The internal communications between the fundamental and applied research operations deteriorated, making it more difficult to commercialize the work of the central research facility and eroding the contributions of central research to the activities of the product divisions.

In a number of respects, the structure of large-scale corporate R&D that emerged in the 1950s and 1960s applied the linear model of innovation rigorously. In this view, innovations were to be developed largely from internal sources, including basic or fundamental applied research within the firm. This type of research could be conducted in a relatively isolated part of the organization and be simply "handed off" to the divisional laboratories or to manufacturing engineers for application. This organizational application of the linear model yielded mixed results. For Bell Labs, situated within a quasi-monopolistic firm and organized to support intensive interactions among basic research, applied research, and manufacturing, this structure operated effectively until competitive pressures and divestiture of the operating companies radically changed the environment and requirements of research (Mowery, 1988a). In other firms that were less insulated from foreign or domestic competition and that did not cultivate interactive relationships among their research laboratories, this structure was less effective.[18] Increasingly, firms were unable to justify investments in basic research and, in some cases, in R&D of all sorts. Combined with severe competitive pressures from foreign firms, increases in the inflation-adjusted cost of capital, and a slowdown in the growth rate of the domestic economy in the 1970s, the returns to R&D investment may have declined during the mid-1970s,[19] and the rate of growth in real industry expenditures on R&D plummeted. The role of industry as a performer of basic research declined, and many of the central research facilities of the giant corporations entered a period of budgetary austerity or cutbacks. Growing uncertainty over the returns to industry-funded R&D in the late 1970s and 1980s and intensified commercial competition led to the institutional change in R&D organization that began at this time (see Chapters 9 and 11 for additional discussion).

Conclusion

To what extent has the growth of the federal R&D system in the postwar years induced the growth of private R&D spending? The federal role has been strongest in basic research, where a substantial presence has long been justified by the strong uncertainties, long-deferred benefits, and

[18] Graham argued in her analysis of the RCA and Alcoa laboratories that "the problem both corporate laboratories encountered was that, while they could influence actual strategy formulation through informal but effective channels, they encountered heavy opposition at the execution stage. The operating tasks required to develop and commercialize major innovations were quite different from the tasks involved in other forms of corporate R&D activity, and the methods and priorities that were effective for these other activities proved dysfunctional for their radical innovations" (1986, p. 189).

[19] See Baily and Chakrabarti (1988), esp. pp. 42–3, who argue that such a decline did occur, but attribute it largely to exhaustion of technological opportunities. The empirical research on the returns to R&D investment, to say nothing of fluctuations in these returns over time, yields mixed results: Scherer (1983) and Griliches (1986) do not find a decline in the rate of return to R&D, although Griliches (1980) did find such a decline.

difficulties of ensuring use of the results inherent in basic research. Successful basic research should provide a stimulus to further applied research and product development. Higher federal expenditures on basic research should raise the potential profitability of much applied research and development conducted by private industry and thus may have induced an expansion in private R&D expenditures.

The relevant response to this assertion, however, asks what would have been the size and the composition of private R&D spending had the federal government not undertaken its postwar R&D programs? Surely, some portions would have been undertaken by private industry (which was already financing some of its own basic research before the Second World War); therefore, there must have been some substitution effects. But how large were the possible substitution effects as compared with the complementarity effects? What can be said about the relative size of those effects with respect to specific industries (or product groups) and with respect to the separate components of basic research, applied research, and development? To what extent could the federal government have stimulated greater private R&D spending through different procurement practices? What other consequences might have flowed from such practices? How can we measure the benefits of federal R&D expenditures? The answers to these and other questions simply are not available.

Another interaction between federal and private R&D expenditures may have been significant. A large, well-financed federal R&D program increased the demand for a limited supply of professional engineers and scientists. Although that demand must have raised the rate of entry and, eventually, the supply of such trained persons, it also raised their wages and salaries and increased the cost of privately financed R&D. Such effects may have been sizable in those industry sectors where military R&D was concentrated, especially aircraft and electrical equipment. Indeed, comparisons of the pre- and post-1940 pattern of research employment (Mowery, 1981) suggest that federal funding was associated with some displacement of research activity away from sectors receiving little or no federal research funds, such as chemicals and petroleum, and toward the sectors that did receive massive defense-related federal R&D support (instruments, electrical machinery, and transport equipment). A more tenuous conjecture concerns the effectiveness of professional personnel employed in large federally funded R&D projects in the military and space sectors who later shifted to civilian employers (for example, with the decline of NASA expenditures after the completion of the Apollo program). Were engineers who had worked on programs where small performance improvements were sought almost regardless of cost effective designers of products for civilian markets where cost considerations and sensitivity to nuances of consumer preferences were likely to be far more significant?

Have large federally supported "crash" programs shaped the approach and influenced the (perhaps implicit) trade-offs of U.S. engineers and product designers in ways that are dysfunctional for highly competitive consumer markets, such as consumer electronics?

Although these thoughts are speculative, comparisons with other countries provide some support for concern over the commercial implications of defense R&D spending. Japan and West Germany have had very small military budgets since the end of World War II, and in both countries the ratios of civilian R&D to GNP have been substantially higher than in the United States for many years. Although international differences in classification systems render comparisons extremely difficult, U.S. federal R&D expenditures appear to include a far smaller share of activities that could be regarded as "advancement of knowledge" than is included in government R&D expenditures for Japan, West Germany, France, or the United Kingdom (see National Science Board, 1981, pp. 214–15).

The allocation of federal R&D resources during the postwar era has been motivated primarily by national security considerations. Although it is possible to examine the economic effects of such an allocation, the basic rationale is noneconomic. Obviously, the reasons for this military orientation of federal R&D are not inherent in the federal R&D system but are the product of strategic and geopolitical considerations. These figures do suggest, however, that unless it can be shown that military R&D has been generating truly gigantic benefits to the civilian sector (and that probably cannot be shown), the true opportunity costs to the U.S. economy of high levels of defense R&D spending have been very high. The relative economic performance of the United States, West Germany, Japan, and other advanced industrial economies in the past few decades does not support the presumption that large expenditures on military R&D have improved this nation's economic strength. Moreover, recent efforts by the military services to broaden their support of commercial as well as military research may create as many problems as they solve (see Chapter 8).

Appendix

The two tables included here (Tables 6.12 and 6.13) give the federal outlays for research, development, and R&D plant from 1940 to 1985. Although these tables are from the same series, and NSF updates the series continually, the tables are not strictly comparable.

In Table 6.12, the numbers before 1953 are not directly comparable with those after. This is due to changes in reporting. Some of the changes are noted in the footnotes to the table. In addition, in 1958, NSF broadened the definition of "development," but apparently the numbers were corrected back to 1953 only.

Table 6.12. *Federal expenditures for research, development, and R&D plant, by agency, fiscal years 1940–73*
(*dollars in millions*)

Agency	1940	1941	1942	1943	1944	1945	1946	1947	1948	1949	1950
Total, all agencies	74.1	197.9	280.3	602.4	1,377.2	1,590.7	917.8	899.9	854.8	1,082.0	1,082.8
Departments											
Department of Agriculture	29.1	28.3	29.9	30.7	32.1	33.7	36.8	39.2	42.4	50.5	53.0
Department of Commerce[a]	3.3	3.1	3.2	5.2	5.2	5.0	5.0	4.8	8.2	12.5	12.0
Department of Defense, total	26.4	143.7	211.1	395.1	448.1	513.0	418.0	550.8	592.2	695.4	652.3
Department of the Army[b]	3.8	18.7	68.4	149.0	161.3	134.0	114.0	100.0	116.4	136.6	123.1
Department of the Navy[b]	13.9	24.6	58.9	130.5	176.6	243.0	183.0	293.8	287.5	332.9	310.8
Department of the Air Force[b]	8.7	100.4	83.8	115.6	110.2	136.0	121.0	157.0	188.3	225.9	218.4
Advanced Research Projects Agency[c]	—	—	—	—	—	—	—	—	—	—	—
Departmentwide funds[c]	—	—	—	—	—	—	—	—	—	—	—
Defense agencies[c]	—	—	—	—	—	—	—	—	—	—	—
Department of Health, Education, and Welfare[d]	2.8	3.0	3.2	3.2	3.3	3.4	3.5	10.1	22.8	27.9	39.6
Department of the Interior	7.9	9.5	13.5	17.0	20.7	18.0	17.0	20.3	31.4	38.2	32.1
Department of Transportation[a]	—	—	—	—	—	—	—	—	—	—	—
Other agencies											
Atomic Energy Commission	—	—	—	—	—	—	—	37.7	107.5	196.1	221.4
Environmental Protection Agency	—	—	—	—	—	—	—	—	—	—	—
Federal Aviation Agency[a]	—	—	—	—	—	—	—	—	—	—	—
Manhattan Engineering District[e]	—	—	—	77.0	730.0	859.0	366.0	186.0	—	—	—
National Aeronautics and Space Administration[f]	2.2	2.6	5.0	9.8	18.4	24.1	23.7	35.2	37.5	48.7	54.5

Table 6.12. *Cont.*

Agency	1940	1941	1942	1943	1944	1945	1946	1947	1948	1949	1950
National Science Foundation	—	—	—	—	—	—	—	—	—	—	—
Office of Economic Opportunity	—	—	—	—	—	—	—	—	—	—	—
Office of Scientific Research and Development	—	5.3	11.0	52.2	86.8	114.5	36.8	5.6	.9	—	—
Veterans Administration	—	—	—	—	—	—	—	—	—	—	—
All other agencies	2.4	2.4	3.4	12.2	32.6	20.0	11.0	10.2	11.8	12.8	17.7

Agency	1951	1952	1953	1954	1955	1956	1957	1958	1959	1960	1961
Total, all agencies	1,300.5	1,816.2	3,101.0	3,147.9	3,308.3	3,446.0	4,461.9	4,990.6	5,806.4	7,744.2	9,287.0
Departments											
Department of Agriculture	52.4	57.1	54.9	55.4	72.0	87.7	97.0	111.8	124.7	131.4	147.7
Department of Commerce[a]	16.9	10.1	13.6	10.6	9.9	20.4	19.8	17.8	30.1	33.1	35.5
Department of Defense, total	823.4	1,317.0	2,454.8	2,487.2	2,630.2	2,639.0	3,371.4	3,664.2	4,183.3	5,653.8	6,618.1
Department of the Army[b]	161.6	318.0	743.3	815.7	1,012.8	702.4	782.1	873.5	890.9	1,108.9	1,306.0
Department of the Navy[b]	363.8	476.0	678.3	664.7	591.9	635.8	784.9	854.1	1,034.7	1,300.6	1,631.0
Department of the Air Force[b]	297.9	523.0	1,033.2	1,006.8	982.2	1,278.9	1,780.0	1,894.0	2,134.5	2,978.0	3,440.6
Advanced Research Projects Agency[c]	—	—	—	—	—	—	—	3.0	80.9	226.3	206.6
Departmentwide funds[c]	—	—	—	—	43.3	21.9	24.4	39.6	42.3	40.0	33.9
Defense agencies[c]	—	—	—	—	—	—	—	—	—	—	—
Department of Health, Education, and Welfare[d]	53.4	64.1	65.2	62.5	70.2	86.2	143.5	180.3	252.8	324.2	374.1
Department of the Interior	32.1	32.8	35.2	39.1	31.9	35.7	42.3	48.9	72.2	65.3	75.1

Agency	1962	1963	1964	1965	1966	1967	1968	1969	1970	1971	Estimates	
											1972	1973
Other agencies												
Atomic Energy Commission		242.6	249.6	378.1	383.1	385.4	474.0	656.5	804.2	877.1	985.9	1,111.1
Environmental Protection Agency	—	—	—	—	—	—	—	—	—	—	—	—
Federal Aviation Agency	—	—	—	—	—	—	—	—	4.2	27.6	41.2	52.9
Manhattan Engineering District[e]	—	—	—	—	—	—	—	—	—	—	—	—
National Aeronautics and Space Administration		61.6	67.4	78.6	89.5	73.8	71.1	76.1	89.2	145.5	401.0	744.3
National Science Foundation		.1	.5	2.1	3.6	8.5	15.4	30.6	33.7	54.1	64.2	82.7
Office of Economic Opportunity	—	—	—	—	—	—	—	—	—	—	—	—
Office of Scientific Research and Development	—	—	—	—	—	—	—	—	—	—	—	—
Veterans Administration	—	—	3.3	4.6	5.1	5.3	6.1	9.4	12.8	16.8	18.6	23.1
All other agencies		18.2	14.3	13.9	11.8	21.1	10.4	15.3	23.5	22.2	25.4	22.6
Total, all agencies	10,386.8	12,012.1	14,707.0	14,888.8	16,017.9	16,859.1	17,048.9	16,347.6	15,735.8	15,992.4	16,733.9	17,326.9
Departments												
Department of Agriculture	155.7	172.5	183.4	205.7	236.3	269.8	286.2	283.8	298.6	318.9	360.7	360.7
Department of Commerce[a]	47.5	70.4	84.5	85.8	71.2	80.5	81.6	78.4	127.9	122.9	157.4	203.1
Department of Defense, total	6,812.0	6,848.8	7,517.0	6,727.6	6,734.6	7,680.1	8,163.6	7,868.4	7,587.9	7,706.0	8,286.2	8,441.5
Department of the Army[b]	1,243.5	1,421.2	1,413.6	1,428.9	1,485.2	1,734.0	1,539.5	1,609.8	1,771.6	1,670.6	2,048.1	2,068.2

Table 6.12. *Cont.*

| Agency | 1962 | 1963 | 1964 | 1965 | 1966 | 1967 | 1968 | 1969 | 1970 | 1971 | Estimates | |
											1972	1973
Department of the Navy[b]	1,561.0	1,573.6	1,724.2	1,419.4	1,548.6	1,941.9	2,104.1	2,108.8	2,172.4	2,477.9	2,547.9	2,562.5
Department of the Air Force[b]	3,672.9	3,539.1	3,951.1	3,404.8	3,194.2	3,487.0	3,987.8	3,626.3	3,150.1	3,025.6	3,197.8	3,271.6
Advanced Research Projects Agency[c]	192.9	—	—	—	—	—	—	—	—	—	—	—
Departmentwide funds[c]	141.7	14.6	21.1	9.9	9.9	9.9	7.2	9.2	5.9	4.5	18.5	46.2
Defense Agencies[c]	—	300.4	406.9	464.7	496.7	507.3	525.0	514.2	488.0	527.5	473.8	493.1
Department of Health, Education, and Welfare[d]	512.1	632.4	793.4	737.9	879.4	1,075.0	1,283.1	1,220.0	1,261.3	1,326.8	1,520.0	1,760.9
Department of the Interior	86.7	102.7	102.0	118.8	149.3	168.7	195.1	204.2	159.8	185.1	225.8	267.7
Department of Transportation[a]	—	—	—	—	165.7	239.3	219.1	208.0	262.6	477.8	397.2	334.3
Other agencies												
Atomic Energy Commission	1,284.3	1,335.6	1,505.0	1,520.0	1,451.9	1,456.9	1,594.3	1,654.0	1,616.0	1,604.9	1,580.0	1,619.5
Environmental Protection Agency	—	—	—	—	—	—	—	—	70.2	101.0	157.7	180.7
Federal Aviation Agency	53.7	74.7	74.0	96.4	—	—	—	—	—	—	—	—

Manhattan Engineering District[e]	—	—	—	—	—	—	—	—	—	—	—	—
National Aeronautics and Space Administration[f]	1,257.0	2,552.3	4,171.0	5,092.9	5,933.0	5,425.7	4,723.7	4,251.7	3,753.1	3,381.9	3,181.0	3,192.4
National Science Foundation	112.6	153.1	202.9	206.3	240.9	294.8	333.6	342.3	324.1	373.9	440.3	489.9
Office of Economic Opportunity	—	—	—	4.2	49.4	36.7	41.0	77.1	79.3	148.7	124.0	113.5
Office of Scientific Research and Development	—	—	—	—	—	—	—	—	—	—	—	—
Veterans Administration	30.8	33.1	34.1	40.4	42.2	46.4	47.4	54.0	61.7	67.9	77.6	81.8
All other agencies	34.3	36.5	39.7	52.5	54.1	77.2	80.2	105.7	133.3	176.6	226.0	280.9

[a]The Department of Transportation, as of 1966, includes the Bureau of Public Roads and the Office of Transportation Research and Development (formerly in the Department of Commerce); the Federal Aviation Agency; and the U.S. Coast Guard (formerly under the Treasury Department).
[b]Includes pay and allowances of military R&D personnel beginning in fiscal year 1953, and support from procurement appropriations of development, test, and evaluation, starting with fiscal year 1954.
[c]Starting with 1963, Defense Agencies include the Advanced Research Projects Agency (ARPA), and other agencies such as the Defense Atomic Support Agency and Defense Communications Agency. With the exception of ARPA, these agencies were previously included in departmentwide funds. Starting with 1963, departmentwide funds include Military Assistance, Civil Defense, and Emergency Funds only.
[d]Federal Security Agency prior to fiscal year 1952.
[e]This agency, under the Department of War, is shown separately to distinguish funds for this atomic agency project from other R&D funds.
[f]National Advisory Committee for Aeronautics prior to fiscal year 1958.
Source: National Science Foundation (1972), pp. 178–9.

Table 6.13. *Federal outlays for research, development, and R&D plant, by agency, fiscal years 1975–85 (dollars in millions)*

Agency and subdivision	1974	1975	1976	1977	1978	1979	1980	1981	1982	1983	Estimates 1984	Estimates 1985
Total, all agencies	15,297.1	19,550.8	21,020.9	22,882.9	25,127.9	27,041.0	30,635.8	34,065.9	35,766.8	37,959.4	44,786.9	50,832.7
Dept. of Agriculture, total	381.5	425.6	468.8	537.8	572.4	630.5	687.6	782.5	828.4	858.8	909.1	919.3
Agricultural Coop. Serv.[a]	NA	1.2	1.4	NA	NA	NA	1.6	1.3	1.7	2.1	2.2	1.4
Agricultural Marketing Serv.[b]						.9	1.3	1.2	1.5	.6	1.5	
Agricultural Res. Serv.[c]	210.5	232.8	247.4	294.6	318.4	331.2	371.6	425.9	436.1	469.4	486.8	497.5
Coop. State Res. Serv.[d]	85.2	95.6	104.2	120.2	134.9	156.6	174.2	199.0	219.8	220.4	243.0	244.9
Econ., Stat., & Coop. Serv.[e]	NA	NA	NA	NA	NA	35.6	NA	NA	NA	NA	NA	NA
Economic Research Serv.	18.1	22.2	23.6	30.5	32.4	NA	NA	38.0	37.0	36.8	43.1	46.7
Econ. & Stat.[f]	NA	NA	NA	NA	NA	NA	31.1	NA	NA	NA	NA	NA
Forest Service	65.6	72.5	90.3	92.5	86.7	105.7	100.6	101.8	116.0	111.1	108.2	104.5
Human Nutrition Info. Serv.			NA	NA	NA	NA	NA		3.8	5.8	7.9	7.6
National Agricultural Library		.1										
Off. of Inter. Coop. & Devt.		NA	NA	NA	NA		6.4	6.9	4.6	4.1	7.2	7.1
Off. of Transportation		NA	NA	NA	NA	.5	.8	.9	.9	.8	1.0	1.0
Stat. Reporting Serv.	.6	1.2	2.0	NA	NA	NA	NA	7.5	7.0	7.6	8.2	8.5
Depart. of Commerce, total	188.2	224.6	233.3	238.2	272.7	307.1	360.6	346.8	286.5	335.2	359.2	287.3
National Bureau of Standards	42.5	47.2	49.1	53.1	59.0	64.8	77.1	84.4	87.6	94.0	96.3	108.0
Natl Oceanic & Atmos. Admin.	109.5	127.7	134.5	132.6	164.7	190.1	210.6	209.0	174.1	222.0	244.3	165.2
Other Commerce	36.3	49.7	49.8	52.5	48.9	52.2	72.9	53.5	24.8	19.2	18.5	14.1
Dept. of Defense, total	8,979.7	9,363.5	9,445.5	10,308.0	10,935.4	11,733.1	13,706.1	15,993.0	18,482.9	21,373.5	26,030.3	31,472.9
Army	2,308.6	2,083.0	1,969.6	2,195.0	2,464.3	2,536.2	2,852.9	3,123.7	3,414.4	3,848.5	4,257.8	4,821.6
Navy	2,715.8	3,126.3	3,320.1	3,582.6	3,919.4	3,926.4	4,507.9	4,916.9	5,394.7	6,023.5	7,007.3	8,858.8
Air Force	3,442.3	3,567.6	3,625.2	3,902.2	3,969.9	4,428.0	5,323.6	6,756.6	8,209.1	9,640.9	13,347.3	14,111.8
Defense Agencies	485.2	556.9	507.5	610.5	555.1	814.2	981.4	1,160.0	1,420.0	1,817.3	2,412.1	3,626.8
Defense Civil Preparedness Agency	2.3	3.0	2.2	1.2	2.9	NA	NA	NA	NA	NA	NA	NA

Director of Test & Evaluation	25.5	26.8	20.9	16.5	23.9	28.3	40.4	35.7	44.8	43.3	55.8	53.9
Dept. of Education, total	NA	NA	NA	NA	NA	136.5	120.9	111.8	150.1	111.5	134.7	126.3
Dept. of Energy, total	NA	NA	NA	3,593.1	4,413.0	4,956.8	5,660.2	6,125.9	5,785.4	5,641.9	5,911.8	6,027.3
Dept. of Health, Ed., & Welfare, total	1,960.6	2,168.2	2,615.0	2,622.2	3,070.2	NA	NA	NA	NA	NA	NA	NA
Alcohol, Drug Abuse & Mental Hlth. Admin.	112.6	114.1	145.1	167.2	179.9	NA	NA	NA	NA	NA	NA	NA
Natl. Institute of Education	96.9	82.8	69.8	59.7	74.8	NA	NA	NA	NA	NA	NA	NA
NIH	1,435.4	1,684.4	2,118.4	2,105.0	2,507.1	NA	NA	NA	NA	NA	NA	NA
Office of Education	66.3	53.1	56.8	30.3	25.8	NA	NA	NA	NA	NA	NA	NA
Other HEW	234.6	233.8	225.0	260.1	202.6	NA	NA	NA	NA	NA	NA	NA
Dept. of Hlth. & Human Serv., total	NA	NA	NA	NA	NA	3,172.7	3,554.1	3,997.5	4,052.1	4,118.6	4,567.2	4,923.7
Alcohol, Drug Abuse, & Mental Hlth. Admin.	NA	NA	NA	NA	NA	184.7	218.1	251.1	292.0	289.8	297.6	339.1
NIH	NA	NA	NA	NA	NA	2,713.4	3,029.3	3,392.2	3,475.0	3,562.9	3,989.0	4,299.8
Other HHS	NA	NA	NA	NA	NA	274.5	306.8	354.3	285.0	265.8	280.6	284.8
Dept. of Housing & Urban Development, total	58.4	58.7	60.3	69.0	59.3	74.3	65.8	54.1	37.0	30.9	31.5	31.8
Dept. of the Interior, total	194.8	266.0	319.7	304.0	339.9	404.3	431.5	436.9	394.9	412.7	421.7	375.5
Bureau of Mines	66.7	82.7	113.7	103.7	104.2	121.4	130.8	109.0	105.2	102.0	97.6	75.0
Geological Survey	68.7	95.2	115.7	112.2	128.7	144.2	145.2	168.2	150.1	171.4	171.6	154.4
Other Interior	59.4	88.1	90.4	88.1	107.0	138.7	155.5	159.7	139.7	139.3	152.6	146.2
Department of Justice, total	40.5	43.8	39.9	33.7	33.5	45.9	45.3	26.1	36.6	27.6	34.7	30.2
Off. of Justice Assist., Res. & Statistics	34.5	39.2	35.2	27.6	27.1	35.5	35.1	19.2	30.4	21.1	25.3	22.6
Other Justice	6.0	4.6	4.7	6.2	6.3	10.4	10.2	6.9	6.2	6.5	9.4	7.6
Department of Labor, total	22.5	25.4	27.8	28.1	97.6	109.2	137.7	61.6	29.4	16.8	18.1	19.3
Department of State, total	24.8	28.6	27.0	44.1	57.5	3.2	2.2	1.8	1.5	1.5	1.6	1.7
Agency for Inter. Dev.	23.2	27.4	25.4	41.8	54.6	NA	NA	NA	NA	NA	NA	NA
Other State	1.6	1.2	1.6	2.3	2.8	3.2	2.2	1.8	1.5	1.5	1.6	1.7
Dept. of Transportation, total	363.7	339.2	335.7	363.5	377.3	372.4	391.0	432.1	360.0	282.3	462.4	499.0
Federal Aviation Admin.	115.8	113.7	114.6	102.8	100.2	111.4	109.7	125.9	110.9	99.5	213.0	276.0

Table 6.13. Cont.

Agency and subdivision	1974	1975	1976	1977	1978	1979	1980	1981	1982	1983	Estimates 1984	Estimates 1985
Federal Highway Admin.	33.5	26.8	42.9	53.0	52.9	48.9	53.4	59.1	42.5	32.5	45.0	48.5
Federal Railroad Admin.	38.3	51.1	48.5	57.3	62.4	58.0	63.5	55.0	25.6	18.5	22.0	18.5
Natl. Highway Traffic Safety Admin.	44.4	36.2	33.8	49.5	68.5	53.6	60.3	60.8	60.2	51.1	57.8	60.8
Urban Mass Trans. Admin.	57.8	60.9	48.2	52.1	52.5	50.5	58.9	61.9	69.8	36.5	71.8	51.3
Other Transportation	73.9	50.6	47.7	48.8	40.8	49.9	45.2	69.4	51.0	44.2	52.8	43.8
Dept. of the Treasury, total	1.1	1.7	3.8	5.0	9.9	9.6	10.9	10.8	13.6	15.6	16.7	28.1
Other agencies												
Agency for Inter. Dev.	NA	NA	NA	NA	NA	80.3	114.3	166.1	188.6	225.2	305.4	380.8
Energy Res. & Dev. Admin.	1,825.0	2,246.6	2,553.7	NA	NA	NA	NA	NA	NA	NA	NA	NA
EPA	172.2	218.6	265.6	283.0	312.5	388.9	384.7	344.3	336.2	312.5	251.7	277.2
NASA	3,256.2	3,266.5	3,669.0	3,449.1	3,432.1	3,395.2	3,605.7	3,705.5	3,252.9	2,646.2	3,600.3	3,477.3
NSF	584.7	600.4	669.1	654.7	738.6	804.6	848.2	905.0	1,015.1	994.7	1,143.6	1,378.2
NRC	46.1	58.5	76.9	107.8	131.7	145.4	182.8	216.0	208.6	244.0	198.7	179.1
VA	85.7	97.0	109.5	112.8	123.9	123.1	138.6	144.3	140.7	164.7	176.2	218.3
All other agencies	111.3	117.9	100.0	109.0	150.5	148.1	187.5	203.7	166.2	145.3	162.0	179.3

Note: NA (not applicable) indicates that the agency or agency subdivision did not exist as such in that year.
An asterisk indicates an amount less than $50,000.

[a] Includes the programs of the Farmer Cooperative Service for fiscal years 1967–76.
[b] Fiscal year 1979 was the first year in which Congress appropriated funds to AMS.
[c] Includes the former Agriculture Research Service of the Science and Education Administration for fiscal years 1978–80.
[d] Includes the former Cooperative State Research Service of the Science and Education Administration for fiscal years 1978–80.
[e] Includes programs of the Economic Research Service, the Statistical Reporting Service, and the Farmer Cooperative Service for fiscal years 1977–79.
[f] Includes programs of the Economic Research Service and the Statistical Reporting Service for fiscal year 1980.
Source: Federal Funds for Research and Development, Fiscal Years 1980, 1981, and 1982 (Washington, D.C.: NSF, 1982), vol. 30, pp. 163–4; Federal Funds for Research and Development, Fiscal Years 1983, 1984, and 1985 (Washington, D.C.: NSF, 1984), vol. 33, pp. 168–9.

7

The U.S. commercial aircraft industry

Previous chapters have examined the historical development of the U.S. R&D system, stressing the importance of organizational structure for innovative performance in the transformation of this system from one financed largely by private funds to one (after World War II) in which federal monies financed a larger share of research. A more detailed consideration of this transformation, the operation of the postwar system, and the implications of both for policy, requires a narrower focus, however. The U.S. commercial aircraft industry presents an excellent subject for such a sectoral study. The industry has been in existence for most of this century, and therefore allows one to trace the effects of different policy regimes on innovative performance and industry behavior in the long run.

In addition, of course, the industry's importance for national security means that it has been at the center of the transformation of the U.S. R&D system, as federal funds (largely for research and testing of military aircraft) now account for a substantial majority of the R&D performed by the firms active in developing and producing commercial aircraft. Other aspects of federal policy toward this industry, including the role of the National Advisory Council on Aeronautics (some of whose functions were absorbed by the National Aeronautics and Space Administration) and the Civil Aeronautics Board (whose remaining functions now are carried out by the Transportation Department), merit particular attention in view of their potential implications for technology policy in other industries. Finally the product development process in this industry has undergone a dramatic transformation in the last fifteen years, as multinational collaboration in the development and production of commercial aircraft has grown.

Innovation and economic performance in the U.S. commercial aircraft industry

The U.S. commercial aircraft industry has long been a major beneficiary of federal research and development programs managed by NASA and the armed services. Government policy in the aircraft industry not only has supported precommercial research in civilian and military aircraft technologies, but has also aided the adoption and application of the results of that research.

The U.S. commercial aircraft industry has been innovative and internationally competitive throughout the postwar period.[1] In 1986, total aerospace industry sales (including missiles and spacecraft) amounted to nearly $105 billion ($43 billion in 1972 dollars), more than 2 percent of the gross national product. Within this total, sales of military and civilian aircraft, engines, and parts were valued at $55.4 billion ($22.6 billion in 1972 dollars).[2] The contribution of aircraft to U.S. foreign trade in 1986 was important as well; exports of aircraft, engines, and parts equaled $19.8 billion ($8 billion in 1972 dollars), the largest single category of U.S. manufactured exports.

The aircraft industry is a major investor in research and development. Expenditures for R&D (nearly 77 percent of which was financed by federal funds in 1986) amounted to 17.5 percent of the value of net sales in 1985, a level exceeded only by the electronics industry. The aircraft industry also has important links (through its demand for components and parts) with other high-technology industries.[3] Indeed, a central reason for the rapid technological progress characteristic of this industry is its ability to draw on and benefit from technological developments in numerous other industries.[4]

The ability of the commercial aircraft industry to benefit from technological developments in other industries reflects the fact that a given aircraft or engine design integrates a number of complex subsystems, including electronics, hydraulics, and materials technologies. The interaction of these individually complex systems or components is crucial to the performance of a design, yet often is difficult to predict. Considerable technological uncertainty thus pervades the development of a new airframe or engine design. This uncertainty makes the systems integration and design phases critical to the introduction of a successful new product. Therefore, R&D investment within the industry is dominated by the integration of components and prototype design and testing, rather than by basic or fundamental research.

[1] This section draws on discussions in Mowery and Rosenberg (1982); and Mowery and Rosenberg (1985).
[2] All figures are from Aerospace Industries Association (1987).
[3] A 1981 study of aeronautics R&D by the Office of Science and Technology Policy concluded that "the aeronautics industry is characterized by high research intensity and a wide technology base. That is, aeronautics depends on R&T (research and technology) performed within the aeronautics industry and on R&T performed by virtually every other high-technology industry" (1982, vol. 2, p. V–28).
[4] A study by the International Trade Administration found that the aircraft industry ranked third among U.S. manufacturing industries in 1980 in its level of "embodied research intensity," that is, R&D expenditures incorporated in purchased inputs. The aircraft industry was exceeded only by missiles, spacecraft, and electronics in this measure. See U.S. International Trade Administration (1983), p. 42.

In addition to the dynamic character of commercial aircraft technology, the great differences among foreign and domestic airlines in preferences and fleet requirements (both of which also change over time) contribute to the length of the design phase in aircraft innovation. To accommodate the broadest possible group of purchasers, major firms produce dozens of "paper airplanes" before the decision is made to launch the development of a specific design. Steiner cites "the excruciating pain of trying to achieve a common denominator among varying airline requirements. All commercial programs go through a similar process and the engineers must work with a great many airlines, not just the few who are most likely to become launch customers" (1982, p. 14).

In the design of the Boeing 727, this process took two and one-half years and produced at least nine separate complete designs for the aircraft. The design-definition phase for the Boeing 767 lasted nearly six years. Once a producer decides to introduce a specific design, however, speed is essential.[5] Being first to market with a new aircraft design is an important competitive advantage in most instances (the unfortunate history of the British Comet, the first jet-powered commercial aircraft, is an exception to this generalization).

Another reason for the importance of product design in this industry is the fact that an aircraft design is produced for a remarkably long time. The Boeing 727 was produced for twenty years, and the manufacture of the DC-8 extended from 1957 through 1972. Although these aircraft were produced over a lengthy period, their designs were modified considerably, through "stretching" the fuselage to accommodate additional passengers, or retrofitting an airframe with new engines.

The phenomenon of stretching as applied to jet transports from the Comet to the 767 is a classic example of a process that is not very "interesting" technologically but that nevertheless is of vital economic importance. Although stretching an airframe appears to produce dramatic improvements in operating costs, this process is unsustainable without the complementary development of power plant technology and, occasionally, wing technology. Technological improvements in engines during the turbine era have increased thrust per pound of engine weight by over 50 percent in twenty years. The performance improvement is even more dramatic when measured in fuel consumption per hour per pound of thrust. In 1950, about 0.9 pounds of fuel was required for each hour-pound of thrust. The development of the turbofan engine in the early 1960s reduced this figure to around 0.75 pounds fuel per hour-pound of thrust. With the development of high-bypass-ratio turbofan engines in the late 1960s, fuel requirements dropped to 0.6 pounds of fuel per hour-pound

[5] "When the market is ready, the successful manufacturer may have to *go*. The eventual prize sometimes goes to the company which is fast on its feet" (Steiner, 1982, p. 31; emphasis in the original).

of thrust. This 30 percent decline in fuel requirements has direct implications for increasing the deliverable payload of an aircraft through fuselage stretching.

As the profitability of stretching aircraft fuselages has become better understood, commercial aircraft increasingly have been designed to facilitate stretching. Although airplane designers generally design to conform to the capabilities of existing engines, they typically expect improvements in engine performance during the lifetime of an airframe design, and therefore attempt to design flexibility into the airplane. The design of aircraft with high potential for stretching requires, among other things, the development of wing designs that will allow significant increases in aircraft payload without major modifications. In some cases, this feat may involve the substitution of new materials such as composites or aluminum-lithium alloys for older ones in an existing wing design. Production facilities also must be designed to accommodate variations in fuselage length.

The economic significance of stretching an aircraft design is difficult to overstate. It allows the high fixed costs of design and development to be defrayed over additional sales in a new market segment; the incremental costs of stretching an aircraft design rarely exceed 25 percent of the original development costs. Thus, design decisions influence both the success of the initial model and the potential for stretching that may enable a single aircraft design to serve additional markets.

Other incremental modifications are made throughout the life of a given aircraft or engine. Such changes rely heavily on information gained from close monitoring of operating experience after the introduction of an aircraft. The importance of this monitoring function and of product support (spare parts supply and field service) makes a global marketing and product support organization critical to market acceptance of a new aircraft design. The need for a global product support and marketing network also acts as a barrier to entry of new firms into the aircraft industry.[6]

Another source of entry barriers is the high and rapidly growing cost of new product development. Development costs have risen dramatically, increasing (in constant dollars) at an average annual rate of nearly 20 percent from 1930 to 1970, considerably greater than the average annual rate of growth in aircraft weight of 8.5 percent. Development of the Douglas DC-3 in the 1930s cost roughly $3 million (Miller and Sawers, 1968, p. 267). The DC-8, introduced in 1958, cost nearly $112 million, while development of the Boeing 747, production of which began in the early 1970s, cost $1 billion. More recently, development of the Boeing 767 is

---

[6] Moreover, the high fixed costs of supporting such a network create a strong incentive for producers to be active in the widest possible range of market segments. Potential purchasers are influenced also by the lower maintenance costs and spare parts inventories associated with standardization around the products of a single manufacturer of airframes or engines.

estimated to have cost $1.5 billion, while estimates of the development costs for a new-technology 150-seat transport range as high as $2 billion. The V2500, a new high-bypass-ratio engine, required roughly $1.5 billion for development. The rapid growth of such costs means that an increasing proportion of the costs of introducing a new aircraft is incurred during the phase of greatest uncertainty concerning market prospects and technical feasibility.[7]

In addition to their sheer magnitude, which is appreciated best by comparison with total stockholders' equity of a firm such as Boeing (in 1984, roughly $2.7 billion), these high fixed costs result in a falling short-run average cost curve. The behavior of costs in the industry is governed by two other factors. The first is the relatively small production runs of most aircraft. Since the introduction of the commercial jet transport in the early 1950s, only five aircraft designs (the DC-9/MD-80 and the Boeing 707, 727, 737, and 747) of twenty-three have sold more than six hundred units. The aircraft business is not one characterized by high throughput. Although average annual production rates typically are low, they are subject to wide fluctuations, with the peak production rate being as much as eight times as large as the trough output rate.

A final important dimension of cost behavior in the industry is reduction in variable costs as a function of cumulative output – the well-known learning curve, first documented in the production of airframes in World War II (Hirsch, 1956; Alchian, 1963). Cost reduction over the course of an aircraft's production history is dramatic: Most estimates suggest that a doubling of output reduces unit costs by as much as 20 percent.[8] The learning phenomenon also contributes to the importance of stretching aircraft designs, since the bulk of the cost reductions from the movement down the learning curve in the production of the original design can be applied to an essentially new aircraft.

The record of technical progress

The U.S. air transportation industry is the primary beneficiary of technological progress in commercial aircraft. Accordingly, one index of the rate of technical change in commercial aircraft is the growth of productiv-

---

[7] Partly in response to these dramatic increases in development costs, the subcontracting of production of new aircraft and engines has grown substantially in recent years and increasingly involves foreign firms as partners of major U.S. aircraft and engine producers. The role of Japanese firms as partners in recent multinational joint ventures in airframe and engine development is discussed in Mowery and Rosenberg (1985).

[8] As McCulloch (1984) has noted, the high fixed costs that characterize the aircraft industry's cost structure, as well as the strong learning effects, can give rise to pricing below average costs.

   In addition to such "predatory pricing," of course, the presence of strong learning effects means that support or protection of a domestic market can move domestic firms rapidly down their learning curves, effectively operating as export subsidies, in the fashion outlined by Krugman (1984).

ity in air transportation, and this indicator suggests that technical change in modern commercial aircraft has been dramatic. Kendrick (1973) concluded that the average annual rate of growth in total factor productivity in air transportation was 8 percent during 1948–1966, higher than for any other industry. Fraumeni and Jorgenson (1980) found that total-factor productivity growth in air transportation was exceeded only by that of telecommunications.

Productivity growth in air transportation reflects more than innovation in commercial aircraft alone. Air traffic control improvements, innovations in ground-based navigational equipment, airfield expansion and modernization, and other enhancements of the overall air transportation network, many of which were financed by the Federal Aviation Administration (FAA), also have been important. Direct measures of aircraft performance therefore have some advantages over productivity data from the air transportation industry for assessing technological progress in commercial aircraft.

Two indexes of commercial aircraft performance are seats multiplied by cruising speed (AS*V_C) and direct operating costs (DOC) per available seat mile.[9] Table 7.1 displays the evolution of the two aircraft performance measures for a sample of piston and jet engine aircraft during 1938–83. With the introduction of successive generations of aircraft, AS*V_C has risen, and costs per available seat mile (in 1972 dollars) have fallen. The sharp drop in operating costs resulting from the introduction of the DC-3 stands out clearly in the table.[10] Another major drop in seat–mile costs came with the introduction of the wide-body transports (such as the Boeing 747, the Lockheed L-1011, and the McDonnell Douglas DC-10) that incorporated high-bypass-ratio jet engines. The latest generation of aircraft, including the Boeing 757 and 767 and the Airbus A300, have higher direct operating costs per available seat mile than did the first wide-body aircraft because of the smaller number of seats in these transports.

Cruising speed and capacity (AS*V_C) declined sharply with the introduction of four-engine transports immediately after World War II and dropped further still with the introduction of jet-powered transports. Gains in speed and capacity have been obtained at the expense of operating costs; the first wide-body transports were unusual in combining major increases in available seat velocity with significant declines in direct operating costs per seat mile. This record of performance improvements in commercial aircraft can be summarized in the estimate by Rosenberg et

---

[9] These measures are employed by Miller and Sawers (1968) and by Rosenberg, Thompson, and Belsley (1978).

[10] As Phillips (1971) noted, the seat–mile costs of the DC-3 aircraft were "so much lower than those of alternate aircraft that even with a relatively low load factor its passenger mile costs were often lower than those for other planes" (p. 94).

Table 7.1. *Measures of aircraft performance, 1938–83*

	AS*V$_c$^{a}		DOC (1972 dollars)^b
B-247		(1938)	10.82
DC-3 (1940)	3,700	(1939)	7.47
B-307 (1952)	9,400	(1950)	3.10
DC-7C (1964)	25,200	(1959)	2.65
B-707 (1959)	73,000	(1959)	2.61^c
B-727-100		(1964)	2.01^c
B-727-200 (1983)	63,000		1.89
B-737-200 (1983)	45,000		2.22
B-747 (1983)	211,000		1.30
B-757 (1983)	77,300		1.54^c
B-767 (1983)	91,300		1.65
DC-9 (1966)			2.68^c
DC-9-80 (1983)	62,100		1.59
DC-8 (1960)			1.86
DC-8-61 (1983)	88,600		2.23^c
DC-10-10 (1983)	131,290		1.57
L-1011-500 (1983)	115,200		1.74
A300-B4 (1983)	84,120		2.73

^{a} Data for pre-1983 period taken from Rosenberg et al. (1978). Data for 1983 from Civil Aeronautics Board, vol. 17 (1984).
^{b} Data for pre-1983 period taken from R. Miller and D. Sawers (1968), Appendix T. Data for 1983 taken from Civil Aeronautics Board, vol. 17 (1984).
^{c} First year of operation.

al. that between the appearance of the monocoque airframe in 1933 and the introduction of the 747, costs per seat mile declined tenfold (Rosenberg, Thompson, and Belsley, 1978), while passenger capacity and speed rose by a factor of 20.[11]

Another measure of technical progress estimates the resource savings that result from the application of improved technologies. A calculation of the "social savings" resulting from technological progress in commercial aircraft compares the costs of air transportation in 1983 using the contemporary U.S. fleet in scheduled domestic service with the cost of that vol-

[11] Improvements in propulsion technology have been responsible for much of the progress in aircraft performance. Fuel consumption per hour per pound of thrust has dropped by at least 20 percent during the postwar period (see Boeing Commercial Airplane Company, 1976, p. 41). Moreover, as temperatures have increased and new materials have been employed, the thrust-to-weight ratio of modern turbofan engines has increased by nearly 50 percent during 1960–80. See National Research Council (1985), p. 123.

ume of air travel if DC-3s were employed exclusively.[12] The choice of the DC-3 for comparison is a conservative one, since the operating costs for that aircraft are lower than other contemporary designs. Moreover, by 1939, the base year for the comparison, DC-3 operating costs had declined from their level in 1933, the aircraft's first year of operation. In 1983, on the other hand, both the Boeing 767 and 757 were still relatively new aircraft (1983 was the first full year of operation for the 757) and therefore exhibited operating costs above their long-run level. In addition, of course, the substitution of the twenty-one-seat DC-3 for the current fleet of larger aircraft almost certainly would produce gridlock at the nation's airports because of the huge increase in flights, landings, and takeoffs that would be necessary. This analysis also ignores the value of more rapid travel. The calculation may somewhat overstate the actual savings, however, since the higher costs of transporting current traffic loads in a fleet of DC-3s would be reflected in much higher prices for air transportation and, consequently, lower levels of demand.

Despite these caveats, the calculation suggests that transportation of the 1983 volume of passenger traffic with 1939 technology would cost nearly $24 billion (in 1972 dollars), rather than the current costs of more than $5.8 billion (also in 1972 dollars). According to this measure of technical progress, then, innovation in commercial aircraft during 1939–83 reduced the cost of transporting today's levels of domestic air passenger traffic volume by more than 75 percent.[13]

An additional aspect of technical progress in aircraft is revealed in Table 7.1, which presents operating costs (in 1972 dollars) for both the year of introduction and 1983 for such aircraft as the Boeing 727, the DC-8, and the DC-9. An important element of technical change and performance improvement in commercial aircraft occurs during the operating life of a given airframe design, in the "beta phase" of the innovation process.[14] For the Boeing 247, the first monocoque fuselage passenger aircraft, seat–mile operating costs declined by more than 25 percent during 1933–40. The Lockheed Electra L-188, a four-engine turboprop, exhibited an average annual rate of cost decline of roughly 7 percent, and operating costs for the Boeing 707 declined at an average annual rate of 8.7 percent.[15]

---

[12] The general concept of "social savings" is discussed extensively in Fogel (1964), and critically evaluated in David (1975).

[13] Direct operating costs per seat mile for the DC-3 in 1939 were taken from Phillips (1971); direct operating costs per seat mile and available seat miles for the 1983 fleet were taken from Civil Aeronautics Board (1966–84), vols. I–XVII. The calculations were based on available seat miles rather than actual revenue passenger miles flown. Therefore, they ignore possible differences in load factors between the 1939 and 1983 aircraft fleets.

[14] For further discussion, see Enos (1962) and Rosenberg et al. (1978).

[15] For additional discussion, see Rosenberg et al. (1978) or Mowery and Rosenberg (1982).

Successive stretches of the fuselage of the DC-8, as well as modifications in the wing design, increased AS*V_C from 62,500 for the original DC-8 design to nearly 90,000 in 1983.[16] Similarly, direct operating costs for the DC-9 declined by nearly 50 percent during 1966–83 because of a succession of stretches of the fuselage and the employment of new, fuel-efficient engines.

These reductions in operating costs reflect modifications in aircraft design and improvements in aircraft utilization and maintenance, both of which incorporate important elements of learning in use (see Rosenberg, 1982). Learning by doing characterizes manufacturing processes in which workers and managers improve their skill in the making of the product, and this learning is responsible for the declining cost curves we described here. In addition, however, considerable learning occurs in the course of aircraft operations, reducing the operating costs of the aircraft in use after its manufacture. Much of the reduction in operating costs for commercial aircraft is associated with the accumulation of a body of experience with an aircraft's or engine design's operating characteristics. Only through extensive use is detailed knowledge acquired about engines' operations, their maintenance needs, their minimum servicing and overhaul requirements, and the like.

Such learning by using is significant for several other reasons. It is not unique to commercial aircraft, but characterizes a number of complex capital goods and even software technologies. Learning by using also means that the product support networks of established producers of airframes and engines are important sources of innovations. Careful monitoring of aircraft performance is necessary so that subsequent models of the same design can incorporate the lessons learned from the operating experiences of early models. Airlines, along with technologically sophisticated purchasers in other industries, are major sources of suggestions for change in aircraft design, maintenance, and even production practices. The integration of after-sales maintenance and marketing data with design engineering that the firms in this industry have developed to take advantage of their users' experience is an excellent example of the ways in which the characteristics of this industry's product technology have influenced the organization of R&D (see von Hippel, 1976).

---

[16] AS*V_C figures for the DC-8 are taken from Rosenberg et al. (1978); that for 1983 is from the Civil Aeronautics Board (1966–84). The DC-8 airframe has proved to be so rugged that the original engines recently have been replaced with fuel-efficient CFM56 engines, reducing the aircraft's operating costs and extending its operating life greatly. Indeed, the ease with which the DC-8 can be stretched and reengined has led some observers to conclude that McDonnell Douglas was wrong to close the production line and destroy the tooling for the DC-8 (see Demisch, Demisch, and Concert, 1984).

R&D investment

Although the technology and the characteristic pattern of innovation within the commercial aircraft industry are unusual, the aspect of this industry's development that most clearly distinguishes it from other U.S. manufacturing industries is the structure and amount of public support for innovation. In this section we examine the public and private support for innovation in commercial aircraft. Two issues are especially important in the context of our analysis in Chapter 6 of the changing structure of the U.S. R&D system and the discussion in Chapter 9 of new forms of R&D organization: (1) the relationship between civilian and military R&D funding and innovation, and (2) the role of the federal aeronautics research agency, NACA and NASA, in commercial aircraft innovation.

R&D investment data

Analysis of R&D investment in the commercial aircraft industry requires consistent time-series data. The modest size of the pre-1945 R&D investment, the substantial shift in the technology of commercial aircraft as piston engines were replaced by turbojets, and the absence of reliable data for that period prevent the analysis of pre-1945 data. Appendix I describes the construction of the time series in Table 7.2 and Figure 7.1.

Table 7.2 and Figure 7.1, respectively, contain tabular and graphic representations of R&D investment during 1945–82 in terms of 1972 dollars. Table 7.2 also reports estimates of the cumulative R&D investment from public and private sources.[17] Annual R&D expenditures from all sources rose by more than 224 percent in real terms, from $963 million in 1945 to roughly $3.1 billion in 1982. Military research funding increased from $820 million in 1945 to $2.1 billion in 1982, and if anything, this latter figure may overstate total military research funding, as a result of the adjustment of the post-1969 figures for independent R&D (IR&D). Military R&D investment grew rapidly in the aftermath of World War II and the Korean War mobilization, reaching a plateau in the 1950s and early 1960s. After 1962–63, however, military research funding declined through

---

[17] These "R&D capital stock" estimates were not depreciated for several reasons. The knowledge resulting from the public research investment does not depreciate. The physical research plant employed by NASA and the armed forces does depreciate. Obtaining a reliable time series for the physical capital portion of this public investment proved impossible, however. As for the private R&D investment stock, were this analysis considering the "R&D capital stock" from the point of view of an individual firm, depreciation of this stock would be appropriate, as is frequently done in analyses of private R&D investment (see, e.g., Grabowski and Mueller, 1978). Since this stock is summed across all of the firms in the industry, however, the "spillover" justification for depreciation of this component of the R&D capital stock seems weak.

Table 7.2. *Annual and cumulative R&D investment, 1945–82*
(1972 dollars in millions)

Year	NACA/NASA	Federal Civil Aeronautics R&D (incl. NASA)	Military R&D	Total federal R&D	Industry-financed R&D
1945	79.16	81.79	820.58	902.37	60.69
1946	84.28	86.56	952.16	1,038.72	63.78
1947	60.61	62.63	705.05	767.68	74.75
1948	79.25	83.02	683.02	766.04	90.57
1949	100.95	104.76	788.57	893.33	133.33
1950	97.01	111.94	822.76	934.70	169.78
1951	108.58	127.85	1,185.64	1,313.49	287.22
1952	195.16	219.34	1,884.28	2,103.63	478.41
1953	129.25	170.07	2,574.83	2,744.90	576.53
1954	92.44	134.45	2,793.28	2,927.73	576.47
1955	77.30	123.36	2,587.17	2,710.53	526.32
1956	81.21	160.83	2,562.10	2,722.93	562.10
1957	77.04	200.31	2,654.85	2,855.16	604.01
1958	68.18	201.52	2,780.30	2,981.82	539.39
1959	71.01	224.85	2,569.53	2,794.38	501.48
1960	46.58	216.89	2,196.51	2,413.39	478.89
1961	56.28	220.78	2,295.82	2,516.59	441.56
1962	62.32	152.97	2,286.12	2,439.09	430.59
1963	92.05	200.84	2,776.85	2,977.68	326.36
1964	115.38	192.31	2,663.46	2,855.77	417.58
1965	137.10	205.65	2,505.38	2,711.02	474.46
1966	143.23	329.43	2,621.09	2,950.52	579.43
1967	169.41	453.86	2,441.21	2,895.07	714.29
1968	207.27	326.06	2,429.09	2,755.15	815.76
1969	248.85	398.62	2,111.75	2,510.37	701.61
1970	217.72	263.68	2,410.96	2,674.63	678.76
1971	218.75	294.79	2,282.44	2,577.23	536.10
1972	236.00	331.00	2,429.60	2,760.60	513.40
1973	296.12	367.08	2,082.63	2,449.71	419.73
1974	241.53	305.82	1,800.81	2,106.63	378.16
1975	249.60	308.43	1,571.56	1,879.99	306.81
1976	245.65	309.90	1,779.50	2,089.40	344.46
1977	270.00	336.43	1,953.17	2,289.60	376.83
1978	291.33	354.00	2,338.99	2,692.99	515.68
1979	317.63	373.32	1,936.97	2,310.29	624.23
1980	313.90	367.15	1,933.35	2,300.50	688.00
1981	268.92	323.11	2,021.81	2,344.92	733.81
1982	248.79	287.85	2,102.72	2,390.57	732.14
Cumulative R&D	6,095.85	9,013.21	77,335.93	86,349.14	17,493.47

Sources: See text.

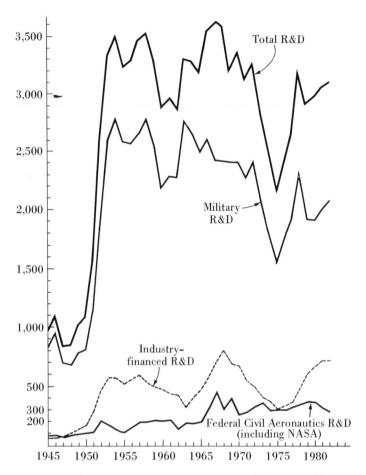

Figure 7.1. Annual R&D investment, 1945–82 (1972 dollars, in millions). *Source:* See Appendix, Chapter 7.

the late 1960s. Throughout the postwar period, the military portion of total annual R&D expenditures has not fallen below 65 percent.

NASA research funding has grown slowly since 1945 and has remained essentially constant since the late 1960s. The diminishing importance of NACA research funding in aircraft also is apparent in Table 7.2. NACA/ NASA research support exceeded industry-financed industry R&D investment in 1945, but by the mid-1950s NACA accounted for less than 20 percent of industry-financed R&D expenditures. By the late 1970s, however, as industry-financed R&D declined in real terms, the relative importance of NASA funding increased substantially, even as the rate of growth of that funding declined. Other federal agencies supporting aeronautics R&D include the Atomic Energy Commission, which funded research on nuclear propulsion of aircraft and space vehicles, and the Federal Aviation Administration, which supported research on avionics and the supersonic transport during the 1960s.

Industry-financed research expenditures fluctuated around an essentially flat trend during this period, in some contrast to the pattern of privately financed R&D in U.S. manufacturing overall. Figure 7.1 clearly indicates the successive waves of investment in the development of the three generations of airframes and engines during the postwar period: R&D expenditures grew rapidly during the early 1950s, the period of development of the first commercial jet aircraft; during the late 1960s, as the first wide-body transports and high-bypass engines were developed; and during the late 1970s, with the development of the most recent generation of smaller aircraft equipped with high-bypass engines.

The cumulative 1945–82 R&D investment in aircraft from all sources amounts to nearly $104 billion in 1972 dollars. Of this total, almost 75 percent, $77 billion, was provided by military sources. Industry-financed R&D during the period amounted to $17.4 billion, roughly 15 percent of the total. Federal nonmilitary research funding was a small portion of the total investment, totaling some $9 billion. Clearly, this enormous public investment was not intended solely to support technological innovation in commercial aricraft; national security considerations dominated the vast majority of the expenditures. Nonetheless, the federal investment in military aircraft technology has had a significant impact on the course of innovation in commercial aircraft.

The role of NACA and NASA

The commercial aircraft industry is unique among manufacturing industries in that a federal research organization, the National Advisory Committee on Aeronautics (absorbed by the National Aeronautics and Space Administration in 1958), has for many years conducted and funded research on airframe and propulsion technologies. Both NACA and NASA have been cited by scholars as models for publicly supported, precommercial research cooperation between industry and government (Nelson, 1981, 1982). In order to assess the implications of NACA and NASA for other industries, it is necessary to examine the development and structure of the research program.

Established in 1915, NACA was intended to "investigate the scientific problems involved in flight and to give advice to the military air services and other aviation services of the government (Ames, 1925). Although it was founded shortly before U.S. entry into World War I, NACA did not confine its research solely to military aircraft, but worked on problems of aerodynamics and aeronautics common to both military and commercial sectors.

Using experimental facilities at Langley Field, Virginia, and after 1940 at Moffett Field, California, and Cleveland, Ohio, NACA was an important source of performance and other test data in aeronautics. The committee pioneered in the construction and use of large wind tunnels, completing one in 1927 that could accommodate full-scale airframes. This and other facilities provided a steady stream of test results that led to major improvements in airframe design. The famous "NACA cowl" for radial air-cooled engines reduced wind resistance and cut airframe drag by nearly 75 percent. NACA research also demonstrated the superior performance of airframes with retractable landing gear and led to important modifications in the positioning of engines in aircraft wings.[18] Total appropriations for NACA from 1915 to 1940 amounted to $81 million in 1972 dollars, less than one-third of NASA's annual appropriation for aeronautics research in the late 1970s.

Before World War II, NACA operated primarily as a test center, providing excellent facilities to both civilian and military users. Significantly, and in contrast to the postwar period, the prewar NACA owned few test aircraft.[19] Reflecting its limited budget and staff, however, NACA carried out very little research during this period that could be described as "basic." Indeed, one account of the development of the jet engine characterized the United States before 1940 as a backwater of research in theoretical aerodynamics, attributing the failure of American engineers to appreciate the possibilities of jet-powered aircraft to their ignorance of aeronautical design theory (see Constant, 1980).

As World War II approached, NACA focused increasingly on military aircraft design, to the partial exclusion of civilian aircraft research. After World War II, during which NACA work was exclusively military, the structure of the aeronautics research system in the United States changed considerably. Major aircraft procedures had acquired substantial in-house

---

[18] "By a comprehensive survey of the net efficiencies of various engine nacelle locations, the optimum position in the wing was found. This N.A.C.A. engine location principle, together with other refinements, had a revolutionary effect on military and commercial aviation the world over. It changed military aviation tactics, made long-range bombers possible, and forced the development of higher speed pursuit planes. In the commercial field it permitted the speeding up of cruising schedules on the air lines from 120 miles per hour of the Fords to the 180 miles per hour of the new Douglas planes. The overnight transcontinental run became possible and the air lines vastly increased their appeal to the public. Even in the midst of the depression, air line traffic boomed" (Hunsaker, 1941, p. 139).

[19] "The old NACA was strictly a research, test, and advisory organization. It built, modified, and owned few aircraft and in the main only tested aircraft submitted to it for evaluation, or 'debugging' " (Legislative Reference Service, 1966, p. 107).

facilities of their own during the war;[20] NACA's research infrastructure was now less critical. Military support of industry R&D also grew in importance after World War II. Despite expansion in its annual budget, which by 1944 exceeded the cumulative total of appropriations during 1915–40, NACA declined in importance. The agency remained an important sponsor of fundamental academic research, however, and continued to conduct empirical research.

During the early postwar period, NACA expanded its research activities in rocketry. Then, in 1958, in the wake of the Soviet launch of Sputnik, NACA was absorbed by the National Aeronautics and Space Administration. As NASA undertook a massive expansion of space exploration activities, its aeronautics research declined in importance. A 1966 Senate study noted, "Space budget demands have probably hampered what might have been expected to be a normal growth of the level of effort in aeronautics within the agency" (Legislative Reference Service, p. 20). In the aftermath of the Apollo program, as NASA's operating budget increasingly was hostage to the fortunes of the space shuttle, budgetary pressures on aeronautics research programs mounted. Appropriations for aeronautics research continued to grow during the 1970s, but more slowly than had been true of the 1960s. Moreover, the modest growth in real spending for NASA aeronautics programs during the 1970s and 1980s masked an apparent decline in the R&D component of NASA's aeronautics research program.[21]

Despite its reduced importance after World War II, NACA/NASA played an important strategic role in supporting research on commercial aircraft technologies. NACA/NASA projects frequently involved two or more erstwhile competitor firms, encouraging some pooling of research efforts and results within the industry. Further, NACA sponsored a liberal system of cross-licensing of patents, disbanded in 1975 because of the objections of the Antitrust Division of the Justice Department. That system

---

[20] The National Research Council's surveys of industrial research laboratories before and after World War II convey some idea of the expansion of the aircraft industry's in-house research capabilities. The in-house research staff at Douglas Aircraft grew from 22 in 1940 to 111 in 1946; the research staff at the Glenn Martin Company grew from 42 to 76; Lockheed's grew from 10 to 314; Consolidated Vultee's grew from 12 to 195; United Aircraft, which included Pratt and Whitney, Hamilton Standard, and Sikorsky, increased its research staff from 80 to 732; and Curtiss-Wright expanded its research employment from 14 in 1940 to 149 in 1946. These figures are even more impressive in view of the fact that these firms' military aircraft sales, especially to Britain and France, had already expanded considerably by 1940. See National Research Council (1940, 1946).

[21] National Research Council, Aeronautics Science and Engineering Board (1982). The other components of the NASA aeronautics budget are "Construction of Facilities" and "Research and Program Management." Growth in NASA aeronautics R&D expenditures includes increases in the costs of staff, management, and construction, at the expense of research programs.

aided the development of a widely shared technology base within the
U.S. commercial aircraft industry.[22]

Both NASA and NACA did more than simply support research yielding
results that were diffused widely within the industry; they underwrote a
portion of the costs of the research infrastructure associated with innovation in airframes and engines. The net social loss associated with private
firms' pursuit of duplicative, parallel R&D programs has been noted by
Hirshleifer (1971) and Nelson (1981), among others. Industrywide research facilities of the sort maintained by NASA and NACA can reduce a
portion of this duplication. Of course, NASA test facilities were and are
by no means the only ones available to U.S. commercial aircraft firms.
Individual firms maintain extensive testing and design facilities, to preserve the proprietary nature of some data and test results. Nonetheless,
NASA facilities complement the privately funded R&D infrastructure and
reduce the total costs of R&D to the industry. Estimates prepared by a
subcommittee of NASA's Advisory Committee on Aeronautics in 1981
suggested that if the NASA aeronautics research program were termi-
nated and private commercial aircraft and engine firms individually supported only one-half of the NASA research programs of relevance to them
during 1982–91 and collaborated on 18 percent of these programs, the
net additional costs of maintaining parallel and duplicative research programs would amount to nearly $1 billion in 1972 dollars.[23]

Military-sponsored research

A final source of external support for commercial aircraft innovation is the
research and procurement of the U.S. armed forces. As the data in Table
7.2 indicate, military sources have provided the vast majority of the large
research investment in the aircraft industry during the postwar period.

---

[22] Miller and Sawers (1968) described the Manufacturers' Aviation Association (MAA) licensing system as a system "under which all aircraft manufacturers agreed to let all their
competitors use their patents. No member can have a patent monopoly on any inventions
which his staff can make, or even for any invention that he may license from an outside
inventor. If he takes an exclusive license, the patent has to be available to the other
members of the MAA; but the original licensee can claim that he should be granted
compensation by the other licensees. Manufacturers apparently believe that it is a good
bargain to give up their right to a patent monopoly in return for the protection from
litigation with other companies in the industry that the right to use their patents brings"
(pp. 255–6). Roland (1985) discusses the origins of the cross-licensing agreement (pp. 37–
43).
[23] See the "Draft Interim Report of the Ad Hoc Informal Subcommittee on NASA Aeronautical Projects," NASA Aeronautics Advisory Committee (1983). These estimates should
be viewed as illustrative of general orders of magnitude, rather than precise figures. In
addition, of course, any assessment of the net benefits resulting from the investment in
NASA research infrastructure must consider the potential returns from alternative investments of public funds.

With the possible exception of IR&D, this research investment was not intended to support innovation in any but military airframe and propulsion technologies. It has nevertheless yielded indirect but important technological spillovers to the commercial aircraft industry, notably in aircraft engines. From the Pratt and Whitney Wasp of 1925 to the high-bypass turbofans of the 1980s, commercial aircraft engine development has benefited from and frequently has followed the demands of military procurement and military-supported research. The development of the first U.S. jet engine was financed entirely by the military. More recently, military-supported research on turbofan engines for the C-5A transport influenced the development of the high-bypass engines that power the latest generation of commercial transports, including the Airbus Industrie A300, A310, and A320, as well as the Boeing 737-300, 747, 757, and 767.

Military–civilian technological spillovers have been most important in aircraft propulsion technologies. The development of commercial aircraft also has benefited, however, from military-sponsored research and procurement in airframes. The importance of technological spillovers in airframe design and development has fluctuated over time, as we noted in Chapter 6. After World War II, the development of jet-powered strategic bombers and tankers allowed airframe makers to apply knowledge gained in military projects to commercial aircraft design, tooling, and production. The Boeing 707, for example, was based closely on the design of a tanker, the KC-135, developed by Boeing to provide in-flight refueling for the strategic bombers (the B-47 and B-52) developed previously by the firm. A major share of the development costs for the 707 was borne by the KC-135, as a comparison of these costs with those for the DC-8 reveals:

> Douglas lost $109 million in the two years 1959 and 1960, having written off $298 million for development costs and production losses up to the end of 1960. Boeing did not suffer so badly. They wrote off $165 million on the 707 by then; some of the development costs may have been carried by the tanker program, which also provided a few of the tools on which the airliner was built. (Miller and Sawers, 1968, pp. 193–4)

Increasing divergences between civilian and military aircraft technologies, as well as the absence of major defense procurement and development programs in large transports since the late 1960s, have reduced the amount and significance of military–civilian technological spillover. Spillover from military to civilian applications remain significant in the areas of propulsion, avionics, and flight-control systems, but their importance has declined. Both aircraft and engine producers therefore must rely more heavily on industry-financed R&D. Assumption of a greater share of this financial burden by the private firms in the industry has increased considerably the financial risks of developing new aircraft.

Industry-financed R&D

The commercial aircraft industry's R&D contribution has been a strikingly small share of total industry R&D throughout the postwar period, despite rapid growth in this research investment. Industry-financed R&D expenditures throughout 1945–82 rarely accounted for more than 30 percent of total R&D. Industry expenditures grew substantially as a share of nonmilitary research expenditures during the early postwar period, reflecting the growth of large in-house research establishments and soaring development costs for commercial aircraft. From 42 percent of nondefense R&D spending in 1946, the industry share rose to nearly 64 percent by 1969. During the 1970s, however, the NASA research budget grew substantially relative to that of industry.

The composition of expenditures

Table 7.3 presents data on the composition of R&D expenditures in the aircraft industry (including both military and commercial aircraft) from both public and private sources for the 1945–69 period. Although these data cover only 1945–69, the shares of the R&D categories are quite stable, and these data therefore should depict industry R&D investment patterns accurately during the 1970s and 1980s as well. One of the most striking findings is the small portion of total industry R&D (both privately and publicly funded) that goes to basic research. That category accounted for less than 10 percent of total R&D expenditures from 1945 through 1969. Moreover, the industry-financed share of basic research also is less than 10 percent: Industry-financed basic research accounts for less than 1 percent of total aircraft R&D during this period. Public sources, primarily the Air Force, Navy, and NASA (in the 1960s), supported most of the basic research in this industry.

Applied research accounts for a greater share of total research investment; industry supported 34 percent of this class of R&D expenditures, substantially exceeding its share of basic research. Development expenditures are by far the largest share of total R&D investment throughout 1945–69, never falling below 60 percent of the total. Military funds account for the largest share of development expenses. The Air Force alone supported more than 50 percent of all development expenses during 1953–66, and development expenditures accounted for more than 70 percent of total Air Force research support during the entire 1945–69 period. In-

Table 7.3. Composition of R&D expenditures in aircraft, 1945–69 (nominal dollars)

	Industry-financed basic research	Military-funded basic research	Federally funded nonmilitary basic research	Total basic research	Industry-funded applied research	Military-funded applied research	Federally funded nonmilitary applied research	Total applied research	Industry-funded development	Military-funded development	Federally funded nonmilitary development	Total development
1945	2	15	5	22	20	41	6	67	18	238	20	276
1946	2	19	6	27	25	55	7	87	22	323	25	370
1947	3	16	5	24	33	44	6	83	29	261	20	310
1948	4	16	7	27	42	46	8	96	37	265	29	331
1949	6	18	9	33	62	50	10	122	56	292	36	384
1950	9	18	9	36	86	51	10	147	76	292	46	414
1951	17	25	11	53	170	70	12	252	153	406	51	610
1952	29	40	19	88	286	111	21	418	257	645	91	993
1953	35	57	13	105	353	161	14	528	317	930	69	1,316
1954	35	65	9	109	354	101	10	545	319	1,051	56	1,426
1955	33	61	8	102	332	173	9	514	298	996	66	1,360
1956	36	63	9	108	356	175	10	541	319	1,013	89	1,421
1957	39	67	9	115	387	188	10	585	298	1,087	84	1,518
1958	36	74	8	118	358	206	9	573	319	1,196	97	1,615
1959	32	70	8	110	329	198	9	536	347	1,150	108	1,555
1960	31	61	5	97	310	170	6	486	322	988	118	1,384
1961	30	65	7	102	300	182	7	489	297	1,051	70	1,390
1962	30	66	6	102	303	183	15	501	278	1,064	84	1,420
1963	29	85	11	125	290	238	28	556	269	1,375	100	1,733
1964	30	82	14	126	301	229	29	559	272	1,330	92	1,693
1965	33	78	17	128	329	217	35	581	258	1,265	96	1,656
1966	41	81	19	141	406	227	23	656	365	1,338	211	1,914
1967	51	73	23	147	509	204	27	740	457	1,202	309	1,968
1968	58	76	29	163	577	211	33	821	519	1,236	207	1,962
1969	53	70	37	160	533	195	43	771	480	1,129	266	1,875

Source: Booz, Allen and Hamilton Applied Research, Inc. (1971), Table C-15.

dustry funds never accounted for more than 15 percent of total development expenses.

Table 7.4 presents the shares of total R&D investment accounted for by various segments of an aircraft. Although airframes account for the largest single share of total R&D investment from all sources – 40–45 percent – avionics absorb a larger share of R&D total investment than do engines throughout the postwar period. Surprisingly, in view of the rapid growth in the sophistication and cost of avionics during the period, the share of total R&D accounted for by avionics is quite stable. Consistent with the preceding discussion, most aircraft industry R&D expenditures are devoted to the integration of the components and subsystems of an aircraft, rather than to their separate development. To some extent, this characteristic of aircraft R&D investment also reflects the fact that the costs of developing many of the major components and systems in an aircraft are borne by other industries. Although these costs are reflected in the cost of components, they are excluded from aircraft industry R&D investment data.

R&D investment: Conclusion

During the postwar period, the commercial aircraft industry has benefited from substantial direct (NASA and NACA) and indirect (military research and IR&D) federal financial support for research. The size of the federal R&D investment, as well as the existence of a dedicated civilian technology development program, renders the aircraft industry unique among U.S. manufacturing industries. Both NACA and NASA were centers for generic research and reduced the costs to industry of R&D through operation and construction of testing and research installations. Moreover, both civilian and military research programs encouraged the wide diffusion of technological knowledge within the aircraft industry, supporting the development of a readily accessible industry knowledge base. In this way, the federal programs operated in a fashion that closely resembles the cooperative R&D programs in the Japanese economy.[24]

Nonetheless, federal R&D priorities in the aircraft industry resemble the broader pattern of federal research funding throughout the U.S. economy, insofar as they were motivated throughout the postwar period primarily by national security requirements. The civilian share of the total federal R&D investment (largely NASA funded) is, after all, only slightly more than 10 percent. Technological development in this industry, as in others, has relied heavily on technological spillovers from military to ci-

---

[24] For additional discussion of Japanese cooperative R&D programs, see Okimoto (1983) and Peck and Goto (1981). The analogy between U.S. aeronautics R&D and these Japanese programs is developed in greater detail in Mowery and Rosenberg (1985).

Table 7.4. *Aeronautical R&D funds used by industry, classified by aircraft component (annual expenditures in millions of dollars)*

Fiscal year	Airframe	Engine	Avionics	Total
1945	118	66	79	263
1946	153	85	102	340
1947	138	76	91	305
1948	148	82	99	329
1949	184	102	123	409
1950	212	117	141	470
1951	332	184	221	737
1952	550	306	366	1,222
1953	716	397	477	1,590
1954	759	422	505	1,686
1955	715	397	476	1,588
1956	749	416	499	1,664
1957	815	453	543	1,811
1958	834	463	556	1,853
1959	795	441	530	1,766
1960	711	395	473	1,579
1961	730	406	486	1,622
1962	729	405	485	1,619
1963	852	473	568	1,893
1964	843	468	562	1,873
1965	845	469	563	1,877
1966	982	546	655	2,183
1967	1,056	587	703	2,349
1968	1,098	610	733	2,441
1969	1,026	570	685	2,281

Source: Booz, Allen, and Hamilton Applied Research, Inc. (1971), Table C-21.

vilian applications. Such spillovers now appear to be less significant, however, and their very direction may have been reversed in a number of aircraft technologies.

The demand for innovation: The role of government regulation

The federal government played an important role in supporting aircraft industry research, thereby expanding the supply of relevant technology.

In addition, however, federal policies affected the speed with which innovations were embodied in commercial aircraft innovations. Civil Aeronautics Board (CAB) regulation from 1938 to 1978 supported rapid adoption of commercial aircraft innovations. Indeed, U.S. government policy toward the industry throughout the postwar period is unusual in its impact on both the supply and the demand for application of that knowledge in innovation.

The policies of the Post Office in the 1929–34 period and those of the Civil Aeronautics Board during 1938–78 created strong incentives for rapid adoption of innovations in commercial aircraft. Airmail transport operations were transferred from the Post Office to private contractors in 1925 after passage of the Kelly Air Mail Act. Bids were opened to private contractors, who were paid on a weight basis. During the ensuing five years, congressional reductions in airmail postal rates resulted in greater airmail volume, while payments to airmail operators remained unchanged. As a result, airmail contractor profits increased considerably.[25] Reflecting the growth of the mail-carriage aircraft market, such aircraft as the Boeing 40 were designed primarily for mail rather than passenger transport.

Following passage of the McNary–Watres Act of 1930, Postmaster General Walter I. Brown encouraged the growth of a smaller number of large trunk carriers who would derive more of their revenues from passenger transport. The act changed the method for computing payments for mail carriage from a pound–mile basis to a space–mile basis; payment was made whether or not mail was carried in an aircraft. Extra payments were made to carriers that used multiengine aircraft, radio, and other navigational aids. The final major section of the McNary–Watres Act was to be its undoing, as it conferred substantial discretionary powers on the Postmaster General to alter route structures or merge carriers, when "in his judgment the public interest will be promoted thereby." Brown orchestrated the merger of Transcontinental Air Transport and Western Air Express into TWA and worked to develop a small number of financially strong, transcontinental carriers who would provide a strong market for larger, more comfortable passenger transports. These policies coincided with rapid growth in passenger traffic and the introduction of the monocoque fuselage air transports, the B-247 and the DC-2, which were of great importance in the development of the commercial aircraft and air transportation industries. Although Brown partially achieved his goals, his tactics produced a furor that resulted (well after his departure from office) in the Air Mail Act of 1934, mandating divestiture by aircraft pro-

[25] Smith (1944) states that "compensation to carriers rose from 22.6 cents an airplane mile prior to July 1, 1926, to 73.6 cents a mile for the second half of 1927. . . . by the end of 1928, however, payments were up to 92 cents a mile, and by the end of 1929 the government was paying the operators $1.09 a mile for carrying the mail" (p. 125).

ducers of their transport subsidiaries and stipulating that mail contracts would pay carriers on a per-ounce basis only and would be awarded strictly to the lowest bidder.

Continued congressional dissatisfaction with air transportation safety and regulatory policy led to the establishment of the Civil Aeronautics Board in 1938. Through its issuance of operating certificates and its oversight of airline fares, the board effectively controlled pricing policies of airlines and entry into or exit from air transportation during 1938–78. These powers were used throughout the postwar period to prevent entry into scheduled trunkline air transportation and to prevent price competition. The CAB also controlled the award of routes to airlines; in general, multiple carriers were allowed to operate only in "major" city-pair markets (such as New York to Los Angeles or New York to Chicago). Less important routes often were monopolized by a single carrier.

CAB regulation led to intense service-quality competition. One result of that competition was rapid adoption of new aircraft designs by the major carriers, in the belief that early introduction of state-of-the-art aircraft was an effective marketing strategy where price competition was prohibited.[26] The drive to be first with a new design was one of the central motives for the willingness of major airlines to make early purchase commitments to aircraft manufacturers as a means of obtaining the earliest possible delivery. The importance of an early position in the delivery queue also allowed aircraft manufacturers to defray a portion of the costs of developing a new aircraft through advance payments by airlines seeking early delivery. Thus, CAB regulation encouraged a rapid pace of innovation and adoption in the commercial aircraft and air transportation industries.

Rapid innovation and adoption, however, and the associated impressive productivity growth in U.S. domestic air transportation, came at considerable cost. Consumer welfare also was impaired by the lack of variety in service quality and price. Government regulation restricted the range within which consumers were free to trade off price against quality. The U.S. General Accounting Office (GAO, 1977), employing a model based on Keeler (1972), concluded that an efficient, deregulated air transportation system would have cost consumers $1.4–$1.8 billion (in nominal dollars) less during each year between 1969–74. Since lower fares would lead

---

[26] Jordan's study (1970) compared California's intrastate air carriers (not regulated by the CAB, and subject to price competition and easier entry) with the interstate carriers in the speed of adoption of cabin pressurization and jet aircraft: "The trunk carriers were consistently the first to introduce each innovation. In fact, they introduced all but two of the over 40 aircraft types operated by all three carrier groups between 1946 and 1965. In addition, they adopted these innovations rapidly and extensively. The local carriers, on the other hand, were slow to introduce the two innovations and their rates of adoption were low" (p. 53).

to more traffic, the GAO calculation almost certainly understated the total annual costs. In other words, a cost equal to nearly two-thirds of the total annual R&D investment flow in this industry (in 1970, slightly more than $3 billion in nominal dollars) was borne by the traveling public as the cost of the regulatory framework that encouraged rapid diffusion of commercial aircraft innovations.[27]

The direction of innovation was also affected by this regulatory structure. The growth of the U.S. market for commuter aircraft was stunted by CAB policies. Weak demand for aircraft with sixty or fewer seats reflected the fact that the route structures developed by the major carriers emphasized long-haul, "point-to-point" service. Indeed, for much of the regulated period, trunk carriers subsidized their short-haul routes from profits earned in long-haul service, restricting further the possibilities for entry into short-haul service. Throughout the postwar period, the development of short-haul aircraft with more than nineteen seats was confined largely to Europe and Canada, where Fokker, Aerospatiale, Shorts Brothers, British Aerospace, DeHavilland, and other firms developed commuter aircraft. Rapid growth in the U.S. commuter market since 1978 has primarily benefited these and other foreign producers.

Deregulation of domestic air transport in 1978 affected the market for aircraft and engines in several ways. Service-quality competition has declined greatly in importance. As a result, major U.S. airlines are less eager now to adopt new aircraft without significant improvements in seat–mile operating costs. The early years of the deregulated era also were characterized by upheaval in the U.S. airline industry as low-cost entrants jeopardized the position of established carriers. An enduring characteristic of the deregulated era is likely to be a much greater reluctance of major airlines to commit funds (in the form of advance orders, etc.) to major new aircraft development. Aircraft producers now are less able to share the risks of new product development with major customers. The exit of Lockheed from commercial aircraft manufacture and the cautious policies of McDonnell Douglas in new product development may be among the legacies of deregulation of U.S. air transportation.

Evaluating technology policy in commercial aircraft

Federal policy toward research and innovation in the U.S. commercial aircraft industry affected both the supply of innovations and the incentives for their embodiment in new commercial aircraft. An evaluation of

[27] Despite their protection from entry during the period of regulation, the airlines earned, on average, only a normal rate of return on capital; as Keeler (1972) noted, "It would appear that with fares set at high, cartel levels, the airlines have competed away profits through excess capacity" (p. 421). Service-quality competition caused costs to rise to the level of fares, as Douglas and Miller (1974) noted, and largely prevented airlines from profitably exploiting their protected position.

this policy structure must take account of the costs of both the "supply-push" and "demand-pull" components. Measuring the economic benefits of technical change in commercial aircraft is hampered by the absence of reliable time series on operating costs and performance characteristics. The estimate of the "social savings" from aircraft innovation concluded that the cumulative investment of $26 billion from industry and federal civilian R&D programs yielded an annual flow of social savings, as of 1983, of $18 billion in 1972 dollars. If CAB regulation played a central role in the rapid adoption of new commercial aircraft, however, the costs of such regulation should be included in any evaluation. An illustrative computation of the costs and benefits (primarily lower operating costs) of this federal policy structure (Mowery, 1986b), found that when the costs to consumers of CAB regulation are included, the estimated social rate of return on the substantial public and private R&D investment (including some share of military R&D spending, to account for spillovers), is negative, regardless of assumptions concerning the length of time needed to adopt commercial aircraft innovations or the fraction of military R&D that yielded commercial spillovers. Despite its positive impact on the adoption of commercial aircraft innovations, then, the costs to consumers of CAB regulation appear sufficiently large to offset the positive returns to the public R&D investment yielded by improvements in aircraft performance.

These illustrative computations employed a limited definition of benefits. Benefits resulting from technological improvements were restricted entirely to operating cost reductions, rather than improvements in aircraft safety or speed. The omission of improvements in aircraft speed would indeed understate benefits in a comparison of an all-piston engine fleet with an all-jet fleet. In fact, however, the average cruising speed of the U.S. domestic fleet has increased only modestly during 1966–84, reflecting the widespread adoption of jet aircraft by 1966. Incorporating estimates of the value of savings in travel time does not significantly affect the results.

More significant, perhaps, is the failure of the estimates to consider the larger benefits to the national economy of federal policy's support for the U.S. commercial aircraft industry. Throughout the postwar period, the United States was the largest single market for commercial aircraft. Although formal protection of the U.S. commercial aircraft market was modest during the postwar period, the importance of close producer–purchaser contacts in the finance, design, and performance-monitoring phases of new aircraft development conferred substantial advantages on U.S. producers in this market.[28] By supporting U.S. domestic demand

---

[28] The study by Phillips (1971) of the demand by trunk airlines for transports found that controlling for other performance characteristics, regardless of the national identity of the

for long-haul commercial aircraft, CAB regulation enabled U.S. producers to gain experience in the production and design of aircraft with a large foreign as well as domestic market.

Federal support for research, as well as for diffusion and adoption of innovations, in the domestic commercial aircraft market thus may have enhanced the international competitiveness of the industry and expanded its export markets. In view of the fact that commercial aircraft now represent the largest single category of manufacturing exports from the United States, this impact on competitiveness was extremely important. To assess the significance of such benefits, however, one must compare the income and other benefits of job creation in the commercial aircraft industry with those that would have resulted from the employment of the commercial aircraft industry labor force in other economic sectors. The human resources and physical capital devoted to the production of commercial aircraft would not have remained unemployed in the absence of federal policies supporting research and the adoption of commercial aircraft. Although CAB regulation aided U.S. producers of large commercial transports, it also discouraged domestic demand and innovation in the commuter segment of the aircraft industry, contributing to U.S. producers' failure to enter that global market.

International collaborative ventures in commercial aircraft

Changes in the technology policy structure we discussed earlier in this chapter have brought about considerable change in the organization of product development and manufacturing activities in the commercial aircraft industry during the past decade. This industry was one of the first major U.S. manufacturing industries to pursue international collaborative ventures in the development, manufacture, and marketing of its products. In this section we analyze the causes and consequences of this shift, a topic to which we give more extensive attention in Chapter 9.

Since the early 1970s, the product development and manufacture process within the U.S. commercial aircraft industry has been transformed from one carried out largely within U.S. firms to one involving collaboration among U.S. and foreign firms (Mowery, 1987). With few exceptions, no commercial aircraft or engine introduced since 1975 has been developed or manufactured solely by one of the major U.S. producers.

As we noted previously, the commercial aircraft industry was the ben-

producer, foreign commercial transports were less attractive than those manufactured in the United States to the U.S. domestic airlines during the postwar period (p. 102).

eficiary of a unique federal policy structure for much of the postwar period. The changes discussed earlier in three critical components of this
domestic policy structure, however, severely affected the industry. Deregulation of domestic air transportation in 1978, a decline in the commonality of military and civilian aircraft technology, and some erosion in
the aeronautics research and technology budget with NASA – all combined with steady growth in development costs – made market demand
more uncertain and increased the financial risks borne by aircraft and
engine producers.

The U.S. aircraft industry during the 1970s and 1980s was also affected
by developments in the world market. One of the most important was the
decline in the rate of growth of demand for commercial air travel in the
United States, relative to the rest of the world (notably, the industrializing nations of East Asia). Between 1950 and 1970, U.S. airlines purchased
67 percent of the aircraft produced by U.S. firms, and the United States
accounted for 57 percent of total world revenue passenger miles flown in
1971. During the 1970s, however, reflecting demographic factors as well
as slower U.S. economic growth, air travel in the United States grew at
an annual rate of 5 percent, well below the average of 9 percent in other
regions. Between 1977 and 1982, only 40 percent of all orders for new
commercial aircraft were placed by U.S. carriers.

The U.S. market for commercial aircraft is still the largest single market
within the world market, but it no longer constitutes an absolute majority
of world demand. Moreover, current trends are expected to continue,
resulting in a decline in the U.S. share of world air traffic to roughly 36
percent by 1990.[29] Because of the steady increase in development costs,
a new commercial aircraft or engine cannot achieve financial success without substantial foreign sales. Penetration of foreign markets, always important to U.S. firms, now is essential. But the sheer size of the U.S.
market means that U.S. sales are critical to the commercial success of
foreign aircraft as well.

Growth in the foreign market for aircraft, engines, and components,
increased use of trade-distorting subsidies to finance development and
sale of commercial aircraft, and the desire of foreign producers to eliminate the tariff on U.S. imports of aircraft, engines, and components resulted in a unique trade document, the Agreement on Trade in Civil
Aircraft, negotiated under the auspices of the General Agreement on Tariffs and Trade (GATT) and effective as of January 1, 1980. The agreement
abolished all customs duties on aircraft and components and instituted

---

[29] Data on world and U.S. market demand are taken from National Reearch Council (1985).

multilateral controls on government procurement and public subsidies for the development and sale of aircraft.[30]

U.S. exports of aircraft parts and components grew rapidly after the signing of the agreement: Exports of components and other parts grew at an average annual rate of 36 percent from 1977 to 1982, from roughly $2 billion to more than $4 billion. Exports of aircraft engines increased from slightly more than $200 million to more than $800 million during the same period (U.S. Department of Commerce, 1984, p. 31). Reflecting this rapid expansion in components trade, U.S. content in many aircraft produced by foreign firms now is substantial. Approximately 30 percent of the value of the Airbus A300, for example, is considered to be U.S.-produced components,[31] while estimates of the U.S. content of the Embraer Bandeirante, produced in Brazil, range around 40 percent. Because many joint ventures depend on extensive international flows of components and parts, the treaty has supported the rise of international collaboration. Indeed, a major factor behind U.S. support for the agreement was the desire of major U.S. producers to expand their offshore procurement of components.

International collaboration within this industry has focused on product development and manufacture, reflecting the fact that the critical competitive assets are product design and manufacturing expertise. Access to foreign markets, risk sharing, and access to low-cost capital are the major motives for collaboration between U.S. and foreign commercial aircraft firms. Market access is especially important in this industry because foreign markets for commercial aircraft, like those for telecommunications equipment, are characterized by heavy government involvement (as owners of the service enterprises, be these Postal Telegraph and Telephone [PTTs] entities or airlines, or as owners of producers of telecommunications or aircraft equipment). Foreign governments in many cases are increasingly interested in collaborating with U.S. firms in order to support an established aircraft production and design capability or to develop such a capability through technology transfer.

In most cases, collaboration between U.S. and foreign aircraft firms has

---

[30] For a more detailed discussion of the agreement, see Piper (1979, 1980).

[31] Airbus Industrie is currently working to reduce the U.S. content in its new aircraft design: "To ensure that the European partners obtain a bigger share on the A320, the past reliance on U.S. manufacturers will be reduced. There are two other reasons for this trend: with the experience of the A300 and A310 behind it Europe now feels more technically able to produce its own equipment. Secondly, the Europeans believe that they have lost aircraft sales due to the amount of U.S. equipment which the aircraft contained. They cite a potential contract for ten A300s with Libya which was blocked because Libya is on the U.S. embargo list" (Reed, 1984, p. 33). Current estimates of the U.S. content of the A320, for example, are as low as 20 percent. See "U.S.-European Trade Talks Focus on Subsidy Issues," *Aviation Week and Space Technology*, March 31, 1986, p. 36.

resulted in outflows of technology from U.S. to foreign firms. Technology transfer between U.S. and foreign firms within these collaborations, however, is not a one-way flow. Boeing and General Electric, for example, have transferred technology to foreign firms through their joint ventures. The "balance of trade" in other ventures, such as the failed collaboration between Saab-Scandia Aircraft of Sweden and Fairchild of the United States, or the International Aero Engines consortium, may be more even.

International collaborative ventures have not yet produced serious competitive threats to the major U.S. aircraft and engine firms. Technology transfer within these ventures is insufficient to enable foreign participants to enter the world commercial aircraft industry as a "prime contractor" in the near future. Indeed, the rise of the European Airbus Industrie consortium, which has motivated much of the international collaboration in the U.S. commercial aircraft industry, owes little to collaboration between U.S. and European firms in commercial aircraft production or development. In this case at least, international collaboration appears to be a result, rather than a cause, of intensified international competition with U.S. firms.

International collaborative ventures do appear to have increased competitive pressures, however, on the U.S. firms producing components and parts for commercial airframes and engines. International collaboration is contributing to the broader expansion of worldwide sourcing of components and parts, which benefits many U.S. firms, as we noted earlier. Nevertheless, continued international collaboration will in the long run require U.S. parts and components producers to improve their technological and competitive performance and may result in increased international collaboration within this segment of the U.S. industry.

Conclusion

The effects of federal R&D investment on the postwar commercial aircraft industry were enhanced by the conjunction of research support with a regulatory policy that facilitated the rapid diffusion of innovations, albeit at considerable cost to consumers. What lessons if any does the experience of the commercial aircraft industry have for technology policy in other industries?

NASA and NACA illustrate the importance of strong in-house expertise within an industry served by a publicly funded program in generic basic and applied research. As we have noted elsewhere, the importance of this "receiving mechanism" has been overlooked by the neoclassical analytic paradigm. The internal expertise of firms in the commercial aircraft industry and their direct participation in NASA research projects facilitated their absorption and utilization of the results of NASA-sponsored research. NASA's widespread dissemination of technical data, the Manufacturers' Aviation Association patent-licensing scheme, and the liberal licensing requirements for patents obtained with federal military research funding all enhanced the intraindustry diffusion of technical data and results.[32]

Indeed, a significant portion of industry-financed R&D investment supports the absorption and adaptation of research and technological developments funded by either NASA or the military services.[33] The commercial aircraft industry is an excellent example of an industry in which high spillovers from one firm's knowledge base to other firms are associated with high levels of research investment, as a means of absorbing such spillovers (Cohen and Levinthal, 1989). The experience of the aircraft industry suggests that this aspect of R&D investment behavior may be influenced by policy as well as by industry structure, by technology, or by market demand.

The NASA and NACA research programs departed from the policy prescriptions of the neoclassical model of research and development in another fundamental way. Although it was important in both NACA and NASA aeronautics R&D, basic research by no means constituted the sole or even the primary focus of these research programs. As we noted earlier in this chapter, NACA provided little direct funding for basic research (by comparison with the aeronautics research establishments of such nations as Germany and Great Britain) before World War II. During the postwar period as well, the research programs of NASA and NACA have extended well beyond basic research into research concerned with the demonstration of the feasibility of a specific combination of systems or materials.

[32] The unusual combination of high concentration and occasional dramatic changes in the market shares of firms in the commercial aircraft industry noted by Phillips (1971) also may reflect the existence of an industrywide knowledge base that was accessible by a number of different firms. Rather than a single firm establishing an unchallengeable technological lead, through much of its history the industry was characterized by recurrent technological "leapfrogging" of one firm by another. While Phillips attributes this tendency to the existence of a substantial exogenous research effort funded by NASA and the military, the ease with which incumbent firms could tap that external knowledge pool also has been important.

[33] Terleckyj (1984) suggests that because a portion of self-financed research investment within the industry was devoted to the absorption of the results of publicly funded research, the public research investment does not contribute statistically to the explanation of productivity growth in the air transportation industry: "It is also possible that the private R&D expenditures made to adapt the results of government R&D to private products already incorporate the effects of government R&D. The military R&D which is represented in the government and to a large degree in the total R&D expenditure for aircraft and parts by itself does not produce products sufficiently developed for private use" (p. 32). In the absence of the public R&D program, however, innovation and productivity growth in the industry would suffer.

By virtue of its ability to pursue both basic and precommercial technological "proof of concept" research, the NASA R&D program was able to exploit the links between basic research and other stages of the research process that contribute to successful innovation. In pursuing research activities that extended beyond basic research, NACA and NASA were able to exploit the interactive relationships among the early stages of the innovation process.

Further insight into the factors that contributed to the success of NACA/ NASA research programs is provided by consideration of a major failure in commercial aircraft R&D programs, the supersonic transport (SST). The federal SST program, aimed at developing a commercial supersonic transport, represented a sharp departure from historical civil aeronautics research policy in several important ways. The program was administered by the Federal Aviation Administration rather than by NASA. More important, the SST program was intended to produce two prototype aircraft and was empowered to provide government financing or loan guarantees for the start-up costs of commercial production.

The SST program was motivated by the perceived threat of the British–French Concorde to American dominance of commercial aircraft and by the desire to use technological "spillovers" from the development of the B-70 strategic bomber. The SST prototype development contract was awarded to Boeing on the strength of a design that the firm claimed would meet the performance requirements stipulated by the FAA, in contrast to the usual design and development process for commercial aircraft, in which the airlines are major participants. Mounting technical and cost problems, as well as growing opposition from environmental groups, led Congress to kill the program in early 1971.

The SST program attempted to apply the military procurement model to the development of commercial aircraft; the federal government conducted a design competition and proposed to support the development efforts of the winning prime contractor. Such policies were feasible in military aircraft procurement because the federal government was the sole customer. In the military "market" it is eminently sensible for the ultimate purchaser to specify in detail the operating and design characteristics of aircraft to be purchased. The attempt to develop a successful commercial SST through the same government procurement mechanism was almost certain to lead to designs and decisions that would suppress ordinary commercial considerations. Similar suppression of commercial considerations characterized the joint Anglo–French Concorde venture.

Both the SST and Concorde experiences represented attempts to exploit military spillovers in commercial aircraft in the form of improved technical performance capabilities. Doing so, however, involved the suppression of normal commercial judgments and considerations. The

American SST was never built, and only sixteen Concordes were constructed after an extraordinary development effort costing several billions of dollars. The indiscriminate pursuit of military spillovers thus turned out to be a recipe for commercial disaster when optimal design requirements of the military and civilian sectors were sharply divergent.

The history of federal research investment in the commercial aircraft industry suggests that public R&D programs can exert a powerful and positive influence on the innovative performance of an industry. The unique circumstances of the commercial aircraft industry must be kept in mind clearly, however, before applying lessons from this industry to other sectors. Its contribution to the military strength of the United States has meant that military procurement and R&D support have exerted a substantial influence on innovation in the commercial aircraft industry. As we noted in Chapter 6, with the possible exception of microelectronics during the 1950s and 1960s, few other industries in the United States have benefited so greatly from military–civilian technological spillovers. The foundation of NACA and the continued support of aeronautics research in NASA reflected the perception that a strong civil aircraft technology base also yielded benefits for military aircraft.[34] In this respect, the NACA/NASA aeronautics research programs anticipated elements of the more recent Sematech effort we discussed in Chapter 6.

Nonetheless, the combination of support for R&D in technology verification, rather than basic research alone, with regulatory support for adoption has considerable potential for more general application. Much of Japanese industrial policy, after all, has applied similar principles. Nevertheless, the particular policy instrument that operated to support such diffusion, CAB regulation, was hardly an efficient or costless one. Nor was this policy framework planned consciously to support innovation, or one whose distributional consequences (especially those of CAB regulation) were even well understood before the 1960s and 1970s. Indeed, had the distributional consequences been more visible or more clearly understood, deregulation might have occurred sooner.[35]

Significant changes in federal policy toward the commercial aircraft industry, as well as changes in the global technological and competitive environments, have contributed to the development of a complex international network of research and product development collaborations. Although their longer-term implications for competitiveness and innovation are still unclear, thus far U.S. firms appear to have reaped considerable

---

[34] The recent report of the Office of Science and Technology Policy, *Aeronautical Research and Technology Policy*, adopts this view of NASA's role.

[35] Noll and Owen (1983) suggest that economic analyses of the distributional and efficiency impacts of regulation played a major role in a number of deregulatory policy episodes of the 1970s.

commercial and technological benefits from them. If these ventures continue to expand in a broader array of U.S. industries, they will create major challenges to managers and policymakers, as we note in Chapter 9.

Appendix
Estimates of R&D investment in commercial aircraft, 1945–83

Data on R&D investment during 1945–69 were taken from the 1971 study by Booz, Allen, and Hamilton Applied Research, Inc., for the NASA/ Department of Transportation analysis of technological change in the commercial aircraft industry. This source provides a detailed breakdown of aircraft industry R&D expenditures by source, by research activity (e.g., basic versus applied), and by functional area of research (e.g., propulsion). The data were discussed at length in Mowery and Rosenberg (1982) and were employed in modified form in Terleckyj's analysis (1984) of productivity growth in air transportation. The Booz–Allen data also separate industry-financed research expenditures from expenditures covered by federal reimbursements for military procurement and development contracts. Before 1959, such reimbursements were restricted to allowable overhead charges on military research, development, and procurement contracts. After 1959, however, reimbursement was allowed for "independent R&D" (IR&D) as a part of the overhead costs of military contracts (see Levy and Terleckyj, 1983; Aerospace Industries Association, 1984; Terleckyj, 1984). Although it represents an important source of federal support for industrial research in firms supplying the armed forces, IR&D typically is reported by those firms to the National Science Foundation as industry-financed research investment.

The post-1969 data are less detailed and lack the functional and other disaggregated breakdowns provided in the Booz–Allen study. Data on the Department of Defense, NASA, and other federal research support for aeronautics were taken from *Aerospace Facts and Figures* (Aerospace Industries Association, 1984). Industry-financed R&D expenditure data after 1970 were taken from the product field data compiled by NSF on the "aircraft and parts" industry (SIC 372).[36] The NSF data have several problems: They do not include basic research activity, and the IR&D reimbursements received by firms in the industry presumably are reported as industry-financed research investment. To deal with these

---

[36] Although these product field data also report federally funded research, the category is restricted to publicly supported R&D carried out within industry and therefore understates the total public R&D investment. The NSF data are collected only for alternate years after 1977. The 1978, 1980, and 1982 entries for industry-financed R&D in Table 7.2 therefore were based on linear interpolations.

problems, the reported basic research expenditures for the aerospace industry (a broader category than aircraft and parts) were added to the figures and the sum was deflated by the average share of reimbursed R&D expenditures for industry-financed and industry-reimbursed R&D investment for the 1945–69 period, as reported in the Booz–Allen study. The excluded portion of "industry-financed" R&D investment was added to reported military R&D expenditures.

PART IV

New environment, new research organizations

8

The changing context of innovation, 1980–present

The R&D system that emerged from wartime underwent little change during 1945–80. Federal funds provided most of the financial support for R&D, and industry dominated its performance. The role of industry as a performer of basic research relative to that of universities declined during this period, and the relative importance of military and space-related research experienced some sizable swings; but otherwise the overall structure of the U.S. R&D system was remarkably stable. Beginning in the 1970s and emerging with particular force in the 1980s, however, several developments have created increasing pressure for structural change within the U.S. R&D system. Changes in the international economic environment within which U.S. firms operate and in the financial and organizational requirements of innovation have been largely responsible for the quickening pace of change in the U.S. R&D system.

In this chapter we discuss the forces of change and examine the new environment for commercial innovation that they have produced. In Chapter 9 we consider several of the resulting shifts in the structure of the research system, including the growth in multinational collaborative ventures and the rise of domestic research collaboration within the U.S. economy. Because of its recent successes in commercializing new technologies, the frequent reference to it as a model for U.S. managers and public policymakers,[1] and what we perceive as the increasing pressures for change within it, we also discuss Japan's R&D system in this chapter.

Changes in the international environment

A flood of reports and commentary has highlighted several of the most important causes of the restructuring of the U.S. R&D system – the increased openness of the U.S. economy to international trade, more rapid rates of international technology transfer, and growth in U.S. imports from new sources. These changes have intensified competitive pressures on U.S. firms. Faster technology transfer has reduced the ability of U.S.

[1] Illustrative of this is the title of Ezra Vogel's book, *Japan as Number One: Lessons for America* (1979).

firms to reap the benefits of privately or publicly financed R&D that is performed within the American economy.

International trade has nearly doubled as a share of GNP during the past two decades, as imports have risen from roughly 6 percent to 11–12 percent of GNP. Aho (1988) estimates that 70 percent of U.S. manufacturing output faces international competition in the form of imports or competition in export markets. Since 1945, U.S. exports from both the manufacturing and nonmanufacturing sectors have been R&D-intensive goods. Earlier studies (Gruber, Mehta, and Vernon, 1967; Keesing, 1967) documented the significant relationship between the R&D content of U.S. manufactured products and the role of these products in U.S. exports. According to a recent Organization for Economic Cooperation and Development (OECD) study (1986), U.S. exports depend on R&D-intensive industries to a greater extent than the exports of other industrial nations. Within the nonmanufacturing sector, the recent study of international trade in services by the Office of Technology Assessment (1987) found that exports of services tend to rely on relatively (by comparison with the rest of the nonmanufacturing sector) high-skill employment.

The importance of export markets for many of these R&D-intensive industries has grown considerably during the past two decades. As product demand in world markets for many high-technology and other goods has become more homogeneous across geographic regions, the U.S. share of world demand for these products has declined. This decline in the U.S. share of global markets has made penetration of foreign markets by U.S. firms essential to commercial success in many industries (especially in view of the growing costs of product development). U.S. firms now must develop strategies for more rapid and effective penetration of foreign markets.

Even as the importance of international trade and R&D-intensive exports within the U.S. economy has increased, access to many foreign markets for the exports of U.S. high-technology firms has been restricted by nontariff barriers of various types (see Chapter 10 for additional discussion of trade issues).[2] In part, the growing significance of nontariff barriers[3] reflects the fact that tariff-based restrictions to market access have been

---

[2] Access by many foreign firms to the U.S. market also has been restricted by nontariff measures. Examples include the "voluntary" export restraint agreement of Japanese auto producers that limits their exports to this market; increasing restrictions on U.S. government procurement in defense authorization and appropriations bills ("Buy American" amendments); the recent United States–Japan Semiconductor Agreement governing the pricing of semiconductor memory components; and the web of bilateral agreements restricting U.S. imports of steel. According to Tyson (1988), the share of U.S. manufactured imports affected by nontariff barriers grew from 20 percent in 1980 to 35 percent in 1983.

[3] Olechowski (1987) estimated that 17–19 percent of the imports of developed nations (by value) were covered by nontariff barriers. Olechowski also concluded that the use of non-tariff barriers increased significantly during 1981–5 (p. 125).

reduced to insignificant levels in many industrial economies through successive rounds of multilateral trade negotiations. Additionally, however, foreign governments in many industrial and developing nations now are promoting the development of domestic technological capabilities more aggressively than before. These programs often rely on such policies as "directed procurement" (favoring particular firms in government procurement contracts), demands for "offsets" (production of the components for a complex capital good by firms within the purchasing nation), or other restrictions on foreign investment (e.g., mandatory licensing of technology). As part of this effort to enhance domestic technological capabilities, a number of governments, including the European Economic Community and its member governments, have also expanded funding for research and development for commercial applications, as in the Esprit, Eureka, Airbus, and British Alvey programs. As we note in Chapter 10, the growing strategic presence of governments within high-technology industries and the increased importance of technology-intensive products within trade flows have made national trade and technology policies much more interdependent in recent years.

Whether because of or in spite of this growing government role, the technological capabilities of foreign firms have grown. Figure 8.1 displays the convergence in the shares of GNP devoted to R&D investment by the United States and four other industrial nations during 1961–85. The data in this chart include defense-related R&D; when this substantial portion of U.S. R&D investment is excluded (Figure 8.2), the data suggest that the United States has devoted a smaller share of its GNP to nondefense R&D investment during 1971–86 than Japan or West Germany. Moreover, this comparison suggests that the proportionate U.S. national investment in nonmilitary R&D has fallen further behind those of Japan and West Germany in recent years.

Another indicator of the relative technological strengths of the U.S. and other industrial economies is the speed of adoption and level of utilization of advanced manufacturing technologies in the United States and elsewhere. Flamm (1988a) and others[4] suggest that robotics technologies have been adopted more rapidly in such economies as Sweden, West Germany, and Japan and are utilized in greater numbers (on a per capita basis) in the manufacturing sectors of these nations than is true of the United States. This evidence of U.S. lags in adoption suggests that the gap between "best practice" and "current practice" in the United States may be greater than is true of other industrial economies. Still another indicator of the stronger performance of some foreign firms in commercializing and exploiting new technologies is the estimate by Clark et al.

---

[4] See also Mowery (1988b) and Mansfield (in press).

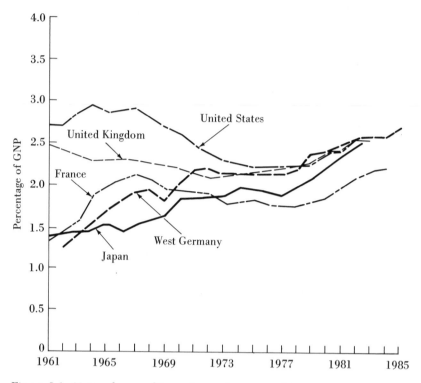

Figure 8.1. National expenditures for performance of R&D as a percentage of gross national product by country. (These are gross expenditures for performance of R&D including associated capital expenditures [except for the United States, where total capital expenditures data are not available]. Estimates for 1972–80 show that the inclusion of capital expenditures for the United States would have an impact of less than 0.1 percent per year.) *Source:* National Science Foundation (1985).

(1987) that Japanese automobile firms require one-half as much time to bring a new model to market as do U.S. automobile firms.[5] Not only are many foreign competitors now technologically equal or superior to U.S. firms, they also have in some cases proved more adept at realizing the commercial returns to these technological capabilities.

The technological capabilities of firms from developing nations, especially firms from the "newly industrializing countries" (NICs), have also improved. Although R&D investment data are not available for these economies, a recent OECD study (1988) notes that the most rapid growth

[5] See also Mansfield (1988) and the discussion of Japanese R&D in this chapter.

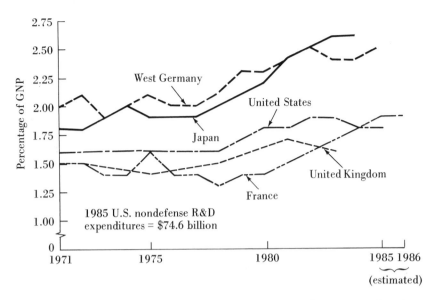

Figure 8.2. Nondefense R&D expenditures as a percentage of gross national product by country. *Source:* National Science Foundation (1987).

in NIC exports during 1964–85 occurred in the technology-intensive industries of telecommunications equipment and electrical machinery.[6] To be sure, this dramatic rate of increase reflects the low level of NIC exports of these goods in 1964, but the share of high-technology exports within total NIC exports also expanded from slightly more than 2 percent in 1964 to 25 percent in 1985.

The improved technological capabilities of foreign firms and economies have, consistent with the arguments we presented in Chapters 4 and 5, strengthened the "receiving mechanisms" in these economies for the absorption and utilization of science and technology from foreign sources. This factor and the development of a number of powerful institutions for the international transfer of technology (e.g., multinational corporations) have increased the pace at which industrial technologies move across international boundaries within the global economy (OECD, 1979; Mansfield and Romeo, 1980; Mansfield, 1985; Abramovitz, 1986; Baumol, 1986). Baumol, among others, has suggested that the increased speed of international technology transfer is responsible in part for the tendency for productivity growth rates within the industrial economies of the world to

[6] The OECD study included as NICs Singapore, Taiwan, South Korea, Hong Kong, Brazil, and Mexico.

converge in recent years. The OECD study of NIC exports noted the contribution of faster international technology transfer to growth in NIC exports of sophisticated manufactured goods:

> A potentially radical change between past and future trends lies in the fact that the diffusion of technologies is becoming increasingly disconnected from the trade in products which embody the technologies. Such an evolution may open new opportunities for those NICs which are succeeding in the development of a technological infrastructure and an industrial organisation which will allow them to respond quickly to the evolution of world demand, especially in the fast-growing sectors. (OECD, 1988, p. 8)

More rapid technology transfer and the growing technological capabilities of firms in these nations mean that in contrast to the 1960s and 1970s, much low-wage foreign competition in manufacturing is no longer low-productivity competition. Process and product technologies in some industries within low-wage competitor nations now approach or exceed those of the United States in quality and cost effectiveness. This new international environment, in turn, increases the payoff to more rapid adoption by U.S. firms of advanced product and process technologies.

Another implication of the increased number and enhanced technological capabilities of foreign firms and nations is that sourcing of both industrial R&D and components has become truly international in scope. In the area of R&D, the example of high-temperature superconductivity, first demonstrated by a Swiss and a German scientist working in a Swiss industrial research laboratory operated by a giant American multinational corporation (IBM), is merely one illustration of a trend that includes Texas Instruments' software engineering laboratory in India and Toyota Corporation's long-established automobile design research center in southern California. The international diffusion of process and product technology (as well as the development of computer-aided design [CAD] and manufacturing [CAM] technologies) means that firms can now parcel out separate activities or components on a truly international basis. As a result, it is increasingly difficult to pin a national label on a product that incorporates numerous components or subassemblies.

The present situation in the computer industry is a good example of the growth and consequences of global sourcing. American industry appears to dominate the world market, especially the mainframe market, with about 80 percent of total sales. On closer inspection, however, the situation is much more complex. Most semiconductor memory chips and disk drives are produced in Japan. Many American computer terminals are made in Korea. Although Japanese manufacturers have not made major inroads in the sale of personal computers in the U.S. market, over 80 percent of the U.S. market for personal computer printers in 1984 was held by Japanese firms. If we look at a single product like the IBM personal computer, the picture is also much more complicated than it appears at first glance. Many of the components for the personal computer were produced by foreign firms. The IBM PC employs Intel microprocessors that were produced by Hitachi, a TDK power supply from Japan, and an Atlas monitor from Hong Kong. As we note in Chapter 10, the complex and varied national origins of the components in these products have greatly complicated trade policy in recent years.

Within this emerging international division of labor, countries can specialize in the manufacture of individual components for complex products, rather than the entire product.[7] Newly industrializing countries that are generally regarded as far from the technological frontier – India, Brazil, Mexico – can establish niches in specific portions of high-technology industries. In other industries, export strategies that rely on the local assembly and integration of advanced components from abroad (components that often are produced by firms in industrial nations) have proved successful. Korean shipbuilders once imported Japanese marine engines and complex navigational components in the same way as Brazilians currently manufacture aircraft (see Moxon et al., 1985; Mowery, 1987) with American engines and electronic components.

A number of firms in industrial nations now produce very complex capital goods for global markets by purchasing components from suppliers in a number of different countries. Boeing, for example, is increasingly a designer of aircraft and an assembler of components made elsewhere, often overseas. IBM is coming to occupy a similar role, as a designer and assembler of computers that incorporate numerous foreign-produced parts and rely on operating systems and applications software produced and maintained by the firm. Both firms sell their products globally with the aid of large international marketing and product-support staffs. In other industries, such as semiconductors and biotechnology, relatively young firms have pursued similar strategies that separate design from production. American and a growing number of Japanese firms operate "silicon foundries," producing application-specific integrated circuits (ASICs) to meet the specifications of independent design firms. In biotechnology, domestic and international collaboration between small firms and larger enterprises in pharmaceuticals and other industries also is common (Pisano, Shan, and Teece, 1988).

Some authors have suggested that the movement by firms in technology-

---

[7] This development should be revealed in growing intraindustry trade between developed and developing nations, reproducing the widely remarked growth in such trade among industrial nations. Intraindustry trade among industrial economies also includes considerable trade in finished goods as well as components.

intensive industries toward global sourcing or even (as in the case of the silicon foundries) toward a role that is limited to design and excludes production is a dangerous trend.[8] Many of these critical commentaries raise two sets of concerns: (1) U.S. firms following these strategies will become "hollow corporations," engaged in financial legerdemain, employing a small number of highly paid R&D, financial, and sales personnel, and displacing high-wage production workers; and (2) these hollow corporations, divorced from day-to-day management of manufacturing operations, will lose their technological and ultimately their competitive edge.

Although these arguments have received wide circulation, there is little evidence to suggest that they apply equally to all manufacturing industries. The first argument applies to all forms of structural change in this economy – as U.S. firms pursue lower-cost production strategies and adjust to international competition, their employment mix will inevitably change. It is widely accepted that public and private policies should be developed to address the distributional consequences of these changes, including more effective assistance to displaced and imminently displaced workers. The second proposition, concerning the "loss of the technological edge," is consistent with the discussion in Chapters 4 and 5 concerning the importance of in-house R&D for the exploitation of the complementarities between innovation and manufacturing operations. The argument, however, overstates the extent to which U.S. firms have become "hollow," and may also exaggerate the importance of manufacturing, as opposed to marketing or product support, as the only critical competitive asset and source of profit (see later in this chapter and Chapter 9 for additional discussion).

Carried to its logical conclusion, this second argument would lead to complete vertical integration of all operations, hardly a universally cost-minimizing strategy and one that differs from those of industrial firms in such nations as Japan. Moreover, there is little empirical evidence to suggest that all technologies or industries depend equally on in-house production of a majority of inputs or components to maintain their technological and therefore their competitive prowess. One can cite examples of corporate "hollowing" and competitive decline that have resulted from extensive outsourcing, but examples also exist of the successful application of international sourcing strategies by U.S. firms that have preserved their technological edge and domestic employment. In our opinion, the underlying determinants of the success or failure of these strategies have

---

[8] See "Special Report: The Hollow Corporation"; Cohen and Zysman (1987); Bluestone and Harrison (1988). For an empirical analysis that contradicts some of the conclusions of Bluestone and Harrison concerning the distribution of household incomes and individual earnings, see Blackburn and Bloom (1988).

not yet been rigorously identified or tested (see Teece, 1986, for a conceptual discussion).

Changes in the technological environment

Along with changes in the economic environment within which U.S. firms operate, technological change during the past decade has created new challenges and opportunities for the organization of R&D. Continued growth in development costs, technological convergence, shorter product cycles in some industries and technologies, and advances in computer-based information and manufacturing technologies, including CAM and CAD, have all contributed to the search for new forms of R&D organization.

The costs of the research and development necessary to bring a new product or process to market in many high-technology industries have continued to rise at a rapid rate: As we noted in Chapter 7, commercial aircraft development costs have risen at an annual rate of nearly 20 percent for decades, despite dramatic advances in the application and productivity of the capital equipment used in the R&D process (e.g., supercomputers – see later in this chapter).[9] Similarly rapid growth in development and marketing costs has characterized the telecommunications equipment, computer, and microelectronics industries. The financial risks of innovation thus are increasing, which means that firms in some industries require markets substantially larger than can be provided by a single Western European nation or even in some cases by the huge U.S. domestic economy. Rising development costs place severe strains on the ability of firms to sustain ambitious R&D programs and increase the importance of penetration of foreign markets to ensure commercial success.

Another source of cost pressure on R&D programs is a form of technological convergence, in which technologies that formerly were peripheral to the commercial and research activities of a firm have become central. The increased interdependence of telecommunications and computer technologies is perhaps the best-known example of such convergence, but others include the growing importance of biotechnology within pharmaceuticals and food processing, as well as the greater salience of computer-based machine vision technologies within robotics equipment.[10] Technological convergence means that firms must develop expertise quickly in a

---

[9] See Mowery and Rosenberg (1982).
[10] The neologism "mechatronics" has been coined in Japan to refer to the fusion of electronic and mechanical technologies. Examples include computer numerically controlled machine tools and industrial robots. See Kodama (1986).

broader array of technologies and scientific disciplines, further straining R&D budgets and human resources. Much recent experimentation with new forms of R&D organization has been driven by the desire of firms to monitor a broader range of technologies without simultaneously incurring vastly higher costs.

Increases in the pace of innovation in some industries are contributing to higher costs and risks. For technological and other reasons, long lead times are often involved in the innovation process. Long lead times postpone the prospect of full recovery of financial commitments. Not only are uncertainties about technological factors particularly great during these prolonged periods of development, but large financial commitments are frequently required during the stages when uncertainties are greatest. Rapid technological change raises the risk of investing in long-lived plant and equipment, since capital equipment becomes obsolete more quickly. As product life cycles shrink in some industries, risks increase and the timing of commitments of large amounts of resources to the development process becomes even more crucial. The earliest innovators have frequently wound up in the bankruptcy courts.

The strategy of a rapid imitator, of a "fast second" that can benefit from the mistakes of the pioneer, has much to commend it, especially when rapid rates of technical change are expected to continue. Technologically complex products experience numerous difficulties in their early stages that may take years to iron out. Although the first commercial jet, the Comet I, was introduced by a British firm (DeHavilland), well before American entry into the commercial jet age, the pioneer reaped few if any profits. As it happened, substantial improvements in jet engines following the Comet's introduction allowed U.S. firms to develop commercial jets that were significantly more reliable, had larger passenger capacities, and offered higher cruising speeds. These improvements proved to be decisive. The British, often criticized for being too slow to innovate, suffered in the commercial aircraft industry in the early 1950s because they innovated *too rapidly*. Timing proved to be crucial. The advantages in some sectors of being a technological follower, able to observe the technological opportunities and errors of leaders, have been exploited by a number of Japanese firms (as we discuss later in this chapter).[11]

The risks of pioneering new technologies are even more serious in electronics, where the technology is changing very rapidly and where all par-

---

[11] The optimal strategy for a firm is complicated by the fact that there may also be "first mover" advantages, as in technologies in which learning phenomena are important and yield firm-specific knowledge that does not flow easily from pioneer to follower firms. See Lieberman and Montgomery (1988). Nevertheless, the presence of learning effects in semiconductors did not prevent Japanese firms from exploiting the "fast second" strategy successfully in this industry.

ties expect that it will continue to change rapidly. Under these circumstances, the decision to commit resources to large-scale development of a new component design, for example, is extraordinarily difficult. Since potential purchasers of electronics products also expect rapid technological change to continue, it takes a great deal of effort, or very low prices, to persuade them of the wisdom of buying now rather than later.

On the other hand, the effects of higher development costs and intensified international competition on the structure of R&D and product manufacture will also be influenced by developments in some process technologies. For example, advances in computer technology could slow the rate of increase of development costs in high-technology industries. CAD and CAM techniques may make it possible without extensive prototyping, inferring the most efficient methods of manufacturing the product directly from design data.[12] Indeed, this is already happening:

> For machining, this integration is reflected in the automatic output of numerical control programmes; in electronic components by the automatic generation of production "masks"; in casting (of metals) by the automatic design of moulds; and for the future, in assembly by the automatic production of robot programmes to assemble complex components. (OECD, 1985, pp. 122–3)

CAD and CAM may reduce development costs and accelerate the transfer of product prototypes to large-scale manufacture. It may also make possible better-designed products. Computer-assisted engineering (CAE) makes it possible to test and evaluate the performance of a prototype that has been designed but not yet built.

The computer and the microprocessor are also bringing automation into the research process itself. In pharmaceuticals, automation makes it possible to monitor toxicological tests on large populations of animals. Drug tests can be conducted more quickly, and the time that elapses before certain new drugs can be brought to market has been drastically reduced. Supercomputers increasingly are applied to the synthesis and simulation of the properties of molecular structures in pharmaceuticals research.[13]

---

[12] Exploitation of the potential of CAM and CAE for dramatic improvement in development costs and cycles, as well as in product quality, typically requires extensive organizational change within the firms adopting these technologies. In many cases, for example, products must be redesigned to exploit the full advantages of CAM. Such redesign efforts may require much closer cooperation between research and manufacturing experts. Interestingly, many gains attributed by U.S. firms and experts to CAE and CAM were attained without the use of these technologies by some Japanese firms through organizational restructuring and changes in the management of the production process. See Abegglen and Stalk (1986); Cyert and Mowery, eds. (1987).

[13] See Wyke (1987): "Genetic engineering allows researchers to make enough protein to enable them to determine its structure by means of a technique known as x-ray crystallography. Computers make the millions of measurements needed to build up a three-

In the slightly more distant future, large computers could streamline a number of time-consuming experimental procedures that contribute to high development costs. For example, large computers may replace wind tunnels for experimentation with new aircraft designs. Supercomputers have already been used to design the wings of both the Boeing 767 and the European Airbus 310 and 320. New airfoil designs can be, in effect, "flown," modified, and subsequently "flown" again – all on the supercomputer – until optimal performance and design are achieved. Computers are now being used "to simulate systems whose complexity approaches that of the real world." Such techniques are already being applied in elementary particle theory, in astrophysics, in automobile design, in the exploitation of oil reservoirs, in modeling the behavior of metals under stress, and many other fields.[14]

The ultimate effect of these new computer-based technologies on the costs and risks of innovation is uncertain. Although they may reduce development costs, their application could shorten product life cycles even further. Additional shrinkage in product life cycles in some industries would increase the financial risks faced by firms. On the other hand, CAD, CAM, and CAE may also provide an effective bridge between product cycles, making it possible for successive product designs to use a common manufacturing and engineering base of knowledge, design data, and equipment. This development could provide some financial benefits for the firm with a technological lead and could reduce product costs for consumers. For example, Boeing and other commercial aircraft firms, such as Airbus Industrie, have become increasingly sophisticated and successful in exploiting these technologies to increase commonality among their products. This reduces development costs and allows a firm to market a "family" of aircraft to airlines concerned with reducing parts inventories, training, and maintenance costs.[15]

Emerging manufacturing technologies may have other surprising effects in the context of the changing international division of labor. For a number of years, the labor-intensive stages of production in many U.S. high-technology industries have moved offshore to the NICs where labor

dimensional view of these molecules and thereby identify the receptor, the working part of the protein.

"A drug designer can then do one of two things. If the protein is a goodie, he can design a synthetic drug which stimulates the natural physiological response: an agonist. If the protein is a baddie, he can develop a drug which blocks that response: an antagonist. He can use computerised graphic displays of molecular structures to determine the best one, producing the effect he wants.

"Eventually, drug companies would like to design most of their drugs using computers" (p. 11).

[14] *Science*, May 3, 1985, p. 568.

[15] See Mowery (1987) and Chapter 7 for additional discussion of product families in the commercial aircraft industry.

is cheaper; this process has been partly responsible for the rapid economic growth of some of these nations and has facilitated the emergence
of the new international division of labor in some sectors that was discussed earlier. New forms of automation, robotics, and flexible manufacturing systems could reduce labor requirements and reverse this flow.
These technologies could enable manufacturing activities that have recently moved to Southeast Asia or northern Mexico to become cost effective within the United States (see Cyert and Mowery, 1987; Sanderson,
1987). "Labor-saving" technologies thus could expand manufacturing employment in the industrial economies. For these advanced production
technologies to have this effect, however, U.S. managers and workers
must be able to evaluate and adopt these technologies more quickly and
efficiently. In fact, U.S. scientific leadership in many fields has not been
reflected in comparable leadership in the speed or effectiveness of adoption of a number of new manufacturing technologies.

Technological developments in telecommunications, CAE, and CAD/
CAM may also have reduced somewhat the competitive advantages of the
large multinational firm and its strategies of internal development of new
technologies and direct foreign investment to exploit these technologies.
The growth of these multinational firms was in part a response to new
technologies (e.g., the railroad and the telegraph) that reduced the costs
and enhanced the reliability and speed of information transmission, storage, and processing (Chandler, 1977). In combination with other technological and organizational changes, declines in information costs in the
late nineteenth century created economies of scale and scope within the
firm that led to increased size and diversification. Eventually, these firms
developed extensive multinational operations. Recent innovations in the
technologies of information transmission, storage, and analysis have lowered information costs still further and have contributed to the growth of
new organizational structures for R&D, production, and marketing in some
industries. Advanced telecommunications and computer technologies
support the exchange of technical, testing, and other data among research
and development teams in different locations and/or firms. The use of
CAD and CAM in both development and production has also simplified
the "spinning off" of tasks to other foreign or domestic firms in product
design and manufacture.

Implications for R&D organization

These changes in the technological and competitive environment have
important implications for U.S. competitiveness in high-technology markets. Elsewhere, we have argued that the "fit" between the structure of
a national R&D system and its environment influences the effectiveness

of that system. The changes discussed earlier in this chapter appear to have lowered the social and private returns reaped by the U.S. economy from the postwar R&D system, which was based in part on federal funding of basic and applied defense-related research performed primarily in industry or in the universities.

During much of this period, the economic returns to publicly funded research were largely captured by U.S. firms because of their considerable technological lead over foreign firms and because they performed much of the publicly funded research. The relatively benign competitive environment of the 1950s and 1960s meant that U.S. firms were under less pressure to achieve rapid commercial applications of scientific and engineering advances. Moreover, the range of technologies in which firms had to maintain expertise was narrower, and defense research budgets may have yielded more significant commercial applications during that period. Since foreign firms now are more technologically sophisticated and technology is more internationally mobile, however, the competitive advantages that accrued in the past from basic research and a strong knowledge base have been eroded. Faster international transfer of new technologies is undercutting a major source of America's postwar superiority in high-technology markets.

Americans (and especially members of the scientific community) may well have exaggerated the purely economic benefits that flowed from leadership at the scientific frontier. This is not a denial that great economic benefits flow from the conduct of scientific research; rather it is a denial that these benefits necessarily flow in the form of economic advantages to the country conducting such research. Great Britain's experience (see Chapter 5) demonstrates the insufficiency of high-quality science when it is not associated with complementary managerial and engineering skills or institutions. On the other hand, the experience of Japan (discussed in the following section) has forcefully demonstrated the remarkable possibilities for economic growth based on the systematic transfer and exploitation of foreign technologies.

It is easy to exaggerate the extent to which national economic growth depends on a first-rate domestic scientific research capability. This should not be terribly surprising. The fruits of scientific research have always been portable; events of recent decades are rendering technological innovations internationally portable as well. Exploiting this increased mobility of scientific and technological knowledge requires an environment within would-be recipient countries that includes strong commercialization capabilities. These include a considerable level of scientific and engineering expertise (a national analogue to the "absorption mechanism" within the firm that we noted in Chapter 5) as well as other skills that reside at the "downstream" end of the spectrum of activities that make up R&D.

The requirements and structure of research systems that have recently experienced great success in rapid commercialization, such as that of Japan, are not well understood. We examine the evolution and structure of the Japanese postwar research system in the next section. This examination requires consideration once again of the "fit" between the competitive and technological environment of Japanese industry and the structure of the research system. More specifically, will a research system that developed in an era of technological "catch-up" be equally effective within an economy that now is at the technological frontier in many sectors?

The case of Japan

There are at least three reasons for discussing some features of the postwar Japanese national R&D system: (1) Japanese firms have been among the most successful commercial innovators in the postwar global economy and have emerged as a key source of competitive pressure on U.S. firms in many industries; (2) our survey of the structure and institutions of this R&D system leads to the conclusion (shared by others; e.g., Ergas, 1987) that many of these institutions were successful because they supported the utilization of R&D results and findings, consistent with the argument we have made elsewhere; and (3) the changing place of Japan and Japanese innovation within the world economy may lead to significant change in the institutional structure of the Japanese R&D system. Although our analysis of postwar Japanese R&D policy and its management within the firm contains important implications for U.S. policymakers and managers, this brief survey also suggests that wholesale borrowing or imitation by U.S. firms or public institutions of Japanese practices in R&D policy and management may accomplish little.

Japanese firms have on numerous occasions been the leaders in the commercialization of new products, in spite of the fact that the new product, or some essential component, was invented elsewhere. Thus, the United States is the acknowledged source of such inventions as the transistor and the integrated circuit. The sequence of scientific and technological events that culminated in these inventions was clearly based on American leadership. Nevertheless, Japan was responsible for the large-scale commercialization of transistor technology for the radio, and Japanese technical skills in the production of high-quality color television sets effectively destroyed America's earlier dominance in the market for that product. Similarly, although America dominated the early introduction of robotics, Japan by 1984 was employing more than four times as many operating industrial robots as the United States.[16]

---

[16] Based on surveys by the Japan Industrial Robot Association and the Robotics Institute of America; cited in Flamm (1988a). See also Mansfield (in press).

Japan's prowess in quality and design in products ranging from compact automobiles to consumer electronics is sufficiently obvious that little comment is required. The videocassette recorder is a more complex and interesting case. It is one of Japan's largest export items, recently accounting for almost $6 billion per year in export earnings. Its successful commercialization has been overwhelmingly a Japanese effort. Although the earliest conception and much of the early development work were American, Japanese engineering, design, and manufacturing skills were responsible for solving many of the basic problems that needed to be overcome before commercialization was possible.[17] In this respect the VCR may constitute an interesting stepping-stone in Japan's transition from dependence on foreign invention to the status of an independent inventor of complex products.

A number of indicators suggest that in many areas, Japanese firms have progressed during the postwar period from borrowing, modifying, and successfully commercializing foreign technologies to operating at the technological frontier. No single one of these indicators is definitive, but together they are suggestive. Okimoto and Saxonhouse (1987) noted that the ratio of Japanese exports of technology to imports has increased from 0.12 in 1971 to 0.30 in 1983. This indicator reflects historical trends in licensing and therefore includes many royalty payments for technologies purchased years ago. The ratio of technology exports to imports in new contracts alone, however, has risen from 1 in 1972 to 1.76 in 1984. The average annual rate of growth in Japanese payments for imports of technology has declined from 31 percent in the 1950s to 6 percent in the late 1970s, according to Uekusa (1987). Alone among industrial nations, Japan registered an increase, rather than a decrease, in the number of patents received per scientist and engineer during 1967–84, as well as an increase in the number of patents received in foreign countries. A recent report to the National Science Foundation concluded from an analysis of science citation indexes that Japanese contributions to pure science have been rising in the 1980s (Narin and Olivastro, 1986). Qualitative assessments suggest that at the technological level, Japanese firms have attained positions of leadership, or near leadership, in a number of fields, including fiber optics, composite materials, fermentation processes, computer peripherals, memory chips, and computer-numerically controlled machine tools.

This remarkable record of technological achievement has rested largely on R&D funding from private industry, rather than from government. The share of national R&D that is privately financed is higher in Japan

---

[17] See Lardner, "The Terrible Truth about Japan" (1987). The subtitle summarizes Lardner's analysis: "They Didn't Steal Our VCR Technology – They Invented It." See also Rosenbloom and Cusumano (1987).

than in the United States or other industrial countries (see Okimoto, 1986, p. 551). The share of national R&D expenditures financed by the Japanese government was only 22.2 percent in 1983, and this included grants-in-aid to national and private universities. The comparable figure for the United States in 1983 was 46 percent. The large military R&D budget in the United States accounts for much of this difference, but the Japanese share of R&D financed by the private sector is larger than that for the United States even if we consider only nondefense R&D. R&D investment has been high within the Japanese economy and recently has exceeded that of the U.S. as a share of GNP, as we noted earlier.[18] When military R&D expenditures are removed from the figures for both countries, the share of GNP devoted to R&D in Japan has exceeded the American figure since the early 1960s.

Science and technology policy in Japan

How have public science and technology policies contributed to Japan's remarkable economic and technological achievement, and what lessons can scholars and policymakers derive from the Japanese experience? We do not offer a comprehensive survey of these issues here, but wish to point out a number of ways in which Japanese science and technology policies supported domestic utilization and exploitation of research advances for commercial innovation. This policy focus was especially well suited to Japan's status as a technological follower during much of the postwar period. With Japan's emergence at the technological frontier, however, this objective may have to be supplemented by institutions and policies that will strengthen the commitment of resources to basic research. The institutions and policies employed in the "catch-up" era, while still useful, may be far less effective for ensuring progress at the technological frontier. (See Langlois et al., 1988 for a similar argument.)

The speed and scope of the technological transformation of the Japanese economy have been so rapid and dramatic that it is easy to overlook that many of the institutions of this nation's R&D system were developed during the period of technological "catch-up." This period was one during which other industrial economies operated as technological "testbeds" for the Japanese economy. Areas of technological opportunity could be identified through careful observation by both private firms and public agencies of the economic performance of foreign firms and nations. Many of the difficulties of "picking winners" were reduced (although by no means eliminated – the record of Japanese government industrial policy is a very

---

[18] R&D expenditures constituted roughly 1.70 percent of Japanese GNP in the years 1975–78. This ratio rose to 1.80 percent in 1979 and to 2.77 percent in 1985, exceeding the U.S. GNP share of 2.4 percent in that year.

mixed one) by monitoring technological and economic developments in leading industrial economies.

Such monitoring of foreign technological developments required considerable indigenous scientific and engineering expertise, as well as a substantial investment of resources. As we observed in Chapters 1 and 4, the import and exploitation of foreign technologies by Japanese firms required substantial investments in domestic R&D on the part of these firms in order to absorb and utilize the technology: "There exists a clear positive correlation between the amount of payments for technology importation made by an industry or a firm and the R&D expenditure made by it. Those who imported technology heavily also invested heavily in R&D" (Goto and Wakasugi, 1987, p. 271).[19]

Among the important technology policies that were developed during this period was the Ministry of International Trade and Industries' (MITI) role as a monitor of foreign technological developments and as a negotiator of licensing terms with foreign innovators. In this second role, MITI was able to exercise monopsony power, gaining more favorable terms for the import of technology via licenses and other mechanisms:

> The number of firms importing a given technology was restricted to a few either through "adjustments" amongst the Japanese firms or through the policy authorities' "guidance" to check a rise in payments that competition among the importing firms might have entailed. . . . royalty payments on import of the oxidation [basic oxygen furnace] process for steel production from Austria were held down to under 1 cent per ton for Japan through an agreement between MITI and the industry, while the U.S. firms paid up to 35 cents per ton for the import of the same technology. (Goto and Wakasugi, 1988, pp. 189–190)[20]

MITI's influence on Japanese firms was enhanced by restrictions on the convertibility of the yen that allowed MITI and other public agencies to restrict access to foreign exchange for purchases of technology licenses and capital equipment, and by controls on the domestic capital market. MITI also took pains to ensure that foreign technologies licensed to Japanese firms were made available to a number of domestic firms, and in this way aided the intranational diffusion of technologies developed by foreign firms.

Thus, measures to accelerate the domestic diffusion of foreign technologies reinforced intense interfirm competition in the commercial introduction and production of goods embodying these technologies. Domes-

---

[19] See also Caves and Uekusa (1976).
[20] The comparative data on royalty payments for the BOF steel production process were reported in Lynn (1982).

tic technological development was further aided by tariff and nontariff barriers to foreign access to the Japanese domestic market during the 1950s and 1960s. Japanese "borrower" firms were able to develop and to exploit these technologies within a domestic market that was fiercely competitive but substantially protected from entry by most foreign firms that had technological leads over Japanese enterprises. The rapidly expanding Japanese domestic market was an invaluable "springboard" for the eventual export of advanced products in the automotive, electronics, and other industries. Where this market proved to be too small to support economic levels of production, as in commercial aircraft, export-oriented industries did not materialize within Japan (see Mowery and Rosenberg, 1985).

Another important element of Japanese technology policy during the "catch-up" phase, and one that has attracted considerable foreign attention, was government-sponsored domestic research collaboration among Japanese firms. The role of research collaboration appears to have shifted somewhat over time within Japan. Much of the research collaboration of the 1960s took the form of Engineering Research Associations (ERAs) that were based on the British research associations described in Chapter 5 (see Samuels, 1987).[21]

As in Britain, the ERAs were intended to serve the needs of small and medium-sized firms. Government funds in the form of conditional loans (conditions that varied in severity and enforcement) covered a portion of the costs of ERAs and participant firms received tax benefits. Japanese ERAs differed from their British counterparts, however, in focusing on specific technologies or engineering problems, rather than attempting to provide research assistance to all firms in a particular industrial sector. During the 1970s, the research association scheme was used by government agencies and private firms to launch cooperative research ventures with considerably larger budgets in the electronics and computer fields. These so-called national projects were undertaken in part as a response to foreign pressure on the Japanese government to liberalize access to its domestic market in these industries. These projects, which were intended to operate for roughly five years, were accordingly intended to bring Japanese firms up to the technological frontier, a frontier defined largely by foreign firms. Among the best-known of these projects are the Very Large Scale Integrated Circuit (VLSI) project of 1976–80 and the far less successful 3.75 Computer project of 1972–6 (see Okimoto, 1986, 1987). In addition to their larger budgets, these cooperative research ventures enlisted the largest Japanese firms in their industries.

[21] Although Japanese research consortia that receive public funds have captured the attention of foreign observers, Samuels argues that "more than 90% of joint research and development projects [in Japan] are undertaken through contracts, rather than through government consortia or formal joint venture arrangements" (p. 31).

Some U.S. accounts of Japanese cooperative research projects suggest that they focus on long-term research to advance fundamental knowledge of interest to the participants.[22] Other scholars, however (e.g., Okimoto, 1986, 1987), argue that the "national projects" of the 1970s focused primarily on applied research and development. Indeed, it is difficult to see how temporary research projects lasting no more than five to eight years could conduct truly "long-term" research. The contributions of government funds to their operations also were relatively small and did not approach the level of financial support for such projects as the Very High Speed Integrated Circuit (VHSIC) project from the U.S. Defense Department or the Airbus aircraft consortium from the participating European governments.[23] Rather than concentrating on the development of fundamental knowledge, many of these joint research projects appear to have operated to transfer and "debug" the advanced research findings of foreign firms and scientists, to strengthen a shared knowledge base, and to diffuse intranationally these research findings. Okimoto's assessment of the national research projects is worth noting:

> Certainly the most important R&D in Japan takes place outside the framework of national projects – within the confines of company laboratories. . . . At most, the work done for national projects supplements what individual companies are doing. What it provides is a firmer foundation of basic knowledge on which companies can compete. . .
>
> None of the national projects so far have led to momentous breakthroughs in state-of-the-art technology. Nearly all have been designed simply to close the gap with U.S. leaders (1987, pp. 53–4)[24]

Japanese cooperative research ventures also may compensate in part for the lack of other mechanisms for diffusion that operate quite effectively within the U.S. economy. Limited interfirm labor mobility within Japan means that one of the most important mechanisms for the diffusion of new technologies within the United States, the movement of scientists and

---

[22] Peck (1986) has characterized the activities of the VLSI and other national projects as "longer term generic research, leaving product and process development to individual companies" (p. 222).

[23] Okimoto (1987) estimates the total government contribution to the VLSI project to be $150 million (over five years) and the public subsidy to the 3.75 Computer project to be roughly $228 million (also over five years). By contrast, the projected Defense Department contribution to the VHSIC project is more than $500 million, and Airbus Industrie is reported by reliable sources to have received several billion dollars in public funding over the life of the consortium.

[24] Borrus (1988) also notes that "much of the VLSI program was aimed at catching up to the U.S. industry's capabilities in advanced process technology" (p. 127).

engineers among firms, is largely lacking (see Saxonhouse, 1982, 1986).[25]
Research collaboration in these "national projects" appears to have been most successful where none of the participants were at the technological frontier, and therefore all stood to benefit from sharing research findings and (in some cases) access to advanced government-provided research facilities. Even under these favorable circumstances, the traditionally fierce commercial rivalries among the participants meant that research cooperation often assumed many of the characteristics of an uneasy cease-fire, rather than a genuinely cooperative undertaking. Many of the problems of "free riding" (contributing second-rate researchers or equipment to the joint enterprise, resisting full disclosure of corporate technological knowhow, etc.) that have hampered the operations of the U.S. Microelectronics and Computer Technology Corporation were present in Japanese cooperative research ventures as well.[26]

Research collaboration in Japan appears to have been a component of the nation's technological "catch-up" strategy, one intended to improve the distribution and accessibility of advanced technologies and knowledge to Japanese firms. As such, it focused primarily on the adaptation, distribution, and utilization of existing scientific and technological knowledge, rather than the generation of new fundamental knowledge. As we note in the next chapter, this apparent objective of Japanese cooperative research contrasts with the stated objectives of a number of recently established cooperative research ventures in the United States, which have enlisted the participation of firms with very different technological capabilities and have initially concentrated on fundamental precommercial research.

The technological transformation of the Japanese economy may reduce the utility of cooperative research in large-scale "national projects," although the broader ERA program will retain considerable value. There are several reasons to anticipate such a change. As more and more Japanese firms are at the technological frontier in their industries, foreign sources can no longer provide the necessary technological knowledge for

---

[25] Saxonhouse (1986) correctly points out that the contribution of high domestic savings and investment rates to Japan's impressive economic performance often is overlooked. It is unlikely that any set of science and technology policies, however clever, could have proved successful without the essential contribution of these macroeconomic factors.

[26] See Okimoto (1986) for a similar argument. Fong (1988) discusses these tensions at some length, stating that "to begin with, the member companies [in VLSI] vigorously opposed the notion of cooperative research. On the one hand, the companies welcomed the infusion of funds associated with the VLSI project. At the time, the industry was still reeling from the 1973–74 oil shock. Financial resources were strapped, and government assistance was sought after. On the other hand, the companies wanted to have nothing to do with MITI plans for consolidation, joint research, and the cooperative lab.

"MITI was able to prevail over industry in creating the cooperative lab only after the companies realized that without the lab the entire project – including the much-needed subsidies – would be placed in jeopardy" (p. 41).

commercial innovation. The absorption, adaptation, and intranational diffusion of this knowledge were central functions of cooperative national research projects in the past. Moreover, foreign firms in many industries are now less willing to license their technologies to the Japanese firms that have proved to be such strong competitors.[27] As Westney and Sakakibara have noted, Japanese firms are approaching the "limits of followership" (1986, p. 317).

A second reason for change in the role of cooperative research reflects the changed incentives of the prospective Japanese participants. As Japanese firms in the electronics and computer industries have approached the technological frontier, they have become more reluctant to participate in collaborative research projects. Cooperative research for these firms involves sharing of proprietary know-how with less advanced domestic competitors and promises little for them in the way of access to advanced knowledge or research facilities.[28] In addition, the temporary nature of the cooperative national projects and the fact that they were staffed largely by personnel seconded from member firms prevent these projects from performing the long-term basic research needed by an economy at the technological frontier. Some Japanese policymakers have expressed concern over the apparent inability of cooperative research projects to undertake the basic research that they see as necessary in the Japanese economy.[29]

Even as some U.S. observers recommend emulation of Japanese cooperative research policies and institutions, a search is under way within Japan for new institutions to support indigenous basic research and to underpin commercial innovations. Japanese higher education is unlikely to serve effectively in that capacity in the near future. In contrast to their prominent role as performers of basic research within the United States, universities in Japan receive little public research funding and do not have strong research linkages with industry.[30] As we noted in Chapter 6, graduate scientific training and research are largely divorced from one another in Japan; Okimoto and Saxonhouse have stated that "in Japan,

---

[27] As the 1987 study of international trade in services by the Office of Technology Assessment noted, the unwillingness of foreign producers to license advanced microprocessor designs to Japanese firms contributed to the formation of a joint venture between Hitachi and Fujitsu to develop thirty-two-bit microprocessors. See Yoder (1986), p. 39.

[28] See Samuels (1987); this argument was supported in interviews by one of the authors with personnel from MITI and NEC in Japan, May 1988.

[29] Interviews with MITI personnel, May 1988.

[30] "The $4.8 billion that the U.S. government provides in support of R&D in universities and colleges is roughly six times what Japanese universities receive in R&D support from their Government. Not surprisingly, U.S. academic institutions in 1981 awarded six times as many doctoral degrees in the sciences and engineering as Japanese institutions. In biology the United States graduates 36 times the number of Ph.D.s and in chemistry 10 times the number" (Okimoto and Saxonhouse 1987, p. 412).

advanced training takes place within the firm" (1987, p. 412).[31] Although reform of Japanese higher education has been discussed extensively and is likely in the near future,[32] discussion of new institutions in the Japanese research system has focused on two other potential sources of basic research: national laboratories and military research.

Although government basic research laboratories long have been funded by the Science and Technology Agency and by the Ministry of Posts and Telecommunications (MPT) (which, as the administrator of Nippon Telegraph and Telephone (NTT) during its period of public ownership, oversaw the Electrical Communications Laboratory), recent initiatives may expand the role of public laboratories within Japan and strengthen their ties to industry. The "Fifth-Generation Computer" national research project, for example, has spawned a freestanding laboratory, the Institute for New Generation Computer Technology (ICOT), that may be funded beyond the scheduled completion of the advanced computer research project.

As a result of the privatization of NTT and the ensuing bureaucratic struggles between MITI and MPT over the proceeds of the sale of NTT shares,[33] as well as concern over the availability of funding for basic research, the Japan Key Technologies Program (JKTP) was established in 1985. Among the objectives of JKTP, which is funded from the sale of NTT shares, is the establishment of laboratories with a permanent research staff that will work in close cooperation with industry, including the temporary transfer of industry research personnel to positions within these laboratories. The scope for substantial increases in public funding for such institutions is limited (hence the reliance on sales of NTT stock for much of the funding of JKTP) by the severe constraints on the expansion of the Japanese national budget and the likelihood that demands for

[31] Although university–industry links within Japan are less well developed than is true within the United States, the Japanese system of higher education has made very important contributions to the technological performance of the national economy through its training and production of large numbers of engineers. According to Ergas (1987, Table 6, p. 216), Japan graduated nearly twice as many baccalaureate engineers, on a per capita basis, as did the United States in 1982 (respectively, 630 and 350 graduates per million population). Although the per capita stock of engineers in the two economies does not differ greatly, Japanese universities are producing a flow of new engineers that is proportionately much greater.

[32] In 1984, Prime Minister Nakasone appointed an expert group to recommend reforms in the entire educational system in Japan, including the university system. See Marshall (1986), which provides the following assessment: "The program will forge ahead at glacial speed.

"Responding to a foreigner's skepticism about the practical impact of all this [study and reform commissions appointed by Prime Minister Nakasone in 1986], some Japanese leaders said it should be regarded as the first step in a campaign that will take more than 10 years to complete. . . Others said privately there is more noise than substance in the whole program, and doubted that it would amount to much in the end" (p. 270).

[33] See Johnson (1989) and Samuels (1987).

public spending on other objectives (e.g., attending to the needs of a rapidly aging population) will grow in the near future. Nevertheless, research institutions dedicated to the conduct of basic research may become somewhat more attractive than large-scale national cooperative research projects for future research and technology development in Japan.

Another source of funding for long-term research with potential commercial applications that has received growing attention within Japan is increased military spending. As pressures on the Japanese government for greater "burden sharing" and application of advanced commercial technologies in joint U.S.–Japanese defense research projects expand, so too will the Japanese military budget. Indeed, the hitherto inviolable ceiling of 1 percent of GNP on Japanese military spending was recently pierced. The "spillovers" of military research spending for commercial innovation have been cited by several groups as another potential source of indigenous research for commercial innovation:

> Europe and America are paying huge sums of money in the name of military research to outside entities, including private companies, for basic research. We should note that in comparison there is far less basic research in Japanese companies, and a long-term perspective demands greater efforts to spur private sector basic research.[34]

According to Samuels and Whipple (1988),[35] the recent decision of the Japanese Defense Ministry to pursue the development of a new design for the FSX fighter aircraft (in collaboration with U.S. firms) was motivated by MITI's desire to exploit military–civilian spillovers in the aircraft industry. This strategy is unlikely to yield the payoffs that Japanese policymakers seek, but their pursuit of it is nonetheless revealing.

Japanese science and technology policies appear to be entering a period of change and experimentation for reasons that are similar to those producing change in the U.S. national research system. The historic focus of policy on rapid absorption and intranational diffusion of scientific and technological advances from foreign sources must be supplemented by

---

[34] See "Japan's Commitment to 'New Globalism' and Its Choice as a 'New Industrial-Cultural Nation' " (1988). This possibility also has been raised in interviews with MITI personnel, May 1988.

[35] The authors conclude that "increased defense production has emerged in the 1980's as a new strategy for aerospace industrial development, . . . it has emerged because it is a versatile and effective strategy that satisfies the needs and interests of numerous influential groups. . . . Convinced that aerospace can help revitalize the troubled heavy industrial sector and spread high-technology benefits throughout the economy, frustrated in attempts to develop commercial aircraft, anxious to capitalize on new opportunities to exploit domestic technology, and continually pressured by the United States to rearm more vigorously, Japanese policymakers in the 1980s have turned to military spending as a mechanism for industrial development" (p. 305).

efforts to develop more of these advances indigenously, albeit in cooperation with scientists and engineers in other industrial nations. This period of flux points to a shift in the importance of cooperative research projects of the type that have received extensive attention in the United States.

Cooperative research will remain important within the Japanese economy as a mechanism for diffusion and utilization of technological knowledge; as we argued earlier in this chapter, historically it has served this function, and there may be considerable potential for this use of cooperative research in the United States. It is less likely, however, that cooperative research projects will occupy a central position in the efforts of policymakers to develop new institutions for the performance of advanced scientific research. Within Japan, cooperative research has served a somewhat different function from that for which it has been promoted within the United States. Cooperative research in Japan has functioned effectively to serve the goals that we noted should receive greater weight within U.S. science and technology policy, namely, supporting the diffusion and utilization of technological and scientific knowledge. Use of this device by U.S. firms and policymakers to support advances in the scientific or technological frontier, however, is not supported by the Japanese experience – care must be taken to match the instrument to the objective.[36] Indeed, uncritical imitation of this policy overlooks the evidence that Japanese policymakers are now considering policies that have long been central features of the U.S. national research system.

The organization of innovation within the Japanese firm

Although Japanese government science and technology policies have contributed significantly to the dramatic transformation of that nation's economy, the success of these policies has rested on the decisions (especially the investment decisions) of private firms within Japan. In briefly summarizing some key aspects of the management of innovation within the Japanese firm, we wish to point out the compatibility of public policies and the objectives of private firms during the catch-up period. In particular, as we will note, the management of innovation within the Japanese firm has focused on an "incrementalist" strategy of intensive analysis of product features, consumer preferences, and process technology, striving to integrate the manufacturing and development processes as closely as possible. This focus of internal R&D efforts has been supplemented by an intensive scanning of the external environment for scientific and tech-

[36] As we note in Chapter 10, this "match" is particularly important because of the possibility that policies designed to support more rapid intranational diffusion may conflict with those intended to support greater domestic investment in scientific or technological research.

nological advances that could be incorporated in an evolutionary fashion into new products.

Since innovation is the production of new technological knowledge, the basic nature and direction of the R&D process in the context of Japanese firms is determined by the ways in which information is processed and utilized within the organization and the structure of incentives that supports such information processing. We first present three basic characteristics of Japanese organizations, whether the manufacturing department of a firm or the bureaucratic organization of a government ministry, and then discuss their role within the context of the Japanese firm's innovative activities.[37]

1. *Reliance on on-site information:* Instead of relying on centralized information and direction for problem solving, Japanese organizations typically undertake this task in a decentralized manner, relegating it to the lowest possible level of the formal hierarchy. This dispersed problem solving provides considerable autonomy to the operating subordinate unit (for example, autonomous shop control by the work team or the jurisdictional autonomy of the *genkyoku* [original] bureau and its section in the ministerial bureaucracy). In Aoki's view (1986, 1988), the Japanese organization relies heavily on the localized use of on-site information rather than on the hierarchical control of specialized knowledge.

2. *Reliance on horizontal communications:* When problem solving must be dealt with jointly by multiple functional units, direct communication among the relevant units without clear direction from a common superordinate is typical (for example, the "kanban" system in the manufacturing process, the "ringi" system in administrative organization, etc.). Where a supervisor intervenes, he does so as an arbitrator rather than as a controller. The Japanese organization often appears to be a coalition of semiautonomous component units rather than a monolithic entity controlled by a central office.

3. *Ranking hierarchy:* In both manufacturing and bureaucratic organizations, personnel are evaluated by their contributions to collective problem solving rather than on the basis of more abstract measures of individual skills. Promotion often takes the form of transfer to other departments. The intraorganizational transfer of personnel facilitates and reinforces the horizontal communications among functional subunits. Because of the long-term nature of personnel evaluation and the emphasis on internal transfers, the central personnel department of the Japanese organization has much more power than its Western counterpart.

The organization of R&D and the innovation process within the Japa-

---

[37] Much of this discussion draws on Aoki and Rosenberg (1987). See also Aoki (1986, 1988), and Rosenberg and Steinmueller (1988).

nese firm share the three following general features of Japanese organization.

1. *The importance of the engineering department:* Although central research laboratories in many firms are now expanding their shares of the enterprise's R&D budget and have gained in prestige, the engineering department of the manufacturing division in the large Japanese firm continues to play a more significant role in the R&D process than do engineering departments in U.S. firms. The engineering department is generally located at the manufacturing site, and engineers assigned there normally have considerable know-how concerning the manufacturing process.

An important source of such know-how is close involvement with manufacturing operations. Japanese firms' deployment of engineers encourages such involvement and familiarity much more than do the personnel practices of U.S. firms. Based on his intensive field studies of the practices followed in adopting new manufacturing technologies in a number of Japanese and U.S. firms, Jaikumar (1986) concluded that Japanese firms deploy far more engineers on the factory floor than U.S. firms to work with and debug new production equipment and to improve the overall manufacturing process.[38] The primary responsibility of the engineering department's research function is to develop and to extend applications of manufacturing process know-how to related uses.

The importance of the engineering department of the manufacturing division, located on the manufacturing site, as well as its intensive monitoring and analysis of manufacturing processes through extensive use of engineers within the process, serve to strengthen the reliance on the localized use of on-site knowledge. Engineers draw on and apply the existing stock of knowledge rather than generate new research. Perhaps most important, the engineering department supports the close interchange of information between those responsible for product design and those responsible for the manufacturing technology. At the same time, it facilitates communication among professionals who have separate but interdependent responsibilities.

This approach to innovation places great emphasis on process research. The importance of manufacturing process R&D within the Japanese firm is revealed in recent data collected by Mansfield from a survey of one hundred U.S. and Japanese firms (Mansfield, 1988). Whereas two-thirds of firm-financed R&D in Mansfield's sample of fifty U.S. firms was devoted to product R&D, with the remaining one-third being spent on process research, the proportions among his fifty Japanese firms were re-

---

[38] As we noted earlier, these international differences in the use of engineers may well reflect the greater abundance of new engineering graduates in Japan.

versed. More than two-thirds of the industrial R&D in the Japanese firms surveyed by Mansfield went to process R&D.

To understand the role of this process-oriented, incremental engineering research within the innovation process, it is useful to distinguish between two kinds of activities that may initiate innovation – "invention" and "analytic design":

> An invention is a new means for achieving some function not obvious beforehand to someone skilled in the prior art. It therefore marks a significant departure from past practice. Analytic design . . . consists of analysis of various arrangements of existing components or of modifications of designs already within the state of the art to accomplish new tasks or to accomplish old tasks more effectively or at lower cost. It is thus not invention in the usual sense. However, analytic design is currently a more common initiator of the central-chain-of-innovation than invention. (Kline and Rosenberg, 1986, p. 292)

"Noninventive" analytic design is an important and common initiator of innovative activity, one that the Japanese firm is well equipped to perform by virtue of the prominent role played by the engineering department.

This type of research is also well suited to the strategy of the "fast second," monitoring developments outside of the firm and moving quickly to introduce high-quality, lower-cost modifications and designs of products or technologies introduced elsewhere. Much of the innovative success of Japanese firms during the postwar period of "catch-up" relied heavily on this strategy of the "fast second." The intensive collection and analysis of detailed knowledge and information enabled Japanese firms to exploit production-related learning, despite the fact that in a number of cases, these firms were not the inventors of a particular commercial technology or application. Moreover, the intensive cultivation of a firm-specific knowledge base, combined with low levels of interfirm mobility of engineers and scientists, meant that "leakage" of such knowledge to other Japanese or foreign firms was minimized.[39] An interesting question that Japanese firms must face is whether such a strategy will suffice in the future, when Japanese firms are less able to draw on the developments of others and when other firms with lower-cost labor and considerable engineering capabilities, especially the Asian NICs, are able to follow the "fast second" strategy.

　2. *Transfers of researchers and engineers:* If a research agenda formu-

---

[39] This point is an important one, since as Lieberman and Montgomery (1988) note, learning effects are important competitive factors only to the extent that learning does not rapidly diffuse among firms.

lated by the engineering department requires more basic scientific knowledge than it possesses, the research may be undertaken by the central research laboratory. When a research project is commissioned at the central research laboratory, young engineers from the engineering department are normally dispatched to the central laboratory to participate in the research team assigned to that project. After the research team has solved the basic problems, the project is handed off to the engineering department of the commissioning manufacturing division and the engineers are transferred back to the original department. They are ordinarily responsible for the continuation of R&D as well as the implementation of the completed project into volume manufacture. Superior performance in these successive stages may result in the promotion of divisional engineers to managerial positions in the manufacturing division and supports further advancement in the career hierarchy within companies. Many top managers of large Japanese manufacturing companies are former divisional engineers, a fact that reflects the strategic importance of the engineering department.

A researcher who is assigned to the central research laboratory on entry to a firm may move to a divisional engineering department after reaching the age of thirty, usually as a carrier of a development project in which he has been involved. He takes responsibility for moving the project from the development stage to manufacturing. In view of the strategic position of the Japanese engineering department for career advancement, the transfer from central research to the manufacturing division historically has been regarded as a major promotion (this may change if central research laboratories continue to expand their budgets, autonomy, and internal prestige). Several years later, a further promotion may lead to entry into the upper managerial hierarchy.

The close connections between the central research laboratory and the engineering department that are facilitated by the transfer of personnel between the two, as well as the close connections between the engineering department and the manufacturing shops within a division, strengthen interfirm communications and contribute to the utilization of technological and scientific research results.

3. *Ranking hierarchy:* Researchers and engineers within the Japanese firm share the cost of human investment with the firm when they are young. They reap returns to the investment only when and if they are promoted to higher ranks (possibly managerial ranks). Therefore, quitting a firm in midcareer is likely to carry serious financial penalties (the loss of seniority premiums and retirement bonuses). As they are promoted according to their contributions to R&D projects and managerial leadership in the subsequent commercialization of new products, researchers and engineers contribute to company-specific projects rather than developing

individually marketable research capabilities. These arrangements reduce the likelihood that researchers in whom investments have been made by the company will depart before the returns to these investments are reaped by the firm. Therefore, the firm is likely to invest in researchers (by sending them to scientific conferences, or to graduate schools abroad at company expense, etc.). As we have noted, the limited interfirm mobility of researchers that results from these policies may impede the diffusion of new technologies within Japan. In the absence of offsetting policies such as cooperative research, this could impose social costs by retarding the diffusion of new technologies and knowledge, despite the contribution of such limited mobility to the private profitability of firms' investment in the human capital of their research staff.

Japanese firms have been particularly effective in the downstream phases of the innovative process, such as redesign of existing products, instead of concentrating on invention. There have been some notable instances of an increasing emphasis on the importance of innovative analytic design, as in the case of the videocassette recorder. The Japanese firm has made effective use of feedback from marketing to production (feedback from consumers' complaints, opinions, and suggestions leading to product improvement), from production to redesign (through value engineering and value analysis), from product design to analytic design (leading to new products), and so on. The use of such feedback is facilitated by the horizontal communications between adjacent functional units, often facilitated by rotation of personnel between them.

On the other hand, the Japanese firm has been less effective in developing radically new products, although important exceptions exist. One reason for this is that radical innovation requires entrepreneurial leadership, often involving a single individual who is prepared to leave and establish a new firm. Japanese management, however, has generally been more concerned with the efficient use of existing human resources than with possible new market opportunities and focusing R&D on such possibilities. As more and more Japanese firms move toward the technological frontier, this incrementalist strategy may lose some of its effectiveness. The gradual expansion of central research and fundamental research budgets within many Japanese firms is evidence of a shift in industrial R&D strategies to more pioneering research.

The Japanese firm has been most skillful in the development stage of the innovation process – testing and redesign, small modifications of product based on careful engineering attention to detail, and so forth. Engineers at the manufacturing division of the Japanese firm actively scan outside scientific information and use this information to augment their own stock of knowledge. The priority given to the organization and management of these downstream development activities by Japanese firms is reflected in the evidence that in some sectors, Japanese firms can develop new products in half the time required by U.S. firms (Imai, Nonaka, and Takenchi, 1985; see also Clark et al., 1987). An even more remarkable difference in R&D performance was described in Mansfield's recent (1988) survey of Japanese and U.S. R&D. Mansfield found that Japanese and U.S. firms do not differ greatly in the amount of time or money required to bring to market innovations based on technology developed within the firm. Consistent with their postwar experience as careful monitors and exploiters of external scientific and technological developments, however, Japanese firms are far more efficient in exploiting technology developed externally:

> Whereas in the United States the commercialization of an innovation based on external technology takes more time and about as much money as the commercialization of one based on internal technology, in Japan it takes about 10% less time and over 50% less money than the commercialization of an internal technology-based innovation. (Mansfield, 1988, p. 1770)

Managers of the innovation process within the Japanese firm have worked to improve intrafirm lines of communication among research, engineering, and manufacturing operations, while simultaneously monitoring the external technological environment with great care. Supported by public science and technology policies aimed at improving the access of Japanese firms to foreign scientific and technological knowledge, this strategy has been remarkably effective. Both public policy and management strategy have focused on the utilization, much more than the generation, of the knowledge that is essential to innovation. As such, the Japanese example illustrates the importance of this dimension of R&D organization that is often overlooked by neoclassical economists.

The critical challenge for Japanese firms and Japanese government agencies is that of adjusting to the new environment, one in which technological borrowing from other advanced industrial economies may prove more difficult, even as the international transfer and exploitation of technology to NICs is increasing competitive pressure on Japanese firms that have followed the strategy of the "fast second." If the manufacturing process expertise and rapid commercialization capabilities of Japanese firms are maintained, the strategy of the "fast second" could remain viable. At least two potential hazards, however, are present in this approach. The first reflects intensifying competition from firms in such nations as Brazil, Korea, and Taiwan. Just as the United States and other industrial nations served as models of sorts for Japanese firms and policymakers in the 1950s and 1960s, Japan is serving as the model for many firms in these nations that pursue export-oriented strategies. There are relatively few "secrets" of Japanese firms' success at this point, and just as many U.S. firms have implemented many of the lessons learned from their Japanese competitors, so too will firms in the NICs. If these firms continue to develop their indigenous scientific and technological expertise, the "fast second" strategy may be theirs, rather than Japan's.

The second difficulty with the strategy of the "fast second" is a more general one. The manufacturing expertise that has proved essential to this strategy within the Japanese firm simply is not equally critical in all industries, as we noted earlier. Although production expertise, along with astute management and marketing, has proved to be extremely effective in such industries as integrated circuits and automobiles, Japanese firms have been far less successful in penetrating foreign markets in commercial aircraft, software and chemicals.[40] In these and other industries, the key competitive assets may not consist solely or even primarily of production-related ones. As and when these industries become more important in the global economy of the future, Japanese firms will have to develop other strategies and competitive assets. This process has already begun.

Conclusion: The structure of an R&D system in a world of technological equals

Changes in the economic and technological environment are eroding the historical dominance of the intrafirm form of governance of technological innovation within the U.S. economy. The higher development costs associated with many new technologies have reduced the economic benefits that devolved from the generation of scientific or technological knowledge and have greatly increased the risks of commercial innovation. Combined with more rapid product cycles in many industries, the increased importance of foreign markets, and the fact that foreign firms frequently possess critical technological, marketing, or production capabilities, the higher costs of innovation have led a growing number of U.S. firms to seek out foreign partners in the development of new products and processes. Although these joint ventures do indeed spread the risks and costs of innovation and facilitate the penetration of foreign markets by U.S. producers of high-technology products, they also increase the rate at which technology moves across international boundaries. A complementary response to intense cost pressures in R&D and the perceived need to decentralize in-house R&D to make it more responsive to market has been growing research collaboration between U.S. firms and/or research collaboration between firms and universities. International collaborative ventures, do-

---

[40] See Mowery and Rosenberg (1985).

mestic R&D collaboration among firms, and university–industry research collaboration all represent a dramatic shift away from the postwar reliance by large U.S. firms on intrafirm innovation.

The technological and competitive environments of U.S. firms have changed drastically since 1945. Much of the change in the competitive environment is not a negative, but a major positive achievement, reflecting the successful economic reconstruction of Western Europe and Japan, as well as the increasing economic strength of such nations as South Korea, Taiwan, Singapore, and Brazil. These developments were the objective of U.S. foreign and economic policies for much of the past four decades, and on the whole contribute to the stabilization and growth of the world economy. In addition, as Nelson (1988) among others has noted, the thirty-year period of U.S. technological dominance was unprecedented and almost certainly represented a departure from a longer-run trend toward greater technological equality between the United States and the economies of Western Europe and Japan.

Both the United States and Japan face challenges to their national R&D systems that functioned with considerable effectiveness during the four decades following the end of World War II. It is tempting to speculate that adaptation to the challenges of global competition and technological ferment may produce some convergence of the R&D systems of these advanced economies. It is possible, for example, that Japan's research system may shift toward one in which universities, defense applied research, and public and private corporate laboratories devoted to basic research play a more important role. Within the United States, much more emphasis is being placed on better integration of process and product research within the firm and on cooperation among firms in research, both characteristics long associated with Japanese R&D, even as the reliance on military–civilian spillovers and large-scale public basic research funding is receiving more critical scrutiny. Regardless of the eventual outcome, it is clear that the technological and scientific interdependence of these economies and research systems will continue to increase as a result of more rapid transfer of technologies and of the new research institutions being developed. One of the most important emergent structures for U.S.–Japanese technological cooperation and transfer is international collaboration in research and product development, one of the topics covered in the next chapter.

9

International and domestic collaboration in research and development

Chapter 8 described the changes that have occurred during the past three decades in the international competitive and technological environment of U.S. manufacturing firms. These changes, which include the development of Japanese technological competition, have led to considerable experimentation and innovation in the U.S. R&D system. One of the most widespread types of innovation is the effort by firms to develop external sources of research and development expertise. These efforts have resulted in considerable expansion of collaboration in R&D that involves U.S. and foreign firms, as well as U.S. universities. Collaborative ventures obviously represent a considerable shift away from the in-house research and development that dominated industrial research during the first seventy-five years of this century.

The causes and consequences of these new organizational structures are still uncertain, since in most cases collaboration is less than ten years old. Nevertheless, there appear to be important contrasts in structure and motives between the international and domestic research and development ventures into which U.S. firms have entered. One must distinguish among at least three broad categories of research collaboration: collaborative ventures between U.S. and foreign firms; research collaboration among U.S. firms; and domestic university–industry research collaboration. International collaborative ventures focus mainly on development, production, and marketing, rather than precommercial research. Thus far, domestic collaborations among U.S. firms have been concerned with research that is less applied in character and less closely linked to a specific commercial product. In general, however, these domestic collaborative ventures do not focus primarily on basic research despite the intentions and founding aspirations of several of them. Indeed, their role and activities are likely to change over time. Finally, university–industry research collaboration appears to incorporate scientific and engineering research of a more fundamental character. These different forms of collaboration are not substitutes but complements, and their effectiveness depends on a strong in-house research capability.

Public funding from the federal and state governments has supported much of the recent growth in university–industry research collaboration.

With the significant exceptions of Sematech and the National Center for Manufacturing Sciences (see Chapter 6), however, public funding has not been important in recently established U.S. research consortia involving only private firms, nor have U.S. public funds supported the international collaborative activities of U.S. firms. This state of affairs contrasts with that in Western Europe, where public funds have been very important in such collaborative research programs as Alvey in Great Britain or Eureka, Esprit, and Brite in the Common Market countries. Public funds have supported the international Airbus Industrie consortium that involves Western European firms. Research collaboration among industrial firms in Japan also has benefited from public funding.

Advantages of research collaboration

Many of the widely cited advantages of collaborative research are grounded in the neoclassical analysis of R&D investment discussed in Chapter 1 and elsewhere. As Bozeman, Link, and Zardkoohi (1986) note, if research collaboration among firms can lower the costs to any single firm of R&D and if the results of such research are made available to the participants, cooperative research can reduce the severity of the market failure stemming from the limited appropriability of research results. Since the profits from basic research are particularly difficult to appropriate, this argument suggests that cooperation among firms in basic research should be especially effective.

Access to research results at lower cost has been an important motive for the establishment of numerous cooperative research programs and university–industry cooperative research programs in recent years. These programs allow participants to monitor developments in specific technologies or scientific disciplines at lower cost than the development of an independent in-house research capability. The importance of such a monitoring capability has increased in recent years with growth in the costs of research and development. As we noted in Chapter 8, technological convergence, which has made unfamiliar technologies in many industries central to the competitive future of firms in these industries, also has increased the importance of this monitoring function.

Another argument in favor of cooperative R&D concerns its efficiency. Duplication among the research activities of competitor firms (Hirshleifer, 1971) can be reduced through collaboration in research. Moreover, if the research process is characterized by economies of scale, collaboration can lower the costs per unit of R&D. By spreading the costs of R&D among firms, cooperative R&D also lowers the costs to any single firm of the failure of a research program, reducing another disincentive to invest in R&D.

Disadvantages of collaborative research

The benefits of collaborative research rest on a number of assumptions. Critical evaluation of these assumptions suggests that cooperative research ventures are not a panacea and will not be equally useful in all industries. Research collaboration may aid the rapid commercialization or development of many technologies, but collaboration alone is insufficient for commercial success or the realization of an economic payoff.

The first limitation of cooperative research rests on the criticism of the neoclassical framework we set out in earlier chapters. The fruits of research do not consist solely of information that can be utilized for commercial purposes at minimal cost. The output of cooperative research must be absorbed by the participant firms and transformed into commercially relevant knowledge. This transformation typically requires considerable intrafirm expertise (Mowery, 1983; Cohen and Levinthal, 1987). Cooperative research thus is not a substitute for, but a complement to, in-house research. In order to exploit externally performed research, whether this research is performed in a multifirm consortium, a federal laboratory, or a university, participant firms must have some in-house expertise. Some duplication of the in-house research investments of firms thus is inevitable even when these firms participate in collaborative research.

Moreover, to the extent that basic research requires a larger investment in this in-house "absorption mechanism," as the Balfour Committee referred to it (Chapter 5), participants in cooperative research may react to the high costs of exploiting collaborative basic research by shifting the collaborative research agenda away from basic research. These pressures appear to have led such well-established cooperative research institutions as the Electric Power Research Institute to reduce their commitment to basic research, as the discussion in Chapter 1 noted.

The structure of cooperative research programs also may reduce the productivity of the research performed within them. Nelson (1961) has argued that diversity in research projects provides an important hedge against the possibility that any single research project will be fruitless. Yet if all or most firms in an industry participate in a cooperative research scheme, the number of independent lines of inquiry in specific problem areas may decline. Heavy reliance on cooperative research may reduce the diversity of research projects in a sector or technology (although this outcome is not a necessary result of cooperative research), reducing the productivity of the larger research effort. Scott's analysis (1987) of preliminary evidence suggests that the National Cooperative Research Act (NCRA) may have had this effect.

The existence of the research economies of scale that are widely cited as a source of efficiency gains through research collaboration also is not well supported by empirical evidence. The average costs of research experiments at large, specialized research facilities, such as wind tunnels or advanced instrumentation (discussed later in this chapter), will decline with more intensive use. There exists no strong evidence, however, suggesting that all industrial R&D exhibits significant economies of scale (Fisher and Temin, 1974), nor are there indicators that enable one to identify the industries or technologies characterized by R&D scale economies.

Cooperative research that focuses exclusively on basic research offers relatively few opportunities for collusion among competitors in the marketplace. Collaborative research does, however, create some potential for anticompetitive behavior in research and in other areas of business activity.[1] There is little evidence that cooperative research programs have resulted in such collusion in research, development, or other areas of business behavior (e.g., pricing or output decisions), nor need collusion among U.S. firms result in significant market power within an open economy. Nevertheless, such collusion could restrict the diffusion of a technology in the early stages of its development or prevent the development of a diversified portfolio of approaches within a technology. The potential for such abuses is greater in domestic and international ventures that involve applied research, product development, or manufacturing, rather than basic research.

International collaborative ventures

As we noted in Chapter 8, during the past two decades the relative economic and technological strengths of the United States have declined.[2] These strengths are now more evenly distributed among U.S. and foreign firms. Combined with changes in product and process technologies and in the industrial and trade policies of the United States and foreign governments, this new international economic environment has contributed to growth in the number and importance of collaborative ventures between U.S. and foreign firms in product development, manufacture, and marketing, activities that are generally somewhat further "downstream" than those typically included in U.S. domestic research collaborations.

Many of these interfirm alliances involve significant exchanges of technology, and several assessments have expressed concern about the long-term implications of international collaboration for the competitiveness of

---

[1] Collaboration among U.S. automobile firms during the 1960s in applied research on anti-pollution technologies was the target of an antitrust suit by the U.S. Department of Justice that was based in part on these concerns (Office of Technology Assessment, 1981; Brodley, 1982; Alic, 1986).

[2] This section draws on Mowery (1988c).

U.S. industry.[3] Other accounts, as we saw in Chapter 8, assert that collaborative ventures will produce a "hollow corporation," not engaged in producing goods, employing a small number of highly paid financial and marketing executives and few if any production workers ("Special Report," *Business Week*, March 3, 1986). Still others view international collaboration as an essential part of global competitive strategy (Perlmutter and Heenan, 1986; Porter and Fuller, 1986).

International collaborative ventures are not completely novel undertakings for U.S. firms, but those into which U.S. firms have entered during the past decade differ in some significant ways from the joint ventures of the 1950s and 1960s. International collaboration is in part a response to the same factors that have given rise to increased domestic collaboration in research among U.S. firms. Why and how have these factors contributed to the growing resort to international collaborative ventures? How do they influence the types of collaboration between U.S. and foreign firms that have developed in recent years?

Collaboration between U.S. and foreign firms assumes many forms. Many collaborative ventures fit a narrow definition of a joint venture, including separate incorporation as an entity in which equity holdings are divided among the partners. Others, such as partnerships between "risk-sharing" subcontractors and prime contractors, or the purchase by one firm of an equity share in another, do not. In some industries, joint ventures and other forms of collaboration are extensions of subcontracting relationships that cover product development and manufacture; others focus on marketing of products manufactured largely by one partner. The following discussion uses the terms "collaboration" and "joint venture" interchangeably and therefore occasionally denotes as joint ventures organizational structures that do not fit the legal definition of this entity.[4]

An international collaborative venture may be defined as *interfirm collaboration in product development, manufacture, or marketing that spans national boundaries, is not based on arm's-length market transactions, and includes substantial contributions by partners of capital, technology, or other assets.* This definition excludes other forms of international economic activity, such as export, direct foreign investment (which implies

---

[3] Reich and Mankin (1986) argue that "the U.S. strategy [in joint ventures with Japan] seems shortsighted. In exchange for a few lower skilled, lower paying jobs and easy access to our competitors' high-quality, low-cost products, we are apparently willing to sacrifice our competitiveness in a host of industries – autos, machine tools, consumer electronics, and semiconductors today, and others in the future" (pp. 78–9).

[4] The formal structure of collaborative ventures, however, often has little to do with either their management or their success, as Gullander (1976) has noted: "There are indications that the difference between a contractual and an equity relationship is highly exaggerated; sophisticated 'cooperators' seem to downplay the importance of ownership control as compared to management control or control through other means" (p. 86).

complete intrafirm control of production and product development activities), and the sale of technology through licensing.

Joint ventures have long been common in extractive industries such as mining and petroleum production (see Stuckey 1983) and account for a significant share of the foreign investment of U.S. manufacturing firms since World War II. Several features of recent collaborative ventures, however, differentiate them from prior cases. The number of collaborations, both those involving only U.S. firms and those between U.S. and foreign enterprises, appears to have grown. Joint ventures now appear in a much wider range of industries.[5]

International alliances involving U.S. firms now are appearing in industries in which direct foreign investment or multinational corporate organization was the exception rather than the rule. Commercial aircraft, for example, is an industry in which direct foreign investment was minimal (Hirsch, 1976). Yet as we made clear in Chapter 7, this industry now is among the leaders in international collaboration (Mowery, 1987). Other U.S. industries in which these ventures have assumed considerable importance in recent years include both "mature" (e.g., steel and automobiles) and "young" (biotechnology) industries.

Many recent collaborative ventures include activities, such as research, product development, and production for world markets, that were absent from the ventures of the pre-1975 era, which focused primarily on production and marketing for a specific foreign market. Collaborations that include R&D and product development may result in significant technology transfer. In some cases (e.g., commercial aircraft), most of the technology transfer within international alliances consists of exports of technology from the United States. In other industries, however, such as steel or autos, these ventures are associated with significant U.S. imports of technology.

International collaborative ventures are based on an exchange relationship, but the commodities exchanged often differ from those exchanged

---

[5] Harrigan (1984) found that domestic joint ventures involving U.S. firms had grown during the previous decade. In the 1960s, joint ventures were concentrated in chemicals; primary metals; paper; and stone, clay, and glass industries, but now extend beyond these sectors (see Harrigan 1985). Hladik (1985) found significant growth from 1975 to 1982 in the number of international joint ventures involving U.S. firms, a growth trend that almost certainly continued through 1985. Hladik's conclusions disagree with those of Ghemawat, Porter, and Rawlinson (1986), who compiled a time series of "international coalition announcements" (joint ventures, license agreements, supply agreements, and "other long-term interfirm accords" [p. 346]) covering 1970–82 that displays no upward trend. The differences are likely to be more apparent than real; the Ghemawat et al. data base includes a number of interfirm mechanisms of collaboration that are excluded by Hladik. The possibility thus exists that a shift in the mix of the different forms considered by Ghemawat et al. occurred during 1970–82, as joint ventures and other collaborative agreements increased in importance relative to such alternatives as licensing.

through licensing or export. Some collaborations allow U.S. and foreign firms to pool their technological assets in a single product or product line without merging all of their activities into a single corporate entity. Other collaborative ventures combine one firm's technological capabilities with the marketing or distribution assets of another for a single product. Why are collaborative ventures, rather than alternative mechanisms such as licensing, employed for this exchange?

Alternative channels for the exploitation of technological and other firm-specific assets

Alternatives to direct foreign investment for the exploitation of firm-specific assets include licensing and collaborative ventures. These different channels for the realization of the value of an asset may be substitutes or complements, and firms frequently utilize multiple channels. The advantages and disadvantages of each of these methods depend on the characteristics of the asset in question. These factors also affect the activities undertaken within collaborative ventures, an issue that receives attention later in this chapter.

In many instances, collaborative ventures provide an alternative to licensing for the exchange of corporate assets that are based on a firm's technological capabilities.[6] Markets for the licensing of advanced technologies that exploit firm-specific knowledge often are very thin, however, with few buyers or sellers. The dearth of alternative outlets for sellers or alternative sources for buyers means that opportunistic behavior may hamper the operation of markets for technology licenses.[7] Other impediments to licensing technological assets include the tacit nature of much of the knowledge necessary to exploit the technology, the need to reveal a great deal about a technological advance in order to convince a prospective licensee of the value of the license (Arrow, 1962; Teece, 1986), and the problems of regulating licensor and licensee behavior in a dynamic and uncertain world.

Licensing is likely to be preferred to either direct foreign investment or collaborative ventures in technologies that are not complex, have strong,

---

[6] Caves (1982) notes that "as indicators of these [firm-specific] assets, economists have seized on the outlays for advertising and research and development (R&D) undertaken by firms classified to an industry. That the share of foreign subsidiary assets in the total assets of U.S. corporations increases significantly with the importance of advertising and R&D outlays in the industry has been confirmed in many studies" (p. 9).

[7] In Williamson's terminology, a "small numbers condition" characterizes such markets: "The transactional dilemma that is posed is this: it is in the interest of each party to seek terms most favorable to him, which encourages opportunistic representations and haggling. The interests of the *system*, by contrast, are promoted if the parties can be joined in such a way as to avoid both the bargaining costs and the indirect costs (mainly maladaptation costs) which are generated in the process" (1975, p. 26; emphasis in the original).

well-enforced patents, are relatively mature, and do not rely on "user-active" innovation (von Hippel, 1976), with its requirements for strong links between marketing and product development. Industries in which these features are not characteristic of the technology and means other than licensing are important in realizing value from technology include steel, automobiles, commercial aircraft, and telecommunications equipment. Licensing is an important alternative to international collaboration, however, in pharmaceuticals. Licensing and collaboration often complement one another in segments of the microelectronics and robotics industries and in biotechnology.

Direct foreign investment supports the exploitation of firm-specific technological capabilities but involves high risks and costs. The cost penalties of establishing multiple production facilities argue against direct foreign investment in industries in which production technologies exhibit a large minimum efficient scale or strong plant-specific learning and cost-reduction effects; commercial aircraft (primarily airframes) and steel are examples of such industries. The high fixed costs of establishing an offshore production, distribution, and marketing network may preclude direct foreign investment. Licensing, direct foreign investment, and export all force the innovating firm to bear all of the costs and risks of research and development, which have grown considerably in many industries, as we argued in Chapter 8.

Uncertainties about economic and political conditions in many foreign markets reduce the attractiveness of direct foreign investment. Political barriers have impeded the establishment of wholly owned production facilities in high-technology industries in a number of nations; both the Japanese and the U.S. governments, for example, have opposed direct foreign investment in their domestic semiconductor industries. International joint ventures have substituted for, and in some cases have complemented, Japanese and U.S. firms' direct foreign investment in this and other industries. A number of collaborative ventures in the integrated circuit, automobile, and pharmaceuticals industries have led to the establishment of a wholly owned offshore production or marketing facility.[8]

What advantages does international collaboration have over licensing or direct foreign investment? Many of the contractual limitations and transactions costs of licensing for the exploitation of technological capabilities can be avoided within a collaborative venture. The problem of determining the value of partners' contributions can be reduced through

---

[8] This is consistent with Porter and Fuller's observation that collaborative ventures centered on marketing "may be particularly unstable, however, because they frequently are formed because of the access motive on one or both sides. For example, one partner needs market access while the other needs access to product. As the foreign partner's market knowledge increases, there is less and less need for a local partner" (1986, p. 334).

collaboration. Partner firms make financial commitments to a collaborative venture that back their claims for the value of the assets they contribute; such financial commitments can substitute for the complete revelation of the value and characteristics of the asset that could be necessary to complete a licensing agreement.[9]

The noncodified, "inseparable" character of firm-specific assets that may preclude their exploitation through licensing need not prevent the pooling of such assets by several firms within a joint venture, or the effective sale of such assets by one firm to another within a joint venture. Technology transfer may also be controlled or regulated more effectively within collaborative ventures than in licensing transactions. Joint ventures enable partner firms to "unbundle" their portfolios of technological assets and transfer components of this portfolio, individual components of which may be worthless in isolation, to a partner. The transfer of technology through a joint venture from a technologically advanced firm to a less advanced enterprise may therefore enable the technologically "senior" firm to reap some financial returns to portions of its portfolio of technological capabilities. In many cases, these returns cannot be attained through licensing because of the difficulties of unbundling the firm's technological portfolio through a license. Moreover, monitoring the behavior of the recipient of technology within a joint venture reduces the risk that the transferor will not benefit from any improvements in transferred technologies made by the recipient. Examples of collaborative ventures that illustrate this argument may be found in steel (National Steel and Nippon Kokan), automobiles (Toyota and General Motors), and commercial aircraft (General Electric and SNECMA).

Collaborative ventures offer an alternative to the complete merger of firms as a means of pooling assets. Such ventures fall short of a complete merger of the partner firms, covering only a limited range of functions or products. Partner firms may well be competitors in other product areas.

---

[9] Brodley (1982) summarizes the advantages of joint ventures, defined as separate corporate entities in which all partners hold equity shares, over mergers or market transactions as follows: "By providing for shared profits and managerial control, joint ventures tend to protect the partners from opportunism and information imbalance. The problem of valuing the respective contributions of the participants is mitigated, because they can await an actual market judgment. The temptation to exploit a favored bargaining position by threatening to withhold infusions of capital or other contributions is reduced by the need for continuous cooperation if the joint venture is to be effective. Moreover, a firm supplying capital to the joint venture can closely monitor the use of its contributed capital and thereby reduce its risk of loss. Common ownership also provides a means of spreading the costs of producing valuable information that could otherwise be protected from appropriation only by difficult-to-enforce contractual undertakings. Finally, joint ventures can effect economies of scale in research not achievable through single-firm action. Because of these advantages, joint ventures are especially likely to provide an optimal enterprise form in undertakings involving high risks, technological innovations, or high information costs" (pp. 1528–9).

Collaboration may provide established firms a faster and less costly means than internal development to gain access to new technologies that are not easily licensed. This "technology access" motive for collaboration between established and young firms has been particularly important in industries based on new technologies, such as biotechnology and robotics.

By comparison with direct foreign investment, licensing, or export, collaborative ventures also reduce the financial and political risks of innovation and foreign marketing. The products of a collaborative venture between a U.S. and a foreign firm may well encounter fewer political impediments to market access in the domestic market of the foreign firm than would direct exports from the U.S. firm.

Nonetheless, the potential difficulties of collaborative ventures should not be minimized. Management of these undertakings has proved to be extremely difficult. The amount of technology transfer occurring within collaborations that focus on new product development, for example, may cause conflict in ventures that involve firms with different technological capabilities. The incentives of the partners in such ventures often are opposed, as the senior firm wishes to minimize, and the junior firm to maximize, the amount of technology transfer.

This problem can be illustrated by the case of International Aero Engines, a consortium developing the V2500 jet engine that includes Pratt and Whitney, Rolls Royce, Fiat, Motoren-Turbinen Union, Ishikawa-jima-Harima Heavy Industries, Kawasaki Heavy Industries, and Mitsubishi Heavy Industries. Pratt and Whitney and Rolls Royce, the "senior partners" within the consortium, attempted to minimize the transfer of engine technology within the consortium by designing the engine in modular form and assigning the development of different modules to different participants. Serious problems in the integration of the engine components, however, have led to delays in the delivery of the V2500 engine and to a loss of orders ("U.S., Europeans Clash . . . ," "Pratt and Whitney Expands Role . . ."; Carley, 1988).

Joint product development ventures between erstwhile competitors that cover only one product line among the many produced by the partner firms may also be unstable. Technological change can cause independently manufactured products to become competitors with those jointly developed within the partnership. Such encroachment contributed to the 1977 demise of the collaboration of Pratt and Whitney and Rolls Royce that was intended to develop a high-bypass, high-thrust engine (the JT10D), and contributed to the collapse of a joint venture between Fokker and McDonnell Douglas in 1982. Collaborative ventures that focus on marketing by one partner of the products of another may not endure, as Porter and Fuller (1986) note, since one partner's knowledge of market conditions and demand may lose its value to the other partner.

Why have international collaborative ventures, which represent a hybrid of interfirm and intrafirm modes for the exchange or sharing of technological and other assets, assumed such importance recently, and why do these ventures now incorporate a wider range of activities? The basic answer is simple: Changes in the technological and policy environment (some of which were discussed in Chapter 8) mean that the potential contributions of foreign firms to collaborative ventures now are much more attractive to U.S. firms.

Causes of increased reliance on joint ventures

Changes in the technical capabilities of foreign firms and in the nature of product demand have increased U.S. firms' demand for foreign partners in collaborative ventures. The enhanced technological capabilities of many foreign firms make them more attractive partners in joint ventures with U.S. firms. Foreign firms now are better able to absorb and exploit advanced technologies from U.S. firms in industries in which there remains a substantial technology gap between U.S. and foreign firms. In other industries, foreign firms either are more advanced or are the technological equals of U.S. firms and therefore can contribute managerial or technological expertise to joint ventures with U.S. firms. U.S. firms in the automotive and steel industries and some U.S. firms in the microelectronics industry now collaborate with foreign firms to gain access to superior foreign technologies.

The growth of nontariff trade barriers that was discussed in Chapter 8 has also increased the incentives for U.S. firms to seek foreign partners. Tariff barriers tend to favor direct foreign investment or joint production ventures as means for market penetration, since they affect only the relative prices of domestically produced and imported goods. Nontariff barriers, however, especially procurement policies or technology transfer requirements, favor the use of collaborative ventures that incorporate product research, development, and marketing, as well as manufacture. Purchase decisions of foreign governments play a major role in the export markets for such goods as commercial aircraft and telecommunications equipment. These decisions can be influenced by offsets, the production (or development and production) of components for the purchased product by domestic firms in the purchase nation.[10] Foreign governments also

---

[10] Recent efforts by a number of European governments to sell off publicly owned enterprises, such as the British government's divestiture of British Airways, British Aerospace, and British Telecom, as well as discussion of plans by the Dutch, West German, and Swedish governments to sell all or part of their state-owned airlines, may prefigure a significant change in the character of major foreign markets in some industries. This "trend," however, is a very modest ripple at present and will not dissolve the informal ties and sources of financial pressure and support that enable governments to exert considerable influence on the purchase decisions of "private" corporations.

frequently provide development funding and risk capital to domestic firms as part of industrial development policies. Combined with high and rapidly increasing product development costs in many U.S. industries, such as microelectronics, commercial aircraft, telecommunications equipment, and robotics, the availability of capital from public sources for foreign firms has enhanced their attractiveness as partners in product development ventures.

Just as foreign government trade and industrial policies have created incentives for U.S. firms to collaborate with foreign firms in export markets, nontariff restrictions on foreign access to the U.S. market have led to increased collaboration between U.S. firms and foreign firms wishing to sell in the United States. In several protected U.S. industries, a foreign production presence has been achieved through a joint venture. Examples include the Toyota–General Motors and Nippon Kokan–National Steel ventures. In the wake of the United States–Japan Semiconductor Agreement and Fujitsu's failure to acquire Fairchild Semiconductor, joint ventures may become a more important means for Japanese semiconductor producers to establish a U.S. production base.[11]

Paradoxically, the pursuit by the United States and other industrialized nations of nationalistic policies of support for domestic industries has encouraged the development of consortia spanning national boundaries. Although the postwar growth of multinational firms and direct foreign investment raised the prospect in some assessments of "global firms" to whom national boundaries would mean little or nothing, much of the current wave of international joint venture activity reflects the opposite phenomenon. National governments are able to influence not only production but, increasingly, the product development and technology transfer decisions of firms through the use of trade and other policies.

Many of the technological factors we discussed in Chapter 8 have also influenced recent decisions of U.S. firms to collaborate with both domestic and foreign firms. Firms in industries in which product cycles are becoming shorter, a group including microelectronics, telecommunications equipment, and robotics, may seek rapid market penetration at low cost through collaboration with a foreign firm with an established marketing network. In addition, advanced communications and computer-assisted design and production technologies facilitate the operation of international collaborative ventures.

Factors influencing the structure of international collaborative ventures

One of the most important motives for collaboration is access to markets, whether in the United States or in a foreign nation. The asset provided in

---

[11] See Borrus (1988) for a similar argument.

exchange for market access is technology. The form in which the technology is provided, which is determined by both the motives of the participants and the characteristics of the product, plays a central role in structuring the collaboration. Thus, where the technology is provided in essentially "embodied" form (i.e., in a finished product), collaboration either is unimportant or focuses largely on marketing, as in the pharmaceutical industry (outside of biotechnology).

In more mature high-technology industries, such as telecommunications equipment, microelectronics, and commercial aircraft, the high costs of new product development, demanding requirements for systems integration, and the nature of political barriers to market access all mean that many collaborative ventures have focused on product development. A similar focus characterizes collaborative ventures in robotics between user and supplier firms that exchange proprietary data between the partners. Increasingly complex requirements for technology integration in robotics have also led to a number of domestic and international collaborative ventures among suppliers of robotics and factory-automation equipment that deal primarily with product development. In commercial aircraft, telecommunications equipment, and segments of the microelectronics industry, the desire of U.S. firms for risk-sharing partners and access to foreign capital or technology provides an additional motive to focus collaboration on research and product development.

In other high-technology industries with a large number of new firms, such as biotechnology, much domestic and international collaboration focuses on the marketing and distribution by established firms of the technologies developed by new entrants. This type of collaboration aids entry into new domestic or foreign markets and need not always incorporate joint product development. The major international collaborations in the automotive and steel industries center on the exchange of foreign process technology, managerial expertise, and production systems for access to U.S. markets. These joint ventures accordingly deal with production.

Since technology transfer is at the center of many joint ventures, the management by partner firms of both technological development and technology transfer is critical to the success or failure of international collaboration. The interests of technological leaders, reluctant to allow the transfer of key technological capabilities, differ from those of technological followers, whose participation may hinge on the amount of technology transfer. The success of a project may be undercut by the attempts of "junior" partners, motivated by their desire to maximize technology transfer and learning, to participate in all aspects of the project, rather than specializing in a particular area or activity.

The importance of technology transfer as a source of cohesion within ventures between a dominant and a subordinate firm nevertheless means that these ventures often are more durable and successful than those among technological equals (Killing, 1983). Evidence from the commercial aircraft industry, in which international collaboration has been widespread for more than a decade, strongly supports this hypothesis. Ventures of technological equals, such as those between Rolls Royce and Pratt and Whitney in the JT10D jet engine project, Fokker and McDonnell Douglas in the MDF100 commercial aircraft project, and Saab and Fairchild in the SF340 commuter aircraft project, frequently have failed to bring a product to market or have been unable to achieve commercial success with a product after its introduction. A major venture of technological equals in telecommunication equipment, AT&T-Philips, also has been rumored to be near dissolution ("AT&T: The Making of a Comeback," p. 62). Ventures between technologically dominant and subordinate firms, however, such as the CFM International venture between General Electric and SNECMA of France and the collaborative ventures involving Boeing and the Japan Commercial Transport Development Corporation appear to be more durable.

The organizational structure of international collaborative ventures, especially those involving joint research and product development, raises additional challenges. There is no optimal management structure for a collaborative venture; the appropriate design will depend, among other things, on the character and magnitude of the contributions of the participants. In collaborations of technological equals, an autonomous management structure charged with the responsibility for a wide range of design, marketing, production, and product support is preferable. This type of management structure often is costly, since it duplicates some or all of the management structure of the member firms. Nevertheless, the experience of recent collaborative ventures clearly indicates the importance of strong links between the product development and design team and the organization charged with responsibility for marketing and product support. The organization managing the collaborative venture, be it the single dominant firm or an independent hybrid of the parent firms, must retain control of a number of downstream activities. On the other hand, in collaborations involving a senior and a junior firm, financial and organizational structure appears to be less important, so long as the technologically more advanced firm retains overall control of technology and management decisions.

Finally, the case of the Anglo–French Concorde partnership, where total project costs rose from $450 million in 1962 to $4 billion by 1978, illustrates the need for building cost controls into the structure of a collaborative venture. This issue is important because of the weaker incentives for participants to minimize shared costs. In the Airbus and other joint ventures with less disastrous financial consequences than Concorde, fixed-price contracts between a central management organization and the partner firms have preserved incentives for partners to minimize costs. Profit sharing, rather than cost sharing, is crucial.

Public policy implications of international collaborative ventures

Although the full impact of international collaboration will not be apparent for some time, a comparative analysis of international collaboration in U.S. manufacturing (Mowery, 1988a) does not support the critical view of international joint ventures presented in such works as Reich and Mankin (1986); nor is a specific federal policy governing such collaborative ventures advisable. Technology transfer within these ventures is more modest in scope and less uniformly "outbound" than some assessments assume. Just as U.S. industries vary in their trade balances in goods, the net inflows or outflows of technology through international collaborations vary across industries. Requiring balance in technology transfer on an industry-by-industry basis makes no more sense than a requirement for such balance in goods trade.

Restrictions or controls on international collaborative ventures involving U.S. firms do not appear to be an effective means to improve U.S. international competitiveness and in fact might impair competitiveness. The complexity of international collaborative ventures, the fact that the pattern and impact of these ventures vary considerably across industries, and the historical evidence that restrictions on technology transfer are either ineffective or perverse in their impacts (Harris, 1986; COSEPUP Panel on the Impact of National Controls on International Technology Transfer, 1987) all argue against controls on collaborations involving nondefense technologies. Controls on the transfer of technologies and technical data are currently imposed on collaborative ventures in technologies with potential military applications for reasons of national security, and the case for additional controls on civilian technologies is not compelling.

Efforts to restrict international collaboration also overlook the fact that in a number of industries, including steel, automobiles, and portions of microelectronics, international collaboration can improve the international competitiveness of the U.S. participants. In other industries, such as robotics, the competitiveness of U.S. systems engineering and software firms and the ability of large U.S. firms to offer a "full line" of factory automation hardware and software depend on access to foreign hardware through joint ventures and licensing.

A policy concerned specifically with international collaborative ventures in civilian technologies thus is ill-advised. Nevertheless, the incentives for U.S. firms to enter into international collaborative ventures and the payoffs from these ventures for U.S. firms and the U.S. economy are heavily influenced by U.S. antitrust, trade, and research policies. Should these policies be revised in order to reduce the incentives for collaboration between U.S. and foreign firms?

There is little evidence to support the argument that U.S. antitrust policy is a central factor in the decisions of American firms to collaborate with foreign enterprises.[12] International collaborative ventures generally are not substitutes for the collaboration among U.S. firms that might develop in the absence of antitrust restrictions. In the semiconductor industry, for example, the firms that are active in developing domestic R&D collaborations and consortia are among the most active in international collaborative ventures. If U.S. firms were forced to choose between international and domestic collaborative ventures because of antitrust restrictions (see Langlois et al., 1988, for a discussion of the semiconductor case), the opposite relationship would hold, in which firms active in international collaboration did not pursue domestic collaboration.

The primary motive for many collaborative ventures – access to foreign markets – is not affected by restrictions on collaboration between U.S. firms. In other cases, such as the collaborative ventures in the automobile and steel industries, U.S. firms collaborate with foreign firms in order to gain access to technological and other assets that are not available from other U.S. firms. Antitrust policy also has little effect on precommercial research collaboration among U.S. firms in the wake of the National Cooperative Research Act of 1984, and antitrust rarely applies to vertical collaborations between firms and their suppliers.

Antitrust policy has played an indirect role, however, in international collaborative ventures in several industries. The 1983 Modified Final Judgment in the case of *U.S. v. AT&T* opened the domestic U.S. market to foreign telecommunications equipment suppliers and unleashed AT&T to compete in markets outside telecommunications and in foreign markets for telecommunications equipment. As a result, AT&T has entered into international collaborative ventures to penetrate foreign markets for equipment and has developed alliances with domestic (Sun Microsystems) and foreign (Olivetti) producers of computers to aid its entry into businesses outside telecommunications. Joint ventures between the Bell operating companies and foreign equipment producers also might develop as a means of aiding foreign access to the U.S. telephone equipment

---

[12] Nelson (1984) argues that "although I am less easy about joint design and production ventures than I am about generic research cooperation, it does not seem right that such an international venture would receive totally different treatment from that received by two or more U.S. firms in a design and production venture for which the market is clearly international. . . . It seems odd that we would discriminate against a national partnership if each partner judged this venture more promising economically than an international consortium" (p. 84).

market if current judicial restrictions on the activities of the U.S. operating companies were lifted.

Antitrust policy has affected international collaboration in other industries as well. The limited duration of the NUMMI joint venture between General Motors and Toyota is a direct result of the settlement reached in the antitrust suit against NUMMI filed by the Chrysler Corporation. There is some evidence in the commercial aircraft engine industry that the U.S. Department of Justice has allowed international collaboration between competing firms that would not have been allowed between the major U.S. firms, based on an inappropriate distinction between the domestic and international markets for these products (see Mowery, 1987). The evidence is not conclusive in this case, however, and the example appears to be an isolated one.

Restrictions on U.S. imports also have resulted in collaboration between U.S. and foreign firms that was prohibited among U.S. firms for antitrust reasons. The conjunction of antitrust and trade restrictions influenced the joint venture between National Steel and Nippon Kokan. That collaboration was established after the Justice Department quashed the sale of a number of National Steel plants to the U.S. Steel Corporation, based on the department's judgment that the domestic U.S. market was protected from imports.[13] The consequences of this collaboration, however, do not appear to be harmful to the long-term competitiveness of the U.S. firms involved. Indeed, in the absence of such a collaborative venture, National Intergroup (parent firm of National Steel) might have withdrawn entirely from the steel industry. The tendency of trade restrictions to create such incentives for international collaboration is another reason to avoid protectionist policies, rather than an argument for the relaxation of antitrust restrictions in protected industries.

Research and product development subsidies are another potential inducement to engage in international collaboration. But with the exception of spectacular cases of subsidized product development in the commercial aircraft industry (Airbus Industrie, which by some estimates received billions of dollars in public subsidies between 1968 and 1982; see Krugman, 1984), public financial support for recent Japanese and European technology development programs is modest, both absolutely or by comparison with U.S. programs. Moreover, these programs typically focus on precommercial research, rather than the development of specific prod-

---

[13] Hufbauer and Rosen (1986) have noted this tendency, arguing that "a pattern has arisen in which transnational associations raise fewer antitrust concerns than combinations involving two domestic producers. . . . The numerous equity purchases plus one joint venture in the auto industry, as well as several joint ventures in steel, exemplify this phenomenon. While this is the logical consequence of import restraints, it was probably an unintended effect" (p. 62).

ucts. Where the results of these publicly supported research programs are published in the open scientific literature, such programs can in fact benefit nonparticipant U.S. firms, which may gain access to many of the results of the basic research without having to bear the full costs of such research. This possibility, however, requires a greater investment by U.S. firms in monitoring foreign scientific and engineering research and, possibly, a greater willingness to utilize scientific and technological advances developed outside of the firm, as Japanese firms have done with considerable success.[14]

Two of the three major areas of trade policy that affect collaboration – public subsidies and government procurement – are now covered by multilateral agreements ("Codes") under the General Agreement on Tariffs and Trade that were negotiated during the Tokyo Round of trade talks (see Chapter 10 for additional discussion). In addition, the commercial aircraft industry is covered by the Agreement on Trade in Civil Aircraft, which specifies acceptable practices for procurement and development funding. To the extent that international collaboration poses a long-term threat to U.S. international competitiveness and is motivated by the trade-distorting practices of foreign governments, both the Codes and the Agreement on Trade in Civil Aircraft must be strengthened.

The Uruguay Round of trade talks that began in 1986 will consider the treatment of foreign investment, including the "right of establishment" by firms of production and other operations in foreign markets. Since government restrictions on foreign investment provide a significant motive for international collaborative ventures, the development within these negotiations of multilateral rules for the treatment of foreign investment could alter the incentives for international collaboration in some industries.

The development and enforcement of stronger forms of intellectual property protection, another subject of the Uruguay Round negotiations, may also facilitate the licensing of process and product technologies to foreign firms, increasing the attractiveness to U.S. firms of an alternative channel for the exploitation of technical capabilities in such industries as biotechnology. In view, however, of the limited importance of patent, copyright, and trade secret protection for the establishment or preservation of a technological advantage (Levin et al., 1987), stronger intellectual property protection probably will have a modest impact on international collaboration in most U.S. manufacturing industries.

The growing role of bilateral negotiations in U.S. trade policy, especially negotiations over access to foreign (frequently Japanese) markets, may lead to additional collaborative ventures between U.S. and foreign

---

[14] See Chapter 8; also see Mansfield (1988) and Rosenberg and Steinmueller (1988).

firms. Recent bilateral negotiations between the U.S. and Japanese governments, according to some observers, have produced understandings that stipulate, among other things, that U.S. firms shall attain a specific market share in the foreign market (see Bhagwati, 1987; Prestowitz, 1987; World Bank, 1987). Achievement of this outcome in many markets, especially the domestic Japanese market, requires either direct foreign investment by U.S. firms, which is slow, risky, and costly, or the formation of long-term collaborations between U.S. and foreign firms. The bilateral talks in semiconductors that led to the United States–Japan Semiconductor Agreement of 1986 have been followed by negotiations over construction services and may lead to further talks covering other industries. If these talks and the associated government monitoring of trade outcomes expand, so too will international collaborative ventures.[15] Trade policy influences international collaboration between U.S. and foreign firms, but the results of such collaboration increasingly may affect trade policy as well. As the national origins of the components in a central office telephone switch, jet engine, or robot become more blurred and complex, national trade policies that are predicated on the protection or promotion of goods with a high domestic content will be unworkable, as we note in Chapter 10.

Which U.S. industries are likely to rely on international collaboration as a permanent component of their global competitive strategies? Industries in which collaboration in product development is motivated by a desire to reduce risk, to gain access to technology, or to deal with the effects of a significant government role in procurement or in the resolution and regulation of international trade disputes, will continue to rely on international collaboration. These industries include telecommunications equipment, commercial aircraft, and (potentially) semiconductors. The reluctance of Japanese firms to assume ownership of additional production capacity and the continued restrictions on foreign access to the U.S. market mean that international collaboration in the steel industry is likely to continue. International collaborative ventures will remain significant in the U.S. auto parts industry as a result of the substantial obstacles that U.S. firms face in gaining access to Japanese management and production systems and to Japanese markets.

In other U.S. industries, international collaboration may be more transitory. The wave of collaborations between major Japanese and U.S. automobile firms that expanded U.S. production of Japanese auto designs, for example, may have peaked. The major Japanese producers now have

---

[15] According to one account, the March 1988 agreement between the U.S. and Japanese governments easing access by U.S. firms to Japanese public construction projects has resulted in an extensive set of joint ventures between U.S. and large Japanese construction firms (Rubinfien, 1988).

established production facilities in the United States, bypassing the barriers to their access to this market. International collaboration that is motivated by market access concerns in industries in which governments are not major customers may also decline in importance in the long run. Industries in which these motives figure prominently include biotechnology, segments of the robotics industry, and pharmaceuticals.

Domestic research collaboration

Along with international collaboration in product development and manufacture, domestic collaboration in research has expanded dramatically within the U.S. economy during the past decade. Research collaboration between industry and universities has also grown rapidly, although industry's financial contribution to university research still is dwarfed by that of the federal government. Private research collaborations also have sprung up – examples include the Microelectronics and Computer Technology Corporation, the Software Productivity Consortium, and numerous smaller domestic joint ventures. Although the proximate causes of these collaborative undertakings may resemble some of those responsible for international collaboration, domestic research collaborations appear to differ considerably from international ventures in focus and structure. In this section, we discuss university–industry research collaboration and compare research collaboration among firms and collaboration between industry and universities.

University–industry cooperation

During the past decade, financial support from industry has established a number of research facilities on university campuses to conduct research with potential commercial value. Stanford University has the Center for Integrated Systems, with financial support from twenty corporations, which is devoted to developing large-scale integrated microelectronic circuits; MIT has the Whitehead Institute, with a huge private endowment, which is devoted to biomedical research; MIT also has a ten-year research contract with the Exxon Research and Engineering Company to support research in the field of combustion. Hoechst AG of West Germany has given the Massachusetts General Hospital, a teaching arm of the Harvard Medical School, $50 million for the support of basic research in molecular biology.

Important initiatives are coming from the federal government as well as private industry. The National Science Foundation has embarked on a program to establish a number of engineering research centers on university campuses. The centers focus on engineering research that is in many cases interdisciplinary, often linking engineering research with such traditional scientific disciplines as biology and physics, and emphasizing advanced computer applications. The financial structure of these centers, which resembles that of the NSF university–industry research centers, also is relatively novel, since it combines "seed-money" support from the federal government (as well, in many cases, as state and local governments) with major contributions from private corporations that are affiliated with the centers. A number of these centers already exist. Columbia University has a center for telecommunications; the University of Maryland and Harvard University, centers for the application of advanced computers to the design of communications systems; MIT, for the improvement of manufacturing processes in the biotechnology industry; and Purdue University, for automated manufacturing systems.

The development of these novel institutions has raised concerns within universities that the university's commitment to basic research will be eroded by an increasing focus on short-term, less fundamental research problems because priorities will be determined more and more by commercial considerations. Closely connected is the concern that scientists will lose their intellectual autonomy, which is to say their freedom to determine their own research agenda, as private industry comes to play a more prominent role in financial support. Protection of this autonomy has long been a serious concern of science policymakers; in fact, peer reviews and other protective arrangements were introduced when the federal government became a massive patron of university research after the Second World War, in response to very similar concerns (we discuss these later).

In considering the advantages and disadvantages of research collaboration between U.S. universities and industry, several points must be kept in mind:

1. The phenomenon of the university–industry research collaboration is not new, as we have noted in Chapters 4 and 6. Research collaboration between universities and enterprises in both the agricultural and manufacturing sectors is more than one hundred years old in the United States. Indeed, industrial funds have accounted for a declining share of university research expenditures through much of the postwar period. In 1953, industry financed 11 percent of university research, a share that declined to 5.5 percent in 1960 and 2.7 percent in 1978. By 1985–6, estimates suggest that industrial funds accounted for 5–7 percent of university research.[16] Industrial

---

[16] See National Commission on Research (1980), pp. 8–9; cf. Government-University-Industry Research Roundtable (1986), 15–16.

funds are unlikely to exceed 8–10 percent of total U.S. university research budgets in the foreseeable future.

2. In several respects, the recent growth in university–industry research cooperation represents a renewal of linkages of long standing. As we noted in Chapter 4, American state universities have a long history of performing highly applied engineering research and extension services for industrial and state government sponsors. The significant role of state governments as sponsors of recent cooperative research initiatives is also not new, as Chapter 4's discussion of the significant state government role in the pre–World War II era noted. To a great extent, the recent development of closer research ties between universities and industry represents the restoration of a linkage that has been weakened in recent years, rather than a fundamental departure.

3. There is a vast array of forms of research collaboration between universities and industry, making generalizations virtually impossible. Moreover, as we note later, the relationship between university research and commercial technology varies considerably across industries. No single model or description of the constraints, advantages, and disadvantages of such collaboration is likely to be accurate for all university–industry collaborations.

4. Many of the issues raised by research collaboration between industry and universities are not new, but resemble those raised in earlier periods by the expansion of external research support from other sources. For example, concerns over intellectual property rights, excessive growth of salaries for faculty specializing in particular disciplines, and other issues raised in recent discussions of university–industry research relationships were important topics of debate in the context of research contracts with nonprofit foundations and the federal government.[17]

A fundamental motive for closer ties between university and industrial research is the fact that U.S. universities account for a growing share of total U.S. basic research. The relative importance of university and industrial performers of basic research has shifted dramatically during the postwar period. In 1953, industry accounted for 58 percent of the com-

---

[17] The Association of American Universities (AAU) noted in a 1985 report that a major policy statement on faculty conflicts of interest between externally sponsored research and other responsibilities of university faculty was issued by the American Association of University Professors and the American Council on Education in 1964 as a result of concerns over research sponsored by the federal government (AAU, 1985, p. 10).

bined basic research budget (from all sources) of the universities and industry; in 1978, universities accounted for 76 percent of the combined basic research budget of universities and industry (National Commission on Research, 1980, pp. 8–9).

Moreover, in recent years such flagships of industrial basic research as the Du Pont Central Research Laboratories, the RCA Sarnoff Laboratories, General Electric's central R&D facility, and even Bell Telephone Laboratories (in the wake of the 1984 divestiture of the operating companies) have either been closed or have reduced their commitment to basic research. Increasingly, universities occupy the central position in the performance of basic research within this economy. The importance of sustained interaction among the various stages of the invention or innovation processes means that new organizational linkages between universities and industry are needed, in order to increase the economic rewards from the growing basic research investment within universities.

From private industry's point of view, there is a growing awareness that an increasing number of fields of research at the universities hold out significant promise of generating findings that may be of great commercial significance. Close proximity to the university scientific community offers firms better access to knowledge that may have great value in the marketplace. The ability to tap into such new knowledge sources, and to convert that knowledge into new and improved products before one's competitors or potential competitors, is an immense attraction. Even in the absence of any proprietary control over the new research findings, a lead time over the competition of several months can often be converted into a decisive competitive advantage.

There are a number of fields in which university research is working at intellectual frontiers that have great potential commercial payoffs. Recent discoveries in high-temperature superconductivity are one example, although the commercialization prospects of these discoveries are perhaps the most distant of the fields that are currently the object of university research. A partial list of other fields would include artificial intelligence, robotics and remote sensing, computers, microelectronics, lasers, composite and other new materials, and biotechnology.[18] Past and prospective research in each of these fields provides a basis for strong industrial interest in strengthening its connections with university science.

The connection between university research and commercial technology appears to be particularly close in the area of biotechnology, which

---

[18] According to the *Economist*, the commercial importance of university biotechnology research has led the U.S. pharmaceuticals industry to increase its financial support of biotechnology research in universities by 90 percent per year in recent years: "American industry now pays for 40% of the $13 billion-a-year biomedical research bill" ("Mismanaging Drug Research," Nov. 21, 1987, p. 67).

influences the character of many university–industry research relationships in this field. This close relationship is due in part to the nature of biotechnology. Recombinant DNA and genetic engineering techniques in many ways represent radical scientific breakthroughs that are being transferred to industry and reduced to practice. In Gomory's terminology, biotechnology is a "ladder" technology, that is, a case in which "the new idea is dominant and the product forms itself around the new idea or new technology. Those who understand that idea or technology are often scientists, and they therefore play leading roles in its introduction" (Gomory, 1988, p. 11).[19] A great many other industrial technologies, by contrast, develop through a process of cyclic, incremental improvement (a process in which many Japanese firms excel, as we pointed out in Chapter 8), in which the application of basic science is more gradual and less direct.

A central influence on the establishment of these new facilities is the growing necessity of a multidisciplinary approach to important problems in both science and technology. The growing importance of multidisciplinary research approaches is another reflection of the phenomenon of technological convergence we discussed in Chapter 8. Multidisciplinary research has developed historically from the emergence of problems at the research frontier of a particular discipline (e.g., cell biology) that required a better understanding of the role of certain processes that were the specialty of scientists in a different discipline (e.g., chemistry). The outcome – biochemistry – was a natural outgrowth of the changing requirements of an expanding body of research knowledge. Similarly, geophysics emerged as an independent subdiscipline of geology when it became possible to apply the methodologies that had been developed in physics to the understanding of the structure and the dynamics of the earth (as well as other planets). The introduction of new techniques of instrumentation has led, time and again, to a beneficial crossing of traditional boundaries between physics and chemistry.[20]

---

[19] Another example of a ladder technology cited by Gomory is the transistor. In contrast to biotechnology, of course, the transistor was first developed within industry. The different origin of these two major scientific discoveries may reflect the shifting role of industry and universities as basic research performers noted earlier.

[20] "The advent of new instrumentation of unprecedented power has required chemists either to develop instrumentation in the traditional fashion of physicists or else to enter into close collaboration with physicists in order to address the microscopic properties of complex molecules, materials, and interfaces. For their part, condensed-matter physicists, propelled by instrumentation, theory, and technology toward materials of increasing complexity, find themselves often confronting questions requiring increased chemical insight and techniques for their answers. Finally, new complex materials displaying remarkable new chemical and physical properties have nucleated a coalition among synthetic chemists, physical experimentalists, and theoretical physicists from deep within their respective fields, far from the traditional interface. Each of these currents has already created new fields and produced new discoveries in established fields. As the principals continue

The need to exploit the knowledge and the methodologies of more than one discipline has become apparent not only at the level of basic science but in applied sciences and engineering as well. In recent years, medical science has benefited not only from such "nearby" disciplines as biology, genetics, and chemistry, but has drawn on research in nuclear physics (magnetic resonance), electronics, and materials science and engineering. Important recent advances in pharmaceuticals have been based on such fields as biochemistry, molecular and cell biology, immunology, neurobiology, and scientific instrumentation. The new pattern of innovation is, by its very nature, multidisciplinary. Success requires close cooperation among an increasing number of specialists.[21]

The development of multidisciplinary university research institutes provides important support for these new cross-disciplinary research problems and opportunities. Moreover, these institutes can train young scholars and prospective industrial researchers in new techniques and research perspectives. Interdisciplinary research institutes are hardly a novel feature in the postwar landscape of American higher education. Major research initiatives in area studies, in computer science, and in materials science, for example, were launched with federal research funding during the 1950s and 1960s. Many of the research institutes spawned by these initiatives, especially in computer and materials sciences, have emerged as freestanding departments in new "disciplines." The novel aspect of recent interdisciplinary research institutes, as in university–industry research collaboration generally, is the source of the research funds, rather than the presence of significant extramural research funding.

The changes in the competitive and technological environment we discussed in Chapter 8 have also increased the payoff to university–industry research collaboration. Faced with spiraling R&D costs, greater demands to monitor a broader array of scientific and engineering fields, and increased competitive pressure from other U.S. and foreign firms to get products to market rapidly, U.S. firms have had to develop research relationships with an array of external institutions that could complement

---

to collaborate and to learn one another's language, there is reason to expect much more" (Physics Survey Committee, 1986, p. 54).

[21] "This new environment is an intensely interdisciplinary one in which the intuition and skill of the chemist are combined with the knowledge of biochemists, pharmacologists, and computer scientists as well as other researchers in universities, industry, and the government. . . . One of the clearest trends is that the biological sciences will play a pivotal role in drug discovery and development. . . . Developments in biochemistry have encouraged greater exploitation of enzymes as specific targets for drugs. The recent success in synthesizing angiotensin-converting enzyme inhibitors as antihypertensives is one of the first examples of drug design based upon structural and functional information on enzymes" (*Outlook for Science and Technology*, pp. 591–2).

and enhance the payoff from their in-house R&D activities.[22] Such relationships provide lower-cost windows on emerging technologies, allow firms to detect emerging commercial opportunities more rapidly, and spread the risks of failure among a larger number of research performers and research budgets. In addition, rotation of research personnel from the firm to external research institutions provides an important means to transfer research know-how and findings from external sources to the firm and can improve the attractiveness of the firm's laboratories to researchers.

Teaming with a university, rather than with a consortium of other firms or a publicly funded national research laboratory, allows the firm additional advantages beyond those already noted. By virtue of their unique mission as educational as well as research institutions, U.S. universities are critically important sources of scientific and engineering personnel. Participant firms can employ these collaborative ventures as "filters" for hiring research personnel, observing the performance of potential researchers before making employment commitments. Moreover, the demonstrated importance of people as a key vehicle for the transfer of scientific and technological knowledge means that the hiring by firms of the graduates of these programs facilitates the transfer of knowledge and technology from university to industry even more effectively than does the rotation of industry personnel through university research facilities.

The increasingly interdisciplinary character of technological and research challenges makes this training and hiring benefit particularly important. Increasingly, firms in the semiconductor, biotechnology, or robotics industries need individuals with interdisciplinary research experience and training. Such interdisciplinary research and educational activities are notoriously difficult to establish within universities with internal funds alone, although the departmental structure of U.S. universities makes this task easier than in many Western European universities.[23] Industrial

---

[22] A recent OECD study quotes a Xerox Corporation research executive's description of the firm's investment in the Center for Integrated Systems at Stanford University: "Xerox's contribution to CIS is very small compared to what we are investing internally in the same kind of research. For little additional investment we enlarge our perspective by participating in a broad program of basic research. We envision opportunities for joint interaction with the university and with other companies, as well as the ability to recruit students. On a per-dollar basis it should be a good investment" (quoted in OECD, 1984, p. 47).

[23] "Among the factors cited to explain West Germany's slow entry into commercial biotechnology is an educational system that prevents the kind of interdisciplinary cooperation that is viewed by most experts as essential to the development of this field. In particular, the traditional separation of technical faculties from their arts and sciences counterparts means that process technicians, usually located in the technical schools, rarely come into contact with colleagues holding university appointments in biochemistry or microbiology" (Office of Technology Assessment, 1984, p. 424).

research funds, like federal government research funds in the 1960s and 1970s, provide important resources for universities to establish such interdisciplinary research and education programs. Finally, by providing research and instrumentation funds for university faculty who otherwise might depart for industrial employment, industry research funds sustain the supply of scientific and engineering personnel in a way that private firm consortiums cannot.

Omitted from this discussion of the industrial benefits of university–industry collaboration are technological innovations developed in university laboratories and "handed off" to industrial collaborators. Although the wide variety of university–industry collaborative programs makes generalization hazardous, the weight of anecdotal evidence (see the Office of Technology Assessment, 1984, 1985; Government-University-Industry Research Roundtable, 1986; and other reports) suggests that collaborative ventures that focus on applied development work or on technological "deliverables" in many cases are less successful. The benefits of collaboration discussed earlier are longer-term benefits that rely on the establishment of a relationship lasting a number of years.[24] Although many firms are unable to adopt such a lengthy time horizon in their internal R&D planning and strategy, the lower costs of external research collaboration may support a longer-term perspective in at least this portion of the firm's research portfolio. Within collaborative relationships of this type, intellectual property issues often are of secondary importance, in contrast to the predictions of the neoclassical analytic paradigm.[25]

As we noted earlier, one exception to this pattern appears to be biotechnology. Blumenthal et al. (1986) report that small biotechnology firms do appear to rely heavily on university research as a basis for patent ap-

---

[24] Hercules and Enyart (1983) report from their survey of chemicals companies and academic researchers that the following four areas of collaboration had very high potential payoffs and currently lacked sufficient activity: (1) lectureships by academic scientists at industrial sites; (2) student interns at industrial sites; (3) continuing education programs at industrial sites; and (4) corporate support for employees to obtain advanced degrees (p. 7). None of these involve significant transfers from universities to industry of intellectual property or other deliverables.

[25] Consistent with this assessment, Gray and Gidley (1986) found in their analysis of evaluations of the first six NSF-funded university–industry research centers that "both faculty and industry respondents rated general expansion of knowledge as the most important goal and the more short-term goals of patent and product development as the least important" (p. 26). Describing firms' expectations at the inception of these cooperative research undertakings, Gray and Gidley found that "the benefits seen [by industry respondents] as most likely to accrue to companies were improved research projects in the company (mean, 2.60; 1 = scarcely likely, 4 = almost certain) and better personnel recruitment (mean, 2.54). Patentable products (1.62) and commercialized products (1.75) were seen as benefits which were 'somewhat' to 'scarcely likely' to accrue through Center participation" (p. 29).

plications and trade secrets. This is consistent with Gomory's description of biotechnology as a "ladder" technology. The authors concluded that

> small firms seem to constitute the greatest gamble for universities. On the one hand, the financial benefits of these relationships could be very large, since these UIRRs [university–industry research relationships] seem to produce many more patent applications per dollar invested than do relationships with large firms. . . . On the other hand, it is far from certain that applications for patents held by universities will ever produce profitable licenses. Moreover, the amount of research support provided by these relationships is small compared with UIRR's with larger firms, and the potential threats to university values seem greater. Compared with large companies in our study, small firms are more likely to support faculty with significant equity in their companies, are more likely to report the occurrence of trade secrets, and tend to fund projects of very short duration. (p. 246)

Just as the spiraling costs of R&D in industry during an era of financial stringency have increased industrial interest in closer research relationships with universities, the combination of soaring equipment and facilities costs and diminishing federal support has aroused academic interest in research collaboration with industry.[26] Federal outlays on R&D plant and equipment have been declining for many years. Such outlays reached their peak in the middle of the 1960s and then declined drastically, rising again in real terms in the late 1970s (although never approaching the earlier peak levels) and then declining again in the 1980s (see Table 9.1). Indeed, for some forms of research capital, federal support has totally collapsed. Although there was considerable support for research facilities of a bricks-and-mortar kind during the 1960s, such programs essentially ended about twenty years ago.[27] Nevertheless, private industry financial

---

[26] Although the soaring costs of research instrumentation pose some threat to the health of academic scientific research, many of the most widely used scientific instruments originated within the university scientific research community where they were developed by working scientists or engineers in response to some specific experimental or observational requirement. Once developed, these instruments were taken up by commercial manufacturers and made available for use in other scientific disciplines and in private industry. The computer is, of course, a classic example, and is distinguished mainly by being the most widely diffused of all scientific instruments. Many of the developers of this technology were academics attempting to develop a technology for reducing the extremely time-consuming computational requirements of their research, typically involving solutions to systems of differential equations. See Ritchie (1986).

[27] Continued deterioration in the quality of such facilities could erode the substantial benefits that flow from the close integration of graduate training and high-level research that has distinguished the U.S. system. The well-equipped European research laboratories

Table 9.1. *Federal outlays for R&D plant, fiscal years*
1960–83
(dollars in millions)

Year	Current dollars	Constant 1972 dollars[a]
1960	443.8	637.9
1961	539.1	766.2
1962	555.2	777.9
1963	673.6	928.3
1964	948.1	1,292.0
1965	1,077.4	1,436.9
1966	1,047.8	1,361.5
1967	792.7	997.9
1968	723.8	879.4
1969	657.0	762.5
1970	578.9	635.9
1971	612.7	640.8
1972	564.4	564.4
1973	638.4	611.2
1974	704.6	628.8
1975	829.7	673.1
1976	800.6	607.1
1977	800.2	568.5
1978	1,107.8	736.9
1979	1,202.8	735.8
1980	1,481.7	833.3
1981	1,606.7	822.8
1982	1,376.1	639.7
1983	1,299.9	581.9
1984	1,639.2	707.8
1985	1,688.9	706.4
1986	1,481.2	603.6
1987 (est.)	1,769.9	702.3
1988 (est.)	1,888.4	723.5

[a] GNP fiscal year implicit price deflators used to convert current dollars to constant 1972 dollars.
Source: National Science Foundation, *Federal Funds for Research and Development: Fiscal Years 1986, 1987 and 1988,* and earlier years.

support of university research remains modest. Industry provided about 19 percent of the funds for all basic research (Table 9.2) in 1984, but it funds a much smaller percentage of the basic research performed at the universities – around 6 percent of the total.

A comparison of two forms of domestic research collaboration in microelectronics

In this chapter we have discussed and compared two broad categories of domestic cooperative research activity – consortia of private firms and research cooperation between industry and universities. In this section, we briefly compare the two types of cooperative research in an industry in which research collaboration has grown rapidly in recent years, namely, microelectronics.

University–industry collaborative research programs in microelectronics include the Semiconductor Research Corporation (SRC), which funds research at a number of universities, and the Stanford University Center for Integrated Systems (CIS), which is based in a single university. Roughly sixty firms participated in the SRC and twenty were members of the CIS as of late 1986, according to the Government-University-Industry Research Roundtable (1986). Member firms in both organizations are granted access to all research findings and results through licenses, briefings, and so forth, and often are encouraged to send technical personnel to university research facilities for extended periods of time. Rather than developing applications for immediate transfer to industry, these programs perform research, train technical personnel for industry, and expose firm employees to advances in the scientific and technological frontiers.

Unlike research collaboration between universities and small firms in biotechnology, the SRC does not appear to focus on tangible "deliverables" from university research. In many ways, collaborative research organizations like the SRC operate as "catch-up" mechanisms for U.S. private industry, enabling more rapid and effective utilization of advanced scientific and technological findings by participant firms. Just as many Japanese cooperative research projects operated to bring Japanese firms up to a technological or scientific frontier that was historically defined by foreign firms and laboratories, university–industry cooperative research projects within the United States can bring U.S. firms closer (through

such as CERN, or the national research laboratories such as the Max Planck Institutes in West Germany, do not train beginning research personnel. This has contributed to a relative shortage of qualified, high-level European researchers. The loss of university access to instrumentation of the highest quality in America or the concentration of such instrumentation in a very small number of locations would be a serious threat to the system for training research scientists that has been built up in the United States in the postwar years.

Table 9.2. *Sources of funds for basic research by sector: 1953, 1960, 1965–84 (dollars in millions)*

		Current dollars			
Year	Total	Federal government	Industry	Universities and colleges	Other nonprofit institutions
1953	441	251	153	10	27
1960[a]	1,197	715	342	72	68
1965[b]	2,555	1,809	461	164	121
1966	2,814	1,978	510	197	129
1967	3,056	2,201	492	223	140
1968	3,296	2,336	535	276	149
1969	3,441	2,441	540	298	162
1970	3,549	2,489	528	350	182
1971	3,672	2,529	547	400	196
1972	3,829	2,633	563	415	218
1973	3,946	2,709	605	408	224
1974	4,239	2,912	651	432	244
1975	4,608	3,139	705	478	286
1976	4,977	3,436	769	475	297
1977	5,537	3,823	850	527	337
1978	6,392	4,445	964	605	378
1979	7,257	5,044	1,091	711	411
1980	8,089	5,559	1,265	805	460
1981	9,217	6,236	1,585	909	487
1982	9,886	6,588	1,805	983	510
1983 (est.)	10,610	6,970	2,025	1,075	540
1984 (est.)	11,850	7,775	2,270	1,220	585

		Constant 1972 dollars[c]			
Year	Total	Federal government	Industry	Universities and colleges	Other nonprofit institutions
1953	742	421	259	17	45
1960[a]	1,729	1,030	497	103	99
1965[b]	3,416	2,415	620	219	162
1966	3,660	2,571	665	256	168
1967	3,853	2,774	622	281	176
1968	4,001	2,837	649	335	180
1969	3,985	2,829	623	346	187

Table 9.2. *Cont.*

		Constant 1972 dollars[c]		
			Universities	Other
		Federal	and	nonprofit
Year	Total	government	Industry	colleges	institutions
1970	3,895	2,733	578	384	200
1971	3,836	2,644	570	418	204
1972	3,829	2,633	563	415	218
1973	3,766	2,589	573	391	213
1974	3,757	2,589	567	386	215
1975	3,720	2,540	562	388	230
1976	3,770	2,604	581	360	225
1977	3,939	2,718	607	374	240
1978	4,250	2,956	641	402	251
1979	4,438	3,085	667	435	251
1980	4,548	3,128	709	453	258
1981	4,727	3,199	813	466	249
1982	4,749	3,160	872	471	246
1983 (est.)	4,886	3,205	938	494	249
1984 (est.)	5,229	3,427	1,006	537	259

[a] Data for 1954–59 can be found in *National Patterns of R&D Resources, 1953–1977* (NSF 77-310).
[b] Data for 1961–64 can be found in *National Patterns of Science and Technology Resources, 1981* (NSF 81-311).
[c] Based on GNP implicit price deflator.
Source: National Science Foundation.

such mechanisms as personnel transfers and the hiring of program graduates) to a scientific frontier defined by the basic research within university laboratories. This point is an important one because it reduced many of the severe difficulties of defining a research agenda and minimizing "free rider" problems that have afflicted some recent collaborative research ventures in both the United States and Japan that do not enlist the participation of universities. The point also underscores one of our central arguments about interfirm research collaboration: It may well prove most effective in supporting the diffusion and utilization, rather than primarily the generation, of new scientific and technological knowledge. The contrast between the SRC and the Microelectronics and Computer Technology Corporation (MCC) also supports this assessment.

The structure and goals of two of the leading private research consortia,

MCC and Sematech, contrast with those of university-based collaborative research ventures. MCC was established in 1983 as an independent research organization in which firms could purchase shares and participate in programs of research in integrated-circuit (IC) packaging, software engineering, very large scale integration, and advanced computer architecture. Member firms are not allowed access to the results or findings of MCC programs in which they are not participants.

MCC thus has a somewhat anomalous structure and goals: Established to support precommercial, cooperative research, the corporation now performs proprietary research for its members. MCC has encountered some difficulties in defining its research agenda, transferring technology to member firms, and enlisting the full cooperation of member firms. Although it was designed to operate with staff drawn largely from member firms, some firms sent their less able technical employees to staff MCC. This policy was abandoned, and MCC now is staffed largely by its own employees (see Sanger, 1984). One of the primary reasons for the original staffing plan was to ensure rapid and effective transfer and utilization of technology by MCC member firms. Reliance by MCC on its own research staff has made technology transfer more difficult, and this issue has created problems for the consortium. In contrast to university-based collaborative research operations, MCC cannot offer its members the attraction of recruiting graduates from the laboratory and transferring technology and know-how through this channel.

Serious differences have also developed among members in research strategies and goals (for a less pessimistic assessment of MCC, see Peck, 1986). Some member firms have expressed displeasure with the lengthy time frame of MCC's research activities, pushing instead for applied research projects that would yield applications more quickly. Turnover in MCC's membership has been high, the price of MCC shares has been reduced, and the leadership of the Corporation has changed hands since its foundation (Lineback, 1987a, 1987b). As we noted in Chapter 1, MCC appears to be shifting its research agenda somewhat from basic to near-term research.

Many of the difficulties encountered by MCC may prove equally acute for Sematech (see Chapter 6 for a brief overview of the structure and origins of this consortium), which is also designed to operate as a free-standing research consortium with no direct university ties and its own research facilities. The problems of conflicting research priorities and time horizons that have hampered MCC may well afflict Sematech as well.[28]

---

[28] According to one account, however, a much larger fraction of Sematech's research staff is drawn from member firms than is true of MCC. According to Corcoran (1989), roughly one-half of Sematech researchers are on secondment from member firms for two-year assignments, substantially higher than the 15 percent of MCC research staff drawn from member firms. Personnel rotation, if it can be sustained, will facilitate the transfer of findings and results from the consortium's research facilities to the member firms.

The proprietary nature of much of the process technology employed within the semiconductor industry, which is the putative focus of Sematech research, further complicates the consortium's role within this industry. In addition, the establishment of applied research priorities within the venture poses considerable risks, in view of the rapid evolution of process and product technologies and the resulting uncertainties within the industry over future technological opportunities (Waldman, 1987). Member companies may well want different things. Some members of Sematech already have .5 micron facilities, at least in their laboratories, while other members do not. Small firms tend to have different priorities than large ones. There is thus a real danger, inherent in a consortium whose members have different needs and capabilities, that the eventual output of the R&D activity will not be of real commercial value to any large segment of participants.

Although its prospects and ultimate structure are uncertain at present, the research agenda of Sematech does not resemble the precommercial, basic research often advocated by supporters of collaborative research. Moreover, the Department of Defense is a major financial supporter of Sematech, and this inevitably raises concern that its research thrust will be heavily influenced by the requirements of military, rather than civilian, markets.

Conclusion

Changes in the economic and technological environment of U.S. firms, growing national concern over U.S. competitiveness, and increased interest within state governments in the use of innovation for economic development have all led to a considerable increase in international and domestic R&D collaboration. Despite their differences in structure and focus, both domestic and international R&D collaboration have grown rapidly during the past decade. R&D collaboration is relatively new within the U.S. R&D system, and its ultimate consequences are difficult to predict at this time.

International collaboration reflects the rising costs and risks of unassisted product development, the growth of significant technological strengths within foreign firms, and the increasingly prominent role of nontariff trade barriers and other government support for the development of advanced technologies. International collaboration has grown dramatically in a diverse array of U.S. manufacturing industries, although its long-term prospects appear brighter in some industries than in others. The consequences for U.S. competitiveness of such collaboration thus far appear to be fairly benign – in most cases, international collaboration is a response to, rather than a cause of, declining U.S. competitiveness. In other industries, collaboration has assisted U.S. firms in strengthening their technological and production skills.

The growing number and importance of international collaborative ventures do not reflect the discouragement of domestic collaboration by the U.S. antitrust statutes. International collaboration ventures create some complex policy implications, however, in both the trade and technology policy spheres. Along with numerous other factors, international collaborative ventures will accelerate international technology transfer in the global economy of the future. Nevertheless, the technology transfer operating within international collaborative ventures involving U.S. firms will remain a two-way flow for the foreseeable future. Trade policy clearly influences the development of international collaborative ventures. Increasingly, however, trade policy formulation and implementation will be affected by the operation and existence of these ventures – notably, the internationalization of sources of R&D and components. We discuss these policy issues at greater length in Chapter 10.

Much of the domestic research collaboration that has grown in recent years involves the renewal of linkages among state governments, publicly supported universities, and industry that had been languishing for a number of years. The erosion of these links during the postwar period was in part a result of the massive expansion in federal funding of research within both universities and industry. Closer research collaboration between universities and U.S. industry could hasten the translation of basic research findings into commercial products and processes: As we argued in this chapter, interfirm collaboration may assist the absorption and more rapid utilization by firms of the research advances of academic scientists and engineers. This absorption nevertheless requires investment by firms in their internal research operations and personnel as well as in the external research consortium.

The huge size, decentralized structure, and research-intensive character of the U.S. higher education system are unique among industrial nations, and these factors increase the potential payoff from closer research collaboration between universities and industry. Nevertheless, university–industry collaboration, when most successful, does not appear to be a short-term proposition, nor is it (nor should it be) a relationship in which clearly defined "deliverables" figure prominently. Indeed, as Blumenthal et al. (1986) noted, the biotechnology research collaborations that appear to focus most intensively on such deliverables pose the greatest challenges to academic ideals, challenges that in many ways resemble those created two decades earlier by classified defense-related research on university campuses.

Thus far, university–industry collaboration appears to have been slightly more successful than private interfirm consortia in supporting long-term research of a generic, precommercial variety. This conclusion reflects the tendency of such collaborative ventures to shift the research agenda toward applied, near-term research, as well as the absence of the important personnel flows between sponsor firm and consortium that typify university–industry research collaboration. The mixed results of U.S. interfirm collaboration in research, however, stem from factors that are also likely to reduce the attractiveness of such research collaboration within Japanese industries in which individual firms are already at the technological frontier.

As we pointed out in Chapter 8, leading Japanese firms have become increasingly reluctant to furnish their most expert research personnel to such ventures and are far less willing to pool their knowledge with competitors that may be able to quickly employ such knowledge against its provider. The heyday of Japanese research collaboration may already have passed: Such ventures function most effectively as instruments for the diffusion of precommercial scientific and technological knowledge among participants, and therefore are most successful where all participants are on a roughly equal footing and well behind the technological frontier. In other words, interfirm research collaboration may be most effective in an environment of technological "catch-up," rather than one of leadership. U.S. firms typically differ substantially in the level of their in-house expertise, and some members of an industry are likely to be far closer to the frontier than others. Both factors complicate the operation of private interfirm research consortia in the United States, just as they increasingly hamper such consortia within Japan. Both factors may favor the development of university–industry research consortia within the United States.

10

The merger of technology and trade policies

As we noted in Chapters 8 and 9, two of the factors that have changed the environment for innovation are increased global interdependence in the economic and technological spheres, and growing involvement by governments in industrialized and industrializing nations in policies to promote innovation and technological advance. These developments are blurring the boundaries between technology and trade policies. The merger of these two policy areas has important implications for policy formulation in both areas. The growing importance of technology issues within trade policy poses challenges to the structure of U.S. trade policy. These challenges stem from the clash between the dynamic effects of technological change and the largely static conceptualization of trade policies and consequences that underpins U.S. trade policy, as well as the fact that the instruments of government technology policy frequently lie outside the purview of conventional trade policies. The merger of these policies could also lead to restrictions on international scientific communication and cooperation, if policymakers overstate the parallels between international trade in goods and international flows of knowledge and act to limit international scientific and technological collaboration and communication.

An unrealistically narrow or nationalistic view of the sources and contribution of scientific research to commercial innovation may create a form of scientific mercantilism,[1] replacing or (more likely) supplementing protectionist trade policies, that could severely hamper the operation of global and national R&D systems. U.S. government actions to restrict foreign access to domestic commercial R&D also undercut official efforts to improve U.S. firms' access to foreign research projects. Finally, official perceptions of the "reverse spillovers" between military and commercial technologies and the development of policies that address these spillovers (see Chapter 6) will compromise U.S. opposition to foreign government subsidies for the commercial development of new technologies.

---

[1] The results of research, rather than precious metals, are hoarded by a nation as a source of power, and the transfer of research results or technology is seen as a zero-sum game.

Why technological change complicates trade policy

Technological innovation and technology-intensive industries fit uneasily into the framework of trade policy negotiations and enforcement developed over the past four decades by the U.S. government. Several characteristics of innovation and the industries spawned by it are of particular importance:[2] the tendency for costs to fall and product quality to improve over time within technology-intensive industries; the imperfect competition and increasing returns associated with many such industries; and the influence of nontariff trade barriers on the development and operation of these industries.

Many of the technology-intensive industries that now are important sources of exports from the U.S. and other industrial economies are characterized by strong dynamic learning effects. Production costs frequently fall as a function of cumulative production volume or time at a specific site or within a single firm; product quality (e.g., yields of microelectronic chips) may also increase as a result of such learning. More generally, the application of new technologies is characterized by prolonged periods of debugging and learning, meaning that the efficiency of their application will grow over time.

These learning effects have a number of important implications for government policy and firm behavior. They provide one justification for government policies of support for the development of technologies or markets for technology-intensive industries (discussed later in this chapter). "Infant industries" that receive government aid and that are characterized by strong learning effects may become robust adolescents capable of survival without government support. Although efficient capital markets should be capable of providing the support for these industries in their infancy, faith in the perfection of capital markets is not widely shared. The most common forms of direct government support for infant high-technology industries are subsidies for R&D and investment in the development and production of advanced products,[3] restrictions on access to the domestic market by similar goods from foreign producers, restrictions on direct investment in the domestic market by foreign producers, and procure-

---

[2] For additional discussion, see Krugman (1987a, b); see also Aho (1988).
[3] Foreign government research subsidies need not create difficulties comparable to those raised by development subsidies. As was noted in Chapter 9, if U.S. firms and other institutions invest in monitoring of the advances made in foreign research facilities, they are able to reap the benefits of this research without incurring the full costs – monitoring of foreign research and development, after all, was a key factor in the development of Japanese commercial technologies. Both the monitoring of offshore research and the conversion of scientific research results into commercial technologies, however, require a robust domestic public and private research system.

ment policies that favor the domestic producer of a high-technology good. All of these policies distort trade flows.

As Krugman (1987) and others have pointed out, a number of technology-intensive industries are characterized by high fixed costs (typically related to the very high costs of development of new products and processes) and a concentrated market structure. The international commercial aircraft industry, for example, has only three producers of large transports and the same number of firms manufacturing engines for these aircraft. The telecommunications equipment and, possibly, the integrated circuit memory chip industries are likely to develop similarly high levels of concentration in the near future as a result of growing development and production costs. The surviving firms in many instances can exercise significant market power, raising prices above competitive levels.

The strategic competition that currently obtains in industries like commercial aircraft, in which a subsidized Airbus aircraft competes against a nonsubsidized Boeing aircraft in many markets, can be attributed in part to the concern of Airbus Industrie's sponsor governments over losing alternatives to Boeing as a supplier of commercial aircraft. If the alternative to subsidized development and production of Airbus products is a Boeing monopoly in many segments of the market, with prices to match, the economic returns to Airbus Industrie's member governments (and to airline passengers and stockholders the world over) from their subsidies may be greater than estimates of the direct employment and spinoff effects suggest. Similar arguments over the dangers of dependence on monopolistic foreign suppliers are becoming increasingly common in proposals for U.S. government subsidies to the design and production of random-access memory chips. These payments have been justified as a way to preserve U.S. production capabilities and to create competition for Japanese suppliers of these components (see Pollack, 1988).

The combination of trade-distorting policies and strong dynamic effects means that the performance of a firm in such an industry may be influenced by government policies (subsidies or protection of domestic markets) and industry structure in earlier periods. This reality is very difficult to accommodate within a U.S. trade policy enforcement mechanism that focuses primarily on costs, pricing, and subsidies in a static, single-period framework. Allegations of dumping (predatory pricing of exports below average cost), for example, often compare export prices with a constructed average cost of production for a product ("constructed" by the enforcing agency, the U.S. Department of Commerce).[4] Producers of goods characterized by average costs that decline over time, however, may find it profitable to price below average cost in the early generations of a prod-

---

[4] Estimating average costs and profit margins obviously becomes even more difficult in a world of flexible (and volatile) international exchange rates.

uct so as to increase production volume rapidly and reap the cost reductions from learning, thus allowing reductions in price.

Allegations that foreign firms are behaving in a predatory fashion, choosing not to maximize profits, may overlook the potential effects of learning on costs and prices over time. Although the Commerce Department has attempted to use a measure of long-run average costs in some recent dumping investigations (e.g., the investigation of dumping of memory chips by Japanese producers), the practice is not widespread.

Restrictions on access to the domestic market of a foreign firm or government subsidies to that firm in the early stages of production may enable it to penetrate export markets with low-cost, high-quality products after the cessation of government assistance. Allegations of unfair trade or subsidies therefore may not be supported by the behavior and costs of the foreign firm at the time at which the firm has become a successful exporter. Procedures for enforcement of U.S. trade law, which presume an essentially static context, cannot easily accommodate the possibility that trade-distorting government actions in earlier periods are responsible for the challenge mounted by a robust foreign firm to the domestic markets of the firms petitioning for government action.

As is clear from the discussion of the range of policy instruments to which governments resort in supporting them, technology-intensive industries also challenge the historic focus of U.S. bilateral and multilateral trade initiatives on tariffs and border measures and on assurances of procedural regularity and national treatment for foreign firms.[5] The instruments employed by governments in support of technological development extend far beyond the border measures (mainly tariffs) that have been the objects of U.S. negotiations.

Because of their effects on trade flows, domestic subsidies for research or investment, government procurement, intellectual property regimes, patent policies, regional development policies, and other policies that historically have received little scrutiny from trade policymakers are now central to trade negotiations. These nontariff barriers to trade are by no means the exclusive province of foreign governments. During the 1980s, as we noted in Chapter 8, the U.S. government imposed nontariff import restrictions in the steel, automobile, machine tool, semiconductor, and

---

[5] As Aho and Aronson (1985) point out, this focus on tariffs pervades the dominant multilateral agreement and organization charged with oversight of international trade, the General Agreement on Tariffs and Trade (GATT) and the GATT Secretariat. The GATT instrument was negotiated in 1947 as the section concerned with tariffs of the founding agreement for the International Trade Organization (ITO), which was intended to complement the International Monetary Fund and the International Bank for Reconstruction and Development in supporting international trade and economic development. The ITO charter was never ratified by the U.S. Congress, and many of its duties have fallen by default to the GATT Secretariat, formally known as the Secretariat of the Interim Committee for the International Trade Organization.

other industries.[6] Just as the macroeconomic policies of sovereign governments often conflict, these sectoral or microeconomic policies also may clash, producing allegations of unfair trade.[7] In many cases, long-standing domestic policies that were developed with little or no attention to their effects on international trade are now the subject of negotiations among trade policymakers.

The growing importance of nontariff barriers to trade and other internal policies with trade-distorting effects has complicated the tasks of trade policymakers. Negotiations over these policies involve a far larger community of policymakers and domestic interests than talks over border measures, however, which greatly increases their complexity. Tariff negotiations focused on a highly visible barrier, the operation and trade effects of which could be monitored fairly easily. The objectives of such negotiations are also more easily defined in terms of reducing and binding tariff levels. The trade effects of nontariff barriers are more difficult to establish and monitor, which complicates negotiations. Moreover, the specific goals of such talks are more difficult to define in operational terms. Although disciplines covering some of these policies were agreed on in the Tokyo Round codes, the coverage and enforcement of the disciplines contained in several of these Codes, such as those covering government procurement and subsidies, have not always been effective (see Tarullo, 1984; Winham, 1986).

U.S. goals in trade negotiations on nontariff trade-distorting policies generally focus on improving the operation of policy processes in foreign economies. Improvements in these processes include greater "transparency," meaning that policies are formulated through public processes that foreign enterprises can monitor and in which they can in some cases participate (e.g., through hearings or opportunities for comment on proposals), and national treatment, meaning that policies and procedures are applied identically to domestic and foreign enterprises. Definition of and agreement on these desiderata for a specific set of policies, such as technical standards, nevertheless do not preclude the evasion of disciplines by using alternative instruments, for example, government procurement to achieve the same ends. The procedural focus of these negotiations thus can weaken their trade-liberalizing effectiveness.

One alternative to focusing trade policy on transparent and nondiscri-

---

[6] See the estimate by Tyson (1988), cited in Chapter 8, that 35 percent of U.S. imports in 1983 were subject to nontariff restrictions, an increase from an estimated 20 percent in 1980.

[7] International coordination and harmonization of national macroeconomic policies have progressed considerably, albeit haltingly, during the past four years in the wake of the Plaza Agreement of 1985. Similar coordination of sectoral policies, however essential to the maintenance of harmonious trade and economic relations, is likely to be far more difficult, since the range of policy instruments is much greater and their effects are more difficult to trace and monitor.

minatory processes is to stipulate outcomes, as in the United States–Japan Semiconductor Agreement, which fixes a price floor for dynamic random-access memories (DRAMs) and allegedly commits the Japanese government to ensure a specific market share in Japan for U.S. producers of these components.[8] "Managed trade" agreements of this sort, which have also been hammered out in the auto, steel, and textiles industries, among others, are supported by some analysts because they provide stronger protection against allegedly predatory imports and may be more easily enforced (see Choate and Linger, 1988). By restricting imports through some form of a quota or price agreement, these "managed trade" arrangements also provide higher profits to the affected foreign producers, which makes such import restrictions more acceptable to them and reduces the possibility of retaliation against U.S. exporters.[9] These agreements frequently result in higher prices and lower efficiency within the U.S. economy. Moreover, since the agreements tend to be renewed repeatedly, these undesirable effects may persist for years, which reduces pressure on U.S. producers to adjust to import competition.

The Semiconductor Agreement is likely to be especially harmful to the U.S. electronics sector because of the new international division of labor in microelectronics and computer systems (discussed in Chapter 8). U.S. computer makers now depend on foreign (mainly Japanese) suppliers of DRAM components, and new personal computer and workstation designs demand more memory components per unit. The sharp increases in the cost of DRAMs that appear to have resulted from the Semiconductor Agreement thus are a serious competitive impediment to U.S. computer producers, few of whom manufacture their own memory components.[10]

Most Japanese producers of personal computers, by contrast, are vertically integrated into memory production. The Semiconductor Agreement sharply increases the profits of Japanese firms from DRAM sales and provides them with a significant cost advantage in components for competitive computer and workstation designs. Moreover, the profits earned in the DRAM market can be applied to the development of even more sophisticated computers in the future.

The agreement's call for an increase in the Japanese market share of U.S. producers of microelectronic components has led a number of U.S.

---

[8] The allegation has been made in Prestowitz (1988), and in a number of journalistic descriptions of this agreement.

[9] Prestowitz notes that the agreement ". . . amounted to getting the Japanese government to force its companies to make a profit and even to impose controls to avoid excess production – in short, a government-led cartel. For the free-traders of the United States to be asking Japan to cartelize its industry was the supreme irony. Yet it was logical" (p. 62).

[10] According to estimates in Pine (1988), the price of 256K DRAMs has risen within the U.S. from roughly $2.60 at the time the agreement was signed to more than $3.60 in June 1988. The price of 64K DRAMs rose from $.90 to nearly $1.40 during the same period. Prices in Japan for DRAMs remained constant or declined slightly during this period. A more favorable view of the effects of the agreement can be found in Yoffie (1988), p. 36.

components firms to develop strategic alliances and other collaborative ventures with Japanese producers of systems (Steinmueller, 1988). One result of these collaborative ventures is accelerated technology transfer from U.S. to Japanese and from Japanese to U.S. firms. Other U.S. producers may move a growing share of their production or procurement activities to foreign locations where the pricing provisions of the agreement are less easily enforced. This response to the agreement reduces U.S. employment in the computer industry. If the Semiconductor Agreement thus far is an example of successful "managed trade" policy, it is hard to know what defines a failure.

The difficulties of the Semiconductor Agreement underline a critical problem in trade policy for technology-intensive industries. Rapid international transfer of technology and development of foreign sources of supply of critical components mean that the definition of the "national content" of a specific product, be this an IBM personal computer or an Airbus A300, is very difficult. As the national origins of complex products become increasingly blurry, the formulation and administration of national trade policies that attempt to maximize the gains from trade by restricting the import or encouraging the export of specific goods have become difficult and may (as in the case of the Semiconductor Agreement) be counterproductive. Expanding international collaboration in product research, development, and manufacture will increase the reliance by U.S. import-competing industries on foreign sources for technology and critical components, as we pointed out in Chapter 8. Firms in these industries may find import restrictions increasingly onerous, reducing the severity of the clash between the political interests of export industries and import-competing industries within U.S. trade policy.[11]

The increasing salience of technology issues within U.S. trade policy

Regardless of the complications introduced by technology issues for trade policy, recent U.S. government actions and legislation have significantly raised the salience of technology issues within both bilateral and multilateral trade negotiations. Negotiations over the renewal in 1988 of the United States–Japan Agreement on Scientific Cooperation, for example, involved senior personnel from the Office of the U.S. Trade Representative

---

[11] Destler and Odell (1987) argue that industrial opposition to protection has grown: "*There has been a significant rise in aggregate political opposition to product-specific trade protection. . . .* From the mid-1970s through the mid-1980s, there was a clear increase in efforts by trade-dependent groups to block or limit new import restrictions" (p. 125; emphasis in the original). The authors noted that "between the early and mid-1980s, [antiprotection] activity by import-related groups rose sharply, whereas activity by export-related ones was flat" (p. 126).

to an unprecedented extent. The central trade-related issues in the talks on this scientific agreement concerned intellectual property rights within Japan and the assurance of access by U.S. firms to publicly funded research in Japanese laboratories that was comparable to Japanese firms' access to publicly funded research in U.S. research facilities.[12] The increasing importance of R&D and technology policy issues thus caused negotiations over an international scientific cooperation agreement, formerly of concern only within the scientific community, to spill over into the trade policy agenda. The example also underlines the extent to which trade policy issues increasingly concern internal domestic policies, rather than tariff or other border measures.

Technology-intensive industries now play a far more important role in bilateral disputes and negotiations. Although such mature industries as steel and textiles have been a source of significant trade tensions for a number of years, in recent years trade disputes among industrial economies have involved a growing number of high-technology industries. These industries include telecommunications equipment, which has been the object of intensive discussions between the United States and Japan, West Germany, and France, among other industrial nations, over U.S. firms' access to foreign markets; commercial aircraft, where the United States has demanded that the European Airbus Industrie consortium reform its structure and reduce its reliance on government support; and microelectronics, in which tensions between the United States and Japan culminated in the United States–Japan Semiconductor Agreement, followed by sanctions against U.S. imports of Japanese goods in response to alleged Japanese nonobservance of the agreement. The informal discouragement by senior officials of the U.S. Commerce and Defense departments of Fujitsu's proposed acquisition of Fairchild Semiconductor also illustrates the growing interdependence of trade and technology policies in this industry.[13]

U.S. officials employed trade policy as an instrument of technology policy in dealing with the recent proposal by the Massachusetts Institute of Technology to purchase a supercomputer from the U.S.-based joint venture involving Honeywell and Nippon Electric Company of Japan (the treatment by U.S. policymakers of the products of this U.S.-based joint

[12] Clearly, reciprocal access is a concept that is more easily stated than implemented in national R&D systems that differ as sharply as do those of the United States, where publicly funded research accounts for nearly 50 percent of all national R&D and where relatively open institutions like universities play a very important role in basic research, and Japan, in which corporate funding of R&D is far more significant. U.S. firms almost certainly would reject a policy that required assurances of equal access to the research facilities of U.S. and Japanese corporations.

[13] The logic of official opposition to this acquisition was apparently based largely on the perceived need to prevent acquisition of the firm's technological assets by Japan, rather than opposition to acquisition of the firm by a foreign firm. At the time of the proposed acquisition, Fairchild Semiconductor was owned by a French firm, Schlumberger.

venture as Japanese in origin also illustrates the complexity of determining national origin in a technologically interdependent world). Faced with threats from the Department of Commerce to investigate the possibility of dumping in supercomputers, MIT elected to postpone the procurement, instead proposing to seek financial support from the National Science Foundation for a supercomputer research center that would involve U.S. firms and U.S.-based technology.[14] As in other areas of change in federal technology and trade policies, these initiatives of the Reagan administration received strong bipartisan support, illustrated by the inclusion of specific provisions for all three industries in the 1988 Omnibus Trade and Competitiveness Act.[15]

A final important area in which trade policy has been influenced by the evolving agenda of technology policy issues is intellectual property rights. Consistent with the growing concern of federal policymakers over the rapid commercialization and realization of profits from scientific research, the domestic enforcement of intellectual property rights has been strengthened significantly in recent years through the establishment and decisions of the Court of Appeals for the Federal Circuit, which has emerged as a champion of patent-holder rights.

Intellectual property rights now occupy a prominent place on the trade policy agenda as well, however, for several reasons. U.S. firms increasingly depend on exports of R&D-intensive products, which arguably benefit from improved intellectual property protection. Bringing intellectual property issues into trade policy also provides a potentially powerful enforcement mechanism – restriction of access to the U.S. market for the products of nations deemed to provide insufficient protection.

Section 337 of the 1930 Tariff Act and Section 301 of the 1974 Trade Act (the latter section has been broadened considerably and intellectual

---

[14] According to the press release issued by the institute, a letter from Acting Secretary of Commerce Bruce Smart to MIT president Paul Gray stated: "I understand that MIT is considering acquiring a supercomputer from Nippon Electric Corporation of Japan. I am writing to inform you that we have no objection to the acquisition of a foreign-produced supercomputer. However, you should be aware that imported products may be subject to U.S. anti-dumping duty proceedings. A dumping case could be commenced by a private petitioner or by the U.S. government."

MIT provost John Deutch stated that "it became clear important elements of the federal government would prefer to see MIT acquire a supercomputer based on U.S. technology. Since the federal government would ultimately bear nearly all the costs of the machine through research grants to MIT, the preferences of the U.S. government must be seriously addressed" (Massachusetts Institute of Technology, 1987, p. 2); see also Putka (1987) and Sanger (1987).

[15] The act calls for a series of reports on U.S. firms' access to foreign markets for telecommunications equipment; creates a new provision (Sec. 1315) for dealing with subsidized international consortia, widely viewed as a provision directed at Airbus; and creates new provisions for "fast-track" antidumping investigations in industries such as microelectronics in which product life cycles are believed to be short.

property issues accorded greater weight in the 1988 act) provide for restrictions on access to the U.S. market for products that infringe on patents or copyright or market-access restrictions for goods produced by nations not providing comparable protection. As the importance of intellectual property rights within U.S. trade has grown, U.S. trade policymakers have employed the threat of broad sanctions under Section 301 to bring about significant revisions in the intellectual property regimes of such nations as South Korea, Singapore, and Thailand.

Increasingly, the standards employed to assess the sufficiency of protection of intellectual property are the effects of such protection on trade, rather than the extent to which (as in the past) foreign firms are afforded national treatment and due process in patent and copyright infringement litigation within foreign markets. The assessment of the adequacy of foreign nations' protection of intellectual property rights employs as its benchmark the protection of these rights under U.S. law, rather than the adherence of foreign governments to the Paris or Berne conventions or to the procedural norms noted earlier. Faced with the possible restriction of access to U.S. markets, foreign governments have been compelled to revise domestic policies to achieve standards of protection and breadth of coverage comparable to those in the United States. As elsewhere, the case of intellectual property rights illustrates the significant extension of the reach of trade policy issues beyond the borders of trading nations into domestic policy.

Intellectual property rights now are the object of multilateral trade negotiations as well. Frustrated with the limited coverage, weak standards, and minimal enforcement of intellectual property rights provided by major international agreements (primarily the Berne and Paris conventions), the United States and other industrial nations have placed intellectual property rights on the agenda of the Uruguay Round of multilateral trade negotiations. A successful outcome for these negotiations would for the first time make insufficient protection for intellectual property rights grounds for sanctions (including trade retaliation against the offending government) under the provisions of the General Agreement on Tariffs and Trade (GATT). Moreover, the GATT would be called on to define, through reference to other international treaties or existing national statutes, acceptable levels of protection and coverage of intellectual property rights. A successful intellectual property rights agreement in the Uruguay Round could produce a multilateral system of trade-based enforcement of these rights that would resemble the bilateral framework currently employed by the United States.

Despite the considerable U.S. investment of political persuasion and resources in the intellectual property question, the benefits of a successful outcome, especially in multilateral negotiations, may be overstated.

Not all U.S. industries benefit equally from intellectual property protection, yet strong protection now is a high-priority U.S. goal in the Uruguay Round, a multilateral negotiation that spans fifteen different substantive areas. Conventional instruments of intellectual property protection, including patents, trade secrets, and copyrights, are not always sufficient to enable innovators to reap the returns to their investments, as a recent survey of R&D executives by Levin et al. (1987) shows:

> For new processes . . ., patents were generally rated the least effective of the mechanisms of appropriation: only 20 percent of the lines of business surveyed rated process patent effectiveness in excess of 4.0 [on a seven-point Likert scale, for which 7 was the highest rating]. Eighty percent scored the effectiveness of lead time and learning curve advantages on new processes in excess of 4.3. Secrecy, though not considered as effective as lead time and learning advantages, was still considered more effective than patents in protecting processes.
>
> Patents for products were typically considered more effective than those for processes, and secrecy was considered less effective in protecting products than processes. Generally, lead time, learning curves, and sales or service efforts were regarded as substantially more effective than patents in protecting products. Eighty percent of the sample businesses rated the effectiveness of sales and service efforts above 5.0, but only 20 percent considered product patents this effective. (pp. 794–5)

Levin et al. concluded that patent protection was most useful for innovators in the chemicals and pharmaceuticals industries. However, in industries in which the critical sources of profit are marketing or production expertise, patents or other forms of intellectual property protection appear to be of secondary importance, no matter how much these protections are strengthened.

The benefits of improved intellectual property protection relative to other goals in the Uruguay Round, such as improved disciplines on foreign-subsidy practices or on safeguards actions (temporary or "escape clause" restrictions on imports), thus will vary across U.S. industries. Yet a Uruguay Round agreement on intellectual property protection will be one component of a complex package covering fifteen negotiating areas. The benefits of stronger intellectual property protection to many U.S. industries may not outweigh the costs of the concessions in other areas of the Uruguay Round that will be necessary to gain agreement on this contentious issue.

The increasing salience of trade issues within U.S. technology policy

As we have pointed out here and in Chapter 8, the increasing importance of technology as a source of comparative advantage, combined with the growing mobility of both technology and capital, has led many governments to shift their domestic science and technology policies to encourage more rapid commercialization and realization of domestic economic benefits. Rather than emphasizing basic research in the support of civilian R&D, as the federal government has done during the postwar period, many of these foreign programs (e.g., Airbus or the second phase of the Common Market's Esprit program) now support the commercial exploitation of new technologies. The "downstream" orientation of such programs reflects the fact that in an era of rapid international technology transfer, the economic returns to basic research investments may not be realized by the nation or firm undertaking the investment. Public policies to commercialize or to diffuse new technologies within the economy are seen as necessary to increase the national economic returns to public investments in technology.

The U.S. government has not been aloof from this change, as concern over commercialization of new technologies has increased during the 1980s. The Reagan administration entered the White House in 1981 with a pledge to remove the federal government from intervention in the commercialization of new technologies. In this view, the appropriate federal role in civilian technology development was limited to funding of basic research, commercialization of which was best handled by the market.[16]

The contrast between its 1981 posture and the administration's 1987 response to the demonstration of the phenomenon of high-temperature superconductivity (HTS), the formation of Sematech, or the 1988 development of standards and research programs for high-definition television, is dramatic. In these instances, as well as in the National Science Foundation programs for university–industry cooperation, Engineering and Science Research Centers, and other initiatives, the Reagan administration, with strong bipartisan support, proposed or implemented a range of policies designed to increase the national economic returns to the large federal investment in basic research.

This effort represents a considerable shift from the rhetoric of 1981. It also changes the historic posture of federal policies toward commercial technology development. Federal initiatives for commercialization gen-

---

[16] An excellent statement of this view can be found in "Special Analysis K" of the *Special Analyses* volume released with the president's budget for fiscal 1983.

erally have been modest, but where significant, they have supported the commercial development of technologies for which market mechanisms and incentives were deemed to be lacking or insufficient. Examples include the commercial supersonic transport, coal liquefaction and synthetic fuels, "Project Breakthrough" in residential housing construction, and the liquid metal fast breeder reactor.

Recent initiatives, by contrast, focus on raising the national economic returns from commercial development of basic research advances for which the private returns are likely to be high, but only in the absence of faster commercialization by foreign firms. These programs are intended to accelerate the national realization of the commercial benefits in a world in which foreign firms are able to commercialize applications of basic research breakthroughs as rapidly or more rapidly and effectively than U.S. firms. As a result, some recent initiatives to support commercialization of new technologies have acquired a nationalistic or even mercantilistic character.

The public HTS symposium convened in 1987 by the White House Office of Science and Technology Policy and the National Science Foundation excluded foreign participants. The administration's subsequent proposals for increased research funding (the Superconductivity Competitiveness Initiative, released in January 1988) for HTS development did not diverge sharply from historic precedent, being confined largely to increased funding that drew primarily on military sources, but the proposal did include provisions designed to prohibit or restrict foreign access to the results of publicly funded basic research in HTS.[17]

The recent discussions between private firms and the Department of Commerce on commercial development of high-definition television have excluded foreign firms, and the Federal Communications Commission's decision on broadcast standards has been interpreted by some (see "Television on Hold," pp. 17–18) as intended to exclude current Japanese HDTV designs. Both the Sematech initiative and the National Center for Manufacturing Sciences (NCMS; see later in this chapter for additional discussion), which are funded in part with public monies, exclude foreign

---

[17] Under the terms of the proposed amendments to the Freedom of Information Act (FOIA), requests from foreign nationals for research data or results could be denied on the basis of potential harm to the competitive position of U.S. firms. The explanation accompanying the proposals noted that "mandatory disclosure of such information under FOIA could encourage U.S. competitors to exploit the U.S. science and technology base rather than making investments in their own research and development infrastructure. Under Title IV, Federal agencies will be required to withhold information of this nature requested under the Freedom of Information Act where disclosure could reasonably be expected to harm the economic competitiveness of the United States" (U.S. House of Representatives, 1988, p. 2).

participation.[18] The recently announced Pentagon research initiative in HDTV also may exclude foreign enterprises.[19]

Although the increased concern of these proposals with commercial development of the fruits of basic research investments arguably is a positive development, the mercantilistic flavor of many of them is not. Proposals to restrict scientific and technological cooperation at the water's edge fly in the face of the growing interdependence of national R&D systems that we noted in Chapter 8. To the extent that U.S. policymakers design technology initiatives that ignore the increasing interdependence of U.S. and foreign scientific and technological research, both U.S. and foreign technological development will be hampered. Consider, for example, the implications for a multinational firm like IBM, which operates research laboratories throughout the industrial world, of the proposed restrictions on disclosure of the results of publicly funded HTS research to foreign nations. Use by the firm of its network of foreign R&D laboratories would decline, limiting the ability of IBM and other U.S. firms to tap the scientific and technological developments of foreign economies. Such restrictions would reduce the competitiveness of U.S. firms. Proposals to restrict access to U.S. research facilities and findings also overlook the historic futility and ineffectiveness of such restrictions.

Recent initiatives by the Pentagon to support commercial technology development create still other challenges to the historic trade policy posture of the United States. Such programs as Sematech (to which the Pentagon may contribute as much as $600 million over five years in matching funds), the National Center for Manufacturing Sciences (to which the Defense Advanced Research Projects Agency [DARPA] will contribute $15 million – out of a total three-year budget of $40 million – over three

---

[18] Dr. Robert Noyce, chief executive officer of Sematech, made this position clear in a recent interview: " 'What advantage would NEC bring to Sematech? I can think of none,' he said.

"He hastened to point out the obvious threat of Japanese participation. 'If the trade problem were resolved and our technology was not used by foreign countries in a predatory fashion, as with TVs or semiconductors, I'd have no fear of diffusing our knowledge around the world. But now, American knowledge is being used to hurt Americans' " ("Robert Noyce: On Sematech, Chips, and Competitiveness," p. 7).

[19] See Davis (1989) and Waldman (1988), p. 2. Waldman quoted Pat Hill Hubbard of the American Electronics Association, the trade association that announced formation of a loose consortium of sixteen U.S. firms to develop HDTV technology, as stating, "It's too early to tell whether the collective will allow foreign-owned companies [many of which are members of the AEA] to participate in any consortiums that emerge. . . . 'The main purpose of this is to ensure the U.S. gains and retains HDTV research and development capacity, engineering design capability and product manufacturing expertise.' " Waldman's account does not discuss the role of the AEA collective in the Pentagon-funded research initiative in HDTV announced earlier in 1989. Wolf (1989) discusses the concerns of European firms that they will be excluded fom the DARPA program.

years), and the recently announced Pentagon initiative in high-definition television are designed to support the defense industrial base. Military funding for these programs is based on two assumptions: (1) Technological spillovers in process and product technologies and design now flow primarily from commercial to defense applications in these sectors (recall the arguments in Chapter 6); and (2) U.S. suppliers of defense technologies cannot survive without maintaining a strong presence in commercial markets.[20] Research subsidies to support commercial technology development within corsortia that exclude foreign firms therefore are necessary for national security purposes.

Regardless of the validity of the assumptions on which they are based, these initiatives undermine the basis for U.S. opposition to such large-scale foreign technology development subsidies as those of the European Airbus program. Admittedly, Airbus is targeted more precisely on a specific commercial technology (indeed, on a set of commercial aircraft designs) than recent Pentagon programs, and Airbus subsidies support production as well as development. The fact nevertheless remains that the Airbus program is driven in part by the desire of the participant governments to maintain *their* respective national military aircraft industries by supporting the participation of these firms in a major commercial project. The development of similar U.S. programs places trade policymakers and negotiators on a very slippery slope. If the difference between U.S. and foreign technology subsidy programs becomes one of degree, rather than kind, the limits to foreign abuse of subsidies that are imposed by U.S. opposition and persuasion are likely to be eroded still further.

In addition to their implications for U.S. trade policy, of course, restrictions on foreign participation in these programs continue the trend toward technological mercantilism. Indeed, the provisions of the NCMS charter that restrict the international transfer by member firms of NCMS-developed technologies could hamper the ability of U.S. multinationals to manage international R&D operations. Increasing restrictions on foreign participation in U.S.-based research consortia, many if not most of which involve significant public funds (in many cases from state, as well as federal,

---

[20] A recent front-page story in the *New York Times* discussed the growing concern that "the trends that hamper major commercial enterprises – lagging productivity, competition from imports, foreign ownership of American companies and inadequate long-term research – are damaging producers of weapons. In response, the Pentagon is beginning to argue for broad industrial policies that would benefit high-technology industries as a whole, hoping that the rewards would reach sectors of the economy that directly serve the military" (p. D22) The story describes a report by the Defense Science Board that recommended the "formation of an 'Industrial Policy Council' that would be headed by the President's National Security Advisor and would recommend policies to bolster industries that support the military. At the same time, the report said, the Defense Secretary should be made a permanent member of the Economic Policy Council, the Cabinet's group for making economic policy" (p. D22). See Cushman (1988).

sources), will also complicate U.S. efforts (as in the United States–Japan Agreement on Scientific Cooperation) to gain unrestricted access for U.S. firms to similar consortia in other industrial economies. Indeed, the reality of global technological interdependence and the futility of efforts to restrict international movement of technological and scientific know-how are well illustrated by the recent decision of Texas Instruments, a major participant in Sematech, to enter a technology-sharing joint venture with Hitachi of Japan, presumably one of the major technological threats to the firms participating in Sematech.[21] Efforts to impose strict limitations on international transfer or foreign participation simply fly in the face of this interdependence and are likely to undercut the effectiveness of the collaborative research ventures currently under way.

Conclusion

Like military officers who learn and refine the tactics used in the last war, national science and technology policymakers in the United States and other industrial nations are applying the precepts of an earlier era, with results quite the opposite of the intended effects. In developing technology and trade policies that emphasize the capture of the benefits of research for their nations, policymakers paradoxically have encouraged the growth of consortia spanning national boundaries for the commercial development of new technologies (Mowery, 1988c). These consortia themselves contribute powerfully to more rapid technology transfer and the internationalization of the global R&D system.[22]

The focus and structure of federal science and technology policy should be changed in response to these shifts in the technological and competitive environment. If the concerns and philosophy underpinning the initiatives we have discussed here spread more widely within U.S. science and technology policy, the results could be detrimental to the strength of the U.S. science and technology base and to U.S. goals for trade liberalization. It is increasingly important that policymakers examine the consistency of initiatives in the technology and trade policy areas, precisely because of the growing interdependence of these policies. An alternative policy analysis and framework must be developed to supplant that of technological protectionism. Much more must be done to highlight the interdependence of trade and technology policies so as to improve the consistency, and ultimately the effectiveness, of policies in these areas.

[21] According to one account, " 'Sematech is for manufacturing knowledge and expertise,' said Stan Victor, a spokesman for Texas Instruments in Dallas. He added that the purpose of the agreement with Hitachi was different, because it was a 'technology development' program meant to create the most effective designs for the 16-megabit [microprocessor] chip." Hayes (1988), p. C6.

[22] As Nelson (1984) points out, the ability of nations to transform "leading" technologies into "strategic" technologies is declining as a result of these developments.

11

Concluding observations

We have covered a great deal of ground in this volume, beginning with the origins of industrial exploitation of scientific research in the mid-nineteenth century and moving forward to discuss problems of international competition among advanced industrial economies in the late twentieth century. This chapter does not present "lessons" or policy implications of this wide-ranging analysis, but draws together some of the threads of the arguments we have presented in preceding chapters.

Although our span has been wide, we have been concerned throughout this volume with the changing structure of national R&D systems and of industrial research, focusing on the ways in which the structural evolution of these systems is influenced by the requirements of absorption and utilization of scientific and technological research results. The appropriability analysis of research investment and innovation developed within neoclassical economics is useful but incomplete for analyzing the development and structure of the institutions of technological progress and for the development of science and technology policies.

Exploiting the results of scientific and technological research is a complex, costly, and knowledge-intensive process. As we noted in our discussion of the emergence of industrial research laboratories in the United States, the large resource requirements and complexity of this process go some considerable distance toward explaining the structure of the industrial research system within this economy. Moreover, this and other evidence (cited in Chapter 5 and in Mowery, 1983) suggest that cooperative research programs alone are insufficient to transform the innovative performance of technically backward industries and firms; more is needed, specifically the development of sufficient expertise *within* these firms to utilize the results of externally performed research. Where such expertise is lacking, cooperative research organizations often have been unsuccessful in industry. The difficulties inherent in the provision of research on a contractual or arm's-length basis can undercut the effectiveness of these organizations in industries with little or no in-house R&D activity.

Because the structure of R&D institutions must support the utilization of research results, and because the environment within which these institutions operate has changed, this means that the landscape we have surveyed is characterized by change over time and distinct contrasts across national boundaries. During the early twentieth century, the institutions of industrial and academic research in the United States developed very differently from those of Great Britain, with significant consequences for innovative and economic performance. Within the United States, the structure of the national research system was transformed by the demands of national mobilization for World War II. More recently, rising costs and increased competitive pressures appear likely to result in some further restructuring of industrial and public research organizations. The postwar Japanese research system, which differed sharply from that of the United States, proved extremely effective (along with other policies) in transforming the technological base of the Japanese economy and bringing Japanese firms to the frontiers of technological know-how and practice in many fields. Many of the institutions of this research system, however, notably the national projects of cooperative research, may undergo change as the position of Japan within the world economy and of Japanese firms as innovators changes.

These comments point to the great importance of context in evaluating and analyzing the organization of research. We have argued in the preceding chapters that the appropriateness and innovative performance of a given institutional structure may change over time as the environment changes. Moreover, the institutions of research and innovation that are appropriate for one industry or technology may be ineffective within another. For this reason, as well as others, it is difficult if not impossible to arrive at fixed and definitive conclusions regarding the optimal structure for a research organization or a national R&D system. The institutions that appear to be effective in a nation engaged in technological and economic "catch-up" may be less useful in nations that are operating at the technological frontier.

We simply do not know, for example, how much high-quality basic research a national economy requires in order to remain competitive in the global economy of the late twentieth century, in which technological and scientific knowledge move more and more rapidly across national boundaries. It is possible, as we noted in Chapter 8, that in some industries the "fast second" strategy pursued by many Japanese firms could remain viable into the foreseeable future; in other industries, however, this strategy has not proved successful for Japanese firms. Similarly, we have suggested that U.S. firms could benefit from monitoring more carefully the research activities and findings of external and foreign performers of research, yet the exploitation of these external research activities requires extensive in-house technological and scientific expertise. What is the optimal balance of in-house and external scientific and technological research? The answer will depend heavily on the specific context in which the question is posed. The ideal extent of integration within the firm of research, development, manufacturing, and other functions will also vary across industries, technologies, and time. The efforts by U.S. firms in some industries to move production operations offshore appear to have diminished their competitiveness, but in other industries, these strategies have been successful. Generalizations in this area are hazardous.

The performance of national R&D systems is also influenced by numerous factors that have little or nothing to do with the structure of these systems. One of the most important of these, to which we have devoted little attention, is the macroeconomic environment, especially insofar as it affects national rates of savings and capital formation. Domestic diffusion of new technologies in an economy in which 15–20 percent of national income is saved is likely to be considerably more rapid than in an economy in which less than 5 percent of income is saved, simply because of the differences in the cost of capital and in rates of capital formation.

The preceding discussion suggests that the utilization and diffusion of the results of scientific and engineering research should receive greater weight within R&D policy. In addition, a global environment of more rapid technology transfer, and increasingly adept adopter firms in other industrial and industrializing nations, increases the need for rapid adoption and commercialization of new technologies within this economy if the national returns to the large U.S. public investment in basic research are to be maintained. It appears likely that the new international economic environment has reduced the ability of any one national economy to appropriate the economic returns from basic research performed within its boundaries. More aggressive efforts to promote the domestic commercialization of the results of such research are needed. The research activities of foreign firms and nations also need to be monitored more carefully, however, both through active participation in such activities and continual scanning of the scientific and technological horizons. Support for adoption and utilization, in our view, is vastly preferable to efforts to restrict the international flow of basic scientific and technological information and research. This latter approach will impoverish U.S. citizens as surely as restrictions on the international flow of goods and services. In addition, the discussion of the Japanese R&D system in Chapter 8, as well as evidence from other economies, suggests that government policies supporting the utilization of R&D results can yield a high social payoff. (see David, 1986; Ergas, 1987; OECD, 1988; Mowery, 1988b).

Publicly funded adoption-oriented research has a long history in such sectors of the U.S. economy as the aircraft industry (see Chapter 7) and agriculture. Such programs appear to be most effective when the private-sector user community is actively involved in planning the research priorities and in performing a portion of the research, and when the program receives state financial support over a long period. This latter require-ment argues against "flagship" programs that focus on large-scale devel-opment of high-risk technologies. In exchange for providing considerable funding, the political sponsors of these programs demand a great deal in a short time period, which creates a high risk of failure.

An adoption-focused policy orientation appears to have gained some acceptance in recent years. Initiatives such as the reorganization of the National Bureau of Standards into the National Institute for Standards and Technology, the publicly supported efforts at the federal and state levels to improve research collaboration between universities and indus-try, and the expansion of state-level technology-extension programs are all promising, although very few of these initiatives have been sufficiently evaluated to inform the efforts of other program designers. As we noted in Chapter 10, concern with reaping the commercial returns from scien-tific research within the United States also has given rise to some disturb-ing and potentially unproductive efforts to restrict foreign access to U.S. scientific research in certain areas. The focus on adoption also appears inconsistent with simultaneous efforts at the federal level to strengthen both domestic and international protection for intellectual property rights, and may also conflict with efforts to further loosen constraints on interfirm collaboration in commercial development and production of new technol-ogies.

Theory provides little guidance on the appropriate balance between protection of intellectual property rights and support for technology adop-tion. The existence and nature of this conflict must nevertheless be kept in mind in formulating technology policy. The appropriability analysis of R&D suggests that improved intellectual property rights are an important goal, since greater appropriability can reduce the effects of market failure in R&D investment. Strengthening domestic and international protection for intellectual property may do nothing, however, to aid more rapid adoption and utilization of the results of research, and may well impede such adoption. The appropriability framework does not provide a suffi-cient basis for policy; if an alternative "utilization-oriented" framework is to guide national R&D policy, further strengthening of intellectual prop-erty rights, especially in the domestic economy, may be of secondary importance.[1] After all, such high-technology sectors as the U.S. microe-

---

[1] "The premise that stronger [intellectual property] protection will always improve the in-centives to innovate is also open to challenge. Unimpeded diffusion of existing technology is immediately beneficial not only for consumers but also for those who would improve that technology. Because technological advance is often an interactive, cumulative pro-cess, strong protection of individual achievements may slow the general advance. This would not occur in a hypothetical world without transaction costs, in which efficient con-tracts to share information would be made. In reality, however, markets for rights to information are subject to major transactional hazards, and strong protection of a key in-

lectronics industry displayed high profitability, rapid growth, and impressive innovative performance for many years with very weak formal protection of intellectual property.

A similar tension may arise between efforts to reduce impediments to collaboration among U.S. firms in the commercial development and, potentially, the production of innovations,[2] and the goal of more rapid domestic diffusion of new technologies. Allowing firms to collaborate beyond applied precommercial R&D creates some potential for the accumulation and exercise of market power for the new technology, and may thus impede its diffusion.

Admittedly, in some high-technology industries, firms individually or collectively may not have significant market power. A "rule of reason" may be justified in these cases, but the point remains that relaxation of restrictions on collaboration, a policy designed to overcome the possible consequences of market failure and risk in the development of new technologies, may clash with the goal of more rapid domestic diffusion and utilization of these technologies. This argument is especially germane to cooperative research because, as we saw in Chapter 8, this device was employed during much of Japan's postwar "catch-up" period to accelerate domestic diffusion.

The Japanese example suggests that cooperation among firms in precommercial research can support the diffusion of knowledge among participant firms and facilitate their utilization of such knowledge in competitive development of new products and processes. Precommercial research cooperation is not only compatible with but in all likelihood intensifies interfirm competition in commercial product markets (see also Peck and Goto, 1981). Much less is known, however, about the effectiveness and competitive impacts of interfirm collaboration that extends beyond such precommercial research. Indeed, given the short period of time during which the National Cooperative Research Act of 1984 has relaxed somewhat the restrictions on interfirm collaboration in precommercial research, little is known about the technological payoff from, and competitive effects of, precommercial research collaboration within the United States. Moreover, we argued in Chapters 8 and 9 that there are grounds for considerable skepticism about the prospects for Japanese and U.S. domestic collaborative research ventures that do not involve a university and focus on the generation of advanced scientific or technological knowl-

---

novation may preclude competitors from making socially beneficial innovations" (Levin et al., p. 788). See also Levin (1986).

[2] See Jorde and Teece (1988) for one proposal. The Reagan administration's Superconductivity Competitiveness Initiative, released in January 1988, contained a similar proposal for liberalization of the National Cooperative Research Act.

edge, rather than on the reduction to practice of foreign or state-of-the-art science and technology.

Improving the effectiveness of adoption and commercialization of new technologies, however, requires initiatives that extend well beyond the boundaries of conventionally defined science and technology policy. Indeed, given the difficulties that many public programs have encountered in "fine-tuning" the innovation system and commercializing specific technologies, broad policies that are relatively evenhanded in their effects on all sectors may be more attractive and feasible. Since the adoption of new technologies typically places a premium on the skills of the work force, policies to improve the educational preparation of entrants to the work force, to remedy basic skills deficiencies in the employed work force, and to improve job-related training of the employed work force may well yield a far greater payoff (albeit in a longer time frame) than a dozen Sematechs (see Cyert and Mowery, eds., 1987; Council on Competitiveness, 1988; and Osterman, 1988). Policies that increase the national savings rate and lower the domestic cost of capital similarly are likely to exert a far more substantial impact on national innovative performance and productivity growth than tinkering with initiatives in collaborative research.

The structure of the U.S. national research system has benefited some components of the national educational and training system far more than others. Federal R&D policy since World War II has funneled large sums of money in the form of research budgets to U.S. colleges and universities. This structure was immensely beneficial to one sector of the U.S. training and education system – higher education – and did little or nothing for its underpinnings. The primary and secondary educational system received no comparable stream of federal largesse during this period. Continued neglect of the primary, secondary, and job-related skills education and training infrastructure will impose a growing burden on the technological performance of this economy.

The process through which science and technology policy initiatives are formulated and implemented is also in need of overhaul. Within science and technology policy, appeals to national security and economic nationalism create a considerable risk of overwhelming the very limited capacity of the policymaking structure for effective review and informed choice. The experience of the past decade demonstrates that a more effective system is needed within the federal government for assessing the economic and security implications of shifts in technological strength and changes in technology policy. In the absence of some systematic process for establishing priorities, the Sematech, high-definition television, and NCMS initiatives will be but the first of many undertakings that claim public funds under a national security cover. In view of the serious resource limitations within future federal budgets and the complex implications of these ventures and other recent developments for science and trade policies, a much more comprehensive evaluation is needed.

As we noted in Chapter 8, many of the challenges that U.S. policymakers face in the economic, trade, and science policy areas in the late twentieth century flow from the success of farsighted political and economic policies following the devastation of the Second World War. The United States now faces a number of robust competitors whose economic and technological infrastructure in many sectors rivals its own. The rumored decline of the United States is a relative, rather than an absolute, decline – especially in the areas of scientific research and technological innovation. In the long run, this competition of near equals is likely to foster a more sustainable and beneficent environment for global economic growth. But we must recognize that the world has changed and adapt to the new realities of technological and economic competition, rather than try to resist them.

Bibliography

Abegglen, J. C., and G. Stalk. *Kaisha: The Japanese Corporation*. New York: Basic Books, 1986.

Abramovitz, M. "Catching Up, Forging Ahead, and Falling Behind." *Journal of Economic History* (1986): 385–406.

Advisory Council to the Committee for Scientific and Industry Research. *Report*. London: HMSO, 1916.

Aerospace Industries Association. *Aerospace Facts and Figures 1984/1985*. New York: McGraw-Hill, 1984.

Aerospace Facts and Figures 1987/1988. New York: McGraw-Hill, 1987.

Agency for Science and Technology, *Annual White Paper*, Tokyo, Japan, n.d.

Aho, C. M. "Technology, Structural Change, and Trade." In R. M. Cyert and D. C. Mowery, eds., *The Impact of Technological Change on Employment and Economic Growth*. Cambridge, Mass.: Ballinger, 1988.

Aho, C. M., and J. D. Aronson. *Trade Talks: America Better Listen*. New York: Council of Foreign Relations, 1985.

Albu, A. "Merchant Shipbuilding and Marine Engineering." In K. Pavitt, ed., *Technical Innovation and British Economic Performance*. London: Macmillan, 1980.

Alchian, A. A. "Reliability of Progress Curves in Airframe Production." *Econometrica* (1963): 579–93.

Alchian, A. A., and H. Demsetz. "Production, Information Costs, and Economic Organization." *American Economic Review* (1972): 777–95.

Alexander, W., and A. Street. *Metals in the Service of Man*. Harmondsworth: Penguin, 1968.

Alic, J. A. "Cooperation in R&D: When Does It Work?" Presented at the Colloquium on International Marketing Cooperation between Rival Trading Nations. San Miniato, Italy, May 29–31, 1986.

Allen, G. C. *British Industry and Economic Policy*. New York: Holmes & Meier, 1979.

Allen, T. J. *Managing the Flow of Technology*. Cambridge, Mass.: MIT Press, 1977.

American Society for Testing Materials. *The Life and Life-work of Charles B. Dudley, 1842–1909*. Philadelphia: ASTM, n.d.

Proceedings. Philadelphia: ASTM, 1908, 1911.

Ames, Joseph (NACA chairman). Statement before the President's Aircraft Board. Washington, D.C.: USGPO, 1925.

Andrade, E. N. da C. *Industrial Research*. New York: Todd, 1946.

Andrews, P. W. S., and E. Brunner. *Capital Development in Iron and Steel*. Oxford: Blackwell, 1951.

297

Aoki, M. "Vertical vs. Horizontal Information Structure of the Firm." *American Economic Review* (Dec. 1986): 971–83.

Information, Incentives, and Bargaining in the Japanese Economy. Cambridge: Cambridge University Press, 1988.

Aoki, M., and N. Rosenberg. "The Japanese Firm as an Innovating Institution." Stanford University. Center for Economic Policy Research Memorandum no. 106, 1987.

Armour, H. O., and D. J. Teece. "Organizational Structure and Economic Performance: A Test of the M-form Hypothesis." *Bell Journal of Economics* (1978): 196–222.

"Vertical Integration and Technological Innovation." *Review of Economics and Statistics* (1981): 470–4.

Armour, Philip. "The Packing Industry." In Chauncy M. Depew, ed., *One Hundred Years of American Commerce.* New York: Hayes, 1895.

Arrow, K. J. "Economic Welfare and the Allocation of Resources for Invention." In Universities-National Bureau Committee for Economic Research, *The Rate and Direction of Inventive Activity.* Princeton, N.J.: Princeton University Press, 1962.

"Classificatory Notes on the Production and Transmission of Technical Knowledge." *American Economic Review* (1969): 29–35.

Association of American Universities. "University Policies on Conflict of Interest and Delay of Publication." Washington, D.C.: AAU, 1985.

"AT&T: The Making of a Comeback." *Business Week,* Jan. 18, 1988, pp. 56–62.

Bacon, R. F. "The Object and Work of the Mellon Institute." *Journal of Industrial and Engineering Chemistry* (1915): 343–7.

Baer, W., L. L. Johnson, and E. W. Merrow. "Government-Sponsored Demonstrations of New Technologies." *Science* (1977):950–7.

Baekeland, L. H. *Metallurgical and Chemical Engineering* (1917): 394.

Baker, W. J. *A History of the Marconi Company.* London: Methuen, 1970.

Baily, M. N., and A. K. Chakrabarti. *Innovation and the Productivity Crisis.* Washington, D.C.: Brookings Institution, 1988.

Balbien, J., and L. L. Wilde. "A Dynamic Model of Research Contracting." *Bell Journal of Economics* (1982): 107–19.

Baldwin, W. "Contract Research and the Case for Big Business." *Journal of Political Economy* (1962): 294–6.

Barker, Brent. "Decade of Change: EPRI and the Climate for Research." *EPRI Journal* (Jan./Feb. 1983): 4–13.

Bartlett, Howard R. *Research – A National Resource. II. Industrial Research.* Washington, D.C.: National Resources Planning Board, 1941.

Baumol, W. J. "Productivity Growth, Convergence, and Welfare: What the Long-Run Data Show." *American Economic Review* (1986): 1072–85.

Baxter, James Phinney III. *Scientists against Time.* Boston: Little, Brown, 1946.

Beaton, K. *Enterprise in Oil: A History of Shell in the United States.* New York: Appleton-Century-Crofts, 1957.

Beer, J. J. "Coal Tar Dye Manufacture and the Origins of the Modern Industrial Research Laboratory." *Isis* (1958): 123–31.

The Emergence of the German Dye Industry. Urbana: University of Illinois Press, 1959.

Ben-David, J. *The Scientist's Role in Society*. Englewood Cliffs, N.J.: Prentice-Hall, 1971.

Bernal, J. D. *The Social Function of Science*. London: 1939.

Science and Industry in the 19th Century. London: Routledge & Kegan Paul, 1953.

Birr, Kendall. "Science in American Industry." In David Van Tassel and Michael Hall, eds., *Science and Society in the U.S.* Homewood, Ill.: Dorsey, 1966.

Blackburn, M., and D. Bloom. "The Effects of Technological Change on the U.S. Distribution of Income and Earnings." In R. M. Cyert and D. C. Mowery, eds., *The Impact of Technological Change on Employment and Economic Growth*. Cambridge, Mass.: Ballinger, 1988.

Bluestone, B., and B. Harrison. *The Great U-Turn: Corporate Restructuring and the Polarizing of America*. New York: Basic Books, 1988.

Blumenthal, D., M. Gluck, K. S. Louis, and D. Wise. "Industrial Support of University Research in Biotechnology." *Science* (1986): 242–6.

Bode, H. W. "Reflections on the Relation between Science and Technology." In *Basic Research and National Goals: A Report to the Committee on Science and Astronautics, U.S. House of Representatives*. Washington, D.C.: National Academy of Sciences, 1965.

Boehm, G. A. W., and A. Groner. *The Battelle Story: Science in the Service of Mankind*. Lexington, Mass.: Heath, 1972.

Boeing Commercial Airplane Company, Document B-7210-2-418. Seattle, 1976.

Booz, Allen, and Hamilton Applied Research, Inc. *A Historical Study of the Benefits Derived from Application of Technical Advances to Commercial Aviation*. Prepared for the joint Department of Transportation/National Aeronautics and Space Administration Civil Aviation R&D Policy Study. Washington, D.C.: USGPO, 1971.

Borrus, Michael A. *Competing for Control: America's Stake in Microelectronics*. Cambridge, Mass.: Ballinger, 1988.

Bozeman, B., A. Link, and A. Zardkoohi. "An Economic Analysis of R&D Joint Ventures." *Managerial and Decision Economics* (1986): 263–6.

Briggs, A. "Social History 1900–1945." In R. Floud and D. W. McCloskey, eds., *The Economic History of Britain Since 1700*, vol. 1. Cambridge: Cambridge University Press, 1981.

British Association of Scientific Workers. *Industrial Research Laboratories*. London: Allen & Unwin, 1936.

Brock, G. W. *The Telecommunications Industry*. Cambridge, Mass.: Harvard University Press, 1981.

Brodley, J. "Joint Ventures and Antitrust Policy." *Harvard Law Review* (1982): 1523–90.

Brodsky, N. H., H. Kaufman, and J. Tooker. *University/Industry Cooperation*. New York: Center for Science and Technology Policy, 1980.

Brooks, Harvey, and Nathan Rosenberg. "A New Look at Science-Technology Interactions." Unpublished manuscript, Stanford University.

Brown, E. H. Phelps. "Levels and Movements of Industrial Productivity and Real

Wages Internationally Compared, 1860–1970." *Economic Journal* (1973): 58–71.

Brueckner, Leslie, and Michael Borrus. *Assessing the Commercial Impact of the VHSIC Program.* Berkeley Roundtable on the International Economy Working Paper, December 1984.

Burnet, M., and D. O. White. *Natural History of Infectious Disease.* Cambridge: Cambridge University Press, 1972.

Bush, Vannevar. *Science, the Endless Frontier.* Washington, D.C.: USGPO, 1945.

Byatt, I. C. R. *The British Electrical Industry 1875–1914.* Oxford: Oxford University Press, 1979.

Cardwell, D. S. L. *From Watt to Clausius.* Ithaca, N.Y.: Cornell University Press, 1971.

Carley, W. M. "Cancelled Jet Order Is a Setback for United Technologies Unit." *Wall Street Journal,* Feb. 9, 1988, 6.

Carnegie Foundation for the Advancement of Teaching. *The States and Higher Education.* San Francisco: Jossey-Bass, 1976.

Carnot, Sadi. *Réflexions sur la Puissance Motrice du Feu et sur les Machines Propres a Développer cette Puissance.* Paris: Chez Bachelier, 1824.

Carr, J. C., and W. Taplin. *A History of the British Steel Industry.* Cambridge, Mass.: Harvard University Press, 1962.

Carty, J. J. "The Relation of Pure Science to Industrial Research." *Science* (1916): 511–17.

Caves, Richard E. *Multinational Enterprise and Economic Analysis.* Cambridge: Cambridge University Press, 1982.

Caves, R. E., and M. Uekusa. "Industrial Organization." In H. Patrick and H. Rosovsky, eds., *Asia's New Giant.* Washington, D.C.: Brookings Institution, 1976.

Chandler, Alfred D., Jr. *Strategy and Structure: Chapters in the History of Industrial Enterprise.* Cambridge, Mass.: MIT Press, 1962.

The Visible Hand. Cambridge, Mass.: Harvard University Press (Belknap Press), 1977.

"The Growth of the Transnational Industrial Firm in the United States and the United Kingdom: A Comparative Analysis." *Economic History Review* (Aug. 1980): 369–410.

"Commentary: From Industrial Laboratories to Departments of Research and Development." In K. B. Clark, R. L. Hayes, and C. Lorenz, eds., *The Uneasy Alliance.* Boston: Harvard Business School Press, 1985.

Scale and Scope. Cambridge, Mass.: Harvard University Press, 1989.

Chandler, Alfred D., Jr., and S. Salsbury. *Pierre S. Du Pont and the Making of the Modern Corporation.* New York: Harper & Row, 1971.

Choate, P., and J. Linger. "Tailored Trade: Dealing with the World as It Is." *Harvard Business Review* (Jan.–Feb. 1988): 86–93.

Civil Aeronautics Board. *Aircraft Operating Costs and Performance Report.* Vols. I–XVII. Washington, D.C.: USGPO, 1966–84.

Clark, K. B., W. B. Chew, and T. Fujimoto. "Product Development in the World Automobile Industry." *Brookings Papers on Economic Activity* (1987): 729–71.

Clark, Victor. *History of Manufactures in the United States.* New York: McGraw-Hill, 1929.

Clemen, Rudolph. *American Livestock and Meat Industry.* New York: Ronald, 1923.

Cohen, I. B. *Science: Servant of Man.* Boston, Mass.: Little, Brown, 1948.

Cohen, S., and J. Zysman. *Manufacturing Matters: The Myth of the Post-Industrial Economy.* New York: Basic Books, 1987.

Cohen, W. M. "Investment and Industry Expansion: A Corporate Variables Framework." *Journal of Economic Behavior and Organization* (1983): 91–112.

Cohen, W. M., and R. C. Levin. "Empirical Studies of Innovation and Market Structure." In R. Schmalensee and R. Willig, eds., *Handbook of Industrial Organization.* Amsterdam: North-Holland, 1988.

Cohen, W. M., and D. Levinthal. "The Endogeneity of Appropriability and R&D Investment." Working Paper. Pittsburgh, Pa.: Carnegie-Mellon University, 1985.

"Innovation and Learning: The Two Faces of R & D." *Economic Journal* (1989):569–96.

Cohen, W. M., and D. C. Mowery. "Firm Heterogeneity and R&D: An Agenda for Research." In I. M. Crow, B. Bozeman, and A. N. Link, eds., *Strategic Management of Industrial R&D.* Lexington, Mass.: Heath, 1984.

Coleman, D. C. *Courtaulds: An Economic and Social History.* Oxford: Clarendon Press, 1969.

"Gentlemen and Players." *Economic History Review* (1973): 92–116.

Collins, N. R., and L. E. Preston. "The Size Structure of the Largest Industrial Firms." *American Economic Review* (1961): 986–1011.

Comanor, W. S. "Market Structure, Product Differentiation, and Industrial Research." *Quarterly Journal of Economics* (1967): 639–57.

Committee on Commercial and Industrial Policy after the War. *Final Report.* London: HMSO, 1918.

Committee on Finance and Industry. *Report.* London: HMSO, 1931.

Committee on Industry and Trade. *Final Report.* London: HMSO, 1929.

Committee on Science, Engineering, and Public Policy (COSEPUP) Panel on the Impact of National Security Controls on International Technology Transfer. *Balancing the National Interest: U.S. National Security Export Controls and Global Economic Competition.* Washington, D.C.: National Academy Press, 1987.

Condit, Carl. *American Building.* Chicago: University of Chicago Press, 1968.

Congressional Budget Office. *Federal Support for R&D and Innovation.* Washington, D.C.: USGPO, 1984.

Constant, E. W. *Origins of the Turbojet Revolution.* Baltimore: Johns Hopkins University Press, 1980.

Cooper, F. S. "Location and Extent of Industrial Research Activity in the United States." In National Resources Planning Board, *Research – A National Resource.* Washington, D.C.: USGPO, 1941.

Corcoran, E. "Science and Business: Technology Transfer." *Scientific American,* May 1989, pp. 98–100.

Council on Competitiveness. *Picking up the Pace: Commercial Innovation in the U.S. Economy.* Washington, D.C.: Council on Competitiveness, 1988.

Crowther, J. G. *Men of Science.* New York: Norton, 1936.

Cushman, J. H. "Bigger Role Urged for Defense Dept. in Economic Policy." *New York Times,* Oct. 19, 1988, A1 and D22.

Cyert, R. M., and D. C. Mowery, eds. *Technology and Employment: Innovation and Growth in the U.S. Economy.* Washington, D.C.: National Academy Press, 1987.

Danhof, Clarence. *Government Contracting and Technological Change.* Washington, D.C.: Brookings Institution, 1968.

Dasgupta, P., and J. Stiglitz. "Market Structure and the Nature of Inventive Activity." *Bell Journal of Economics* (1980): 1–28.

David, P. A. "Professor Fogel on and off the Rails." *Innovation, Technical Choice, and Growth.* Cambridge: Cambridge University Press, 1975.

——. "Technology Diffusion, Public Policy, and Industrial Competitiveness." In Ralph Landau and Nathan Rosenberg, eds., *The Positive Sum Strategy.* Washington, D.C.: National Academy Press, 1986.

David, P. A., J. Lewis, and F. Nold. "Multivariate Probit Analysis." Stanford Center for Information Processing. Stanford, Calif., 1976.

Davis, B. "Pentagon Seeks to Spur U.S. Effort to Develop 'High-Definition' TV." *Wall Street Journal,* Jan. 4, 1989, 29.

Davis, E. W. *Pioneering with Taconite.* St. Paul, Minn.: Minnesota Historical Society, 1964.

Davis, L. E., and D. J. Kevles. "The National Research Fund: A Case Study in the Industrial Support of Academic Science." *Minerva* (1974): 207–20.

Demisch, W. H., C. C. Demisch, and T. L. Concert. *The Jetliner Business.* New York: First Boston Corporation, 1984.

Denison, E. F. *Accounting for United States Economic Growth, 1929–1969.* Washington, D.C.: Brookings Institution, 1974.

Destler, I. M., and J. S. Odell. *Anti-Protection: Changing Forces in United States Trade Policies.* Washington, D.C.: Institute for International Economics, 1987.

Douglas, G. W., and J. C. Miller. *Economic Regulation of Domestic Air Transport.* Washington, D.C.: Brookings Institution, 1974.

Duncan, R. K. "On Industrial Fellowships." *Journal of Industrial and Engineering Chemistry* (1909): 600–3.

——. "On Certain Problems Connected with the Present-Day Relation between Chemistry and Manufacture in America." *Journal of Industrial and Engineering Chemistry* (1911): 177–86.

Eads, G., and R. R. Nelson. "Government Support of Advanced Civilian Technology: Power Reactors and the Supersonic Transport." *Public Policy* (1971): 405–28.

Edwards, R. C. "Stages in Corporate Stability and Risks of Corporate Failure." *Journal of Economic History* (1975): 428–57.

Enos, J. *Petroleum Progress and Profits.* Cambridge, Mass.: MIT Press, 1962.

Ergas, H. "Does Technology Policy Matter?" In H. Brooks and B. Guile, eds., *Technology and Global Industry.* Washington, D.C.: National Academy Press, 1987.

Erickson, C. *British Industrialists: Steel and Hosiery 1850–1950.* Cambridge: Cambridge University Press, 1959.

Fisher, F. M., and P. Temin. "Returns to Scale in Research and Development: What Does the Schumpeterian Hypothesis Imply?" *Journal of Political Economy* (1973): 56–70.

Fitch, C. *Tenth Census of the United States, II.* Washington, D.C.: Bureau of the Census, 1880.

Flamm, K. "The Changing Pattern of Industrial Robot Use." In R. M. Cyert and D. C. Mowery, eds., *The Impact of Technological Change on Employment and Economic Growth.* Cambridge, Mass.: Ballinger, 1988a.

Creating the Computer. Washington, D.C.: Brookings Institution, 1988.

Fleming, Donald, and Bernard Bailyn, eds. *The Intellectual Migration: Europe and America, 1930–1960.* Cambridge, Mass.: Harvard University Press (Belknap Press), 1969.

Floud, R. "Technical Education and Economic Performance: Engineering in the Late Nineteenth Century." Unpublished manuscript, Birkbeck College, London, 1978.

Fogel, R. W. *Railroads and American Economic Growth: Essays in Econometric History.* Baltimore: Johns Hopkins University Press, 1964.

Fong, G. "Federal Support for Industrial Technology: Lessons from the VHSIC and VLSI Programs." Prepared for the Office of Technology Assessment, U.S. Congress. Washington, D.C.: USGPO, 1988.

"Food Preservation." *Encyclopaedia Britannica.* 15th ed. Chicago, Ill.: Encyclopaedia Britannica, 1975.

Fraumeni, B. W., and D. Jorgenson. "The Role of Capital in U.S. Economic Growth, 1948–76." In G. M. von Furstenberg, ed., *Capital Efficiency and Growth.* Cambridge, Mass.: Ballinger, 1980.

Freeman, C. H. "Research and Development: A Comparison between British and American Industry." *National Institute Economic Review* (Feb. 1962): 21–38.

Galambos, L. *Competition and Cooperation.* Baltimore, Md.: Johns Hopkins University Press, 1966.

General Accounting Office, *Lower Airline Costs per Passenger Are Possible and Could Result in Lower Fares.* Washington, D.C.: USGPO, 1977.

Ghemawat, P., M. E. Porter, and R. A. Rawlinson. "Patterns of International Coalition Activity." In M. E. Porter, ed., *Competition in Global Industries.* Boston, Mass.: Harvard Business School Press, 1986.

Gilfillan, S. C. *The Sociology of Invention.* (1935). Cambridge, Mass.: Massachusetts Institute of Technology, 1970.

Inventing the Ship. 1935. Chicago, Ill.: Follett, 1970.

Glover, John, and William Cornell. *The Development of American Industries.* New York: Prentice-Hall, 1951.

Gomory, R. E. "Reduction to Practice: The Development and Manufacturing Cycle." *Industrial R&D and U.S. Technological Leadership.* Washington, D.C.: National Academy Press, 1988.

Goto, A., and R. Wakasugi. "Technology Policy in Japan: A Short Review." *Technovation* (1987): 269–79.

"Technology Policy." In R. Komiya, M. Okuno, and K. Suzumura, eds., *Industrial Policy in Japan*. New York: Academic Press, 1988.

Government-University-Industry Research Roundtable. *New Alliances in American Science and Engineering*. Washington, D.C.: National Academy Press, 1986.

Nurturing Science and Engineering Talent: A Discussion Paper. Washington, D.C.: National Academy Press, 1987.

Grabowski, H. G. "The Determinants of Industrial Research and Development: A Study of the Chemical, Drug, and Petroleum Industries." *Journal of Political Economy* (1968): 292–306.

Grabowski, H. G., and D. C. Mueller. "Industrial Research and Development, Intangible Capital Stocks, and Firm Profit Rates." *Bell Journal of Economics* (1978): 328–43.

Grad, M. "Evaluation Status and Planning II: Cooperative Research and Development Experiment." Report 77-03, Industrial Program, Applied Science and Research Applications Directorate, National Science Foundation. Washington, D.C.: USGPO, 1977.

Graham, W. B. W. "Industrial Research in the Age of Big Science." Presented at the meetings of the Society for the History of Technology. Washington, D.C., October 1983.

"Corporate Research and Development: The Latest Transformation." *Technology in Society* (1986): 179–95.

RCA and the Videodisc: The Business of Research. Cambridge: Cambridge University Press, 1986.

Gray, D., and T. Gidley. *Evaluation of the NSF University/Industry Cooperative Research Centers: Descriptive and Correlative Findings from the 1983 Structure/Outcome Surveys*. Raleigh, N.C.: Department of Psychology and Center for Communications and Signal Processing, North Carolina State University, 1986.

Greene, A. M. "Conditions of Research in U.S." *Mechanical Engineering* (July 1919): 588.

Griliches, Zvi. "Issues in Assessing the Contribution of Research and Development to Productivity Growth." *Bell Journal of Economics* (1979): 92–116.

"R&D and the Productivity Slowdown." *American Economic Review* (1980): 343–8.

"Productivity, R&D and Basic Research at the Firm Level in the 1970's." *American Economic Review* (1986): 141–54.

Gruber, W., D. Mehta, and R. Vernon. "The R&D Factor in International Trade and International Investment of United States Industries." *Journal of Political Economy* (Jan./Feb. 1967): 20–37.

Gullander, S. "Joint Ventures in Europe: Determinants of Entry." *International Studies of Management and Organization* (1976): 8.

Haber, L. F. *The Chemical Industry 1900–1930*. Oxford: Oxford University Press, 1971.

Hall, A. R. "The Historical Relations of Science to Technology." Inaugural Lecture, London, 1963.

Hamberg, D. "Size of Firm, Market Structure, and Innovation." *Canadian Journal of Economics and Political Science* (Feb. 1964): 62–75.

Hannah, L. "Managerial Innovation and the Rise of the Large-Scale Company in Great Britain." *Economic History Review* (May 1974): 252–71.

"Mergers in British Manufacturing Industry, 1880–1919." *Oxford Economic Papers* (March 1974): 1–20.

The Rise of the Corporate Economy. London: Methuen, 1976.

"Visible and Invisible Hands in Great Britain." In A. D. Chandler and H. Daems, eds., *Managerial Hierarchies.* Cambridge, Mass.: Harvard University Press, 1980.

Harrigan, Kathryn R. "Joint Ventures and Competitive Strategy." Working paper. New York: Columbia University Graduate School of Business, 1984.

Strategies for Joint Ventures. Lexington, Mass.: Heath, 1985.

Harris, J. "Spies Who Sparked the Industrial Revolution." *New Scientist,* May 22, 1986, 42–7.

Hayes, T. C. "Developing a Computer-Chip for the 90's." *New York Times,* Dec. 23, 1988, C6.

Haynes, W. *American Chemical Industry: The Merger Era.* New York: Van Nostrand, 1948.

Hercules, D. M., and J. W. Enyart. "Report on the Questionnaire on Current Exchange Programs between Industries and Universities." Council for Chemical Research, University–Industry Interaction Committee. University of Pittsburgh, 1983.

Hill, D. W. *Co-operative Research in Industry.* London: Hutchinson's Scientific and Technical Publications, 1947.

Hirsch, W. "Firm Progress Ratios." *Econometrica* (1956): 136–43.

Hirshleifer, J. "The Private and Social Value of Information and the Reward to Innovation." *American Economic Review* (1971): 561–74.

Hladik, Karen. *International Joint Ventures.* Lexington, Mass.: Heath, 1985.

Hoddeson, L. "The Origins of Basic Research in the Bell Telephone System, 1875–1915." *Technology and Culture* (1981): 512–44.

Horwitch, M. *Clipped Wings: The American SST Conflict.* Cambridge, Mass.: MIT Press, 1982.

Hounshell, D. A., and J. K. Smith. "Du Pont: Better Things for Better Living through Research." Presented at the Hagley Conference, Wilmington, Del., 1985.

Science and Corporate Strategy: Du Pont R&D, 1902–1980. Cambridge: Cambridge University Press, 1988.

Huettner, David. *Plant Size, Technological Change, and Investment Requirements.* New York: Praeger, 1974.

Hufbauer, G. C., and H. F. Rosen. *Trade Policy for Troubled Industries.* Washington, D.C.: Institute for International Economics, 1986.

Hunsaker, J. C. "Research in Aeronautics." In National Resources Planning Board, *Research – A National Resource.* Washington, D.C.: USGPO, 1941.

Hunsicker, H. Y., and H. C. Stumpf. "History of Precipitation Hardening." In

C. S. Smith, ed., *The Sorby Centennial on the History of Metallurgy*. New York: Gordon & Breach, 1965.

Imai, Ken-Ichi, Ikujiro Nonaka, and Hirotaka Takeuchi. "Managing the Product Development Process: How Japanese Companies Learn and Unlearn." In Kim Clark et al., eds., *The Uneasy Alliance: Managing the Productivity-Technology Dilemma*. Boston: Harvard Business School Press, 1985.

International Association for Testing Materials, American Section, *Bulletin* (1899): 22.

Jaikumar, J. "Postindustrial Manufacturing." *Harvard Business Review* (1986): 69–76.

"Japan's Commitment to 'New Globalism' and Its Choice as a 'New Industrial-Cultural Nation.' " Japan's Choice Research Society (1988).

Jenkins, R. V. *Images and Enterprise*. Baltimore: Johns Hopkins University Press, 1975.

Johnson, C. "MITI, MPT, and the Telecom Wars: How Japan Makes Policy for High Technology." In C. Johnson, L. Tyson, and J. Zysman, eds., *Politics and Productivity: How Japan's Development Strategy Works*. Cambridge, Mass.: Ballinger, 1989.

Johnson, P. S. *Co-operative Research in Industry*. New York: Wiley, 1973.

Jones, R., and O. Marriott. *Anatomy of a Merger: A History of GEC, AEI, and English Electric*. London: Jonathan Cape, 1975.

Jordan, W. *Airline Regulation in America*. Baltimore: Johns Hopkins University Press, 1970.

Jorde, T., D. J. Teece. "Innovation, Strategic Alliances, and Antitrust." Revised draft of paper presented at the Centennial Celebration of the Sherman Act, Berkeley, Calif., Oct. 7–8, 1988.

Judson, Horace. *The Eighth Day of Creation*. New York: Simon & Schuster, 1979.

Kamien, M., and N. Schwartz. *Market Structure and Innovation*. Cambridge: Cambridge University Press, 1982.

Kaplan, A. D. H. *Big Business in a Competitive System*. Washington, D.C.: Brookings Institution, 1964.

Keeler, T. "Airline Regulation and Economic Performance." *Bell Journal of Economics* (1972): 399–424.

Keesing, D. B. "The Impact of Research and Development on United States Trade." *Journal of Political Economy* (1967): 38–48.

Keller, J., G. Lewis, T. Mason, R. Mitchell, and T. Peterson. "AT&T: The Making of a Comeback." *Business Week*, Jan. 10, 1988, 62.

Kendrick, J. W. *Productivity Trends in the United States*. Princeton, N.J.: Princeton University Press, 1961.

Postwar Productivity Trends in the United States 1948–1969. New York: Columbia University Press, 1973.

The Formation and Stocks of Total Capital. New York: National Bureau of Economic Research, 1976.

Kennedy, D. "Government Policies and the Cost of Doing Research." *Science* (1985): 480–4.

Killing, J. P. *Strategies for Joint Venture Success.* New York: Praeger, 1983.

Klein, R., R. G. Crawford, and A. A. Alchian. "Vertical Integration, Appropriable Rents, and the Competitive Contracting Process." *Journal of Law and Economics* (1978): 297–326.

Kline, Stephen J. "Research, Invention, Innovation and Production: Models and Reality." Report INN-1, Department of Mechanical Engineering, Stanford University, 1985.

Kline, Stephen J., and Nathan Rosenberg. "An Overview of Innovation." In Ralph Landau and Nathan Rosenberg, eds., *The Positive Sum Strategy.* Washington, D.C.: National Academy Press, 1986.

Kodama, F. "Japanese Innovation in Mechatronics Technology." *Science and Public Policy* (1986): 44–51.

Krugman, P. W. "Import Protection as Export Promotion: International Competition in the Presence of Oligopoly and Economies of Scale." In H. Kierzkowski, ed., *Monopolistic Competition and International Trade.* Oxford: Oxford University Press, 1984.

"Is Free Trade Passe?" *Journal of Economic Perspectives* (1987a): 131–44.

"Technology-intensive Goods." In J. M. Finger and A. Olechowski, eds., *The Uruguay Round: A Handbook.* Washington, D.C.: World Bank, 1987b.

Kuhlmann, Charles. *The Development of the Flour-Milling Industry in the U.S.* Boston: Houghton Mifflin, 1929.

Kuznets, S. *Modern Economic Growth.* New Haven, Conn.: Yale University Press, 1966.

Lane, H. W., R. G. Beddows, and P. R. Lawrence. *Managing Large Research and Development Programs.* Albany: State University of New York Press, 1981.

Langlois, R. N., T. A. Pugel, C. S. Harklisch, R. R. Nelson, and W. G. Egelhoff. *Microelectronics: An Industry in Transition.* Boston: Unwin Hyman, 1988.

Lardner, James. "The Terrible Truth about Japan." *Washington Post,* June 21, 1987, B19.

Lawrence, P. R., and J. Lorsch. "Differentiation and Integration in Complex Organizations." *Administrative Science Quarterly* (1967): 1–47.

Lazonick, W. A. "Factor Costs and the Diffusion of Ring Spinning in Britain Prior to World War I." *Quarterly Journal of Economics* (Feb. 1981): 89–109.

"Industrial Organization and Technological Change: The Decline of the British Cotton Industry." *Business History Review* (1983): 195–236.

Legislative Reference Service. *Policy Planning for Aeronautical Research and Development.* Prepared for the Senate Committee on Aeronautical and Space Sciences, U.S. Congress. Washington, D.C.: USGPO, 1966.

Lieberman, M., and D. Montgomery. "First-Mover Advantages." *Strategic Management Journal* (1988): 41–58.

Lenz, R. C., J. A. Machnic, and A. W. Elkins. *The Influence of Aeronautical R&D Expenditures upon the Productivity of Air Transportation.* Dayton, Ohio: University of Dayton Research Institute, 1981.

Leonard, W. N. "Research and Development in Industrial Growth." *Journal of Political Economy* (1971): 32–56.

Levin, R. C. "The Semiconductor Industry." In Richard R. Nelson, ed., *Government and Technical Progress: A Cross-Industry Analysis*. New York: Pergamon, 1982.

"A New Look at the Patent System." *American Economic Review* (1986): 199–202.

Levin, R. C., and P. Reiss. "Tests of a Schumpeterian Model of R&D and Market Structure." In Z. Griliches, ed., *R&D, Patents, and Productivity*. Chicago: University of Chicago Press, 1984.

Levin, R. C., A. K. Levorick, R. R. Nelson, and S. G. Winter. "Appropriating the Returns from Industrial Research and Development." *Brookings Papers on Economic Activity* 3(1987): 783–820.

Levine, David O. *The American College and the Culture of Aspiration, 1915–1940*. Ithaca, N.Y.: Cornell University Press, 1986.

Levy, D. W., and N. Terleckyj. "Effects of Government R&D on Private R&D Investment and Production: A Macroeconomic Analysis." *Bell Journal of Economics* (1983): 551–61.

"Government-Financed R&D and Productivity Growth: Macroeconomic Evidence." In Z. Griliches, ed., *R&D, Patents, and Productivity*. Chicago; University of Chicago Press, 1984.

Lewis, W. A. *Economic Survey 1919–1939*. New York: Harper & Row, 1949.

Lewis, W. D. "Industrial Research and Development." In M. Kranzberg and C. Pursell, eds., *Technology in Western Civilization*. Oxford: Oxford University Press, 1967.

Lichtenberg, Frank R. "The Private R&D Investment Response to Federal Design and Technical Competitions." *American Economic Review* (1988): 550–9.

Lineback, J. R. "Can MCC Survive the Latest Defections?" *Electronics*, Jan. 22, 1987, 30.

"It's Time for MCC to Fish or Cut Bait." *Electronics*, June 25, 1987, 32.

Link, A. N. "An Analysis of the Composition of R&D Spending." *Southern Economic Journal* (1982): 342–9.

Livesay, H. *Andrew Carnegie*. Boston: Little, Brown, 1975.

Lucas, A. F. *Industrial Reconstruction and the Control of Competition*. London: Longmans, 1937.

Lynn, L. *How Japan Innovates*. Boulder, Colo.: Westview Press, 1982.

MacDowell, Charles. "The Chemist in the Packing and Allied Industries." *Chemical Age* (June 1921): 217–20.

Maclaurin, W. R. *Invention and Innovation in the Radio Industry*. New York: Macmillan, 1949.

Macrosty, H. W. *The Trust Movement in British Industry*. London: Longmans Green, 1907.

Mansfield, E. F. "Size of Firm, Market Structure, and Innovation." *Journal of Political Economy* (1963): 556–76.

"Industrial Research and Development Expenditures: Determinants, Prospects and Relation to Size of Firm and Inventive Output." *Journal of Political Economy* (Aug. 1964): 319–40.

The Economics of Technological Change. New York: Norton, 1968.

"How Rapidly Does New Technology Leak Out?" *Journal of Industrial Economics* (1985): 217–23.

"R&D Innovation: Some Empirical Findings." In Z. Griliches, ed., *R&D, Patents, and Productivity.* Chicago: University of Chicago Press, 1984.

"The Diffusion of Industrial Robots in Japan and the United States." *Research Policy.* In press.

"Industrial Innovation in Japan and the United States." *Science,* Sept. 30, 1988, 1769–74.

Mansfield, E., and A. Romeo. "Technology Transfer to Overseas Subsidiaries by U.S.-Based Firms." *Quarterly Journal of Economics* (1980): 737–50.

Mansfield, E., J. Rapoport, A. Romeo, S. Wagner, and G. Beardsley. "Social and Private Rates of Return from Industrial Innovations." *Quarterly Journal of Economics* (1977): 221–40.

Mansfield, E., J. Rapoport, J. Schnee, S. Wagner, and M. Hamburger. *Research and Innovation in the Modern Corporation.* New York: Norton, 1971.

Marshall, A. W., and W. H. Meckling. "Predictability of the Costs, Time, and Success in Development." In Universities–National Bureau Committee for Economic Research, *The Rate and Direction of Inventive Activity.* Princeton, N.J.: Princeton University Press, 1962.

Marshall E. "School Reformers Aim at Creativity." *Science,* July 18, 1986, 267–70.

Marx, Karl. *Capital.* New York: Modern Library, 1936.

Capital. Moscow: Foreign Languages Publishing House, 1959.

Massachusetts Institute of Technology, News Office. "MIT Exploring Linked Supercomputer Center." Nov. 5, 1987.

Matthews, R. C. O., C. H. Feinstein, and J. C. Odling-Smee. *British Economic Growth 1856–1973.* Stanford, Calif.: Stanford University Press, 1982.

McCulloch, R. "International Competition in High-Technology Industries: The Consequences of Alternative Trade Regimes for Aircraft." Presented at National Science Foundation Workshop on Economic Implications of Restrictions to Trade in High-Technology Goods. Washington, D.C., Oct. 3, 1984.

"Meat Packing and Slaughtering." *Encyclopaedia of the Social Sciences.* New York: Macmillan, 1933.

Mees, C. E. K. *The Organization of Industrial Scientific Research.* New York: McGraw-Hill, 1920.

"Metal-Working Machinery." *Special Reports of the Census Office,* part IV. Washington, D.C., 1905.

Miles, F. D. *A History of Research in the Nobel Division of I.C.I.* London: Imperial Chemical Industries, 1955.

Miller, R. W., and D. Sawers. *The Technical Development of Modern Aviation.* London: Routledge & Kegan Paul, 1968.

"Mismanaging Drug Research." *Economist,* Nov. 21, 1987, 67.

Moody's Manual of Industrial Investments. New York: Moody's Investors Service, various issues.

Mowery, D. C. "The Emergence and Growth of Industrial Research in American Manufacturing 1899–1945." Ph.D. diss., Stanford University, 1981.

"The Relationship between Contractual and Intrafirm Forms of Industrial Research in American Manufacturing, 1900–1940." *Explorations in Economic History* (Oct. 1983a): 351–74.

"Economic Theory and Government Technology Policy." *Policy Sciences* (Winter 1983b): 27–43.

"Industrial Research and Firm Size, Survival, and Growth in American Manufacturing, 1921–46." *Journal of Economic History* (1983c):953–80.

"Firm Structure, Government Policy, and the Organization of Industrial Research: Great Britain and the United States, 1900–1950." *Business History Review* (1984): 504–31.

"Industrial Research, 1900–1950." In B. Elbaum and W. Lazonick, eds., *The Decline of the British Economy*. New York: Oxford University Press, 1986a.

"Federal Funding of Research and Development in Transportation: The Case of Aviation." Presented at the Symposium on the Effects of Federal R&D, National Academy of Sciences, Nov. 19–20, 1985. Published in *The Effects of Federal Research Funding*. Publication on Demand Program. Washington, D.C.: National Academy Press, 1986b.

Alliance Politics and Economics: Multinational Joint Ventures in Commercial Aircraft. Cambridge, Mass.: Ballinger, 1987.

"Assessing the Effects of Divestiture on Bell Telephone Laboratories." *Technovation* (1988a): 353–75.

"The Diffusion of New Manufacturing Technologies." In Richard Cyert and David Mowery, eds., *The Impact of Technological Change on Employment and Economic Growth*. Cambridge, Mass.: Ballinger, 1988b.

Mowery, D. C., ed. *International Collaborative Ventures in U.S. Manufacturing*. Cambridge, Mass.: Ballinger, 1988c.

Mowery, D. C., and N. Rosenberg. "The Influence of Market Demand upon Innovation: A Critical Review of Some Recent Empirical Studies." *Research Policy* (1979): 102–53.

"Government Policy and Innovation in the Commercial Aircraft Industry, 1925–75." In R. R. Nelson, ed., *Government and Technical Change: A Cross-Industry Analysis*. New York: Pergamon, 1982.

"Commercial Aircraft: Cooperation and Competition between the U.S. and Japan." *California Management Review* (1985): 70–92.

Moxon, R. W., T. W. Roehl, J. R. Truitt, and J. M. Geringer. *Emerging Sources of Foreign Competition in the Commercial Aircraft Manufacturing Industry*. Washington, D.C.: U.S. Department of Transportation, 1985.

Mueller, W. F. "Du Pont: A Study in Firm Growth." Ph.D. diss., Vanderbilt University, 1955.

"The Origins of the Basic Inventions Underlying Du Pont's Major Product and Process Inventions, 1920 to 1950." In Universities National Bureau Committee for Economic Research, *The Rate and Direction of Inventive Activity*. Princeton, N.J.: Princeton University Press, 1962.

Musson, A. E. *Science, Technology and Economic Growth in the 18th Century*. London: Methuen, 1972.

Musson, A. E., and E. Robinson. *Science and Technology in the Industrial Revolution*. Manchester: University of Manchester Press, 1969.

Narin, Francis, and D. Olivastro. "First Interim Report: Identifying Areas of Leading

Edge Japanese Science and Technology." Submitted by CHI Research/Computer Horizons, Inc., to National Science Foundation, May 1986.

NASA Aeronautics Advisory Committee. "Draft Interim Report of the Ad Hoc Informal Subcommittee on NASA Aeronautical Projects." Washington, D.C.: NASA, 1983.

Nason, Howard. "Distinctions between Basic and Applied in Industrial Research." *Research Management* (May 1981): 23–8.

National Academy of Sciences. *Basic Research and National Goals, A Report to the Committee on Science and Astronautics, U.S. House of Representatives.* Washington, D.C.: National Academy of Sciences, 1965.

Physics through the 1900s: Scientific Interfaces and Technological Applications. Washington, D.C.: National Academy Press, 1986.

National Commission on Research. *Industry and the Universities.* Washington, D.C.: National Commission on Research, 1980.

National Research Council.

"Research Laboratories in Industrial Establishments of the United States, Including Consulting Research Laboratories." *Bulletin 16.* Washington, D.C.: National Research Council, 1921.

"Industrial Research Laboratories of the United States." *Bulletin 60.* Washington, D.C.: National Research Council, 1927.

"Industrial Research Laboratories of the United States." *Bulletin 91.* Washington, D.C.: National Research Council, 1933.

"Industrial Research Laboratories of the United States." *Bulletin 104.* Washington, D.C.: National Research Council, 1940.

"Industrial Research Laboratories of the United States." *Bulletin 113.* Washington, D.C.: National Research Council, 1946.

"Research in Europe and the United States." In National Research Council, *Outlook for Science and Technology: The Next Five Years.* San Francisco: Freeman, 1982.

The Competitive Status of the U.S. Civil Aircraft Manufacturing Industry. Washington, D.C.: National Academy Press, 1985.

The Role of the Department of Defense in Supporting Manufacturing Technology Development. Washington, D.C.: National Academy Press, 1986.

Aeronautics Science and Engineering Board, Committee on NASA Scientific and Technological Program Reviews. *Aeronautics Research and Technology: A Review of Proposed Reductions in the Fiscal 1985 NASA Program.* Washington, D.C.: National Academy Press, 1982.

National Resources Planning Board. *Research – A National Resource, II. Industrial Research.* Report of the National Research Council to the National Resources Planning Board. Washington, D.C.: NRPB, 1941.

National Science Board. *Science Indicators, 1980.* Washington, D.C.: NSB, 1981.

Science Indicators, 1982. Washington, D.C.: NSB, 1983.

National Science Foundation. *Federal Funds for Research, Development, and Other Scientific Activities, Fiscal Years 1971, 1972, and 1973.* Washington, D.C.: NSF 1972.

An Analysis of the National Science Foundation's University/Industry Cooperative Research Centers Experiment. Washington, D.C.: NSF, 1979.

Federal Funds for Research and Development: Fiscal Years 1980, 1981, and 1982. Washington, D.C.: NSF, 1982.

Federal Funds for Research and Development: Detailed Historical Tables, Fiscal Years 1967–1983. Washington, D.C.: NSF, 1982.

Federal Funds for Research and Development: Fiscal Years 1983, 1984, and 1985. Washington, D.C.: NSF, 1984.

Science and Technology Data Book. Washington, D.C.: NSF, 1985.

Science Indicators, 1985. Washington, D.C.: NSF, 1985.

National Patterns of Science and Technology Resources. Washington, D.C.: NSF, 1977–86.

Federal Funds for Research and Development: Fiscal Years 1986, 1987, and 1988. Washington, D.C.: NSF, 1987.

Science & Engineering Indicators – 1987. Washington, D.C.: NSF, 1987.

Nelson, C. A. "A History of the Forest Products Laboratory." Ph.D. diss., University of Wisconsin, 1964.

Nelson, R. R. "The Simple Economics of Basic Scientific Research." *Journal of Political Economy* (1959): 297–306.

"Uncertainty, Learning, and the Economics of Parallel Research and Development Efforts." *Review of Economics and Statistics* (1961): 351–64.

"Assessing Private Enterprise: An Exegesis of Tangled Doctrine." *Bell Journal of Economics* (1981): 93–111.

"Government Stimulus of Technological Progress: Lessons from American History." *Government and Technological Change: A Cross-Industry Analysis.* New York: Pergamon, 1982.

"U.S. Technological Leadership: Where Did It Come from and Where Did It Go?" Unpublished manuscript, Columbia University, 1988.

Nelson, R. R. *High Technology Policies: A Five-Nation Comparison.* Washington, D.C.: American Enterprise Institute, 1984.

Nelson, R. R., and S. G. Winter. *An Evolutionary Theory of Economic Change.* Cambridge, Mass.: Harvard University Press, 1982.

Noble, D. F. *America by Design.* New York: Knopf, 1977.

Noll, Roger G., and Bruce M. Owen, eds., *The Political Economy of Deregulation.* Washington, D.C.: American Enterprise Institute, 1983.

"Robert Noyce: On Sematech, Chips, and Competitiveness." *Challenges* (Oct. 1988): 7.

Office of the Director of Defense Research and Engineering. *Project Hindsight: Final Report.* Washington, D.C.: USGPO, 1969.

Office of Science and Technology Policy. *Aeronautical Research and Technology Policy.* Vols. 1 and 2. Washington, D.C.: OSTP, 1982.

Office of Scientific and Engineering Personnel, National Research Council. *Foreign and Foreign-Born Engineers in the United States: Infusing Talent, Raising Issues.* Washington, D.C.: National Academy Press, 1988.

Office of Technology Assessment. *U.S. International Competitiveness: A Comparison of Steel, Electronics, and Automobiles.* Washington, D.C.: USGPO, 1981.

Commercial Biotechnology: An International Analysis. Washington, D.C.: USGPO, 1984.

Demographic Trends and the Scientific and Engineering Workforce. Washington, D.C.: USGPO, 1985.

Research as an Investment: Can We Measure the Returns? Washington, D.C.: USGPO, 1986.

International Competition in Services. Washington, D.C.: USGPO, 1987.

Okimoto, D. T. "Pioneer and Pursuer: The Role of the State in the Evolution of the Japanese and American Semiconductor Industries." Occasional paper, Northeast Asia–United States Forum on International Policy, Stanford University, 1983.

"The Japanese Challenge in High Technology." In R. Landau and N. Rosenberg, eds., *The Positive Sum Strategy.* Washington, D.C.: National Academy Press, 1986.

"Regime Characteristics of Japanese Industrial Policy." In H. Patrick, ed., *Japan's High-Technology Industries.* Seattle: University of Washington Press, 1987.

Okimoto, D. T., and G. R. Saxonhouse. "Technology and the Future of the Economy." In K. Yamamura and Y. Yasuba, eds., *Political Economy of Japan.* Vol. 1, *The Domestic Transformation.* Stanford, Calif.: Stanford University Press, 1987.

Olechowski, A. "Nontariff Barriers to Trade." In J. M. Finger and A. Olechowski, eds., *The Uruguay Round: A Handbook for Negotiators.* Washington, D.C.: World Bank, 1987.

Olson, Sherry. *The Depletion Myth.* Cambridge, Mass.: Harvard University Press, 1971.

O'Neill, H. "The Development and Use of Hardness Tests in Metallographic Research." In G. Smith, ed., *The Sorby Centennial.* New York: Gordon & Breach, 1965.

Organization for Economic Cooperation and Development. *The Impact of the Newly Industrializing Countries on Production and Trade in Manufactures.* Paris: OECD, 1979.

Educational Trends in the 1970's: A Quantitative Analysis. Paris: OECD, 1984.

Industry and University: New Forms of Co-operation and Communication. Paris: OECD, 1984.

Software: A New Industry. Paris: OECD, 1985.

OECD Science and Technology Indicators. No. 2, *R&D, Invention, and Competitiveness.* Paris: OECD, 1986.

The Newly Industrializing Countries: Challenge and Opportunity for OECD Industries. Paris: OECD, 1988.

Science and Technology Policy Outlook: 1988. Paris: OECD, 1988.

Osterman, P. *Employment Futures.* New York: Oxford University Press, 1988.

Outlook for Science and Technology: The Next Five Years. A Report of the National Research Council. Published in collaboration with the National Academy of Sciences by Freeman, San Francisco, 1982.

Pavitt, K. L. R. "On the Nature of Technology." Inaugural Lecture, University of Sussex, Science Policy Research Unit, 1987.

"Introduction and Summary." In K. L. R. Pavitt, ed., *Technical Innovation and British Economic Performance.* London: Macmillan, 1980.

Payne, P. L. "The Emergence of the Large-Scale Company in Great Britain, 1870–1914." *Economic History Review* 20(1967): 519–42.

Peck, M. J. "Science and Technology." In R. E. Caves, ed., *Britain's Economic Prospects*. Washington, D.C.: Brookings Institution, 1968.

"Joint R&D: The Case of Microelectronics and Computer Technology Corporation." *Research Policy* (1986): 219–32.

Peck, M. J., and A. Goto. "Technology and Economic Growth: The Case of Japan." *Research Policy* (1981): 222–43.

Peck, M. J., and F. M. Scherer. *The Weapons Acquisition Process*. Boston: Division of Research of the Harvard Business School, 1962.

Perazich, G., and P. M. Field. *Industrial Research and Changing Technology*. National Research Project Report M-4. Philadelphia: Works Progress Administration, 1940.

Perlmutter, H. V., and D. A. Hennan. "Cooperate to Compete Globally." *Harvard Business Review* (1986): 136–52.

Phillips, A. W. *Technology and Market Structure*. Lexington, Mass.: Heath, 1971.

Physics Survey Committee. *Physics Through the 1990s: Scientific Interfaces and Technological Applications*. Washington, D.C.: National Academy Press, 1986.

Pine, A. "Computer Chip Pact Backfires on U.S. Industry." *Los Angeles Times*, June 6, 1988, IV/1:5.

Piper, Stephen. "The Agreement on Trade in Civil Aircraft." In Subcommittee on International Trade, U.S. Senate Committee on Finance, *Hearings on S. 1376*, 96th Congress, 1st Session, 1979.

"Unique Sectoral Agreement Establishes Free Trade Framework." *Journal of World Trade Law* (1980): 221–53.

Pisano, G. P., W. Shan, and D. J. Teece. "Joint Ventures and Collaboration in the Biotechnology Industry." In D. C. Mowery, ed., *International Collaborative Ventures in U.S. Manufacturing*. Cambridge, Mass.: Ballinger, 1988.

Pollack, A. W. "Chip Makers Will Seek U.S. Aid to Spur Output." *New York Times*, Sept. 10, 1988, D4.

Porter, M. E., and M. B. Fuller. "Coalitions and Global Strategy." In M. E. Porter, ed., *Competition in Global Industries*. Boston: Harvard Business School Press, 1986.

"Pratt and Whitney Expands Role in V2500 Compressor Work." *Aviation Week and Space Technology*, March 16, 1987, 32–3.

President's Commission on the Accident at Three Mile Island. *The Role of the Managing Utility and Its Suppliers*. Washington, D.C.: USGPO, 1979.

Prestowitz, C. *Trading Places*. New York: McGraw-Hill, 1988.

Putka, G. "MIT Cancels Supercomputer Plan, Citing US Pressure to Reject Japanese Bids." *Wall Street Journal*, Nov. 6, 1987, 2:2.

Reader, W. J. *Professional Men*. New York: Basic Books, 1966.

Imperial Chemical Industries: A History. Vols. 1 and 2. Oxford: Oxford University Press, 1975.

Metal Box: A History. London: Heinemann, 1976.

"The Chemicals Industry." In N. K. Buxton and D. H. Aldcroft, eds., *British Industry between the Wars*. London: Scholar Press, 1979.

Reddy, J. V. *The IR&D Program of the Department of Defense.* Peace Studies Program Occasional Paper No. 6. Ithaca, N.Y.: Cornell University, 1976.

Reed, Arthur. "Airbus Talks about A320, Future Projects." *Air Transport World* (May 1984): 33.

Reich, L. S. "Radio Electronics and the Development of Industrial Research in the Bell System." Ph.D. diss., Johns Hopkins University, 1977.

———. "Research Patents and the Struggle to Control Radio: A Study of Big Business and the Uses of Industrial Research." *Business History Review* (Summer 1977): 208–35.

———. "Industrial Research and the Pursuit of Corporate Security: The Early Years of Bell Labs." *Business History Review* (Winter 1980): 504–29.

———. "Irving Langmuir and the Pursuit of Science and Technology in the Corporate Environment." *Technology and Culture* (April 1983): 200.

Reich, R. B., and E. D. Mankin. "Joint Ventures with Japan give Away Our Future." *Harvard Business Review* (March/April 1986): 79–86.

Ritchie, David. *The Computer Pioneers.* New York: Simon & Schuster, 1986.

Rogers, E. M. *Diffusion of Innovations.* New York: Free Press, 1962.

———. "Information Exchange and Technological Innovation." In D. Sahal, ed., *The Transfer and Utilization of Technical Knowledge.* Lexington, Mass.: Heath, 1982.

Roland, A. *Model Research: The National Advisory Committee for Aeronautics, 1915–58.* Washington, D.C.: USGPO, 1985.

Rosenberg, N. "Technological Change in the Machine Tool Industry 1840–1910." *Journal of Economic History* (Dec. 1963): 414–46.

———. ed., *The American System of Manufactures.* Edinburgh: Edinburgh University Press, 1969.

———. "Learning by Using." In Nathan Rosenberg, *Inside the Black Box: Technology and Economics.* Cambridge: Cambridge University Press, 1982.

———. "How Exogenous Is Science?" In Rosenberg, *Inside the Black Box: Technology and Economics.* Cambridge: Cambridge University Press, 1982.

———. *Inside the Black Box: Technology and Economics.* Cambridge: Cambridge University Press, 1982.

———. "Some Reflections on the Interface between Science and Technology." Stanford University, mimeo, 1986.

Rosenberg, N., A. Thompson, and S. Belsley. *Technological Change and Productivity Growth in the Air Transport Industry.* NASA Technical Memorandum 78505. Washington, D.C.: NASA, 1978.

Rosenberg, N., and W. E. Steinmueller. "Why Are Americans Such Poor Imitators?" *American Economic Association Papers and Proceedings* (1988): 229–34.

Rosenbloom, R. S. "The R&D Pioneers, Then and Now." Presented at the Hagley Conference, Wilmington, Del., Oct. 7, 1985.

Rosenbloom, R. S., and M. A. Cusumano. "Technological Pioneering and Competitive Advantage: The Birth of the VCR Industry." *California Management Review* (1987): 51–76.

Rostas, L. *Comparative Productivity in British and American Industry.* Cambridge: Cambridge University Press, 1948.

Rubenfien, E. "U.S. Contractors Forge Alliances in Japan." *Wall Street Journal*, June 28, 1988, 28.

Salter, M. S., and W. A. Weinhold. *Merger Trends and Prospects*. Report for the Office of Policy, U.S. Dept. of Commerce. Washington, D.C.: Department of Commerce, 1980.

Samuels, R. J. "Research Collaboration in Japan." Presented at the annual meeting of the Association of Asian Studies, Boston, Mass.: April 11, 1987.

Samuels, R. J., and B. C. Whipple. "Defense Production and Industrial Development: The Case of Japanese Aircraft." In C. Johnson, L. Tyson, and J. Zysman, eds., *Politics and Productivity: How Japan's Development Strategy Works*. Cambridge, Mass.: Ballinger, 1989.

Sanderson, M. "Research and the Firm in British Industry." *Science Studies* (April 1972): 107–51.

The Universities and British Industry. London: Routledge & Kegan Paul, 1972.

Sanderson, S. W. "Implications of New Manufacturing Technologies in International Markets." Paper presented at the meetings of the American Association for the Advancement of Science, Chicago, Ill., Feb. 14, 1987.

Sanger, D. E. "MIT, Pressed by U.S., Won't Buy Computer." *New York Times*, Nov. 6, 1987, IV S:1.

"Computer Consortium Lags." *New York Times*, Sept. 5, 1984, D1.

Saul, S. B. "The Engineering Industry." In D. H. Aldcroft, ed., *The Development of British Industry and Foreign Competition*. Glasgow: University of Glasgow Press, 1968.

Saxonhouse, G. R. "Japanese High Technology, Government Policy, and Evolving Comparative Advantage in Goods and Services." Prepared for the Japanese Political Economy Research Conference, Honolulu, 1982.

"Why Japan Is Winning." *Issues in Science and Technology* (Spring 1986): 50–62.

Scherer, F. M. "Firm Size, Market Structure, Opportunity, and the Output of Patented Inventions." *American Economic Review* (Dec. 1965): 1097–1125.

"Market Structure and the Employment of Scientists and Engineers." *American Economic Review* (June 1967): 524–31.

"R&D and Declining Productivity Growth." *American Economic Review* (1983): 215–18.

Schmookler, J. "Inventors Past and Present." *Review of Economics and Statistics* (Aug. 1957): 321–33.

Schumpeter, J. *The Theory of Economic Development*. Trans. R. Opie. Cambridge, Mass.: Harvard University Press, 1934.

Capitalism, Socialism, and Democracy. 3rd ed. New York: Harper & Row, 1954.

Schofield, R. *The Lunar Society*. Oxford: Oxford University Press, 1963.

Scott, J. T. "Diversification versus Cooperation in R&D Investment." *Managerial and Decision Economics* (1988): 173–86.

"Firm versus Industry Variability in R&D Intensity." In Z. Griliches, ed., *R&D, Patents, and Productivity*. Chicago: University of Chicago Press, 1984.

Senate Military Affairs Committee, Subcommittee on War Mobilization. *The*

Bibliography 317

Government's Wartime Research and Development. Washington, D.C.:
USGPO, 1945.
Servos, J. W. "The Industrial Relations of Science: Chemistry at MIT." Isis (Dec.
1980): 531–49.
Sharlin, H. I. The Convergent Century. New York: Abelard-Schuman, 1966.
Smith, C. S. "The Interaction of Science and Practice in the History of Metal-
lurgy." Technology and Culture (1961): 357–67.
"Materials and the Development of Civilization and Science." Science, May 14,
1965, 915.
ed. The Sorby Centennial Symposium on the History of Metallurgy. New York:
Gordon & Breach, 1965.
Smith, H. L. Airways. New York: Knopf, 1944.
Society for the Promotion of Engineering Education. Report of the Investigation
of Engineering Education, 1923–29. Pittsburgh, Pa.: SPEE, 1930.
"Special Analysis K" of the Special Analyses volume released with the president's
budget for fiscal 1983. Washington, D.C.: USGPO, 1982.
"Special Report: The Hollow Corporation." Business Week, March 3, 1986, 57–
85.
Steelman, John R. Science and Public Policy. Washington, D.C.: USGPO, 1947.
Steiner, J. E. "How Decisions Are Made: Major Considerations for Aircraft Programs." American Institute of Aeronautics and Astronautics, 1982 Wright
Brothers Lectureship in Aeronautics, Seattle, Wash., Aug. 24, 1982.
Steinmueller, W. E. "Industry Structure and Government Policies in the U.S,.
and Japanese Integrated Circuit Industries." In John B. Shoven, ed., Government Policies toward Industry in the U.S. and Japan. New York: Cambridge University Press, 1988.
"International Joint Ventures in the Integrated Circuit Industry." In D. Mowery, ed., International Collaborative Ventures in U.S. Manufacturing. Cambridge, Mass.: Ballinger, 1988.
Stigler, G. J. "Industrial Organization and Economic Progress." In L. D. White,
ed., The State of the Social Sciences. Chicago: University of Chicago Press,
1956.
"Monopoly and Oligopoly by Merger." In G. J. Stigler, ed., The Organization
of Industry. Homewood, Ill.: Irwin, 1968.
Storck, John, and Walter Teague. Flour for Man's Bread. Minneapolis: University of Minnesota Press, 1952.
Sturchio, J. L. "Experimenting with Research: Kenneth Mees, Eastman Kodak,
and the Challenges of Diversification." Presented at the R&D Pioneers Con-
ference, Hagley Museum and Library, Wilmington, Del., Oct. 7, 1985.
Summers, R. "Cost Estimates as Predictors of Actual Costs: A Statistical Study of
Military Development." In T. Marschak, T. K. Glennan, Jr., and R. Sum-
mers, Strategy for R&D. New York: Springer-Verlag, 1967.
Tarullo, D. K. "The MTN Subsidies Code: Agreement without Consensus." In
S. J. Rubin and G. C. Hufbauer, eds., Emerging Standards of International
Trade and Investment. Totowa, N.J.: Rowan & Allanheld, 1984.
Taylor, F. W. On the Art of Cutting Metals. New York: American Society of
Mechanical Engineers, 1907.

Teece, D. J. "Economies of Scope and the Scope of the Enterprise." *Journal of Economic Behavior and Organization* (1980): 223–47.

"Towards an Economic Theory of the Multiproduct Firm." *Journal of Economic Behavior and Organization* (1982): 39–63.

"Profiting from Technological Innovation: Implications for Integration, Collaboration, Licensing, and Public Policy." *Research Policy* (1986): 285–305.

"Television on Hold." *Economist*, Oct. 1, 1988, 17–18.

Temin, P. *Iron and Steel in 19th Century America.* Cambridge, Mass.: Massachusetts Institute of Technology Press, 1964.

Temporary National Economic Committee, *Large-Scale Organization in the Food Industries.* Monograph 35. Washington, D.C.: TNEC, 1940.

Technology in our Economy. Monograph 22, Washington, D.C.: TNEC, 1941.

Terleckyj, N. "Sources of Productivity Advance: A Pilot Study of Manufacturing Industries, 1899–1953." Ph.D. diss. Columbia University, 1961.

Effects of R&D on Productivity: An Exploratory Inquiry. Washington, D.C.: National Planning Association, 1974.

"The Time Pattern of the Effects of Industrial R&D on Productivity Growth." Presented at the Conference on Interindustry Differences in Productivity Growth, American Enterprise Institute, Washington, D.C.: Oct. 11–12, 1984.

Teubal, M. M., and W. E. Steinmueller. "Government Policy, Innovation, and Economic Growth: Lessons from a Study of Satellite Communications." *Research Policy* (1982): 271–87.

Thackray, A. "University–Industry Connections and Chemical Research: An Historical Perspective." U.S. National Science Board, *University–Industry Research Relationships: Selected Studies.* Washington, D.C.: National Science Foundation, 1982.

Thorelli, H. B. *Federal Antitrust Policy.* Baltimore: Johns Hopkins University Press, 1954.

Tilton, John. *International Diffusion: The Case of Semiconductors.* Washington, D.C.: Brookings Institution, 1971.

Timoshenko, S. *History of the Strength of Materials.* New York: McGraw-Hill, 1953.

Tolliday, S. "Industry, Finance and the State: An Analysis of the British Steel Industry during the Inter-War Years." Ph.D. thesis, University of Cambridge, 1979.

Tyson, L. "Making Policy for National Competitiveness in a Changing World." In A. Furino, ed., *Cooperation and Competition in the Global Economy.* Cambridge, Mass.: Ballinger, 1988.

Tyson, R. E. "The Cotton Industry." In D. H. Aldcroft, ed., *The Development of British Industry and Foreign Competition.* Glasgow: University of Glasgow Press, 1968.

Uekusa, M. "Industrial Organization." In K. Yamamura and Y. Yasuba, eds., *The Political Economy of Japan.* Vol. 1, *The Domestic Transformation.* Stanford, Calif.: Stanford University Press, 1987.

U.S. Bureau of the Census. *Census of the United States: 1910.* Washington, D.C.: Bureau of the Census, 1913.

Historical Statistics of the United States: Colonial Times to 1970. Washington, D.C.: USGPO, 1975.

U.S. Council of Economic Advisers. *Economic Report of the President.* Washington, D.C.: USGPO, 1963.

U.S. Department of Commerce Panel on Invention and Innovation. *Technological Innovation: Its Environment and Management.* Washington, D.C.: USGPO, 1967.

U.S. Department of Commerce, International Trade Administration. *A Competitive Assessment of the U.S. Civil Aircraft Industry.* Washington, D.C.: USGPO, 1984.

"U.S.–European Trade Talks Focus on Subsidy Issues." *Aviation Week and Space Technology,* March 31, 1986, 36.

"U.S., Europeans Clash over Airbus Subsidies." *Aviation Week and Space Technology,* Feb. 9, 1987, 18–20.

U.S. General Accounting Office. *Lower Airline Costs per Passenger Are Possible in the United States and Could Result in Lower Fares.* Washington, D.C.: USGPO, 1977.

University Funding: Patterns of Distribution of Federal Research Funds to Universities. Briefing report to the ranking minority member, Committee on Appropriations, U.S. Senate, Washington, D.C.: Feb., 1987.

U.S. House of Representatives. *Hearings of the Science Policy Task Force of the Science, Space, and Technology Committee of the U.S. House of Representatives.* Washington, D.C.: USGPO, 1986.

Proposed Legislation – Superconductivity Competitiveness Act of 1988. House Document 100-169. Washington, D.C.: USGPO, Feb. 24, 1988.

U.S. Internal Revenue Service. *Statistics of Income for 1933.* Washington, D.C.: USGPO, 1934.

U.S. International Trade Administration, Department of Commerce. *An Assessment of U.S. Competitiveness in High Technology Industries.* Washington, D.C.: USGPO, 1983.

U.S. Senate Commerce Committee Subcommittee on Science, Technology, and Space. *Hearings on the National Technology Innovation Act.* Washington, D.C.: USGPO, 1979.

Varcoe, I. *Organizing for Science in Britain: A Case-Study.* Oxford: Oxford University Press, 1974.

Vogel, Ezra. *Japan as Number One: Lessons for America.* Cambridge, Mass.: Harvard University Press, 1979.

von Hippel, E. "The Dominant Role of Users in the Scientific Instrument Innovation Process." *Research Policy* (1976): 212–39.

Waldman, P. "Sixteen U.S. Companies to Form Groups to Develop Advanced TV Technology." *Wall Street Journal,* Jan. 13, 1988, 2.

Waldrop, M. M. "NSF Commits to Supercomputers." *Science,* May 3, 1985, 568–71.

Warren, K. "Iron and Steel." In N. K. Buxton and D. Aldcroft, eds., *British Industry between the Wars.* London: Scholar Press, 1979.

Weidlein, E. R. "Fifty Years of Science for Human Progress." *50th Annual Report of the Mellon Institute.* Pittsburgh, Pa., 1961.

Weiner, Charles. "A New Site for the Seminar: The Refugees and American Physics in the Thirties." In Donald Fleming and Bernard Bailyn, eds., *The Intellectual Migration: Europe and America, 1930–1960*. Cambridge, Mass.: Harvard University Press (Belknap Press), 1969.

Westney, D. E., and K. Sakakibara. "The Challenge of Japan-Based R&D in Global Technology Strategy." *Technology in Society* (1986): 315–50.

White, L. J. "The Motor Vehicle Industry." In R. Nelson, ed., *Government and Technical Progress: A Cross-Industry Analysis*. New York: Pergamon, 1982.

Wickenden, W. E. "A Comparative Study of Engineering Education in the United States and in Europe." *Report of the Investigation of Engineering Education, 1923–1929*. New York: Society for the Promotion of Engineering Education, 1930.

Williams, T. "Science and Technology." In vol. 11, *The New Cambridge Modern History*. Cambridge: Cambridge University Press, 1967.

Williamson, Harold, ed., *Growth of the American Economy*. New York: Prentice-Hall, 1951.

Williamson, O. E. *Markets and Hierarchies*. New York: Free Press, 1975.

"Transaction Cost Economics: The Governance of Contractual Relations." *Journal of Law and Economics* (1979): 233–62.

"The Economics of Organization: The Transaction Cost Approach." *American Journal of Sociology* (1981): 548–77.

Economic Institutions of Capitalism. New York: Free Press, 1985.

Wilson, C. H. *The History of Unilever*. London: Cassell, 1954 (vols. 1 and 2), 1968 (vol. 3).

Winham, G. *International Trade and the Tokyo Round Negotiation*. Princeton, N.J.: Princeton University Press, 1986.

Wise, George. "R&D at General Electric, 1878–1985." Presented at the conference on the R&D Pioneers, Hagley Museum and Library, Wilmington, Del., Oct. 7, 1985.

Wolf, J. "Europeans Fear Obstacles by U.S. on Advanced TV." *Wall Street Journal*, May 31, 1989, A16.

Wunder, Bernard. Statement before the Senate Commerce Committee, *Hearings on the AT&T Proposed Settlement*, Jan. 25, 1982.

Wyke, A. "Pharmaceuticals Survey." *Economist*, Feb. 7, 1987.

Yoder, S. K. "Hitachi, Fujitsu Link in Microprocessors." *Wall Street Journal*, Oct. 28, 1986, 39.

Yoffie, D. "Chip Shortage: Don't Blame the Pact." *Wall Street Journal*, June 21, 1988, 36.

Zuckerman, Harriet. *Scientific Elite: Nobel Laureates in the United States*. New York: Free Press, 1977.

Index